The Provocative Joan Robinson

SCIENCE AND CULTURAL THEORY

A Series Edited by
Barbara Herrnstein Smith
& E. Roy Weintraub

The Provocative Joan Robinson

The Making of a Cambridge Economist

Nahid Aslanbeigui & Guy Oakes

Duke University Press

Durham & London

2009

© 2009 Duke University Press
All rights reserved
Printed in the United States of America
on acid-free paper ∞
Designed by Jennifer Hill
Typeset in Carter and Cone Galliard
by Achorn International

*Library of Congress Cataloging-in-Publication Data
appear on the last printed page of this book.*

Photograph on previous spread:
Joan Robinson. © reserved;
collection Marshall Library of Economics, Cambridge.

In memory of
PARVIN ASLANBEIGUI, M.D.
1959–2007

✝ CONTENTS ✝

† ACKNOWLEDGMENTS †

Our warmest thanks to Geoff Harcourt, who read an entire draft and wrote elaborate notes, saving us, to paraphrase Joan Robinson, from our headlong errors. We are also grateful to Prue Kerr and Michele Naples, who read parts of a draft and offered helpful suggestions. Two readers for Duke University Press made valuable criticisms on which we acted. The usual caveats apply.

For permission to quote unpublished copyrighted material, we acknowledge the following: Sir Nicholas Henderson for permission to publish from the papers of Hubert Henderson; David Papineau for permission to publish from the papers of Richard Kahn; John Elmen Taussig for permission to publish from the papers of Frank Taussig; Seymour Weissman for permission to publish from the papers of Evan Durbin; by kind permission of the Faculty of Economics, University of Cambridge, to quote from the unpublished papers of Austin and Joan Robinson; King's College for permission to quote from the unpublished writings of Edward Austin Gossage Robinson, Joan Robinson, and John Maynard Keynes, copyright The Provost and Scholars of King's College Cambridge 2009; the Syndics of Cambridge University Library for permission to publish from the minutes of meetings of the Faculty Board of Economics and Politics and the General Board of the Faculties; and The Cambridgeshire Collection, Cambridge Central Library for permission to reproduce Ramsey & Muspratt photographs.

We thank VS Verlag for permission to reproduce part of our essay "The Importance of Being at Cambridge" and the *Journal of the History of Economic Thought* for permission to reproduce in part two of our articles: "Joan Robinson's 'Secret Document': A Passage from the Autobiography of an Analytical Economist" and "The Twilight of the Marshallian Guild: The Culture of Cambridge Economics Circa 1930."

For archival assistance, we are grateful to the archivists and librarians of King's College, the Marshall Library of Economics, the Cambridge University Library, and the Wren Library at Cambridge University and the National Library of Norway in Oslo. For research assistance, we thank Linda Fette Knox, Kristin McDonald, Andre Renaudo, and Linda Silverstein.

Research on this book was supported by Grants-in-Aid-for Creativity and the Jack T. Kvernland Chair, Monmouth University.

Collage with Woman
in Foreground

HERE'S TO YOU, MRS. ROBINSON

Joan Robinson was one of the most original and prolific economists of the twentieth century and unquestionably the most important woman in the history of economic thought. In the latter regard, no one else comes close, not even the abundantly gifted Rosa Luxemburg, the Marxist economist and political leader whose work she came to admire in the 1940s. Her publications in economic theory began in 1932 and ended two years after her death, in 1983. A comprehensive but incomplete bibliography compiled by Cristina Marcuzzo (1996) runs to 443 items, a body of work that covers most of economic theory: production, distribution, employment, accumulation, innovation, and economic growth as well as methodological and philosophical reflections and contributions to the study of economic education. Since 1933, there has been an extensive and lively literature on Robinsonia. It has grown considerably since her death and the centenary of her birth in 1903.[1] A book on her life and work by Geoffrey Harcourt, her Cambridge colleague and friend of many years, and Prue Kerr, her student and friend, is in preparation.

Robinson studied economics at Cambridge University, where she made a career that lasted some fifty years. Her work falls into three research programs, each a product of developments in economic theory at Cambridge: the innovations from the mid-1920s to the early 1930s that led to the theory of imperfect competition, the Keynesian revolution of the 1930s, and the attempts in the 1950s and 1960s to develop a general analysis of long-term economic growth. Her first book, *The Economics of Imperfect Competition* (1933d), achieved international recognition. In the early 1930s, she also became an ardent follower of John Maynard Keynes's new approach to economics. Soon after *The General Theory of Employment, Interest, and Money* appeared in 1936, she published *Essays in the Theory of Employment* (1937a), which refined and extended Keynes's ideas. She followed this book with the *Introduction to the Theory of Employment* (1937b), a Keynesian primer designed to revolutionize undergraduate pedagogy in economics.

Shortly after publication of *The General Theory*, Robinson concluded that neither neoclassical nor Keynesian economics could account for long-term economic changes. However, she was convinced that if Keynes's ideas were reformulated and generalized on the basis of supplementary assumptions, such an analysis would be possible. This was her last major effort: the development of a dynamic theory of capital accumulation that rested on the assumptions of historicity and historical temporality. Its result was *The Accumulation of Capital* (1956), a daunting work of uncompromising formalism and an important stimulus of the "capital controversy," one of the most acrimonious disputes in the history of economic analysis. The debate spanned two decades, produced hundreds of books, articles, and notes, and consumed the energies of its antagonists.[2] To Robinson's dismay and consternation, neoclassical economists admitted the validity of her criticisms but dismissed them as empirically inconsequential and irrelevant. Thus the battle ended not with a bang but a whimper.

Robinson ended her long career covered with honors. In 1971, she delivered the prestigious Richard T. Ely address of the American Economic Association. The year before, no less a figure than Paul Samuelson judged her "one of the greatest analytical economists of our era" (Samuelson 1970, 397). An honorary doctorate from Harvard followed in 1980. Throughout, she remained enmeshed in controversy: denouncing neoclassical economics for failing to address the most serious economic problems of the time, censuring American economic theory for contributing to the nuclear arms race, attacking the government of Margaret Thatcher in Great Britain, and celebrating the communist regimes of China and North Korea. In surveying Robinson's work, Samuelson concluded that a number of her accomplishments would merit the Nobel Memorial Prize in economics, which was created in 1969 (Samuelson 1970, 397). By the mid-1970s, she was under consideration by the Swedish Academy. Although apparently short-listed for several years, she was repeatedly passed over. The reasons offered by her contemporaries varied considerably. Would she be considered on the basis of *The Economics of Imperfect Competition*, her best-known and most successful book? That seemed likely, in which case an award would have been awkward. Edward Chamberlin's doctoral dissertation at Harvard in 1927, revised and published a few months before her book appeared, covered the same ground (1933). But he had died in 1967. Moreover, Robinson had recanted much of the book's argument and mode of analysis (see Robinson 1953). She was an unsparing critic of orthodox economics and rejected its dependence on mathematical models and quantification generally. She exhibited the public persona of a radical of the left, claiming to find virtues in both the Maoist Cultural Revolution and the North Korean totalitarian state of Kim Il Sung. Her writings often gave the impression that her greatest strength lay in polemics rather than in building original theories of her own. She was a woman in a discipline overwhelmingly dominated by men. Finally, she seems to have adopted, or perhaps affected, a Sartre-like pose toward the Nobel Prize by holding it in some contempt. If she did not want it and would not accept it, it would not be surprising if the Swedish Academy was reluctant to offer it (Turner 1989, 214–21).

After her death, Robinson achieved near canonization in the eulogies of numerous economists, including several perennial adversaries whose work was quite remote from the Cambridge tradition. The Robinsonian conduct of intellectual life as a mode of partisan warfare was interpreted as a mark of flinty integrity and selfless dedication to the pursuit of truth, uncompromised by academic ambition (Matthews 1989, 911–15; Goodwin 1989, 916–17). One commentator even saw in her "the stark and deadly simplicity of Antigone" (Walsh 1989, 881). Milton Friedman, not a champion of Cambridge economics, declared that economists would have achieved a rare consensus in judging Robinson the only woman to meet the standards of the Swedish Academy (Friedman 1986, 77). She would not have taken the compliment. In her view, economic theory was an androgynous enterprise, and her work transcended differences of gender.

PROFESSIONAL IDENTITY FORMATION AND ACADEMIC CAREER PRODUCTION

This is a book about Robinson's career in the 1930s. Her professional identity, first as a microeconomist and then as a Keynesian, was formed in acquiring credentials that would qualify her as a Cambridge theorist. In 1930, she had no professional identity and no apparent resources that would enable her to assemble these credentials. Becoming a Cambridge economist called for strategies of academic career production and tactics for executing them. She recruited mentors who would serve as guides, and advocates—allies who would become masters of her apprenticeship. Although she proved to be adept in acquiring supporters, her initiatives also met resistance. Not all economists at Cambridge were prepared to tolerate the zeal with which she pursued objectives and her tendentious approach to teaching.

In early 1933, Richard Kahn, Robinson's best friend on the faculty, was at Harvard, and Robinson kept him up to date on Cambridge economics and economists. Writing on February 20, she ventured the breathtaking speculation that, like women generally, she had no ambition (RFK/13/90/1/127–30). Really? The subject of this letter was Robinson herself and her recent progress in promoting her budding career at Cambridge. It had a major and a minor theme. She was chiefly interested in giving Kahn an account of the latest developments in the allocation of credit for original work in the theory of imperfect competition at Cambridge. This issue first arose in summer 1931. Although Gerald Shove had been working on theories of value and distribution for several years, he was notoriously slow to publish. That summer Kahn told him that Robinson was not only lecturing in his area but writing a book. Initially, Shove was merely uneasy. He was developing new and largely unpublished material in his lectures and saw Robinson as an ambitious, disciplined, and theoretically promising economist. Would she credit him with priority for ideas that he believed were his? In pressing her for assurances on this point, he became increasingly meddlesome and offensive. Robinson was annoyed but also in a difficult position, one requiring subtle diplomacy. She was determined to see her book recognized as an important original contribution. This called for efforts to secure her claims to priority. However, it would be dangerous to antagonize Shove, who would have a voice and a vote in any decision on a lectureship for her at Cambridge. Shove's long intimacy with Keynes was even more worrisome. Robinson had been courting Keynes since early 1932, hoping to become one of the economists on whom he relied for advice concerning his work in progress. Could she risk infuriating Shove without placing in jeopardy her project of becoming a Keynesian? Robinson's tactic was to stand her ground where significant issues of priority were at stake and at the same time present herself to Keynes as his ally—civil, reasonable, moderate, and ready to compromise in their joint effort to mollify Shove and cool his volatile temperament.

The second theme concerned Robinson's efforts to manage the reception of her book before it appeared. An early version of one of her arguments (1932b) had caught the eye of A. C. Pigou, the Cambridge Professor of Political Economy, who detected a mathematical defect in her analysis. Conversations chaperoned by her husband, Austin, also a Cambridge economist, and exchanges of letters ensued. Robinson could not solve Pigou's problem. She could not even understand his objection, and she was not prepared to tell him why: as she later admitted, she was almost entirely ignorant of mathematics. What to do? Pigou's critique could not be ignored or dismissed, and Kahn, her mentor on questions of formal analysis, was in the United States. She temporized, became confused, and tried to change the subject, all the while maintaining a dialogue with Pigou by keeping him engaged in the problem posed by his objection. In this fashion, Robinson placed herself and the problem in his capable hands. The result was a tactical tour de force. It was Pigou, not Robinson, who found an answer to his criticism by demonstrating that her argument was, after all, formally valid. Pigou performed a remarkable reversal of the conventional relationship between novice and senior scientist. He found a flaw in her argument, solved the problem, published his result some three months before her book appeared, and gave her credit for the fundamental elements of his proof. Robinson embraced his solution and accepted the credit. Pigou's imprimatur on a book that had not been published or even completed was a stunning endorsement. Robinson made good use of it, including a reference to his published proof in her book (Robinson 1933d, 100, n.1)

In these episodes, Robinson was engaged in producing resources that advanced her nascent Cambridge career. Throughout the 1930s, she demonstrated impressive skills in selecting and defining objectives that promised substantial benefits. She was flexible in matters of tactics, astute in perceiving opportunities, and deft in exploiting them. In turning to her advantage interventions by others that she neither planned nor anticipated, she was able to simplify and strengthen the operation of her tactics, at the same time confounding her adversaries and weakening their powers of resistance. In managing adventitious events that seemed to jeopardize her chances of success, she translated threats into opportunities that served her purposes.

On Robinson's strategic and tactical sense—the objectives she set in attempting to establish herself at Cambridge and the steps she took to execute them—the archival evidence of the 1930s is unequivocal. Her Cambridge contemporaries, both advocates and adversaries, saw her as a woman of considerable enterprise and energy, determined to achieve success by making a reputation as a theorist. As the ensuing account shows, Kahn took her ambitions seriously and did everything in his power to help her achieve them. Pigou saw her first book in careerist terms. In his view, it would make her a strong candidate for the next university lectureship in economics.[3] He also took a careerist perspective on her work generally and gave her advice on how to write her next book to best advantage.[4] Austin, too, encouraged Robinson's ambitions and accommodated her career plans, in part by agreeing to postpone having children until she had "reorganized economics."[5] Robinson's antagonists took a darker but no less serious view of her aims. Shove saw her work in drafting *The Economics of Imperfect Competition* as a threat to his unwritten book. He believed she had drawn some of her analyses from his unpublished lectures without his knowledge and took measures to extract priority concessions. By early 1935, Dennis Robertson believed that Robinson was attempting to alter the Cambridge curriculum in money in order to strengthen the Keynesian position, denigrate his lectures on monetary theory, and marginalize him generally. The economic historian C. R. Fay shared this view and was much more frank in expressing it: "The assumption has always seemed to me that if she wants it [anything], of course she can have it."[6]

In the ensuing we trace the operation of strategies of career production in three early phases of Robinson's professional life: (1) In early 1932, she was an unlikely candidate for success at Cambridge. A woman in a university dominated by men, she did not have a remarkable academic record, a college fellowship, significant publications, or a powerful patron. She responded to this predicament by proposing a distinctive conception of the condition of Cambridge economics and creating for herself the key role in advancing the research program based on this conception. Appropriating and radicalizing Pigou's idea of economic theory as a box of tools, she developed a fragmentary but uncompromising view of economics as pure theory. In the Robinsonian philosophy of economic science, theory was limited to tool-like techniques or methods of analysis. Although her heroes Alfred Marshall, Pigou, and Keynes had discovered ideas of singular greatness, each had failed to grasp the essential methodological significance of his thought. Who would reinterpret their work and place it on a sound theoretical footing? Who would consummate the Cambridge tradition by reconceptualizing the truths that its innovators had envisioned but failed to understand? The young Joan Robinson, who represented herself as taking the next big step in Cambridge economics. In part 1, we consider the relationship between career production and professional identity construction by examining Robinson's early efforts to imagine and fashion a place for herself in the social and theoretical space of Cambridge economics.

(2) In her first research program, Robinson entered a new area of economic theory and achieved an impressive payoff. The personal costs were low in large measure because she moved quickly to identify local Cambridge assets on which she could draw without undue difficulty. Cultural resources were at hand in the Cambridge practice of collaborative research, of which Robinson became a master. Colleagues became coworkers, critics, editors, or collaborators. They supplied her with ideas, arguments, data, scholarly advice, and mathematical analyses. In tutoring her, filling the gaps in her training, and easing the task of writing an ambitious book, they accelerated her progress from relative ignorance of her subject to a complete book manuscript in less than three years. New intellectual resources were also available. The introduction of the marginal revenue curve at Cambridge was an auspicious event for Robinson, who became the first economist to make serious use of it. At the same time, the Cambridge culture of Marshallian economics provided favorable conditions for work on monopoly. Following Piero Sraffa, Kahn began

research in the area by analyzing the short period in his fellowship dissertation. What could be established by a long-period analysis of imperfectly competitive markets that employed the marginal revenue curve systematically? This was an unexplored question at Cambridge and a promising research problem for an economist on the scene who was capable of moving quickly. In part 2, we consider the relationship between book production and career production by examining the circumstances under which Robinson wrote *The Economics of Imperfect Competition.*

(3) Robinson became an enthusiast of Keynes quite early. In spring 1932, she was attempting to establish a close professional relationship, and by January 1933, she was intent on achieving the status of a client—performing intellectual services for Keynes, basking in his glory, and enjoying the benefits that scientific clientage would bring. She saw in Keynes "the charismatic glorification of 'Reason'" (Weber 1978, 1209). Robinson was seduced by his brilliance and attracted by the prospect of admission into the small circle of his confidants in economic theory. The promise of intellectual adventure—participating in a bold new heterodoxy and following the lead of a thinker who could revolutionize his field with a fundamental breakthrough—was irresistible.

Keynes was slow to respond. He had no interest in doing research on imperfect competition. As his letters to his wife, Lydia, show, he was troubled by Robinson's liaison with Kahn, which was also a danger to Austin's position. Robinson's relations with Robertson, the Cambridge economist with whom Keynes had enjoyed his closest and most rewarding intellectual friendship, were increasingly strained and abrasive. During the 1920s, the etiquette of Cambridge economists was grounded in a principle of liberal civility: unsparing frankness in debate and an absolute distinction between ideas and persons. Intellectual positions but not their advocates were open to criticism. This principle rested on a dichotomy—difficult to sustain, unrealistic, and perhaps ultimately indefensible—between who you are and what you think. In scientific debate and academic disputation, Robinson was not averse to ad hominem tactics that transgressed this etiquette. Moreover, her transgressions exhibited a lack of finesse and tact that suggested malice. As Keynes's contemporary and fellow Kingsman Fay complained to him, "It is a pity she's so bloody rude."[7] Robertson, with whom she clashed on issues of theory and curriculum, was a favorite object of her invective. Any move on Keynes's part that indicated support for the role she was constructing for herself at Cambridge would, it seemed, put him at odds with Robertson.

Robinson persisted. Beginning in 1934, she made it her business to become au courant with the latest developments in Keynes's post-*Treatise* work, a taxing undertaking in view of his intellectual agility and disposition to discard newly acquired views for alternatives that seemed more promising. In this project, she labored under the disadvantage of having little direct contact with Keynes himself. Her response to this problem was to employ his confidants as sources of information on changes in his views. Kahn, who was a frequent guest at Keynes's country house in Sussex, kept her informed by a regular stream of letters that were supplemented by fuller discussions on his return. Because of Sraffa's regular conversations with Keynes on their current research interests, he too was a source of information, which Robinson extracted on their walks around Cambridge and its environs.

Robinson was a believer in a Keynesian revolution even before Keynes himself understood the implications of *A Treatise on Money* (1930) in these dramatic terms. Although she was a partisan of the revolution, Keynes did not acknowledge her as a member of the revolutionary elite until June 1935. At that point, her efforts finally succeeded when he sent her the proofs of *The General Theory* and asked for her help. In 1935, she was one of only five economists to whom he entrusted his new ideas for criticism and revision. Kahn was his disciple and friend. Roy Harrod, Ralph Hawtrey, and Robertson, all of whom were figures of considerable prestige in economics, had known Keynes for many years. In this manner, Robinson entered Keynes's inner circle, a move that placed her at the center of Cambridge economics. The following year, she and Keynes exchanged roles as author and commentator. In spring 1936, he was reading the proofs of her *Essays in the Theory of Employment*. Later, in 1937, she finally convinced him that the fate of *The General Theory* would be decided not by debating the defects of orthodoxy with his contemporaries but by revolutionizing the teaching of economics. As a result of these discussions, he gave his blessing to the *Introduction to the Theory of Employment*, the first textbook in Keynesian economics. Robinson had arrived as an internationally acknowledged leader of the Keynesian revolution. In part 3, we consider the relationship between patronage and career production by examining the tactical history of Robinson's long and ultimately successful courtship of Keynes.

An investigation of the genesis of Robinson's professional identity and the strategies on which her early career was based is best explored from two perspectives. One is historical. Who did what, to and for whom, and on the basis of what intentions and purposes? In what institutional settings and under what circumstances were intentions formed and actions taken? Who won, who lost, and what consequences followed? In this respect, our book is a small-scale local history of certain episodes in Cambridge economics during the 1930s. It is not a collective scientific biography or a sketch for such a study but rather an account of Robinson's early professional world. This social sphere was characterized by rapid changes in theoretical idiom, reconfigurations of alliances, and a transformation of the Cambridge disciplinary culture.

The second perspective is theoretical, in a modest and perhaps even minimalist sense. We offer various analyses that are intended to clarify the history. In this respect, the book is an anthropology of Cambridge economics in the 1930s. Conventionally, anthropology is an investigation of a culture and its artifacts. We pursue this course by investigating the academic and disciplinary culture in which Robinson did her early work. There is an older sense of anthropology embodied in European philosophy (Schnädelbach 1984): *Anthropologie*, an account of what it means to be a certain kind of human being—in our case a Cambridge economist of the 1930s, endowed with the powers and constrained by the limitations of this species of *Homo academicus*. We take this course as well by exploring Robinson's objectives and the strategies she employed to achieve them.

The historical and theoretical perspectives intersect. Although our microtheories are not generally the analyses of the actors themselves, they are based in local knowledge and built close to the ground they cover. We do not stray far from the conduct of Cambridge economists in the 1930s and their stories—what they thought they were doing and wanted to achieve by acting as they did. Much of what follows qualifies as Geertzian "thick description" or Wittgensteinian "perspicuous representation": an account of social interactions and their artifacts considered within the institutional frames and cultural settings in which actors attempted to make sense of their enterprises (Geertz 1973, 1983; Wittgenstein 1953, 1971).

Our microtheories are linked to two lines of investigation in science studies, a loose synthesis and an uneasy coalition of the history, sociology, and philosophy of science. We explore various respects in which the formation of Robinson's identity as a Cambridge economist and her early career moves were results of strategic efforts. On this point, our analysis is a contribution to research on the social constitution of scientific careers and the role of strategy in forming scientific research programs and professional identities. Mario Biagioli has argued that Galileo conceived a new socioprofessional status for the mathematician as natural philosopher and employed the intellectual and cultural assets at his disposal in order to occupy this status (Biagioli 1993).[8] We argue that Robinson imagined a new project of Cambridge analytical economics and mobilized resources at hand to become such an economist. Throughout, our work draws on the thinking of two precursors of science studies, both of whom stress the importance of strategies of identity formation and career production: Max Weber's writings on the role of institutional orders and cultural spheres in setting criteria for selection and success in career paths (Weber 1978) and Erving Goffman's studies on the creation, reproduction, and presentation of social identities (Goffman 1959, 1969).

We also argue that Robinson's professional identity was embedded in a local scientific culture, the changing Marshallian guild—students of Marshall, the father of Cambridge economics, and successive generations of their students—of Cambridge economists in the late 1920s and early 1930s. This argument connects our account to recent work on microsocial geographies of science, which is based on the premise that scientific research programs and the socialization of the scientists who execute them are formed in local scientific cultures. The geography of science has sharpened doubts concerning the "everywhere and nowhere" conception of science and scientific institutions: the view that in the origins and development of scientific research and careers, there are no special or privileged places (Golinski 1998, 80). Microsocial geographies of science take the position that the cultural spaces of science are among the conditions that identify scientific performances that are treated as acceptable or respectable in these spaces. Local cultures distinguish claims that are acknowledged as interesting and promising from those that are rejected as hopelessly confused and scientifically worthless. Sites of research are characterized by distinctive methodological regimes that govern what qualifies as a legitimate scientific move. "Spaces of discursive exchange" define the modes of consensus and disagreement that are possible as well as how they are framed and interpreted (Livingstone 2003, 7). What can reasonably be claimed or questioned in a scientific investigation depends in part on the places from which investigators speak—the connection between location and locution (Livingstone 2007). In sum, an understanding of locales of scientific production is essential to understanding the circumstances under which scientific work is done and scientific careers made.[9] Our analysis proceeds from recent ideas on local cultures in science, transposing them from the natural sciences, the site of their use thus far, to the circumstances of Robinson's career.

SIGNPOSTS AND CAVEATS
An Epistolary Anthropology

To a remarkable extent, Cambridge economists of the 1930s conducted their professional lives in correspondence. Because of the wealth of unpublished sources housed in the University of Cambridge archives, we have been able to write this book largely as a study in epistolary anthropology (Biagioli 1993, 19). We read the story of the formation of Robinson's professional identity in the letters she and her colleagues exchanged at the time. The riches of the archives make it possible to act on the historiographic principle: follow the primary sources of the 1930s.[10] This principle also answers the question of why no accounts of interviews? After all, as of this writing some of Robinson's students and younger colleagues are distinguished economists with memories intact and stories to tell. These are stories of the post–Second World War Robinson. When she was in her fifties, sixties, and seventies, she reminisced on the years of her apprenticeship, remembrances that were refracted through the events of later decades. This book considers Robinson in the 1930s. It is not an investigation of how she may have recalled Cambridge economics of the 1930s after the experiences of a quarter of a century or more. The revisionism of distant recollections—the fact that what is remembered is formed by the experience of a more recent past and recalled from the perspective of the present—suggests that what Robinson and her colleagues wrote in the 1930s outweighs later recollections.

It follows that readers who knew the later Robinson may find it difficult to recognize the young economist of the 1930s—discovering new research programs, honing her skills, and working to establish herself. If that is the case, it should not cause surprise. The battles of the 1930s were fought and on the whole won at the time. Her priorities of the 1930s were not the desiderata of her postwar career. By the mid-1960s, when she was the Professor of Political Economy at Cambridge and an internationally celebrated economist, the question of her professional identity and the problem of how to fashion an academic career had not been on her agenda for decades.[11]

Narratives of Career Strategy and Analyses of Economic Theory

Robinson's enterprise of career production cannot be detached from her projects in economic theory. This means that in telling her story, it is not always sensible to take a path of strict chronological linearity. Robinson and her colleagues were academic intellectuals, passionately devoted to their work. An exploration of her social world does not permit a fine distinction between a narrative of action and an analysis of economic ideas. More often than not, the narrative concerns a problem of economic theory. To advance the narrative, it is necessary to consider the economic ideas in which it is embedded. Robinson's efforts in promoting her career were generally tied to the books or papers in which she was engaged. It is not even clear that she made a distinction between her work in economics and her contemporaneous work in career management. Little sense can be made of Robinson in the 1930s without interweaving her theoretical and strategic interests—the details of her economic thought and the elements of her career planning. It follows that evidence for our account of her strategic projects often unfolds in an analysis of her work in economic theory.

It also follows that the character of the narrative varies with the problems on which Robinson and her colleagues were engaged. In part 2, we show that she embraced the Cambridge practice of economic research as dialogue with considerable élan. It is not possible to tell an intelligent story of how her kinked demand curve (Robinson 1933d, 81) was produced in dialogues with Kahn without explaining what the kinked demand curve is. For the same reason, an account of Pigou's exchange with Robinson over the problem of equilibrium in imperfect markets would be incomprehensible without commentary on technical and theoretical details. Comparable considerations hold for our history of Robinson's attempts to secure Keynes's patronage in part 3. She attempted to gain his recognition in the course of struggling to understand his *Treatise on Money* in 1934, commenting on the proofs of *The General Theory* in 1935, and debating with him in 1936 on the proofs of her *Essays in the Theory of Employment*. The story of her success in winning his endorsement as a leader of the revolution cannot be told without considering some of the details of her theoretical engagement with Keynes and his work.

Contingencies

Robinson did not return from India with a plan to maneuver herself from the margins of Cambridge economics to its center, as if she were Athene bursting fully formed from the forehead of Zeus. The skills she acquired and the strategies she employed were developed against a background of contingencies that proved to be remarkably propitious for the development of her professional identity. She had no hand in their production, nor were they objects of planning on her part. It could not have been otherwise. A plan rests on premises that are not planned. Her strategies were based on assumptions without which they would not have been possible.

Consider the circumstances under which she began work on a long-period analysis of imperfect competition. Sraffa had published his influential article in the *Economic Journal* (1926), spelling out the requirements of a theory of value under conditions of imperfect competition. He was also lecturing on these issues. Shove, Robertson, and Kahn had defined and clarified possible lines of research. the *Economic Journal* symposium of 1930 on increasing returns had appeared, and Cambridge economists had become acquainted with the marginal revenue curve, a new research tool with intriguing possibilities for a diagrammatic analysis. By this point, the outlines of a research program were clear enough to allow for the entrance of a novice and for the execution of a significant piece of work. Although promising terrain and the means for exploring it had been discovered, no one had entered the territory. If Sraffa had acted on the suggestions he made in 1926, if Shove had been a more nimble thinker, or if Kahn had followed Pigou's advice and published his dissertation in a timely fashion, it is unlikely that the conditions under which Robinson took the first steps to establish her professional identity would have been in place.

In the received historiography of interwar economics at Cambridge, the favored genre is the epic. The master narrative is the story of *The General Theory*. Its hero is Keynes, the single charismatic economist of the time. Other dramatis personae appear in their relations to him—as interlocutors, acolytes, or opponents (Ambrosi 2003; Marcuzzo and Rosselli 2005). The story of the development of imperfect competition is told in the same fashion. Piero Sraffa is the principal actor in the drama of renovating economics by abandoning the assumption of competitive markets. Others—Shove, Kahn, and Robinson—have their parts to play, but they follow in his steps (Cozzi and Marchionatti 2001).[12] Both stories are Homeric adventures of ideas. A single theoretician dominates the stage, and lesser figures respond to his innovations.

The picture changes markedly if Robinson is moved to the foreground from her place in the conventional historiography as either Keynes's disciple or Sraffa's follower. In understanding the Cambridge economics of the time, the unit of analysis is no longer the single theoretician but an epistemic community: the Marshallian guild. An account of Robinson as fledgling economist shifts the perspective from heroic deeds of virtuosi to the importance of guild membership. What were the barriers to entry and the criteria for admission? What skills were expected of apprentices? How was performance judged? Because Robinson introduced new sources of conflict into the guild, its social dynamics acquired a new salience. How far could an apprentice venture in testing the limits of guild civility? When the etiquette of the guild was violated, what were the results and how were conflicts adjudicated? In attempting to enter the guild by producing work that was recognized as original, Robinson's priority claims were not uncontested. What tactics in defending credit claims were prudent for aspirants to guild membership? In Keynes, Robinson sought and eventually gained a patron. What effects in the guild did his patronage and her clientage produce? Because of the importance of intraguild friendship in Robinson's early career, collegiality intersected with friendship. What consequences followed when the lines between the personal and the professional were blurred? In sum, the picture of Cambridge economics that emerges when Robinson is moved to the foreground is not an imposing mural of heroes and their deeds but a series of collages that depict changes in the guild as she progresses from novice to master.

†

The Improbable
Theoretician

SUCCESS AT CAMBRIDGE, FEBRUARY 1938

"I am extremely relieved that the matter of Joan's lectureship looks like being settled." This was Keynes writing on February 19, 1938, from his home in London in response to news from Kahn that Robinson had been appointed to a university lectureship in economics at Cambridge (JMK/L/K/94–96).[1] Although Kahn's letter ended Keynes's worries over her candidacy, his delight was hardly unqualified. He had neither participated in the deliberations of the Faculty Board of Economics and Politics that recommended the appointment nor was he consulted. During its meetings on the lectureship in January and February, he was convalescing from a heart attack suffered the previous summer. Moreover, Kahn—Keynes's protégé and colleague at King's College—believed that in taking no notice of Robinson's contributions to economic theory, the board had arrived at its decision in a willfully demeaning fashion.[2] This slight provoked Keynes's anger. With the exception of Kahn, Robinson's chief supporter on the board, only Pigou, the senior member of the economics faculty, had taken "the right line." But what of Keynes's other colleagues? "How the other wretches can have failed to recognize that outside Cambridge she is unquestionably one of the most distinguished members of the staff, without doubt within the first half dozen, I cannot imagine."[3]

In early 1938, the top five economists at Cambridge were Pigou, Keynes himself, Robertson, Sraffa and either Kahn or J. R. Hicks.[4] Pigou was Marshall's handpicked successor as Professor of Political Economy. He was the founder of welfare economics and arguably the most authoritative voice of neoclassical economics in Britain. Keynes made his reputation immediately after the First World War with *The Economic Consequences of the Peace* (1920), a trenchant critique of the political economy of the Treaty of Versailles based on his experience as a member of the British delegation at the Paris Peace Conference. As the term *Keynesian revolution* suggests, *The General Theory of Employment, Interest and Money* (1936) made him the most influential economist of the 1930s. Robertson was a Cambridge pioneer in investigating linkages of money, business cycles, economic growth, and government policy. When the faculty board recommended his appointment to a university readership, it stressed his "exceptional qualifications and world-wide reputation" and his "outstanding distinction as an economist."[5] Sraffa's article of 1926 in the *Economic Journal* produced a sea change in the understanding of Marshallian value theory and marked the beginning of research on imperfect competition at Cambridge. In his fellowship dissertation (1929) and his publications of the thirties (1931, 1933), Kahn constructed theoretical building blocks that were used by Keynes and Robinson.[6] He also reinterpreted conclusions of Pigouvian welfare theory under conditions of imperfect competition (1935) and published innovative work on duopoly (1937). Hicks's analysis of labor markets under long-run competitive conditions developed several important tools for microeconomics (1932). Together with R. G. D. Allen, he introduced British economists to Vilfredo Pareto's conception of utility theory and achieved a groundbreaking reformulation of the theory of demand (1934). Most famously, he was responsible for a popular simplification of Keynes's new ideas in an IS-LM diagram that proved easy to understand and enjoyed international appeal only a few months after Keynes published his book (Hicks 1937).[7] Thus Keynes placed Robinson in extraordinarily select company.

Keynes's assessment was not excessively generous, an appreciation of the dedication shown by an early and enthusiastic supporter of his work. Only three years after beginning serious work on economic theory, Robinson published *The Economics of Imperfect Competition*, which set a new course for the theory of price determination—or, in the Cambridge parlance of the time, value theory. She claimed that her inspiration was Sraffa's critique of the reigning Cambridge theory of value that descended from Marshall, the author of *Principles of Economics* (1890), the canonical treatise of Victorian economic thought. One of Sraffa's main objections to Marshall's theory was its assumption of free competition between economic actors, a premise he regarded as obviously inconsistent with the realities of economic life. Following Sraffa, Robinson analyzed price determination under monopolistic conditions. She also considered the consequences of this analysis for the distribution of income, arguing that under imperfect competition workers are paid less than the market value of their labor. Thus she revived and refined the Pigouvian concept of exploitation (Pigou 1920, 511–19).

The book was an immediate *succès d'estime*, receiving reviews in the major British and American journals. The young Nicholas Kaldor was the reviewer for *Economica* (1934). Shove wrote the review for the *Economic Journal* (1933a). Perhaps the most important review was by Joseph A. Schumpeter, who contributed an eight-page appreciation for the *Journal of Political Economy* (1934). Widely read on both sides of the Atlantic, the book quickly became a standard text in the new research field. A letter of November 9, 1937, from Fritz Machlup to Robinson gives a good sense of the early excitement her work generated. Machlup was a Viennese economist trained in a tradition opposed in many respects to Cambridge principles. He had emigrated to the United States and was teaching at Cornell University. He wrote, "A seminar of eighteen postgraduate students is studying your book *The Economics of Imperfect Competition* and discussing it from cover to cover, paragraph after paragraph. In appreciation of your most stimulating work, the undersigned wish to thank you and to assure you of their admiration."[8]

The Economics of Imperfect Competition was reprinted thirteen times between 1933 and 1965. The reprint of 1942 appeared when demand for higher education and supply of paper were both quite low owing to the war. By the early 1960s, the book had been translated into German, Italian, Japanese, Portuguese (Brazil), Korean, Polish, and Serbo-Croatian (JVR/vii/269). Robinson's work on price theory did not end with *The Economics of Imperfect Competition*. Her essay "Rising Supply Price" (1941) was praised by Samuelson and won the approval even of the "hypercritical Jacob Viner" (Samuelson 1989, 126). The long-term impact of this paper was surprising and quite remote from her intentions. In 1942, George Stigler used her analysis in *The Theory of Competitive Price*, an immensely successful neoclassical textbook studied by thousands of economics students over several decades. As a result, her argument was appropriated to rescue the theory of price determination under conditions of perfect competition, precisely the model she had attacked in 1933 (Aslanbeigui and Naples 1997, 527).

During the 1930s, Robinson also became a zealous partisan of Keynesian thinking. The origins of *The General Theory* lay in dissatisfaction with Keynes's first attempt at a magnum opus in economic theory. This was the two-volume *A Treatise on Money* (1930), a project on which he labored fitfully and with many interruptions and distractions for some seven years. Its flaws were quickly noticed by both friendly and unsympathetic critics. Even as he corrected the final proofs, Keynes was planning a comprehensive revision. On publication of the *Treatise*, a group of young economists at Cambridge—Sraffa, Kahn, James Meade, who was visiting from Oxford, Robinson, and Austin—began discussions. Although their initial intention was to understand the complexities of the book, they quickly moved to a consideration of its defects and how they might be repaired. This was the fabled Cambridge Circus, which arrived at conclusions that eventually moved Keynes to abandon his attempts to revise the *Treatise*. Instead, he would write a quite different book, one that would mark a more fundamental break with the Cambridge tradition. In 1932 and 1933, Robinson argued that the *Treatise* entailed a vision of a new world of economic theory that Keynes had glimpsed but not clearly comprehended. Once he accepted this view, he made the turn from the *Treatise* to the enterprise of developing a theory of monetary production in which aggregate demand played a large role.

In the years of the conception and composition of *The General Theory*, Robinson wrote the first essay on the emerging Keynesian synthesis. Her article "The Theory of Money and the Analysis of Output" (1933e) was the earliest signal to economists not closely connected with Cambridge that fundamental changes in Keynes's thinking were underway. Once *The General Theory* was published, she moved from theory construction to theory translation and extension. Within a year of its appearance, she completed a book that elucidated and refined Keynes's ideas and offered a spirited defense of his methods. *Essays in the Theory of Employment* brought to fruition a plan Robinson made in summer 1934. Her idea was to write rough sketches on the main themes of Keynes's new work as well as problems she could analyze by employing his methods. When circumstances seemed opportune, she would prepare them for publication.[9] She also extended the explanatory range of *The General Theory* by taking up problems Keynes did not pursue, applying its short-period framework to longer-term economic interactions and opening up its closed economy to international trade and finance. Finally, she celebrated the virtues of Keynes's theory by placing it above all competitors. In providing a convincing account of the role of qualitative variables such as expectations as well as a rigorous quantitative analysis of employment, output, and wages, Keynes's work superseded all rivals. Most of the papers in the *Essays* were written in 1936. "The Long-Period Theory of Employment" was first published in a German journal in March, a month after *The General Theory*. "Disguised Unemployment" appeared in the *Economic Journal* three months later. This was remarkably fast work. It was possible only because Robinson kept up to date with changes in Keynes's thinking as he wrote successive drafts of *The General Theory*.

Unlike *The Economics of Imperfect Competition*, the *Essays* was not an immediate commercial or critical success. The first edition was not reprinted. In October 1947, when wartime printing restrictions due to paper shortages had been lifted and postwar university enrollments had increased dramatically, a second edition was published and reprinted the following month. There seems to have been only one early review, published in the *Economic Journal*, where Austin was assistant editor. Robinson's consolation prize was the reviewer: Roy Harrod, the distinguished Oxford economist and enthusiast of *The General Theory*. Harrod praised Robinson for contributing "another volume of great distinction to economic studies" (Harrod 1937b, 326). He was especially taken by "The Long-Period Theory of Unemployment," in his judgment the "*pièce de résistance*" of the book (Harrod 1937b, 328). However, he raised two intriguing objections to Robinson's project of extending *The General Theory* to the long run. She made no attempt to tackle the intractable problem of measuring capital. In addition, both Keynes and Robinson analyzed problems of economic dynamics by employing a static theoretical framework. In Harrod's view, a genuine dynamic analysis was needed, an analysis like the one on which he had been working for some time.[10]

In autumn 1936, Robinson considered writing a more accessible version of Keynes's program for students, who were likely to be bewildered by its antiorthodox polemics, formidable organization, and complex analyses. She also moved quickly on this project, and within a year her Keynesian primer, *Introduction to the Theory of Employment*, appeared. She conceived the book as an exposition of *The General Theory* for beginners, including students who could not be expected to perform brilliantly on the Cambridge Economics Tripos, or honors examination. The *Introduction* is best understood as Robinson's attempt to revolutionize undergraduate economics in a Keynesian direction, socializing students in the language and methods of *The General Theory* at the outset of their training. Robinson understood a basic revolutionary imperative that some of her fellow partisans, Keynes among them, did not appreciate: capture the next generation. The revolution would be decided not in debates over the merits of Keynes's book by academics of the 1930s but in debates by their students. This meant that his adversaries could be vanquished even though they were not refuted or fully persuaded. Classicism would be destroyed when its adherents retired and a new generation educated on Keynesian principles became civil servants, central bankers, and academics. Demand for her bedtime story or "told to the children" (in Keynes 1979, 185) version of *The General Theory* was impressive. The *Introduction* was reprinted twice in 1938, once again in 1939, and several times after the Second World War, by which time the victory of the revolution had been achieved.

MAKING IT: HOW TO BECOME A CAMBRIDGE ECONOMIC THEORIST CIRCA 1900–30

At the beginning of the 1930s, Robinson possessed no profile as an economic theorist, not even in the small Cambridge faculty in which she was known. In 1931, Keynes did not recognize her as an economist. In a letter of May 4 to Lydia, he identified Robinson solely by her conjugal status, as the marital appendage of Austin (JMK/PP/45/190/5).

What were Robinson's credentials in 1930? As a student of Girton College, Cambridge, Joan Violet Maurice read economics, graduating in 1925 with an undistinguished performance on her tripos and receiving a disappointing Second Class (Pasinetti 1987, 212). The following year she married Austin, and the couple sailed to India, where Austin began a two-year appointment as tutor in economics to the young maharajah of the Indian state of Gwalior. If Austin's memory can be trusted, Robinson knew little economics when she completed her studies and did not acquire much more during their stay in India. When he returned to Cambridge and she reappeared as Mrs. Robinson, she attended Sraffa's lectures on advanced theory of value. In Austin's recollections, she was not preparing herself for a career in economic theory but only pursuing current work in the field of her studies (Robinson 1994, 7). In 1931, there seems to have been no reason Keynes should have regarded her as a budding theoretician.

When Robinson began supervising students at the couple's flat, her prospects for a Cambridge lectureship were dim. Between the introduction of the Economics Tripos in 1903 and 1930, there were no official standards for university lectureships in economics. However, the faculty board, which recommended candidates for lectureships to the general board, seems to have employed tacit criteria that functioned as consensual norms for appointment. In 1930, there were five economists at Cambridge who incontestably qualified as theorists. In order of appointment, Pigou, Keynes, Shove, Robertson, and Sraffa.[11] In considering the obstacles Robinson faced, it is useful to examine their pedigrees, the credentials they established as young men prior to their appointments. Then, as now, the socioeconomic locus of British economic theory was the university. This meant that the career prospects of a theorist were tied to the institutional imperatives of academia. It was necessary to build an impressive curriculum vitae by submitting to critical rites of passage. Examination papers, prize essays, and dissertations were trials, tests of merit that decided the fate of academic apprentices by determining whether they were, if not brilliant or original, then at least, in the parlance of the time, sound.

Pigou (b. 1877) was the only member of the economics faculty in 1930 to have entered Cambridge before the Economic Tripos. Admitted to King's in 1896, he had a brilliant undergraduate career, placing Firsts in Part I of the History Tripos and Part II of the Moral Sciences Tripos, which at the time included political economy as well as philosophy. His essay in 1902 on changes in agricultural prices, which was awarded the Cobden Prize, won him a fellowship at King's. As a result of Marshall's management of the selection of his successor in 1908, he was elected to the Chair of Political Economy.

Keynes (b. 1883) took the Mathematics Tripos in 1905, receiving the twelfth highest score in the First Class. After taking his degree, he studied economics with Marshall for one term. Eighteen months at the India Office left him time to work on a fellowship dissertation for King's, a philosophical analysis of probability theory. The examiners rejected the dissertation as not up to fellowship standards. However, Pigou's selection as Marshall's successor transformed Keynes's prospects. Pigou was elected on May 30, 1908. Three days later, the faculty board—Keynes's father was its secretary—authorized a lectureship for Keynes, to be funded from Pigou's professorial stipend. It was Pigou who had suggested some weeks earlier that Marshall write Keynes about such a possibility. Thus Keynes's first appointment was arranged through the joint intercession of Marshall and Pigou and with the assistance of his father. He resubmitted his dissertation in early 1909 and was elected a fellow of King's in March.

Shove (b. 1888) entered King's in 1907 and received a First with distinction in the Economics Tripos of 1911. He was a pupil and intimate of Keynes. Like Keynes, he was one of the chosen few selected for membership in the Society of Apostles, the secret transgenerational Cambridge discussion club that entertained pretensions to the highest levels of intellectuality. Also like Keynes, he was among the Cambridge Bloomsberries, bright young men from King's and Trinity who frequented the salons of the Stephen sisters, Vanessa Bell and Virginia Woolf, in London. Shove's fellowship dissertation, submitted to King's in 1914, failed to win the approval of the electors. Although Keynes registered a strenuous dissent with the electors, the decision stood. When military conscription was introduced in January 1916, Shove gained an exemption based on pacifism and conscientious objection. Keynes gave evidence on his behalf. In 1926, Keynes finally succeeded in arranging his election as a fellow of King's.

Robertson (b. 1890) entered Trinity in 1908 and also became a pupil of Keynes. He wrote verse not only in English, but also in Greek and Latin, winning the Chancellor's Medal for English Verse three years in succession as well as the University Craven Prize. He received a First in Part I of the Classics Tripos (1910) and took another First in Part II of the Economics Tripos (1912). Although his fellowship dissertation for Trinity was rejected in 1913, it won the Cobden Prize the same year. In 1914, he renewed his application and was elected to a fellowship on the basis of a revision of the dissertation, published in 1915 as *A Study of Industrial Fluctuations*.

In 1930, Sraffa (b. 1898) was arguably the most brilliant economist at Cambridge. In the preface to his *Philosophical Investigations*, Ludwig Wittgenstein, not noted for a misplaced sense of intellectual modesty, acknowledged only two debts: Frank Ramsey's critique of his earlier *Tractatus* and a larger obligation to the "unremitting" criticisms of Sraffa, to whom he credited "the most consequential ideas" of the book.[12] Sraffa studied economics in the faculty of law at the University of Turin, where economists were influenced more by Marshall than by Pareto. In 1925, he published a seminal critique of Marshall's theory of value in an Italian journal. The following year, Keynes, in his capacity as editor of the *Economic Journal*, published a considerably altered English version. In 1927, a lectureship for Sraffa was established at Cambridge on Keynes's initiative.

What do these academic profiles of Cambridge economists show? The Cambridge products received First Class degrees. Pigou, Keynes, and Robertson wrote successful dissertations that won them election to college fellowships. Four of the five benefited from patronage, resources placed at the disposal of a young scholar by a more powerful member of the economics faculty. Marshall was Pigou's patron. Both Shove and Sraffa enjoyed Keynes's patronage. And no fewer than three members of the faculty—Pigou, Marshall, and J. N. Keynes—took a hand in arranging Keynes's appointment. Finally, all five theorists were men, a fact that should not pass without comment in view of the status of women at Cambridge before the Second World War.

A MAN'S WORLD

By the 1920s, Cambridge had a long and inglorious history of discrimination against women unique among British universities. One product of this history was an academic caste system based on sex. In 1881, students at Girton and Newnham, the two Cambridge colleges for women, received permission to sit for honors examinations and have their papers evaluated. Performance on the tripos and satisfaction of the three-and-one-half-year residence requirement were the criteria for a Cambridge honors degree. However, the faculty senate decreed that regardless of their tripos performance and notwithstanding the fact that they wrote the same papers set for men, women would not receive degrees. In May 1897, a "grace," or proposal, was introduced to grant qualified women the title or name of their degree but not the degree itself, an arcane distinction that seems to have made sense to the members of the university. The proposal engaged the passions of both graduates and faculty, especially those committed to Victorian conceptions of the natural place of women in the social order and the limits of their intellectual faculties. On polling day, many nonresident graduates traveled to Cambridge for the vote, and the proposal was roundly defeated.[13]

One of the most able and influential opponents of measures to reform women's education at Cambridge was the teacher of Pigou and Keynes, the architect of Cambridge economic pedagogy, and the namesake of the Pigouvian dictum, "It's all in Marshall." Yet Marshall had been an early champion of higher education for women and an ally of Henry Sidgwick in the ambitious project to build and staff Newnham College. He donated money to its construction fund and even married one of its products, his student Mary Paley. In the 1870s, Marshall defended equal education for men and women and supported the movement to permit women at Cambridge to sit for honors examinations. He was also in the vanguard of Cambridge faculty who taught women, lecturing on political economy and political philosophy and preparing them for examinations. By 1885, when he became the Professor of Political Economy, he was singing a song with a more traditional theme. Women's chief responsibilities were by nature domestic. Their education should generally be restricted to part-time study at local colleges, such as Bristol University College, where he had been principal in 1877–84. Marshall viewed granting degrees to women as especially dangerous. It was likely to debase the quality of the university since questions of academic policy as well as many routine matters were settled by polling graduates.

By the 1890s, Marshall embraced social Darwinist views that would severely limit higher education for women. His earlier alliance with Sidgwick and his support for liberal reform were now outweighed by theories of racial degeneration derived from a tendentious reading of Charles Darwin's *The Descent of Man* and Herbert Spencer's *Principles of Biology*. Education would damage women's health by weakening their reproductive systems.

It would have a seductively destructive effect on ethics by encouraging them to pursue lives that conflicted with marriage and motherhood. Marshall envisioned ruinous consequences for the family, which depended on the presence of dutiful wives and mothers in the home. If Cambridge and other British universities encouraged women to pursue higher education, the British "race" would degenerate physically as well as morally. Women university graduates would spell doom in the implacable international and interracial struggle for survival. Britain would be subjugated by other races, which would prove their superiority by confining women to their naturally endowed functions. Women in various fields occasionally outperformed men in honors examinations. Marshall's explanation? They were diligent by nature and endowed with an innate capability for proficiency in examinations that was denied men. Because they lacked male capacities for creativity and originality, this was the upper limit of their intellectual potential. Marshall compared the effects of malperformance by women in the household to a draft horse that was not properly cared for and a steam engine without a sufficient supply of coal (Groenewegen 1995, 507). Although a Cambridge education might open up opportunities for women, the economic value of their domestic functions vastly outweighed any contribution they might make as members of the labor force.[14]

When Joan Maurice entered Girton, commitment by the university to Marshallian views on the dangers women posed for Cambridge and the perils they faced remained largely intact, compromised but not seriously weakened by the suffrage movement and the liberalization of relations between the sexes that followed the First World War. On October 21, 1921, a year before Maurice's matriculation, members of the university were asked to vote on whether to award purely titular degrees to qualified women students or to grant them additional rights as well. Thus the question posed in 1921 presupposed acceptance of the proposal that had been rejected in 1897. Polling day was a volatile event, with elements of a class reunion, political convention, pep rally, and small-scale riot. Voting by opponents of the more liberal measure was encouraged by a wealthy graduate who offered like-minded nonresident alumni vouchers for round-trip train tickets between London and Cambridge at reduced rates. The views of undergraduate men were canvassed the evening before at the Cambridge Union, which debated the proposition that the "house did not consider granting a titular degree met the legitimate aspirations of women students." W. R. Sorley, Professor of Medicine, resurrected Victorian arguments for the inferior intellectual status of women and suggested a darker motive for the movement to extend women's rights in higher education: mobilization of support for radical positions on the woman's question. The motion before the Union was defeated 375 to 185. The next day undergraduates chanted, "We won't have women!" and members of the university defeated the more liberal proposal. After the vote, a group of students rushed from the Senate House to Newnham and attacked the bronze-plated main gate of the college, partially destroying it—an act of political symbolism since the gate was valued for both aesthetic and sentimental reasons. In attempting to invade the college grounds by another entry, they were finally subdued by university proctors and local police. No charges were brought and no student was disciplined (Bradbrook 1969, 165).

The vote of October 21 placed limits on the number of women students, denied them entry to men's colleges, and gave the faculty the freedom to use different syllabi for men and women preparing for the same examinations. As a result of the vote, Cambridge remained the only British university where women were excluded from university lectureships and administrative offices, even at the lowest levels.[15] Women attended university lectures at the pleasure of the lecturer. Faculty had the right to deny women admittance to lectures or segregate them in specially designated seats. No examiner was obligated to read women's papers, and their tripos performance continued to be reported independently of the results of men.

The vote was especially dispiriting for Cambridge women who had academic aspirations. Eileen Power, the medievalist and one of the most distinguished economic historians of her time, was a graduate of Girton, placing Firsts in both Parts of the History Tripos in 1910. After several years of lecturing and supervision at Cambridge, she left for a better position at the London School of Economics (LSE), where the prospects for women seemed more promising. On learning the results of the vote of October 21, she wrote Bertrand Russell, "Cambridge has really cut our throats now: it would have been much better to get nothing than to get the titular degree. . . . Our position in the University [is] exactly where it was. I have never been so bitter in my life" (quoted with elision in Berg 1996, 141). It is not difficult to sympathize with Power's response, especially in light of the apparent incomprehensibility of the distinctions on which the university insisted so strenuously. In 1897, the university declared that there was no connection between women's performance on honors examinations and their degree qualifications. But at that time, tripos performance was the most important requirement for the Cambridge honors degree. In 1921, the university held that it was sensible to grant the name of the degree but withhold the degree itself. Both positions seem anomalous. In 1897, Cambridge created a right to be examined but not a right to university tuition to prepare for the examination; neither did it guarantee that the examination would be read. In approving purely titular degrees for women in 1921, it created "a graduate without a degree" (McWilliams Tullberg 1998, 68). Such reasoning exceeded the limits of Power's tolerance.

Restrictions on women during Joan Maurice's student years were not limited to purely academic matters. The institution of chaperonage, which required an adult female to accompany women students when they left the confines of their college or received extrafamilial male visitors within college gates, was not formally abolished at Cambridge until 1936. Some chaperonage regulations were relaxed following the First World War. For example, unattended women were permitted to meet men in local tea shops, and there were circumstances under which a woman was even allowed to entertain a male student in her rooms if another woman was present. Yet regulations from 1920 governing mixed company in the traditional pastime of boating on the Cam illustrate the tortured scholasticism of redefining rules for the surveillance of women: "Parties may with leave of the Tutor go on the river in punts or boats but not in canoes. Such parties may only take place before dinner (8 p.m. Sundays) and more than one student must be present except that a student may go alone with her brother or her fiancé. No such parties may include more than one punt or boat and no parties may take place on Thursday" (quoted in McWilliams Tullberg 1998, 144).

In November 1925, women were finally admitted to university teaching posts and membership on faculty boards that made most decisions on curricula, lectureship appointments, and examinations. This was the first occasion on which women were allowed to deliver lectures to male students. They remained excluded from competitions for fellowships in men's colleges. Women students did not receive the right to attend university lectures until 1926. During Maurice's student years, this was a privilege that might be granted, withheld, or withdrawn at the discretion of the lecturer (McWilliams Tullberg 1998, 177–78).[16]

THE "ANALYTICAL ECONOMIST":
GENESIS OF A PROFESSIONAL IDENTITY, 1930–31
From Joan Maurice to Joan Robinson

Women at Cambridge in the early 1920s contended with obstacles imposed on them by a sexist academic culture. The university conferred on men advantages that women did not enjoy, endowing them with resources to which women had little or no access. Segregation of women into separate colleges distributed the goods of the university not only unequally but inequitably. What was the significance of these inequities for Joan Maurice? After all, the leading economists of her student years seem to have taken progressive stances on academic rights for women. The question might be posed in another way: in the early 1920s, what were the ideal conditions for women undergraduates in economics at Cambridge? Untrammeled attendance without invidious treatment in all lectures that were listed for men reading for the Economics Tripos, common syllabi for men and women, and freedom from chaperonage. Even under these circumstances, Maurice would have labored under disadvantages owing solely to the fact that she was not a man.

Maurice was not supervised by a high-powered theoretician such as Robertson or Keynes. Her first supervisor was probably Marjorie Robinson. Entering Newnham as Marjorie Powel in 1912 and taking a First in the Economics Tripos during the war, Robinson was a product of the pre-1919 regime of women's education at Cambridge. She had no experience of the more liberal, sophisticated academic socialization that Robertson and Shove enjoyed as students of Trinity and King's. Widely read in the literature of economics, she was, according to her contemporary Hubert Henderson, "content with her role as a teacher" and made "no pretensions to originality or distinction" (Henderson 1940, 162).[17] Marjorie Tappan (later Tappan-Holland), who replaced Robinson as director of studies of both Girton and Newnham in 1923, was most likely Maurice's second supervisor. A Cambridge outsider, she graduated from Bryn Mawr College in Pennsylvania in 1915 and completed a doctoral degree at Columbia in 1917 (Turner 1989, 252, n. 24). Perhaps because of her positions in the two women's colleges and her teaching responsibilities—she also became a member of the faculty board in November 1926 (FB/Min.V. 116)—she had little time for research and publication. Keynes seems to have regarded her credentials as pedestrian and in 1932 voted against her reappointment to a university lectureship.[18]

Excluded from the privileged social spheres of men's colleges, Maurice did not have the valuable informal contacts and close personal relations with leading economists that were such an important element of a Cambridge education. She was not allowed in the rooms of male students or fellows, nor could she dine in the halls of men's colleges or expect invitations to breakfast on weekends or tea from male faculty. This meant that she was barred from sites at which journeymen economists received much of their education. Before he became a recluse, Pigou held Sunday breakfasts for his favored students, some of whom he also invited on mountaineering expeditions at his Lake District cottage. When Shove was Keynes's pupil, they vacationed together. In their undergraduate years, both Pigou and Robertson had been elected to the presidency of the Cambridge Union, the leading university debating society. The Union was a forum for self-presentation in an academic culture that stressed verbal facility and a glib mastery of rhetoric and sophistry as proofs of merit. Women were allowed in the audience but prohibited from engaging in debate. In the development of new ideas, lines between the economics faculty and their students were not finely drawn. Gifted undergraduates had a role in research that is difficult to imagine today. In 1929, Kahn had less than a year of training in economics, yet he was assisting Keynes with final revisions of the *Treatise*. In 1930, Austin was introduced to the marginal revenue curve by one of his pupils. Following the tradition of Cambridge Victorians, who emulated the classical Greek synthesis of strenuous physical and intellectual pursuits, tripos preparation was often a peripatetic exercise. Study was conducted on walking tours in the English countryside scheduled during interterm vacations. Lecturers or fellows selected their favorite students. With books packed, they set out for days or weeks of hiking through the southwest counties or the Lake District, attired in plus fours and tailored walking jackets complete with soft, collared shirts and ties. Reading and discussion took place on breaks from hiking and during overnights at country inns. Maurice's undergraduate life did not include these opportunities. In the 1920s, the homegrown theoreticians—Pigou, Keynes, Robertson, and Shove—were all products of the castelike culture and social organization of Cambridge education. Women were at the bottom of the sociointellectual order. From the standpoint of entitlements, privileges, liberties, resources, and assets—including the excellence or contemptibility of the cuisine served by college kitchens—women lived in the lower depths.[19] Moreover, the lifestyles of Cambridge economists—Pigou, Keynes (until 1925), Robertson, and Shove (until his marriage)—were marked by a pronounced homoerotic complexion. Although it is difficult to characterize with any precision the disadvantages this fact entailed for women, some observations can be made with reasonable confidence. Young men were preferred for intimate relationships as pupils, disciples, and companions. At best, women were treated with diffidence and kept at a respectable distance. In the 1920s, none of the Cambridge theoreticians had selected women as their preferred pupils, protégés, or professional peers.

When did these disadvantages begin to make a substantial difference to Maurice? Not until she returned from India as Mrs. Robinson and began to take seriously a career as a Cambridge economist. This apparently was not her immediate intention when the Robinsons resettled in Cambridge before Austin began teaching in the Easter term of 1929. In July 1928, Robinson had returned to England from India, while Austin remained there until the end of the year. Her correspondence offers evidence of a reflective, well read, intellectually engaged, and energetic young woman with aspirations for economic independence. In a long letter written in late September, a month before her twenty-fifth birthday, she discussed the social functions and moral virtues of common-law or companionate marriage, the foundations of morality, the relationship between tradition, reason, and freedom, and the excesses of the emancipation of women in England, which she interpreted as "only a violent reaction against Puritanism + the immoral morality" of the Victorian era.[20] From her standpoint, an ideal society would institutionalize free divorce, an equal distribution of wealth, and education and independence for women. Thus it is not surprising that she impressed on Austin her personal commitment to self-reliance: "Please I don't want you to earn money to send me round the world. I am a strong believer in the economic independence of married women, + only ask to be allowed to earn some myself."[21] However, she had little conception of her opportunities and ambitions. The main object of her energies at the time was her husband's career. Prior to 1930, two episodes show especially clearly how she invested her efforts in his work, serving in a subordinate role as his willing assistant and factotum: the report on the princely states of India and the attempt to secure a position for Austin at Cambridge.

In spring 1927, the British viceroy of India appointed the Butler Committee to examine relations between the Indian states—princely territories of the Indian subcontinent not under British rule—and the colonial government. The brief of the Butler Committee was to improve economic relations between the states and British India. A Standing Committee of the Chamber of Princes—officials appointed by the princes to represent their collective interest—undertook an independent investigation of two main issues: neglect on the part of the British government of rights of the states established by treaties and inequities that the British fiscal system imposed on the states. The standing committee compiled a substantial two-part report: part 1 covered the political relations between the states and the Crown, and part 2 surveyed economic matters in dispute between the states and the British government of India (The Directorate 1929, xiv–xv). In April 1928, Austin prepared a draft on the economics of the case for the princely states intended for inclusion in part 2 of the report. In late June, his draft was discussed in Delhi by the standing committee. Since his tutorial responsibilities in Gwalior limited his freedom to travel, Robinson went to Delhi in his stead to help finish the draft. At the invitation of the standing committee, she sailed with the committee members to London in order to assist in completing the report and presenting the economic brief. On July 20, two days before arriving in London, she noted that she had written a preface for the report (EAGR/Box 8/2/1/13/13–16).[22] A few days after her arrival, she consulted with William Beveridge, the prominent British economist and director of LSE, who promised to read and comment on the material she gave him (EAGR/Box 8/2/1/13/17–21). The Butler Committee met on July 25 but accomplished virtually nothing and adjourned until October. In the intervening months, Robinson continued her work on part 2. By mid-October, an unidentified note on which she had been laboring had become "our note."[23] However, her work seems to have ended in disappointment. In the presentation to the Butler Committee, the note in question was reduced to a "mangled remnant," and although she had added notes on railways and salt, she was dissatisfied with her results.[24]

When Robinson returned to London in mid-September 1928 from a holiday with her parents in Ireland, a cable from Austin awaited her. His job in India would likely terminate before the end of the year. Could she inquire on his behalf concerning academic positions at Cambridge and Liverpool? Her response was to make an appointment with Robertson, who had visited Austin in India during an Asian tour in 1926–27 (Dennison and Presley 1922, 23). "Cambridge full at present but not hopeless" was his assessment. At that point there was a small chance of a university lectureship and, in a year or two, an excellent opportunity for a fellowship at one of the colleges that would not elect Maurice Dobb because he was a communist. Robinson noted that the Cambridge economists were "all most delightfully + genuinely excited" at the prospect of Austin's return. In addition, professorships were open at Liverpool and Hull.[25] The following day, she wrote a "more lucid account of our prospects." In her view they were good. "The economists though plentiful are bad." Any of three university lectureships at Cambridge might soon be open. Robertson was not happy with Humphrey Mynors because he was lecturing on industry without specialized knowledge of the field. Philip Sargant Florence might leave voluntarily or be pushed out because he was living in London while lecturing at Cambridge. And Sraffa—"the brilliant Italian at King's"—seemed to be incapacitated by the nervous strain of lecturing. She deferred making inquiries at LSE until she heard more from Robertson, who hoped that Austin could be offered a lectureship effective October 1929.[26] It seemed that the lectureship would concentrate on population, an area in which Austin had not lectured. Robinson reacted to this news with considerable enthusiasm, treating both the lectureship and its probable territory as a joint enterprise: "We can get Population well in hand before you have to bother with lectures. It sounds fun. I have my heart in it more than Localisation," on which he had lectured previously.[27] By October 31, she was already working on the literature. "I have bought a fountain pen so as to be able to work at L.S.E. but the books I want are always out. The India Office library is a good spot" (EAGR/Box 8/2/1/13/74–77).

Through her contacts at Cambridge, Robinson followed the deliberations of the faculty board on Austin's chances. The board met on November 6, but no offer was forthcoming.[28] On November 26, it decided to permit Austin to lecture during the academic year 1929–30 in an ex officio fashion, without holding a lectureship (FB/Min. V. 116). On May 10, 1930, the Appointments Committee of the board agreed to offer him a university lectureship, to begin in October (FB/Min. V. 117).

Shortly before Austin's appointment was announced, he commiserated with his wife, who was searching without success for a job near Cambridge: "Yes, you must get a job near Cambridge, + come + keep my nose down to localisation [the subject of a course he was teaching at the time]. But please don't worry about jobs. Everybody is in the same boat."[29] Everyone was in the same boat because the capitalist economy had collapsed.[30] Robinson was looking for a job, not necessarily an academic position. It seems that the only acceptable work she could find was in the university as a supervisor of undergraduates in economics. She was responsible for holding weekly supervisions of pupils, assigning essays, and evaluating the results. There is no reason to suppose that at this point she entertained a vision of herself as an academic economist, much less as an original theorist.

Robinson's return to Cambridge as the wife of a fellow and her supervision of a few students neither diminished the limitations under which she worked as a woman, nor altered her institutional marginality. Lacking a college fellowship, she was not entitled to rooms in a college. Supervising from the Robinson flat, she enjoyed no unmediated contact with Cambridge economists or unfiltered access to theoretical discussions. Yet within some two years, she developed a strikingly clear and confident conception of her professional identity. It was articulated but not publicly announced in October 1932, with many flourishes of Robinsonian hauteur, in a little text that she called "A Passage from the Autobiography of an Analytical Economist."[31] What did this new self-identification mean to her at the time? What happened between March 1930, when she was searching for jobs, and October 1932 that led to this exercise in professional identity production and self-representation, performed in a "secret document" that was not only cheeky but grandiose in its pretensions?

Although records are not at hand, it seems that in 1929–30 Robinson attended Sraffa's lectures.[32] What did she make of his article and lectures, which dismantled the stately edifice of Marshall's value theory? Sraffa argued that logical problems posed by Marshall's analysis of value left economists with three options. One possibility was to retain the assumption of free competition but abandon Marshall's supply-demand apparatus in favor of classical theory (Sraffa 1926, 541). At Cambridge, where Marshall's *Principles* was studied as secular scripture, this seemed not only impractical but unthinkable. A second option was to abandon Marshall's partial-equilibrium framework in favor of general equilibrium; however, the state of economic theory at the time would make this effort fruitless. The last possibility was to "take the path of imperfect competition": to begin with the premise that markets are not perfectly competitive. This was a much more tolerable course, calling for clever retooling of Marshall's machinery. Sraffa himself had sketched the repairs that were called for by developing a rough account of an alternative theory of value, suggestions that amounted to a map of how the landscape of economics would appear when viewed from the perspective of monopoly. This third option—renovating Marshallian value theory by developing a theory of imperfect competition—was the course Robinson pursued.[33]

Robinson's apprenticeship seems to have begun in a fortuitous and perhaps even serendipitous fashion. Her work had its origin in an attempt to resolve several problems of economic theory by using a new analytical tool: the marginal revenue curve, a classic case of simultaneous discovery for which several economists had a legitimate claim to credit. The circumstances that led her to apply the marginal revenue curve to research in imperfect competition on the agenda of Cambridge economics are revealing.

The Origin of *The Economics of Imperfect Competition*: Austin's Account

Austin wrote a remarkably comprehensive and detailed answer to this question, going so far as to recall the microsocial interactions and the constellation of economies of research interests and opportunities that came into play (Robinson 1994). It was early 1930, and he was supervising Charles Gifford, a mathematics student in Magdalene College who had taken up economics and would go on to take a First in Part II of the tripos in 1931. Gifford had written an essay replicating the marginal gross revenue curve in Theodore Yntema's article "The Influence of Dumping on Monopoly Price" (1928). On the day he read his essay to Austin, Robinson had invited Kahn—who was also attending Sraffa's lectures—to lunch with the couple. Austin appeared, as he recalled, "bubbling with excitement over the new concept" and eager to explain it to them (Robinson 1994, 7). In his account, this lunch conversation marked the genesis of *The Economics of Imperfect Competition*. The three began to play a game by using Yntema's curve to solve a variety of problems. As they moved from one question to another, the game became more complex and ambitious.

Ultimately, it centered on a large and fundamental issue: if economists replaced the axiom of perfect competition with the assumption of imperfect competition, what consequences would follow for theories of value and distribution?

The Origin of *The Economics of Imperfect Competition*: Robinson's Account

In the Autobiography, Robinson's more succinct account of the genesis of her research departs from Austin's story in several respects. The lunch with Kahn disappears. Instead, Austin introduced Robinson to the curve, and she was left to ponder its significance. Just as there was no lunch, there was no game the three played with the curve and no flash of insight in which its theoretical promise instantly became apparent. Following her introduction to the curve, she made no use of it until one day Kahn posed a problem to her, and she responded, "Let's see if Gifford's curve will do it for us. And it did. One problem led to another, and all the time Mr. Sraffa's article of 1926 kept nagging at us: —What about the supply curve in an imperfect market?"[34] Austin claimed that Robinson initiated the work and proposed the research questions. In the Autobiography, she and Kahn shared this responsibility: he raised a question, and she suggested they try to answer it by using the curve. If it makes sense to say that *The Economics of Imperfect Competition* was born at a certain point, its birth was in these conversations between Robinson and Kahn.

In the foreword to her book, Robinson acknowledged Austin's contribution on several points. He named the curve, gave her illustrative detail drawn from his work *The Structure of Competitive Industry*, and suggested what finally proved to be the book's title—a matter that was settled quite late in the history of the manuscript in discussions that included Austin, Kahn, and Keynes.[35] However, with the exception of his function as messenger in delivering news of the arrival of the marginal revenue curve at Cambridge, he played no role in its genesis. Therefore, she excised her husband from the origin of the book.

In view of the discrepancies between these two accounts, what can be said with reasonable probability concerning the question of when Robinson was introduced to the marginal revenue curve? The Autobiography begins with the observation that "three years ago" Austin showed Robinson the curve in Gifford's essay. Does this mean she first learned of it in autumn 1929? This seems unlikely.

Kahn became acquainted with the marginal revenue curve through the Robinsons. However, he does not mention it in his fellowship dissertation, submitted in December 1929. In preparing the final draft, he surveyed the recent literature on the economics of the short period and made appropriate revisions (Kahn 1989, 105–7). This was an exercise for which Pigou later chastised him: if he insisted on repeatedly revising his text in light of current research, the dissertation would never be published.[36] If Kahn had seen the marginal revenue curve in 1929, references to some of its discoverers would have appeared in his dissertation, and he surely would have used the concept. In his analysis of individual firms in imperfect markets, the vertical line that determines equilibrium price and output traverses the marginal cost curve precisely at the point where it would have intersected the marginal revenue curve (Kahn 1989, 119–20). The conclusion: he and Robinson had no knowledge of the curve prior to 1930.

In view of the fact that the Autobiography was not typed before spring 1933, this conclusion is supported by Robinson's claim that she learned of the curve three years before: in 1930, three years before her book was published; not autumn 1929, three years before October 1932.[37] When in 1930? From the Autobiography, it is clear that her knowledge of the curve preceded Harrod's paper "Notes on Supply," published in the *Economic Journal* in June 1930.[38] Thus it seems that Robinson first saw the marginal revenue curve after December 1929, when Kahn submitted his thesis, and before June 1930, when Harrod's article appeared.[39]

Robinson's newly minted professional identity was underpinned by a carefully crafted personal mythology that told the story of her beginnings as an analytical economist by recounting her engagement with three books. Their authors, she insisted, were the only men of her time worthy of installation in the pantheon of economic genius. The Autobiography circumscribed and explored the field of analytical economics by examining the concept of economic genius, which was understood on the basis of a peculiar mode of book composition and reception. Was it an accident of history that the three authors she elevated to this status happened to be Cambridge economists? Was it nothing more than an interesting coincidence that their books were the most important texts of her apprenticeship: Marshall's *Principles* (1890), Pigou's *Economics of Welfare* (1920), and

Keynes's *A Treatise on Money* (1930)? In Robinson's account, her professional identity was forged in her innovative reading and reconceptualization of these books.

An economic genius is born when a thinker of striking originality—"a man who thinks of something to think about"—develops a new technique and writes a book about it. However, his achievement is diminished by a failure to understand the technique and the conditions for its use. The genius casts his technique in a theoretical language that is inconsistent with its application. Because there is a sense in which he does not know what he is talking about, he mischaracterizes the technique and gives his book a misleading title. The next move is made by an unsympathetic reader, who points out the inconsistency between technique and theoretical language. As a result, the unsympathetic reader seems to demonstrate that the genius is "talking nonsense."[40] Although the genius may be incapable of breaking this impasse, his technique is more powerful than its creator, possessing an immanent logic that speaks to a sympathetic reader. Enlightened by the critique of the unsympathetic reader, this charitable reader sees what the genius did not: the theoretical assumptions needed to understand his technique. When the sympathetic reader grasps the innate wisdom of the technique and its theoretical requirements, it becomes clear that the genius, after all, "was perfectly right."[41] The economic genius may be compared to an explorer who discovers a new continent but is mistaken in identifying it. The unsympathetic reader points this out. The sympathetic reader, following clues in the explorer's map, corrects his errors and redrafts the cartography of the new methodological world.

Marshall understood the subject matter of his *Principles* as the theory of value.[42] Sraffa demonstrated that Marshall had committed radical and self-destructive logical errors. The sympathetic reader—Robinson (1933d, 16; 1933e, 26)—set matters aright by following the logic of Marshall's technique, which was buried in his footnotes. When Marshallian value theory is reconceptualized as the analysis of the output of a single commodity, the place of the new Marshallian continent in the universe of analytical economics becomes clear.

Pigou wrote a book about resource allocation and committed the colossal error of calling it *The Economics of Welfare*. Precisely because of the magnitude of his mistake, Cambridge supervisors, baffled by his concept of human welfare, advised their students not to worry over this matter and concentrate on the real subject of the book, the allocation of resources.

In the Autobiography, Robinson seemed to have little enthusiasm for applying the concept of economic genius to Pigou. Who were the unsympathetic and sympathetic readers? And what was the inner logic of Pigou's book that would enable the sympathetic reader to see that, like Marshall, he was not writing nonsense? Although these questions are left untouched in the Autobiography, a persuasive case can be made that Robinson regarded J. H. Clapham as Pigou's unsympathetic reader and saw herself and Kahn as his sympathetic interpreters. Kahn's article "Some Notes on Ideal Output," an analysis of resource allocation based on part 2 of *The Economics of Welfare*, attempts to dispose of Clapham's criticisms of Pigou (Kahn 1935, 13). In the Cambridge summer vacation of 1934, Robinson and Kahn were working on a draft of this article. She answered some of his questions, suggested ideas, and urged him not to struggle with the more recalcitrant issues until they met again in Cambridge.[43] Clapham had argued that Pigou's analysis of the laws of returns is incoherent because there are no criteria for deciding whether specific industries operate under conditions of increasing or diminishing returns (Clapham 1922). Kahn claimed it was not difficult to identify industries that produced increasing returns. Public utilities and railroads, which have substantial fixed costs, are obvious cases. Economists agreed that subsidies for such industries were advantageous since they increased the output of industries that benefit from lower utility and transportation costs. Because public utilities and railways generally succeed in eliminating their competition, economists also agreed on the advantages of compelling them to increase their output. Thus the issue that Clapham regarded as an irresolvable conceptual problem was reduced to "an exercise in the control of public utilities." Kahn concluded that "Dr. Clapham's economic boxes were full all the time, but the economists were looking on the wrong shelf" (Kahn 1935, 13). Where were economists looking? On the shelf where they found increasing and diminishing returns industries. What was the right shelf? Presumably where they would find public utilities and railways. Where did Kahn's article take the analysis of the allocation of resources? Back to Pigou's *Economics of Welfare*: "Public Control of Monopoly," his argument for state regulation of private monopolies in order to ensure that their output approximates the socially optimal level. The genius was right after all.

When Robinson turned to Keynes, who mistitled his book on the analysis of output as a whole *A Treatise on Money*, her interest in economic genius was revived. The first unsympathetic reader of the *Treatise* was perhaps the author himself in his "cutting epigrammes about people who write books on money." Although the theoretical implications of his technique may not have been immediately apparent to Keynes, they were quickly grasped by "two or three hardy, self-conceited young colleagues"—members of the Circus. Keynes's sympathetic readers listened to his technique and made the proper inferences. Since the Circus was formed immediately following publication of the *Treatise*, confusion between the author's conception of the book and its actual analysis was quickly cleared up.[44]

In "The Theory of Money and the Analysis of Output," Robinson noted that Keynes failed to see he was investigating the analysis of output and not money. This is the sense in which he did not understand that he had produced "a revolution": a dramatically new theory of the long-period analysis of output (1933e, 24–25). In redrawing the theoretical map of the *Treatise*, she compared his misconceptions to Marshall's errors, which in her view she had also corrected (1933e, 25–26). Thus in each of her three cases, she assumed the role of the sympathetic reader who listens to the technique of the confused and misunderstood genius and, following its voice, places his analysis on a sound footing.[45]

The voice of the Autobiography expresses the identity of a writer who has no doubts about the theoretical program of economics and how it should be executed. Although the style of the text is whimsical, its substance is pedantic in the extreme, suggesting that the writer possesses a Schumpeterian mastery of the entire field of economics. This confident self-presentation is surprising on the part of a relative novice. Lecturing established economists on the basis of two years of informal postgraduate study and little publication called for formidable self-assurance. The presumption of calling to task Marshall, Pigou, and Keynes concerning their most fundamental errors and reinterpreting their books in order to disclose their true theoretical direction required an extravagant measure of chutzpah. Comparable considerations hold for Robinson's short methodological pamphlet, in which she summed up what she had gleaned from her autobiographical reflections on Cambridge economics. It was published by the Cambridge student bookstore Heffer in October 1932, the date she placed on the Autobiography and the month she delivered the manuscript of her book to Macmillan.[46] She gave this fourteen-page text the stunningly ambitious title *Economics Is a Serious Subject: The*

Apologia of the Economist to the Mathematician, the Scientist and the Plain Man. Her main purpose was to write a crisp, convincing account of her ideas on the foundations of economic theory.

The pamphlet was a methodological exercise in the largest sense: a statement that put economists on notice as to their proper business and how they should go about it. What is the basis of the metatheoretical priority of technique or method? How are theoretical assumptions linked to technique? What is the significance of the choice between methodological optimism and pessimism? The attempt to answer these difficult, contentious questions in a short essay was obviously a presumptuous undertaking, not least for a fledgling economist who had published nothing beyond a book review.

In the 1920s, the Marshallian guild did not produce a book or even an article devoted to methodology. The pamphlet marked a significant departure from this practice in several respects. Unlike Robertson and generations of tripos students who followed in his footsteps, Robinson was not content to treat cursory remarks by the godfathers of the guild as the last word on Cambridge metatheory, skipping through the early chapters of Marshall's *Principles* in order to arrive as effortlessly as possible at the analyses that were presumed to constitute the core of the discipline (Robertson 1952, 13–14). In publishing the first purely methodological essay by an economist trained in the tripos, she also broke with the Marshallian tradition of consigning metatheoretical discussions to prefaces, introductions, appendices, and informal observations in correspondence. Moreover, the pamphlet repudiated Marshallian doctrine on the subordinate status of economic theory and its relationship to substantive research. Robinson took dead seriously the mechanistic figures of speech used by Marshall and Pigou, transposing their metaphorical allusions to toolboxes, appliances, and analytical machinery into a methodological principle.[47] As was her wont, she pushed this principle to its ultimate logical conclusion, reducing economics to its methods of research: "The subject matter of economics is neither more nor less than its own technique" (Robinson 1932a, 4).[48]

Robinson maintained that the methods of her time were "only capable of giving unreal answers to unreal questions" (Robinson 1932a, 5). The questions are unreal because they are derived from the logical possibilities of economic method, which abstracts from the properties of economic phenomena. The answers are unreal because their referents are not economic facts but artifacts of method. Any correspondence between the results of theoretical analysis and actual economies is purely fortuitous.

Economic analysis is defined by the position that economists take on the assumptions of their investigations. In choosing assumptions, the analytical economist employs the criterion of "tractability." By employing a given set of assumptions, is it possible to conduct an analysis using existing technique? This is the fundamental methodological issue for the "optimistic, analytical, English economist," who regards the empirical status of assumptions as irrelevant (Robinson 1932a, 6). The "pessimistic, methodological, Continental economist," faced with a decision between assumptions that are tractable but unrealistic and alternative assumptions that are realistic but intractable, chooses the latter. Optimists are model builders committed to the project of abstract theory construction for its own sake. Pessimists believe that only facts are of intrinsic interest: the test of a good theory is not methodological tractability but conformity to facts.

For the optimist, there is a close correspondence between the problems and methods of economics. A method generates the problems for which it can provide solutions. What is the basis of this supposition? The current set of theoretical problems is the work that can be done with existing technique. The possible uses of the existing array of tools determines the agenda of theoretical problems. At any given point, there are as many different problems as there are unresolved tasks that existing tools can be used to perform. The optimist supposes that economic methods bear labels that identify their possible uses. In Robinson's metaphor, which ascribes a voice to economic technique, economists pose questions to their methods, and the methods reply, revealing the problems they can be used to investigate and how to conduct the investigation. If an optimistic English economist fails to state his assumptions clearly, the solution is not to ask him for a more exact account of his premises but to "go behind his back and ask his technique" (Robinson 1932a, 8–9). This is the ultimate basis of the claim that economics is neither more nor less than its technique. On this strict instrumentalist position, economics is reduced to making and applying tools that speak when they are spoken to. Or, in more banal terms, a method entails its applications, in which case the uses of a method can be derived from the method itself. The decisive consideration in economic theory is not economic phenomena and the problems they pose. It is economic method, which constitutes its own objects of investigation, determines how they can be analyzed, and places limits on the conclusions that can be drawn. Just as the tools at the disposal of carpenters determine the materials they can work on and what can be made with them, so the tools of economic analysis define the problems of economic theory and the constraints imposed on their solution.

Because pessimists are not of one mind concerning their doubts about the validity of analytical economics, they are divided into many tribes. Writing as if she were an anthropologist constructing kinship taxonomies of an exotic culture, Robinson sketched a brief typology of pessimists. Methodological pessimists are motivated by precision, eliminating from the analytical toolbox all techniques "which appear to involve conceptions that are not capable of measurement" (Robinson 1932a, 11). They are distinguished from fundamental pessimists, on whom she did not comment.[49] Pessimists, we learn, are not confined to the Continent.[50] English pessimists are classified as either pure or logical. Logical English pessimists prevent the ossification of analytical economics into a dogma by proposing problems that exceed the limits of current technique by a small margin, challenging optimists to extend and refine their methods.

The analytical response to the pessimist is essentially a confession of faith based on a vision: to exploit the limits of existing technique in a piecemeal fashion, moving from one abstract problem to another and solving each by adopting the most exacting standards of current methodology. Analytical economists work in the belief that this program will gradually evolve a method sufficiently complex to take the measure of real economies (Robinson 1932a, 11–12). In this program, technique is the unmoved mover: it answers all questions that are answerable, solves all problems that are resolvable, and produces all explanations that are possible. But there is no explanation of technique. Any putative explanation could be produced only by technique itself. Because the explanans could not be distinguished from the explanandum, any attempt to produce such an explanation would be tautological. The same holds for questions about the validity of technique. How could they be addressed? Only by technique, the validity of which is presupposed and thus lies beyond question.

The Economics of Imperfect Competition rests on this conception of method, employing assumptions that, "in all their naked unreality," are detached from the facts of real economies (Robinson 1933d, 8). Borrowing the mountaineering metaphors favored by Marshall and Pigou, both devoted Alpinists, Robinson issued a warning that the reader who follows her path "will quickly find himself in a mountainous and inhospitable territory" that is "*nur für Schwindelfreie*": heights of analysis reserved for economists who are not intimidated by the possibility of theoretical vertigo. Work at the highest levels of theoretical abstraction is essential to the progress of economic analysis, the objective of which is not knowledge of the real world but the production of tools to build a "working model" of the world (Robinson 1933d, 1).[51]

Truth as conformity to facts is irrelevant to this project. Faced with an inconsistency between a "charming diagram" and the facts, Robinson of course refused to sacrifice the diagram. Acting on an "unscrupulous resolve," she used her technique to "trick" pessimists, convincing them that the deviation of the diagram from the facts it represents was within acceptable limits.[52] Truth in economics has a purely formal sense. An account is true when a given technique is correctly applied to the analysis of facts that are presumed as given. The relation between the presumptive facts of analytical economics and the facts of the empirical world is indeterminate. Because analytical economics brackets empirical reality in order to exploit all the possibilities of technique, its conclusions are purely hypothetical. Should they happen to have empirical value, this is a matter of pure chance. Is this a scientific defect? The merit of analytical economics, Robinson claimed, "lies in its charm." In language that recalls the self-referential aesthetics of Gertrude Stein: "For people who like this kind of thing, this is the kind of thing they like."[53]

The Origin of *The Economics of Imperfect Competition*: The Epistolary Account

Although the accounts by Austin and Robinson shed light on the genesis of her book and the circumstances under which it was conceived, her correspondence with Austin and Kahn is more enlightening on these matters. In her earliest observations on the book, the question of whether she regarded it as a collaborative work or a solo enterprise does not have an unambiguous answer. By October 1932, any hesitation on her part had disappeared. It was her book. The belated Cambridge discovery of the marginal revenue curve, the origins of the book, and the formation of her professional identity intersected in her consciousness. Work on the marginal revenue curve led to the book, and it was her understanding of what she had achieved in writing it that gave her an assured sense of herself as an analytical economist—the successor of Marshall, Pigou, and Keynes who would consummate their theoretical work.

Did the game that Austin recalled actually take place? At the end of July 1930, Kahn and Robinson, the latter with Austin's help, began to exchange notes concerning Hubert Henderson's ideas on products that are jointly produced (wool and mutton, for example) and the effects of changes in the demand for one on the demand for the other.[54] Between November 1930 and March 1931, these notes became increasingly sophisticated, centering on the diagrammatic and mathematical analysis of paradoxes that Kahn posed concerning monopoly output, returns to scale, concavity of demand curves, and price discrimination.[55] It also quickly became a two-person exercise, bearing out Austin's recollections many decades later (Robinson 1994, 8). The idea of writing a book on the material of their exchanges did not occur to Robinson until the end of March: "I am now toying with the idea of producing a complete book of all this stuff."[56] She envisioned a tripartite collaboration of Austin, Kahn, and herself: "It is not I who am bringing out this book. It is a syndicate of you A[ustin] + me."[57] Austin's role would be limited to writing an introduction and adding economic data in order to give the book "a realistic flavour, + give the reader a rest between theorems."[58] Kahn's part would be more substantial. He would contribute a "mathematical appendix" and pose "difficult problems" for her to solve.[59] The drafting would be Robinson's responsibility, a task on which she moved swiftly. By April 1, she had a "rough version of Chapter II of our book." A day later, she announced she would "get on with Chap III."[60]

If Robinson took the initiative in drafting, the reasons are not difficult to fathom. Kahn's work in winter and spring 1931 included lecturing on the economics of the short period, revising his dissertation for publication, playing the role of messenger angel fluttering between Keynes and meetings of the Circus (Moggridge 1992, 532), and writing an article for the *Economic Journal*.[61] Austin had more than a full schedule of lecturing and supervision and had been elected secretary of the faculty board in January 1931. As Robinson told Kahn, he was also "grinding out his stuff" on the structure of competitive industry, which would shortly be published in the Cambridge Economic Handbooks series.[62] This left Robinson a freelance supervisor without a university appointment or other formal connection to Cambridge economics. With domestic help and no children, her chief responsibility lay in household management as performed by an upper-middle-class English matron of the time. Thus the economies of research time operated in her favor. And unlike Austin and Kahn, she had an incentive to pursue a new and promising line of investigation. Without other academic assets, she could achieve distinction at Cambridge only by publishing an impressive original work.

Robinson began to regard the book as her individual project between late March 1931, when she conceived the idea of writing a book on the problems she and Kahn were exploring, and mid-September of the same year, when she asked Robertson to write a preface. She told Robertson she had drafted five chapters and sketched out another ten. She was clearly planning to publish under her name alone:

I feel rather shy about saying so, but I would very much like to ask you to do me a Preface. I hope to get the Prof. [Pigou] to read the stuff + tell us if we have dropped any bricks, but I would rather have you as my Godfather than anyone. You will see from Chap I my general idea (1) on how analysis ought to be done. (2) The importance of monopoly. If you have any sympathy with that point of view perhaps you could make some remarks about it. If you don't feel inclined to do that, but would write a few words giving me your blessing I should value it very much.

But altho' I should have asked you in any case for my private satisfaction I am also actuated by the sordid view that I might find it easier to get a publisher if I appeared under your wing, so you mustn't have anything to do with it if you feel any hesitation at giving the countenance of your name to this stuff. Anyway it won't be finished at best before next term so there is no hurry from your point of view.[63]

In September 1931, Kahn was laboring on two fronts: assisting Robinson on the relationship between a firm's demand for factors of production and productivity and reworking his dissertation. Although their research intersected, there is no doubt they both saw the book as Robinson's.[64]

Robinson and Kahn worked intensively on the book until October 1932, when the manuscript was nearly complete. Not until this point did she understand that she had written a major theoretical work. At the same time, she grasped what the achievement meant to her. Although "literally sick with exhaustion," as she wrote Austin, who was in Africa at the time, she was also quite pleased with herself, sending him a series of observations on the personal and professional transformation she had experienced.[65] Why the robust sense of self-satisfaction? Because she had written "a Damn Good Book," one that had recast the theory of value and placed it on a new footing.[66] "I have found out what my book is about," she wrote Austin. "It was quite a sudden revelation which I only had yesterday. What I have been + gone + done is what Piero [Sraffa] said must be done, in his famous article. I have rewritten the whole theory of value beginning with the firm as a monopolist. I used to think I was providing tools for some genius in the future to use, + all the time I have done the job myself."[67]

Robinson's new understanding of the relationship between writing an important book and establishing a professional identity gave her a sense of self-confidence and an appreciation of her intellectual worth that she had never enjoyed. The Michaelmas term was under way, and as she began to supervise students she discovered that her attitude and approach to teaching had undergone a sea change: "I used to feel 'I must tell these people what economists think'—now I really feel *I* am an economist + I can tell them what I think myself."[68] She anticipated criticism of the book, but she was not apprehensive. Convinced that her analyses were sound and that she had succeeded in specifying the limits within which they applied, she welcomed critics, who would have much to say about her basic concepts and assumptions.[69]

In summing up these shifts in the conception of herself as an economist, Robinson wrote her husband on October 16 that she had experienced "a violent revolution" in her view of economics. On his return, he would find "a Changed Woman." She had become a superb teacher. She had also achieved a deep, discriminating respect for Marshall's work: "I have learned to feel the real reverence for Marshall that Dennis [Robertson] feels, without losing any of my disapproval of his deliberate cheating." The new world of Robinsonian economics was so engrossing that she was determined to postpone having children in order to advance her researches. Finally, she had found the moral courage, or perhaps the presumption, to take credit for a work that was a product of collaboration: "I have recovered my self-respect about the book. You + Kahn + I have been teaching each other economics intensively these two years but it was I who saw the great light + it is *my* book" (EAGR/Box 8/2/1/13/124–26).

Robinson also made the point that she had arrived at "an absolutely clear feeling about how the curvists and the turnipists can work together instead of getting on each other's nerves."[70] Curvists were methodological optimists, economic model builders who employed diagrams in order to achieve maximum theoretical precision. Turnipists were methodological pessimists, economic empiricists who placed the primacy of data collection and the accumulation of facts—or turnips—over theory. This dichotomy was an important theme of her methodological pamphlet, which she completed and sent to Austin by October 20: "I must tell you some more of what I have been up to. I went into a trance (it was almost automatic-writing) + produced a brilliant essay in 3,000 words called 'Economics is a Serious Subject' (in the sense that Mathematics + Physics are serious)."[71] She had already shown it to "the grown ups"— Claude Guillebaud, Shove, Robertson, Keynes, and Sraffa—and in five days, she had found a publisher.[72] The positive reception it received from colleagues convinced her that "it needed saying out loud + not just taking for granted."[73] With the completion of her book and the breathless composition of the methodological pamphlet, Robinson was convinced, for the first time, that she had achieved the status of a serious economic theorist.

STRATEGIST OF ACADEMIC
CAREER PRODUCTION

The Autobiography documents Robinson's conception of her new professional identity. However, it articulates her aspirations in a "secret document"—entrusted, it seems, only to Austin and Kahn. The project of achieving these aspirations required resources of academic career production that would reposition her from the periphery to the center of Cambridge economics. When she began serious work in economics, she had few such resources. Her chief problem was marginality, both intellectual and social. She was a faculty wife who did occasional supervision and a barely visible figure, even in the small world of Cambridge economics. Without a First Class degree, a respectable fellowship dissertation, or publications of signal originality, intellectual marginality was inevitable. She also lacked the academic social standing that would enable her to acquire the appropriate credentials. When Joan Maurice of Girton College became Joan Robinson on Trumpington Street, she did not enjoy easy access to the social spaces of collective theory production, the sites that gave senior economic theorists unencumbered opportunities for discussion during term time. Nor could she expect from them invitations unaccompanied by her husband to off-term vacation visits, reading parties, mountaineering expeditions, or walking tours—the occasions that formed and strengthened ties among Cambridge economists.

Intellectual and social marginality were linked. Without social resources, Robinson could not expect to achieve intellectual visibility. Without intellectual credentials, she lacked the qualifications to acquire a professional standing. Robinson solved these problems in the 1930s. This book is an investigation of the circumstances under which she achieved recognition as an innovative thinker and became a leading figure in the most exciting theoretical movement of the time. How did this happen? In part 2, we consider how she began to establish social and intellectual bases of career production by developing her first research program and recruiting support to execute it. There is an essential preliminary to this account. At this point, we consider a relationship that above all others made Robinson's career at Cambridge possible: her friendship with Kahn.

EXCURSUS

Robinson and Kahn

FRIENDSHIP AND CAREER PRODUCTION

Robinson's career in the 1930s was a work of many hands. However, none of its artificers was more engaged, committed, or consequential than Kahn. Her formation as an economist cannot be detached from their friendship, nor can her progress from the margins of Cambridge economics to its center be understood without considering his efforts on her behalf.

In 1930, Robinson and Kahn began by sharing ideas. By spring 1931, they had become intimate, each giving the other entry to the privileged and private spheres of personal life. By 1932, their relationship was a love affair. Archival material currently available, which does not exhaust extant sources, suggests that it was not consummated earlier than autumn 1938, when Robinson suffered a severe psychiatric breakdown. For much of the period 1932–38, they managed their passions, attempting to arrive at an equilibrium that was unobjectionable in Cambridge and at the same time emotionally tolerable.

In comparison with Kahn, Robinson was the more untutored in economic theory and technique. However, she was the more complete human being, with a capacity for dispassionate self-scrutiny that he did not seem to possess. In December 1932, when their four-month separation occasioned by his visit to the United States began, she was twenty-nine and he was twenty-seven. His adolescent expressions of self-absorption and egocentricity do not stand up well against her understanding of the dangers their relationship posed and the constraints they faced. However, these differences cut in more than one direction. If Kahn's letters are more self-indulgent, they are also more revelatory. As expressions of his day-to-day states of mind, they are not generally products of Cambridge affectation or efforts at cleverness. With a few exceptions, Robinson's letters have a reportorial and breezy tone. She sends Kahn the latest news on their small circle at Cambridge and presents herself as an aspiring member of an exclusive self-selecting elite, dispensing cutting witticisms and casting outsiders into utter darkness.

The history of the friendship between Kahn and Robinson in the 1930s is not a story of smooth transitions along a continuum that began with emotionally colorless exchanges on imperfect competition and ended in bed. It was marked by episodes of doubt, irresolution, and backtracking as well as false decisiveness and confusion as they weighed personal and professional risks. Both had much to lose by giving their passions free play. They were not prepared to ignore the problems their conduct might create for her marriage and uncertain prospects at Cambridge, nor were they willing to compromise the Cambridge careers of Kahn and Austin. The correspondence of early 1933 makes it clear they had decided to subject their erotic relationship to instrumental controls by weighing the costs of acting on their feelings. This decision called for compromises they found difficult. Both partners were sometimes miserable even as they remained intent on convincing themselves that they were, or might be, happy. Above all, it seemed necessary to sustain the illusion that they had found a solution to their most intractable difficulty: how could a space be created for the breakthrough of their erotic desires in a social world in which it had no legitimate place?

Although historians of economic thought have taken note of the friendship between Robinson and Kahn, little detail has been forthcoming, and some accounts are mistaken or misleading. Marcuzzo writes that they met when he was working on his dissertation, following which a friendship developed that "shaped their intellectual and emotional lives" for more than fifty years (Marcuzzo 2003, 545). Her only hint at the character of the friendship is an excerpt from a letter Kahn wrote after Robinson's death: "I first got to know Joan in 1928 and ever since then we have both enjoyed life in various aspects of that word."[1] Annalisa Rosselli's essay on Robinson and Kahn gives no indication that they had an erotic relationship before he left for the United States. Her examination of their early correspondence details Robinson's preoccupations with her career at Cambridge, her revisions of *The Economics of Imperfect Competition*, and Kahn's views on social and academic life in America. Although he had "very strong feelings towards Robinson at the time," she responded to his "amorous sentiments" with "fond, humorous indulgence." Rosselli claims that the American correspondence is of interest because of "the points" that brought them together at this time. Readers are left to speculate on what these points might be. Their letters from 1934 to 1939 receive little attention since they are said to concern only family life and Cambridge. There is no mention of the breakup between Robinson and Austin following her psychiatric illness in 1938–39. Instead, readers are told that Austin drew away as his absences became longer and more frequent (Rosselli 2005a, 263–68). Austin's biographer Alec Cairncross claims that Austin and Robinson did not drift apart until the end of the Second World War. Kahn is mentioned in passing as a friend, like Nicholas Kaldor, with whom she enjoyed postwar vacations (Cairncross 1993, 172).

In their friendship, Robinson and Kahn did not distinguish personal and professional considerations. With the exception of the beginning of their acquaintance, when they were classmates but not yet friends, work on economic theory penetrated personal life, and friendship was interwoven with science. Although the formation of their friendship seems to have been independent of Robinson's ambitions, its consequences for her career at Cambridge would be difficult to exaggerate. Kahn, a potential competitor in developing a new theory of imperfect competition, became the selfless helpmate—dependable, loyal, devoted, and ideally placed to give her access to Cambridge economic theoreticians. In her efforts to gain proximity to Keynes and win his confidence, it was Kahn who used his close relationship to Keynes to smooth her path. Although their friendship was not instrumentally grounded, it produced benefits, not least in Robinson's project of career production. Thus the significance of this excursus for an account of Robinson's early career.

The beginnings of the friendship between Robinson and Kahn intersect with the genesis of her professional identity, the period between March 1930 and April 1931. In the first piece of correspondence between the two—March 15, 1930—she congratulated him on his election as a fellow of King's. The letter was addressed to "My dear Kahn" and included a footnote: "Excuse this form of address. I cannot deal with any more Richards" (RFK/13/90/1/1–2).[2] To name is to place in a social category. Robinson did not yet have a settled place for Kahn in her social framework. However, "Kahn," with variations, he would remain through the 1930s. She also signed herself in full formal fashion:

Yours with the best of wishes
Joan Robinson

In letters to friends, she was "Joan" or "J." However, she also noted when she expected to return to Cambridge from vacation, which indicated she might not remain "Joan Robinson" for long. A few days later, she sent him more specific information about her travel arrangements and proposed a meeting in London, where both their parents had homes. She planned to visit her family during the first week of April. Would he be in London then as well? Her postscript—"N.B. Please refer to us as Joan + Austin"—suggests that Kahn had addressed the couple as Mr. and Mrs. Robinson.[3] Although Robinson's Autobiography shows that they became acquainted with the marginal revenue curve between December 1929 and June 1930, it seems that they did little work together with the curve before summer 1930 (see Rosselli 2005a, 260). When Keynes's *Treatise* was published at the end of October, they became members of the Circus. Research with the marginal revenue curve and the elucidation and critique of the *Treatise* are evidence of more frequent contacts. The character of these contacts was friendly but not intimate.

On March 30, 1931, Robinson wrote Kahn that she was considering writing a book on the problems they had been discussing (RFK/16/1/59–62), and in early April she sent him a draft of a chapter.[4] Kahn's response on April 10 shows that the complexion of their exchanges had changed.

My dear Joan,
I have not time now to get into detailed criticism, and neither of us, I imagine,

will have much time for that for some days now. But I feel that I must write at once and congratulate you on making such a firm beginning—and also to thank you. For it is tremendously pleasant to see it all rolling off—or at least beginning to roll off (it is going to be quite a big work)—so beautifully. I am so very pleased it has begun.

I shall have a good deal to say about individual passages when I think that there is undue compression or that the exposition might be made clearer in some other way. Except for these occasions, when you appear—quite occasionally—to be taking rather a lot for granted in regard to the responsiveness of the reader, the general effect I felt was very pleasing indeed.

I was awfully glad to see you yesterday—thanks so much.

Yours

R.F.K. (JVR/vii/228/1/13–14)

Kahn declared his delight with Robinson, his pleasure in her work, and his gratitude, even if it is not clear exactly what he was grateful for. That she had begun the book superlatively? That he had seen her the previous day? No matter. He and Robinson were together, they were working together, and Kahn was happy.

This new turn in the relationship did not escape the attention of their immediate social circle. Keynes's letters to Lydia illuminate the impression the two made on a discerning observer. Keynes was generally alert to forces that might dislodge Kahn from the career path he had envisioned for his protégé. Infatuation with a woman was not what Keynes had in mind, especially not a liaison with the wife of a Cambridge colleague. In a letter to Lydia on November 21, 1931, he referred with some asperity to Robinson as Kahn's "beloved Joan." Expecting Kahn to bring her to a social occasion that Sunday, he noted pointedly that he had invited Kahn but not Robinson to supper (JMK/PP/45/190/5). On January 17, 1932, he wrote that he planned to attend "one of Kahn's high dinner parties" that evening. Sraffa and Colin Clark were among the announced guests. But: "I expect to find Joan, not yet mentioned, as well" (JMK/PP/45/190/5). Only two weeks later, he gave a more alarming account of developments. That evening after tea he had gone into Kahn's rooms for paper: "His outer room was in darkness, but there closeted in his inner room were he and Joan alone, she reclining on the floor on cushions. We were all embarrassed—they were so much like lovers surprised, though I expect the conversation was only The Pure Theory of Monopoly.[5] I wish I knew how open of their feelings they are to one another. But it seems to me a desperate affair, and how is it to end?"[6] Were Robinson and Kahn discussing her book? or were they enmeshed in a "desperate affair" that could only end disastrously? Keynes was unsure and troubled. Formally, Robinson and Kahn were not violating university regulations. But, as Keynes saw, their conduct might provide grounds for suspicion, compromising them as well as Austin.[7] On February 19, he gave Lydia a sense of the tensions in the sociodrama played out by Kahn, Robinson, and Austin. The occasion was a small party, again given by Kahn, after one of Keynes's evening lectures. "Joan and Austin were there. Joan rather white, silent and sad, I thought. Austin went away early, without even asking Joan to come with him. Joan stayed until late, and I am sure Kahn was going to walk home with her. I feel it is a drama, but a concealed one, and having (has it?) no solution" (JMK/ PP/45/190/5).

By early 1932, expressions of anxiety over their future appear frequently in the correspondence of Robinson and Kahn. Although unwilling to offer any assurances about their immediate future, she urged him not to take a "dramatic view" of their circumstances, especially since there was no possibility of "drastic" measures the next term.[8] What did she mean by drastic measures? What were they contemplating? A declaration to Austin? Was she considering divorce? These possibilities hardly seem likely. An open affair would jeopardize the careers of Kahn and Austin and end Robinson's hopes of establishing herself at Cambridge. Also unlikely was divorce, which would have been ruinous for all parties.[9] The issue quickly became moot. On receiving a Rockefeller Foundation grant for study in the United States, Kahn made plans to take leave during the Michaelmas term 1932—thus Robinson's reference to "next term." Moreover, their worries about the future were quickly suspended owing to a serendipitous appointment that called Austin to Africa for some six months. In early 1932, the archbishop of York asked Pigou to recommend a candidate for membership on a commission of enquiry sponsored by the International Missionary Council, one of the many religious agents of the British empire in Africa. The brief of the commission was to examine the impact of copper mining on local African life and the work of Christian missions in the copper belt of the British territory that is now Zambia. Pigou nominated Austin, who took leave for the Michaelmas term and sailed for Cape Town on July 1 (Cairncross 1993, 51). Since Austin's work in Africa would coincide with Kahn's visit to the United States, he and Robinson would lose an opportunity to have more than five months of relative freedom. Kahn quickly decided to postpone use of the Rockefeller grant to the end of 1932 in order to take advantage of Austin's absence. Keynes captured the significance of this episode quite nicely in a letter to Lydia:

You know that Kahn is supposed to be going on his travels to America next [academic] year. But two days ago he rang me up to say he thought he would like to stay at Cambridge next term to finish some theory he is at, and go to America after Christmas. When I get back I hear that Austin is to go to Africa on a mission for five months and will be *away* from Cambridge all next term. The human heart! To finish something he is at! However it is very dangerous. If Austin is away for several months, what will happen do you think?[10]

Robinson and Kahn made good use of Austin's absence. In correspondence they exchanged information about their respective schedules in order to determine when they would both be in Cambridge or London. At Cambridge there was also the new asset of Austin's unoccupied rooms in Sidney Sussex College, where they could enjoy uninterrupted privacy. In an undated note following a vacation with relatives after Austin's departure, Robinson wrote, "Here I am back again + all well. Come round after lunch to A's [Austin's] room in S[idney] S[ussex]" (RFK/13/90/2 /134). The pair indulged in fantasies of perfect freedom, envisioning what they might do and where they might live if circumstances permitted. In playfully imagining their life together, Robinson suggested that "Copenhagen would suit us better than Oxford when we decide to emigrate."[11] The following week, she pictured Kahn teaching her calculus on a hillside in Austria, where they vacationed together in August and September.[12] There were also lovers' quarrels characteristic of a highly eroticized friendship. Apparently they had discussed the relative merits of eighteenth-century English poetry and Shakespeare's sonnets, Robinson contending for Shakespeare and Kahn exhibiting questionable aesthetic judgment in speaking for the later poetry. "I am not annoyed," she insisted. "But it is absurd to prefer the 18th Century to Shakespeare's sonnets. A penny whistle has more clarity and perhaps more charms than an orchestra it's true—but still. Would you send a kind word to Margaret [Braithwaite]—it's a shame to visit my sins on her head. 'Do not remember evil against me.'"[13]

The amusements of a fantasy life and inconsequential lovers' spats aside, Robinson did not stray far from the realities of career production.

By summer 1932, they included her efforts to court Keynes through ingratiating herself with Lydia. Two days before she asked Kahn not to remember evil against her, she reminded him that she intended to write Lydia shortly with an invitation to a performance of a Greek play. He was instructed to mention the play in conversation with the Keyneses in order to "prepare the way."[14] During Austin's absence, Robinson wrote and published *Economics Is a Serious Subject* as well as "Imperfect Competition and Falling Supply Price." Most important, she completed a draft of *The Economics of Imperfect Competition*. Austin disembarked at Southampton on December 19, 1932. Two days later, Kahn sailed from the same port to the United States, where he remained until mid-April 1933.

Robinson's papers include an undated outline for a novel that was never written. In view of her relationship with Kahn during the 1930s, its theme is of some interest. A young woman, working at a monotonous office job and renting a grubby room, feels that her life is empty and wonders what she is living for. Her few moments of pleasure are limited to occasions on which a fatherly boss praises her work or compliments her on a new hat. Without enthusiasm, she allows herself to drift into a sexless friendship with a young man—"a sweet tormented idealistic youth" who, for reasons that are not made clear, is not an appropriate candidate for marriage. Is he half Indian? Is his mother mad? Because he is devoted to the young woman and completely undemanding, she finds it easy to respond to him even though he seems to hold no attraction for her. Then she meets a conventionally acceptable young man with a good job and the promise of security, a home, and a conventional middle-class life. A worldly wise sister or girlfriend advises her to take the opportunity and marry. Although the heroine attempts to find the prospects of marriage desirable, she is troubled by the scene she must enact: ending her relationship with the "half caste" and "throwing him back into his tormented loneliness." She sees that it would be folly to allow a momentary episode of painful leave-taking to jeopardize a solution to the problem of her life. And yet it does. The problem of the novel revolves around what happens next and how the characters act out the denouement. The point of the story, Robinson notes, "is to show the importance of a feeling which is not 'in the proper'—which does not fit into a pigeon hole of accepted notions" (JVR/vii/424/17–18).

Although Robinson and Kahn shared feelings that did not fit the pigeonholes of Cambridge conventions, she was determined to achieve academic success within their boundaries. The correspondence between Robinson and Kahn during his American visit is an especially rich source of clues to the ways in which she resolved, or at least managed, this dilemma. The lovers decided to ratchet down expressions of their erotic feelings in order to bring their emotional life under control. They would share their hopes and desires. But in the main, erotic emotions would be closeted. They followed this regimen of dispassion within quite different degrees of latitude. Kahn was the more expressive correspondent. Like the romantic, emotionally tormented youth of Robinson's unwritten novel, he seems to have been very lonely, and his dependence on Robinson was pathetic and extravagant. Her letters, while not devoid of sentiment, are much more businesslike and journalistic. Robinson's reserve may have been due in part to her reluctance to broach delicate private matters in correspondence.[15] Several features of the changing emotional quality of their relationship appear in the American letters.

(1) The decision to subject their passions to self-conscious and selective disattention was made before Kahn sailed for the United States. It was a relief to them both and seemed to ease their anxieties. In January 1933, Kahn was living at the International House at the University of Chicago, a hotel-like apartment building for foreign graduate students and visiting scholars. Between January 20 and 24, he wrote one of his characteristically effusive letters. His purpose was to reassure Robinson that he had achieved a new and more healthy perspective on their relationship. She should not worry because he had finally succeeded in placing her in "the right setting":

> We spend a great deal of the time talking about you. My dear, you must not mind that. I hope at least you won't. It is such a great pleasure. But it is not a case of wicked indulgence—it is inevitable. When I am feeling gloomy it cheers me up, and above all gives me strength, and when I am cheerful I feel that I am giving expression to my good spirits. Bless you for being such a comfort. I do hope you don't mind. There is nothing to fear. I am almost certain that I have now got you in the right setting, and when I look at the future my heart does not shrink. The more I meet people the more (this sounds like economics) difficult I find it to believe that I can claim to know anybody like you. But it is true, isn't it, not just a mistake? The fact *is* true; but it is the future as well that helps me along (you *do* know, don't you? That when I talk about the future I *am* being sensible); and as a result the present isn't at all bad. (RFK/13/90/1/67–72)

These remarks presuppose a background of conversations on a future defined by restrictive options that neither found tolerable. They escaped this future by fabricating an illusion they could believe in. They had not been expelled from the paradise of Venusberg because they had not entered it. Could they create a demiparadise of their own? Kahn seems to have thought so. Erotic salvation within the mundane world of Cambridge would be achieved by heroic efforts of emotional honesty: an intellectual performance in which they took cognizance of their passions but also put them in "the right setting"—a perspective from which they would not become dangerous by violating Cambridge norms. It was necessary to feel the power of erotic love and yet deny its force, to admit their passions but refuse to act on them. Robinson and Kahn seem to have contrived a solution to their problem on terms later made famous by F. Scott Fitzgerald. It required that they "hold two opposed ideas in the mind at the same time, and still retain the ability to function" (Fitzgerald 1956, 69).

A month later, Kahn was at Harvard, happily observing that he was no longer anxious or nostalgic for the halcyon days of Michaelmas, when Austin was in Africa: "I can't help it if my feelings about you only grow stronger. You must not let it upset you. I could do everything for you but I cannot accomplish the impossible. And I realize it is no use concealing it from you: if I thought it would help I would try; but I am right surely? The important thing is that, though stronger my feelings are different. That restlessness has gone, and everything is going to be lovely. And I do so want to get on with my work. I shall be very busy."[16] If his feelings for Robinson had grown stronger, why was he no longer plagued by anxieties over the future? On Kahn's interpretation of his own pacification, it was because he had accepted resignation. He and Robinson would not become Tristan and Isolde, embracing a cosmic passion with all the risks it entailed. They settled for a more banal solution: compromise with the requirements of careerism and a surrender to the conventions of Cambridge. Robinson encouraged this compromise. She had been more responsive to the dangers of erotic transgression and urged him not to enter the magic garden of his dreams in which she became an imaginary demigoddess and not a flesh-and-blood, all-too-human being. If he embraced the Robinson of Trumpington Street in Cambridge and not the "wraith" of his hyperactive imagination, she agreed that they had no reason to worry.[17]

(2) Robinson was sensitive to Kahn's worries, mood swings, homesickness, and extravagant distaste for the United States. From the beginning of his visit, she advised him on how to handle himself as well as American "grubbiness." In making her presence felt even at a great distance, she was able to ease his daily confrontations with unhappiness. Kahn, on the other hand, was much more self-absorbed. In some letters he seems fascinated by the experience of inspecting his ephemeral emotional states. He left Cambridge confused, ambivalent, deeply troubled by the prospect of a long separation from Robinson, and unbalanced by loss of the institutional underpinnings that made his life as a fellow of King's so agreeable. How did he overcome the disturbing moments of depression and emotional volatility? He addressed this question in a revealing letter written only a few days after he arrived in Chicago:

Isn't it lovely that everything is going so well? I could not believe it was true that I was being so cheerful when we parted in town. I thought at least it must be because I had not taken in that I was going. I had not taken it in, but now I have and I continue in an angelic frame of mind. In fact in a curious kind of way I am enjoying it and quite often I feel that it would have been a pity not to have come. You must not mind that it is thinking about you that helps me such a lot to do so well. Not that I think about you all the time. But it is an enormous comfort to be able to do so whenever I want to. Please may I go on? I am so grateful to you for being such that it is a pleasure. It is turning out so much better than I expected and I know that you are the reason. You are a dear. I have my bad moments, of course, but they amount to far less, and are far less frequent than one could possibly have foretold. In fact it is my firm belief that I would suffer far more from exasperation, annoyance, and despair as a result of living in this impossibly inhuman country if I had not this to fall back on. Moreover, your advice to regard it as a visit to the Zoo was more practical than I imagined at the time. But you must not mind if I tell you something about the animals—monstrosities most of them, a few exotic, and some almost human to a degree that, as a human being myself, I find disquieting. Disquieting but not upsetting. For the extraordinary thing is that most of the time I do not feel anything to regret for having come.[18]

(3) Because Robinson and Kahn could remain in touch only through correspondence, they were understandably delighted when letters arrived and upset when the post was delayed.[19] Before moving on to Harvard, Kahn made arrangements to use Schumpeter's residence as his mailing

address. Since they were both acquainted with Schumpeter from his visits to Cambridge, Kahn was concerned that Robinson would not write as frequently as she had done during his Chicago stay. He explained his arrangements and appealed for understanding: "Please don't be bashful about writing to me c/o Schumpeter. All my other letters are going there too, so no matter how many you write they won't be noticed. In any case, he doesn't know your writing: and I shall probably let him know I am looking at your proofs. It was only after great hesitation I decided to adopt his address; so I should be terribly anguished if I had made an unfortunate decision. So please."[20] Kahn understood that their relationship could be misinterpreted—or, more dangerously, correctly interpreted—by third persons. But it was not his use of Schumpeter's address that troubled Robinson, as her reply of February 3 shows: "It is very encouraging to hear that you are doing so well. Bless you— + please don't apologise. I am certainly not put off writing by the idea of Schumpeter. That isn't the kind of thing that worries me" (RFK/13/90/1/88–93). Presumably the source of her concern was the possibility that her letters were an insecure repository of secrets that might be revealed by unreliable or malicious readers. This consideration would explain her cool, composed tone in correspondence. It would also explain why she did not harbor the same worries about the overheated emotional temper of Kahn's side of the correspondence. His letters were addressed to her at Trumpington Street, where her post was not subject to surveillance.

(4) Despite their preoccupations with research and one another, Robinson and Kahn did not forget Austin. He was kept clearly in focus, if not in the foreground of their attentions at least close by. As early as Christmas day, only four days after Kahn had sailed, Robinson was already relaying news of Austin, his health, and their conversations about his African assignment (RFK/13/90/1/22–23). In a postscript to her letter of January 18, 1933, she told Kahn that Lionel Robbins was scheduled to speak to the Marshall Society and relayed Austin's comments: "What a pity Kahn won't be here—But it is a good thing he should go away, then everybody finds out how much they miss him" (RFK/13/90/1/57–58). On February 11, she wrote that Austin had read Kahn's paper for the Harvard Economics Club and was "very keen it should be published as the first manifesto of the Trumpington Street School" (RFK/13/90/1/115–18).

In response, Kahn expressed interest and delight in all things Austinian. He recalled seeing Austin at the Southampton docks on the day of his embarkation: "I was thrown into a terrific state of excitement when I heard that Austin was coming down to the docks. And I was awfully pleased to see him. I am so much looking forward to hearing him in Cambridge when I get back."[21] A few days later, he pumped Robinson with a litany of questions about Austin. What of his paper for the Marshall Society and the progress of his lectures for ordinary degree students? Had he bought a car? Had he completed his paper on imperfect competition?[22] "Give him my affectionate love," Kahn wrote.[23] Quite understandably, Robinson had remained silent on these matters. In a relationship that was "beyond time, place and all mortality," Kahn's queries seemed contrived and inconsequential in the extreme.[24]

HOMECOMING?

The tensions created by efforts on the part of Kahn and Robinson to conventionalize their erotic life are nicely documented by a misunderstanding over the date of his return to England. On January 31, 1933, Robinson said she had seen one of Kahn's friends, who asked "anxiously" when he was expected back. This question was on Robinson's mind as well. Although she wondered whether he had begun to think about it, she urged him to consider only his own "financial + psychological convenience" in setting the date of his voyage. "We can easily be perfectly all right as far as I can see. I must say I miss you horribly but I feel quite equal to coping" (RFK/13/90/1/84–87). Kahn was annoyed by her question, which he regarded as "superfluous": "Have I begun to think about coming back? What do you take me for?" Yet he was coy and noncommittal. The winged chariot of time, which he had cursed on so many occasions, no longer troubled him. He was pleased with the final stage of his American visit, in a "beautiful frame of mind," and "not particularly restless." A decision about his voyage did not seem pressing. Should he sail immediately after Passover, which ended April 18? In that case, he would appear in Cambridge some two weeks after the beginning of the Easter term. Kahn, whose emotional well-being at Chicago and Harvard had depended on Robinson and the space she filled in his active romantic imagination, found it impossible to make up his mind. "I suppose," he wrote, "I shall get back sooner or later."[25]

Robinson's response to Kahn's blasé attitude toward their reunion was a studied silence. However, he seems to have been determined to extract a reaction and raised the issue again in mid-March when he was in New York. Although he was considering sailing late in the third week of April, he had made no decision.[26] She would not be drawn. In a third letter at the end of March, he returned to the question. Keynes was contemplating a holiday at the beginning of May. In that case, Kahn would be expected to lecture in his place, which would call for an earlier arrival. He found the uncertainty over what the faculty might expect of him "horribly perplexing." Yet he still did not settle a date for his return.[27] Robinson's apparent lack of interest in Kahn's return caused an angry response. Although his letter is not extant, the two radiograms she sent him in New York are evidence that he had become sufficiently overwrought for her to telegraph twice. The first telegram, on April 16, read, "Dont Be Hysterical Everyone Expecting You By Majestic All Well Love, Joan" (RFK/13/90/1/227). Two days later, she wrote, "Joan expects you sail eighteenth Don't worry" (RFK/13/90/1/228). Her letter of April 19, presumably written the day after he sailed, gives an account of what transpired prior to his departure. A misunderstanding over small matters had become magnified:

My dear I am so sorry to have caused you so much distress. I thought that my line was to be perfectly natural and simply to accept your plans. When I wrote some time ago that you had only to consult your own convenience I regarded it as a final pronouncement. You really ought to have learned by now that when I seem to you to be hyper-subtle it is just that I am not attending. But I ought to have known how you would be feeling, and I am most sincerely penitent at giving you such trouble. If you will forgive me for being dense I will forgive you for being hysterical. I fear my cable was not very well thought out—I was hurrying to catch a train at the time. (RFK/13/90/1/235–36)

Robinson was in London to see Lydia perform in a play at the Old Vic on April 24 and attend a lecture by Hawtrey at the Royal Statistical Society the next day. Because Austin had decided not to come to London, she had an extra ticket for the performance that she hoped Kahn would use, a fact she mentioned as evidence that his impression of her indifference was groundless.[28] She had called Kahn's family, hoping to find him there. When she learned that he had not yet arrived, she asked him to let her know when he planned to come up to Cambridge should they fail to connect in London. Robinson was struggling to find the terms that would reestablish their intimacy: "Please don't see any hidden meaning in this remark for there is none."[29] On April 24, before seeing the play, she closed her letter with a plea: "Love to you my dear. Don't be any crosser with me than you can help for being so dense" (RFK/13/90/I/230–32). By May 1, she was back in Cambridge with a letter from Kahn, now in London. Harmony had been reestablished in their little universe. Robinson was relieved that she had been forgiven. There was "nothing further to explain so we needn't wrangle when we meet" (RFK/13/90/I/233–34). On May 7, Keynes, Kahn, and the Robinsons lunched in Cambridge. Afterward, Keynes offered Lydia the following observation: "I had a slight feeling that Joan and Alexander, though thick friends, were just a little less *intimate* than before the long interval" (JMK/PP/45/190/5).

THE MUNDANE LIFE, 1933–37

Keynes's perception was perhaps not mistaken. Kahn's return marked the beginning of a long period of intimate friendship and collaboration. Its temper was more serene than the turbulent, sharpened feelings of 1932–33. Robinson's letters revolved around work, family life, friends, and the prospect of spending time alone with Kahn. When either of the two was not in Cambridge—generally during university vacations—she coordinated their respective itineraries and forwarding addresses so that they could correspond and arrange meetings, either in London or on returning to Cambridge. Although his letters from June 1933 through September 1938 are not extant, their content can occasionally be gleaned from her replies.

It is evident from Robinson's side of the correspondence that neither of the lovers was restless in the sense of Kahn's American letters. Even Keynes was relaxed about the liaison and regarded the following episode as innocent: "I went to see Alexander this morning and found him lying on the floor of his inner room with Joan—no socks on and unshaven. But you mustn't suppose wrongly. They were on the floor because that is the only convenient way of examining mathematical diagrams, and there is a Jewish Feast on to-day during which to wear socks or to shave is against the law of Moses."[30] In fact, they were doing theoretical work together. She was preparing a paper to read at Keynes's Political Economy Club the following year—either "Euler's Theorem and the Problem of Distribution" (1934a) or "What Is Perfect Competition?" (1934b). And for some time they had been engaged in a dialogue about duopoly, on which Kahn was working.[31]

When Keynes found Robinson on the floor in Kahn's rooms, he did not know she was pregnant with her first child.[32] Her pregnancy did not seem to change their relationship. They remained affectionate, discussed their work, planned meetings around Austin's absences, and stayed connected during vacations. Austin remained a presence in the background as she tried to juggle the various professional and domestic demands on her time so that she and Kahn could meet privately.

On March 26, 1934, Robinson informed Keynes that she was expecting a baby, news that she had earlier confided to Kahn and Sraffa (JMK/UA/5/3/124–30). On March 29, while on Easter holiday in Essex, she wondered about his reaction: "I haven't had Maynard's reaction to my letter even if he has written as the forwarding arrangements are a bit weak. I am staying here over Easter + will come to town on Tuesday. Austin continues to be vague about his movements so I can't say beyond that" (RFK/13/90/2/1–2). She went into labor on May 27, updating Kahn about her condition the same day: "I have been put to bed + the nurse sent for but nothing has happened so far. It may be a false alarm. I don't think it would do any harm if you rang up in the morning for news. There seems to be a provision of nature that one's not alarmed—like being eaten by a tiger" (RFK/13/90/2/12–15). On the same day, a note from Austin notified Kahn of Ann's birth: "Ann appeared, with a slight excess of punctuality in the course of my college meeting this afternoon. Joan is, I am told, quite fit. I have seen her for a moment + she was still drowsy but quite cheerful. Ann (at the moment) is best regarded as taking after her father + when her time comes to lecture she will certainly not be inaudible. I am backing her against all comers for the Economics Tripos of 1956" (RFK/13/90/2/14–15). Austin was not on the scene for Ann's arrival, and his information about his wife's condition was sketchy and indirect. Two days later Robinson herself wrote Kahn, "while nibbling your delicious grapes + feeling very well." She ruled out a visit since it was regarded as unorthodox for the new mother to see friends.[33]

Between 1934 and 1937, the form and substance of the friendship seem to have remained settled. With a probationary lectureship, an ambitious publishing program, a new course of lectures on applications of monetary theory, a baby, and success in gaining Keynes's endorsement as a leader in the Keynesian revolution, Robinson was a busy woman. By the beginning of 1937, she was pregnant with her second child, Barbara, who was born on October 9, 1937. Robinson was on leave during the Michaelmas term but taught her normal academic load during Lent and Easter. On December 8, 1937, she wrote Kahn a characteristic letter. Although she knew little about Austin's schedule, he was generally at his college in any case. She intended to write her mother about spending a week or so with her family in London beginning on December 23 and asked Kahn for a note on his holiday plans so that they could arrange to meet (RFK/13/90/2/194–95).

THE BREAKDOWN

During Robinson's pregnancies and her introduction to motherhood, she attempted to balance the imperatives imposed by the production and management of her career against the values of what Tolstoy called "real life"—the intimate world of friends, a husband, a lover, and children. Motherhood obviously imposed professional limitations. On August 30, 1934, she noted that she would not read a paper at Oxford because of her "young suckling child" (RFK/13/90/2/64–71). However, she also shared with Kahn the witticism that on showing Ann, age three months, her article on Euler's Theorem, "she didn't remember much about it"—evidence that she was working on this paper during her pregnancy.[34]

The first nine months of 1938 must have been especially hectic. In addition to managing a household, Robinson gave three sets of lectures over the Lent and Easter terms and published two articles and a book review. As she vacationed with her relatives in August, however, her letters showed no signs of fatigue or stress. "Time here floats sweetly by," she observed on August 18 (RFK/13/90/3/10–11). No longer troubled by doubts about her ability to resume original theoretical work after returning from life as a mother, she was content with an intellectually vacuous existence, at least for an interval. Moreover, she was relaxed about the immediate future. Although her plans for September were uncertain, she asked Kahn to keep his calendar open for the end of the month.[35] And yet on the weekend of October 1–3, Robinson suffered a catastrophic psychiatric breakdown, causing her to be hospitalized in a nursing home for a few months. What happened between early September, when she was enjoying her children and a soft life of idleness, and the beginning of October? The first sign of distress was a letter of September 11 to Kahn about her travel plans:

We are now all set to return to Cambridge arriving Friday 16 [September]. Austin is driving taking 2 days + Ann + I are going by train + spending Thursday night at K.P.G.[36] I shall have to spend the time there with the family. If I get in before the car party I will ring up—if not see you sometime on Saturday. But perhaps you could send a word to catch me at K.P.G. saying where you are. Future plans are quite vague—but any way it's not much good making our plans till Hitler has made his. I am still expecting another May 21 but it's really not much good thinking about it. (RFK/13/90/3/26–27)

What happened on May 21? Why did Robinson suppose that Hitler's plans in September might have a substantial bearing on her own? May 20–22, 1938, was the weekend of the May Crisis, when war between Germany and Czechoslovakia seemed imminent. On Friday, May 20, the Czech government recalled its army reservists to active duty, fearing a German attack amidst rumors of German troop movements along the Czech-German border. Tensions were magnified by an incident in which Czech police shot dead two Sudetens—Czech ethnic Germans. The rumors of German troop movements were never confirmed, the Germans insisted they had no plans to invade, and the sense of crisis dissolved by Saturday evening.[37]

Hitler's plans for Czechoslovakia seemed to have been made no later than November 1937, when he delivered one of his monologues on German destiny, international affairs, and military strategy to his senior generals. Germany faced a historic choice between vitality and impotence. The critical issue was not to redress national boundaries as they were defined by the Treaty of Versailles that ended the First World War but *Lebensraum*, the problem of national living space. Within its post-Versailles frontiers, Germany could not achieve its destiny. New natural resources were indispensable. Britain's domination of the high seas ruled out overseas colonies. Germany's fate lay in the east, which meant that a move against Czechoslovakia was inevitable. Hitler reportedly claimed that British and French leaders did not take the existence of Czechoslovakia seriously. It was merely an artifact of the Treaty of Versailles, which dismantled the Austro-Hungarian Empire. The fate of the unsustainable multiethnic Czech nation, with its large German population in the northwestern provinces, would be settled by the chief central European power: Germany. Hitler had his eye on both Austria and Czechoslovakia, the annexation of which would enable Germany to feed an additional five to six million people (Robbins 1968, 171–72). Although the Sudeten Germans were not critical to his calculations, their aspirations for inclusion in the new German empire and the agitation of the Sudeten German Party had significant propaganda value. In summer and early autumn 1938, the European press and foreign ministries in Prague, London, and Paris did not see the Czech crisis in terms of Hitler's political metaphysics. It was understood as a set of issues that revolved around the interests of Sudeten Germans. Would home rule within the limits of a Czech nation meet their legitimate aspirations? Was secession, the formation of a Sudeten German nation state, called for? Or should the Sudeten regions of Czechoslovakia be annexed by Germany? How should these determinations be made: by a plebiscite conducted in Sudeten areas? And irrespective of questions of political process, what response to the demands of the Sudeten separatist movement was consistent with the existence of an independent Czech state sufficiently powerful to defend itself against Germany?

Robinson's observations were made on September 11. Hitler was scheduled to give a much-anticipated address on the Czech crisis the following evening. In this speech, he declared that the status quo in Czechoslovakia, where he claimed that 3.5 million Germans were denied self-determination, was insupportable. Germany would not abandon its compatriots, and he refused to accept anything less than full rights. Although this was not a new position, in London the tone of the speech was regarded as ominous. It seemed that Hitler's patience was exhausted, and Germany might strike soon. But instead of announcing a decision to attack, he made the vague suggestion that the Czech government had an obligation "to discuss matters with the representatives of the Sudeten Germans and in one way or another to bring about an understanding" (quoted in Robbins 1968, 262–63).[38]

The offer of negotiation was music to the ears of the British prime minister, Neville Chamberlain, whose policy toward Germany was appropriately called appeasement. It was an equivocal position, perhaps not internally consistent, and based on the following assumptions: (1) Like all British interwar foreign policy, appeasement rested on two political axioms: the sanctity of the empire and the avoidance of general war. Both were unquestioned even as British power waned, severely damaged by the human and economic losses of 1914–18 and eroded by the failure of the economy to achieve robust levels of investment and employment in the 1920s and 1930s. (2) Because of the excesses of the Treaty of Versailles, Germany had legitimate complaints. They should be addressed—but prudently and without encouraging the Nazis' appetite for territorial expansion. (3) As a great power, Germany deserved what German politicians and journalists of the time called its place in the sun. This meant that Germany should enjoy a relatively free hand in central Europe, its major sphere of influence, where it would also serve as a bulwark against Soviet communism. (4) Rapprochement with Germany was high on the foreign policy agenda of Chamberlain's government. It called for resolution of political and economic conflicts that had placed the two nations at loggerheads for almost half a century. In the interest of achieving this objective, British policy in Europe should not antagonize Germany. (5) The territorial integrity of Czechoslovakia should be defended. For Britain this was not a matter of treaty obligations but democratic principles and its own political prestige as the most powerful democratic nation in Europe. In light of the dramatically successful German annexation of Austria in March—achieved without firing a shot and consummated by Hitler's triumphal entry into Vienna—Britain's failure to enforce its traditional principles would encourage the conclusion that it was finished as a great power. This meant that Britain was compelled to assert its support for Czechoslovakian independence even though it lacked the military resources and the will to make good on this claim. (6) Germany also had legitimate interests in Czechoslovakia. They should be addressed in negotiations that would not threaten war, damage relations between Germany and Britain, lead the Czechs to believe they had been abandoned, or encourage them to suppose they enjoyed unconditional British support.

It was in the context of this policy that Chamberlain wrote the king the day after Hitler's speech. He proposed a dramatic personal visit to Germany, during which he and Hitler would resolve the Czechoslovakian problem and arrive at a British-German understanding. The cabinet approved Chamberlain's visit on September 14, and the request for an invitation to meet Hitler was received in Berlin the same day. The following afternoon Chamberlain was greeted by Hitler at his Berchtesgaden villa in the Bavarian Alps. Annexation, which was proposed by Chamberlain, dominated the discussion: the inclusion of some three million Sudeten Germans in the Reich. Sudeten autonomy or home rule within current territorial boundaries was no longer considered viable. Although the logistical and human difficulties of transferring populations into and out of Sudeten territories were thorny, Hitler seemed to accept the idea in principle. Chamberlain agreed to discuss the matter with his cabinet.

When Chamberlain returned to London on September 16, he received a hero's welcome and a letter from a grateful king. After discussions with the full cabinet, Chamberlain and Lord Halifax, the foreign minister, met in London with their French counterparts on September 18. They hoped to finesse a general principle of self-determination for Czech ethnic minorities and the possibility of a plebiscite by securing the agreement of the Czech government to an ad hoc solution: rectification of Czech frontiers with Germany, secession of Sudeten territory, and transfer of Czechs out of Sudeten areas into other parts of Czechoslovakia. The Czech government was persuaded to accept the British-French proposal. On the afternoon of September 22, Chamberlain met Hitler again, this time at Bad Godesberg on the Rhine. Chamberlain proposed methods for implementing the plans they had discussed in Berchtesgaden. Hitler responded by performing one of his more risky, audacious, and, in the end, successful diplomatic maneuvers. He rejected Chamberlain's proposals and made demands that exceeded the Berchtesgaden agreement, assuming the improbable role of representing the interests of Polish, Hungarian, and Slovak minorities in Czechoslovakia, all of whose claims, he insisted, were no less compelling than those raised by the Sudetens. The British delegation was confused and disappointed. Chamberlain had taken great political risks in proposing a revision to the Treaty of Versailles in order to meet Hitler's demands. Now Hitler wanted more. What would the outcome be? Hitler was ready with an answer to this question. His staff had prepared a map that had redrawn Czech-German national frontiers based on language. By October 1, Czech administrative and military personnel would withdraw behind these new borders and be replaced by Germans. A plebiscite would be held in the Sudeten areas by November 25. It would include all Sudetens who had left the country and disqualify all Czechs who had relocated there since 1918. When Chamberlain demurred, Hitler repeated his familiar threat that there were two ways to settle the Czech question: a peaceful solution based on his new map or a military solution, which the western democracies would find intolerable. The Godesberg meeting ended in an apparent impasse at 1:45 am on September 24.

After Chamberlain returned to London to meet with the cabinet and the French on the Godesberg proposals, Hitler flew to Berlin, where the stage was set for another major address on Czechoslovakia, scheduled for the evening of Monday, September 26. Although he expressed appreciation for Chamberlain's efforts to resolve the crisis, his peroration was chilling. Unless the Czech government agreed by Wednesday at 2:00 pm to carry out his terms for the evacuation of Sudeten areas by October 1, Germany would declare war on Czechoslovakia. The British public and its government concluded that this was tantamount to a declaration of general war. As in 1914, Germany would attack the western democracies. Londoners anticipated German air attacks and the use of poison gas. The response was mass distribution and fitting of gas masks. Men worked day and night digging defensive trenches in public parks, and hospitals prepared for heavy civilian casualties. Londoners with cars drove their children to the safety of the country. In order to check a panic in ticket reservations and overuse of the railway system, the BBC broadcast an official denial that the government intended to nationalize the railways. Because of the large volume of calls, the British telephone system malfunctioned. The number of marriages at registry offices increased by 500 percent. There was also a large increase in sales of forms for preparing wills, metal boxes for deeds and cash, and one-way bus tickets out of London. Panic buying of provisions occurred at groceries (Madge and Harrison 1939, 94–96).

At 8:00 pm Wednesday evening, Chamberlain delivered a radio address to the nation. Finding the Czech refusal to accept German terms baffling and Hitler's timetable unreasonable, the prime minister expressed the incomprehension of much of the British public: "How horrible, fantastic, incredible it is that we should be digging trenches and trying on gas-masks here because of a quarrel in a far-away country between people of whom we know nothing. It seems still more impossible that a quarrel that has already been settled in principle should be the subject of war" (quoted in Robbins 1968, 306).

This was the political background of an uncharacteristically hysterical letter Robinson sent Sraffa that same evening. She did not write as a social scientist or as an actor in the political drama but as a spectator who saw the demonstrations in London for and against a more aggressive response to Germany as political theater played on a world-historic stage: "I wrote you a long letter and then stupidly posted it by ground instead of air. I was imploring you to come here as fast as you can + not miss the most amazing spectacle of centuries. I also urged that this is definitely the place you will find most interesting if the war starts."[39] That afternoon she had been in Whitehall, where she saw "an immense procession of Communists and the League of Nations Union demanding (in effect) an ultimatum to Germany." The demonstrators were surrounded by sympathetic crowds and pitted against a smaller contingent of British fascists, some of whom she believed were political mercenaries hired for the occasion by the British Fascist Party. The socialists demanded immediate conscription. "Simple minded" Tories were puzzled. In considering the response of the British public to the crisis, Robinson saw "a united nation—in a sense which does mean something—demanding war + the Premier making desperate effort after desperate effort to save himself from being pushed into it. Does this sample whet your appetite?"[40]

The Czech crisis was resolved, at least for the time, by the Munich conference of September 29–30. The heads of government and foreign ministries of Britain, France, Germany, and Italy agreed to German annexation of all Sudeten territory. Evacuation of Czech populations would begin October 1 and be completed by October 10. German military occupation of Sudeten areas would begin the day after the agreement was signed, October 1. Final frontiers would be resolved by a plebiscite. The Munich agreement seems to have marked the beginning of Robinson's acute psychiatric disintegration. As her correspondence shows, she was in London at the peak of the panic over the imminence of war. Shortly after Wednesday, September 28, she returned to Cambridge. The only archival details currently available on her breakdown are letters from Kahn and Austin, both of whom wrote Keynes independently and confidentially as close friends and colleagues, giving him early reports of the bare facts. On returning to Cambridge, Robinson was obsessed by the Czech crisis, about which she talked incessantly. As the week passed, "all her emotional problems boiled up + entered into her outpourings." She was unable to sleep—Austin claimed that by Monday, October 3, she had not slept for more than a week. By this point, "the continued strain resulted in storms that were too violent for us to allow her to endure."[41]

Austin and Kahn had both been in touch with Karin Stephen, a close friend of Robinson, a physician, and a Freudian psychoanalyst trained in Britain and the United States. Her husband, Adrian, was also a psychoanalyst and the brother of Virginia Woolf and Vanessa Bell. Adrian (b. 1883) had been a contemporary of Keynes at Cambridge. Karin (b. 1889), a student and fellow of Newnham, had studied philosophy with Bertrand Russell, her uncle by marriage.[42] These connections made the Stephens members of the Cambridge-Bloomsbury aristocracy. Before her psychiatric problems became severe, Robinson had written Karin a letter as a pretext to encourage the offer of a professional consultation. Kahn claimed that Robinson would have rejected such an offer from any other psychiatrist. The pretext was apparently too heavily veiled, and no consultation took place.[43] On the basis of telephone reports from Austin and Kahn, the Stephens compared Robinson's symptoms to those of Woolf. On arriving in Cambridge on Sunday, October 2, they "insisted that she had reached a state at which she must be under expert + continuous supervision + restraint."[44] On Monday, she was given a sedative injection and driven to Brooke House, a clinic and nursing home for mental patients at Clapham in London. Her initial treatment was ten to twelve days of "narcosis"—a continuous regime of drugs intended to induce sleep and break the pattern of behavior that Austin described as "distraught + stormy."[45]

EXPLANATIONS AND REEXAMINATIONS

Shortly after Robinson's breakdown, Kahn, Austin, and Keynes all ventured explanations. In Kahn's view, the Czech crisis was responsible. The Munich agreement, he thought, made war with Germany inevitable. One casualty, Robinson herself, was a victim of the "state of acute neurosis into which the whole country was driven" by the horror of another war.[46] At the same time, she experienced "an exultation at the prospect of the downfall of Fascism." These emotions drove her into a "frenzy," a condition exacerbated by the result of the Munich conference, which made it clear that "the Fascists and Neville Chamberlain were after all going to triumph." But by that point she would not relinquish her conviction that democratic forces would finally prevail, presumably through a British and French guarantee of military support for Czechoslovakia. In response to the Munich agreement, she refused to read the newspapers.[47]

Keynes, who had not seen Robinson in the weeks preceding the breakdown, replied to Kahn's unsettling news on October 10. He provided a more ambitious analysis, not only a diagnosis but a therapeutic program and a prognosis as well.

My dear Alexander,

I am frightfully sorry to hear your news. I thought Joan's letters excited and rather incoherent and one passage in the last one unintelligible, but not such as to arouse in me any suspicions. The strain of combining babies with so much intellectual work is at the bottom of it. I have often in recent times thought that her mind was *racing*. But rest will do wonders. In Virginia's case the symptoms were bad headaches, an unwillingness to take nourishment and delusions which were (except one, so far as I remember) quite mild. [48] The mental specialists never did anything for her, neither the old-fashioned nor the new-fashioned. I should say that complete rest, good nourishment, the avoidance of seeing people and exciting conversations (Leonard has always attached prime importance to the last) is what is wanted.

You must have had a frightful time one way and another. But be of good courage. I should say, from what you tell me, that the prognosis for Joan is good.

Lydia sends her love.

Yours

JMK

We expect to return to London next Sunday and to Cambridge later in the week.

The *conflict* between the desire to avoid war and the desire to defeat Fascism has run many people's feelings to pieces. (RFK/13/90/3/101–102)

If Keynes had recently noticed that Robinson's mind was often "racing," if he found her letters not only excited but somewhat incoherent and in at least one case unintelligible, it is surprising that these aberrations failed to arouse his suspicions. His explanation is more remarkable. The arch anti-Victorian appealed to a conventional late nineteenth-century cliché, diagnosing Robinson's problems as a result of strain. Women did not have the resources required for the physiological effort to bear children and the intellectual effort to write books on economic theory.[49] Or did they? In his afterthought, Keynes seemed to dispose of the "not both books and babies" nostrum of his father's generation and embrace Kahn's view of the prospect of war as the real explanation. Like many of her British contemporaries, Robinson went to pieces over a political or moral dilemma: the conflicting imperatives of preserving peace and defeating fascism.

Austin gave a more detailed and nuanced explanation in his letter of October 4 to Keynes, notifying him of the breakdown the day after Robinson was taken to London. His account began with the Czech crisis, the minor roles played by Robinson's father and her sister Nancy in events of September, and the impact of family conflicts over appeasement. General Sir Frederick Barton Maurice, who had been a senior staff officer in the First World War, was a leading figure in the efforts of the British Legion to assist the Chamberlain government in resolving the Czech crisis.[50] The legion, an organization of British ex-servicemen founded in 1919 under royal patronage, offered to place ten thousand legionnaires at the disposal of the German government as neutral observers and supervisors of the transfer of Sudeten territory. The offer was made to Hitler with the knowledge of the Chamberlain government. Although the entire contingent of legionnaires was apparently prepared to sail for Germany after the Godesberg talks, the Munich agreement made the offer moot.[51] Nancy Maurice was the private secretary, aide, and confidante of Major General Sir Edward Spears. As a member of Parliament in the 1930s, Spears was a leading figure in the Conservative opposition to Chamberlain's policy of appeasement.[52] Robinson seems to have labored under an illusion of personal political responsibility and power. She thought it was her task to resolve conflicts over foreign affairs in her family and acted on the fanciful belief that her domestic contributions to political clarification would make a difference to the outcome of the Czech crisis. In Austin's view, Robinson's obsession with the Czech crisis intersected with "all her emotional problems." The political events of September were a cause in the sense of a catalyst, a contingent factor lighting the fires that caused her emotional problems to "boil up" in an uncontrollable fashion: "To the world I am merely saying that she had a severe nervous breakdown brought on by the political crisis."[53] This is what Austin was saying, but he knew better. The real story of her breakdown was more obscure and also more disturbing. What were the emotional problems to which he alluded but did not identify in his letter to Keynes?

This question is answered in a strained and guarded exchange of letters between Austin and Kahn, initiated by Austin the day he wrote Keynes. In the exchange, it is clear that the Cambridge commitment to rigor, lucidity, and unsparing honesty could not withstand Robinson's breakdown. The event portended a crisis in the relationship between her husband, to whom she did not want to remain married, and her lover, with whom she enjoyed a liaison fraught with danger. Austin and Kahn struggled to reexamine their lives in the wake of her collapse, trying to reestablish their little world of intimacy and conviviality on more stable ground.

Austin's first letter broached—obliquely, with some fastidiousness, but unequivocally—Kahn's friendship with his wife: "There are some things that I think that it is rather easier to write than to say. So please forgive me writing this. I think we must all feel that when we get Joan back again to normal, everything must be done not to put her in the position of strain in which any further breakdown is to be feared." He did not expect "violent upheavals" in their lives or "drastic measures of any sort," and he did not encourage them. Instead he proposed a therapeutic reconsideration of their relationships, a two-track, quasi-psychoanalytic dialogue that he and Kahn would conduct with Stephen independent of one another. They would each write Stephen in complete candor and be prepared to accept her counsel: "I am going myself to try to put down on paper for Karin everything that seems to me relevant + my own feelings + thoughts about them. Do you feel at all inclined to do the same? With her help I have great hope that we can find a way out that will bring happiness to us all."[54]

Why did Austin find it difficult to speak with Kahn, his close colleague, professional ally, and friend of some eight years? Why did he make an effort to establish emotional distance between them by putting in a letter what could have been said in conversation? What was his reason for avoiding a face-to-face talk? These questions can be posed from another perspective. What did Kahn and Robinson share that might threaten another breakdown after the Robinson-Kahn-Austin triadic relationship was steered back to normal? Austin's letter seemed to imply that Kahn's friendship with Robinson was objectionable because it was dangerous ground for conversation and hazardous to her health. If it was necessary to eliminate all threats of subsequent breakdowns and if Austin regarded the friendship as one of these threats, his letter can be understood as an attempt to alter its course by pushing it to the margins of her life.

Kahn responded on October 6. He too hoped to avoid disruptive changes in their lives. Above all, he wanted no part in "melodramatic action merely for its own sake." At the same time, he saw that circumstances could not remain as they were.

If we can arrange matters to the true interests of Joan's peace of mind, I should certainly not want to leave the place where I have friends and a way of life, though it is obvious that, so far as I am concerned things would have to be different from what they have been.

But Joan's peace of mind, as you say, must be the criterion. Your suggestion about Karin is excellent and I will certainly do as you suggest. I take it that your idea is that our reflective comments should be for Karin's private eyes and not for yours or mine. I feel, at the same time, that, perhaps at some later stage, we ought to aim at a candid discussion between ourselves, difficult though it may be.

I blame myself now that I have never in the past given you an opportunity for such a discussion. (EAGR/Box 9/2/1/17/66–67)

Austin had ended his letter in the hope that, with the help of Stephen, the three would find a "way out." Out of what? Presumably the subterranean conflicts and the repressed emotional turmoil that had ended in the breakdown. Once this solution was found, what would happen? Although the seemingly prelapsarian innocence of the 1930s might be beyond recovery, they would arrive at an arrangement that would make them all happy. Kahn stressed the sincerity with which he shared Austin's faith in their collective happiness and added some striking assurances: "There is one thing to be remembered. I have always found a great feeling of fondness for you, and now I always shall. And another thing is that Joan has always been faithful to you, and has never, as far as I know, felt tempted to be otherwise" (EAGR/Box 9/2/1/17/66–67).

Why did Kahn think he and Austin should have a candid discussion? Why would such a discussion between old friends prove difficult? What delicate matters called for uncommon candor? And why did Kahn hold himself responsible for failing to provide an opportunity for this conversation? Was there some piece of dangerous interpersonal knowledge critical to their relationship that Kahn possessed but Austin did not? Why was Kahn reluctant to share his private reflections with Austin, with whom he was on close terms, but prepared to reveal himself to Stephen? Consider also the several items Kahn said he remembered. Why would he find it necessary to reassure Austin of his feelings for him and insist that they were not in jeopardy? Only if there were facts that might place their relationship in doubt. Why did he believe it was important for him to provide guarantees of Robinson's fidelity to her husband? Only if there were some reason to suppose guarantees were needed. How could Kahn presume to know that Robinson had always been faithful? Only if he knew Robinson better than her husband knew her. How could his knowledge of Robinson extend to her beliefs about her marital fidelity? Only if he knew that he was the only person who might cause her to become unfaithful.

When Austin replied to Kahn, the exchange had reached a critical juncture. Austin's first letter disclosed his sense that Kahn's friendship with his wife was suspicious and possibly objectionable. Kahn's letter made it clear that he understood how Austin saw the friendship. By that point, most of the cards were on the table. The next move was Austin's. Would he make it by pursuing the dialogue into more perilous territory? Would he speak or at least write to Kahn in a more straightforward fashion about the friendship and the changes he expected? He would not. Further disclosures on Kahn's part were emphatically discouraged. Standing on the brink of a full exposé of the friendship, its extent and intensity, and what might be done about it, Austin stepped back. Their mutual understanding was left as it stood at this point. The fundamentals were clearly avowed. Other admissions were either made tacitly or couched as studied ambiguities. Details were neither offered nor expected.

Austin also stepped back from the view that the trauma of Robinson's marriage with him and her friendship with Kahn was the decisive factor in the breakdown. Instead he moved in the direction of Kahn's more comfortable explanation, the Czech crisis and "Joan's thoughts about the war."[55] Were Austin's position on the Czech crisis and his support for appeasement a source of Robinson's obsession over the political developments of late September? In that event, the emotional problems that boiled up during the weekend might have included a conflict between Robinson and her husband over European politics. Austin explained himself to Kahn in a letter of October 6. After noting that the personal memoranda he and Kahn were writing were intended for Stephen alone—he would let her "judge whether there is anything we ought to have out together"—he turned to the explanation Kahn preferred.

I hope that you may be right, + believe that there is a considerable probability that you are, in thinking that it was the strain of deciding one's attitude to war, + not other underlying matters which brought Joan to this state. I think I probably tend to exaggerate the things which happened to be on the top of her mind during the stress of last Sunday night. I had been feeling that it was not only the facts of war, but also the contrast between her own brave attitude and my very cowardly one which had contributed to her distraction, + I had been led to ask myself why I had thought + felt what I did. I think the fact it is incredible that [illegible] of my generation shall feel that there can be nothing for which it is justifiable again to reinforce upon us the strains of 1914–8, and that we have tended to deny ourselves the strong principles which could lead us to say again "I would rather die than submit to this." (RFK/13/90/3/107–13)

Austin understood his position on the issue of war as an unseemly readiness to compromise principles in order to escape painful consequences, even though he believed that the principles in question were fundamental imperatives on which no compromise could be justified. During the Munich conference, Harold Nicolson, former diplomat and current National Labour Party MP, wrote H. A. L. Fisher, the historian and warden of New College Oxford. Nicolson described the confused national response to Chamberlain's resolution of the Czech crisis: "I have a nasty feeling that I shall not approve of the results of the Munich conference. People seem unable to differentiate between physical relief and moral satisfaction" (quoted in Gilbert and Gott 1963, 80). Austin was one of these people. In his diagnosis of his own thinking, he had confused relief from the stress of enduring the prospect of another war with the conviction that the Munich agreement was ethically acceptable. In his conversations with Robinson during the weekend of her breakdown, he had assumed that in order to avoid war with Germany in autumn 1938, any measure that promised success was morally tolerable. As he perhaps understood later, some measures might be contemptible and cowardly if they sacrificed the Czechs. Measures might also be politically self-defeating if they increased the chances of a later and more disastrous war by strengthening Germany's resources and rewarding its aggressive behavior. This meant that certain policies to avoid war, such as appeasement, might be more objectionable on both moral and political grounds than war itself. Austin felt, somewhat obscurely, that his misjudgments during the Czech crisis were anchored in deeper moral weaknesses in his character, which he regarded as grounds for more shame and self-reproach than his morally flaccid position on the war: "I had been wondering how far Joan was feeling acutely conscious of this, + how far that contributed to her worries."[56] If Austin's fears were justified, his moral failings may have troubled Robinson more deeply than the compromises entailed by his apparent belief in appeasement at any ethical price. A comparison with her principled antiappeasement stance would have been devastating. There was a more serious worry. These considerations might have forced her to the conclusion that her husband was a morally contemptible human being.

These unsettling reflections notwithstanding, Austin invited no dialogue with Kahn, either on appeasement and war or on any aspect of Kahn's friendship with Robinson. "Please don't answer this," he wrote. "I think we shall make it difficult for both of us to be natural again + to be real and follow normally. I feel sure that we are good enough friends to work out a way to our own joint happiness + to Joan's. Never at any time, even when I have been worried + unhappy about our own relation to Joan, have I really wavered in heart + affection towards you."[57] Were candid conversations with Kahn important to Robinson's recovery, the prevention of subsequent breakdowns, or the reestablishment of a status quo between Kahn and himself? Austin had no interest in pursuing these questions. He would leave to Stephen, the impartial professional therapist, the question of whether there were matters that they "ought to have out together." An exchange of hard, unpleasant truths was likely to complicate efforts to reestablish interpersonal conditions approximating normality. Even though they were good friends and would find a path to their collective happiness, certain matters were best left unexpressed. Comity and truthfulness, it seems, were conflicting values.[58]

The perspective and emotional tone of the letters on Robinson's breakdown written by Austin and Kahn, both to Keynes and to one another, are quite different. Robinson's illness left Kahn in a desperate state, and he made no effort to conceal this. His concern was for Robinson, not for the impact of her breakdown on him. Austin's letters are emotionally more detached. His account to Keynes is clinical and dispassionate. In writing to Kahn, he presumed that Robinson's drive to London was quiet and comfortable; under sedation, she slept most of the way and was now safely in the hands of medical specialists. Although he was not under medical care, he apparently thought he should have been: "I do feel that it is rather important that Karin should help me tidy myself up," he wrote, and he anxiously awaited her arrival in Cambridge. Austin was struggling to create an appearance of normality in his professional life at Cambridge that would make it unnecessary to reveal the truth to his colleagues. He was chiefly concerned to show that he was "behaving with decency" even though he suffered from lack of sleep as well as "nerves + hysteria."[59] His main task seems to have been self-maintenance and rehabilitation. As he assured Keynes, "I am here in Cambridge, + prefer to remain here, where I have Piero + Kahn when I want them, + an utterly normal College knowing nothing of my problems." He was certain Keynes would understand if the *Economic Journal*, which required no urgent business, was left dormant for a few days.[60]

In his letter of October 6 to Kahn, Austin set out his protocol for contact with Robinson: none. For the present, friends and colleagues could do nothing useful and should not attempt to get in touch with the patient. "In fact," he claimed, "I gather that the removal of all outside associations is rather desirable" (RFK/13/90/3/107–13). Notwithstanding Austin's instruction, Kahn quickly took matters in hand. Very shortly after Austin ended their exchange, he composed his memorandum for Stephen, wrote her, and met with her as well in order to learn whether he could be of help through letters or visits. He also raised with Stephen the question of whether he might help pay for Robinson's medical care. Stephen assured Kahn that Austin would not be told about her contact with him or his offer of financial assistance. If at some point Robinson would benefit from correspondence or visits, he would be informed.[61]

Like the barking dog in the Sherlock Holmes story, Stephen's letter is perhaps most illuminating in what it does not contain. Although she considered the Austin-Kahn-Robinson triad in discussing the sources of Robinson's problems, there is nothing about her political passions or her reaction to the Czech crisis. Stephen made it clear that once Robinson began to recover, she would advise her on what to do about Austin and Kahn. There is no indication that she proposed to consult with her patient on how to think about a European war. From Stephen's professional standpoint, the significant source of Robinson's problems was her relationships with her husband and her lover.[62]

Kahn was determined to cover some of Robinson's medical expenses or at least assure himself that the burden would not fall solely on Austin. His discussion with Stephen on this matter produced no results. Austin had told Kahn that he had no financial difficulties for the present.[63] However, Kahn was troubled. Although he had no specific knowledge of Austin's resources, he supposed they would be quickly exhausted by the cost of Robinson's care. His solution was a clumsy effort to interest Keynes in becoming Austin's lender, but without seeming to make this suggestion. He had an outstanding loan of £500 from Keynes, which he had invested. The day after he received Stephen's letter, he repaid £250, hoping to return the balance soon. The prospect of war had encouraged him to liquidate some of his investments, which explains the availability of the £250. He noted that he had intended to make this repayment during the Michaelmas term in any case. "I mention that I am merely carrying out an old intention because I do not want you to feel that I am asking you to turn your attention to needs much more pressing than mine. It *may* be, however, that you might, at some time, feel inclined to offer Austin some assistance."[64] In suggesting this possibility, Kahn framed the matter of financing Robinson's care in purely economic terms. Expenses should be regarded as a "capital expenditure"—presumably an investment in human capital that would prevent loss of value in a significant university resource. In view of the intellectual capital that Robinson represented, it was necessary to finance its upkeep, "if necessary, by special measures." Thus the rationale for a loan to Austin, which Kahn quite implausibly said he was not proposing.[65]

THE DEATH OF ALEXANDER

Robinson's recovery was slow. A month after her hospitalization, she asked the medical staff of Brooke House to reestablish her connection with Kahn. Ilene Chennell, her physician and the assistant medical officer of the clinic, wrote him that although her condition had improved considerably, she understood that she was not yet well enough to receive letters. However, she worried about Kahn and was eager to receive news from him. Chennell asked for a "reassuring line," which she would pass on to Robinson.[66] By the following month, Robinson was well enough to write Kahn a note and to keep in touch through either her aunt Francis or Chennell, with whom she encouraged him to speak freely. Robinson and her physician had reached an understanding on matters that should be held in absolute confidence; Chennell was "perfectly reliable in every respect."[67]

The medical staff of the clinic offered no explanation for Robinson's breakdown. She was not interested in explanations or arriving at her own theory, unlike Keynes, Austin, and Kahn. She believed that the most intelligent course was to dismiss the matter: "I think it is best to write off altogether the queer week end of Oct.1–3rd—but in dreams I have cleared out what ever grit there was in the masking so no one need worry about how or what or why this sad accident occurred."[68] Robinson was convinced she could recover without considering exactly what this "sad accident" was and how and why it happend. Instead of an explanation, she shared a metaphorical account of her dreams with Kahn. Although her frictional metaphor of grit and masking tape did not identify the source of her difficulties, it presumably resolved them to her satisfaction. If the events of October 1–3 were an imponderable mystery, they were not open to the simple explanation of political hysteria. Neither Robinson nor Chennell seems to have had a word to say about her reaction to the Czech crisis. In her correspondence from the clinic with Kahn, however, Robinson connected the breakdown with her marriage to Austin and the difficulties it created for her friendship with him. "Please give my love to Piero," she wrote in concluding her note, without a word of greeting for Austin.[69]

Cairncross mentions that Robinson's physician advised Austin not to see his wife until six months after the breakdown (1993, 171). The first substantial communications from Robinson to Kahn, two long letters written between January 2 and 18, 1939, show that the physician's recommendation reflected the patient's wishes. By this point Robinson was convinced that her marriage had ended, in spirit and in the flesh, if not in law: "I have put it frankly to the Dr that it is better for me not to see Austin except for a few 'token' meetings at a superficial level, until the Easter vac (I am day-dreaming already of a family party in the Lakes with me stepping over the pass for a few days climbing with you + Piero—but it [is] naughty to look so far ahead)."[70]

Chennell's position was that Austin should not visit her patient at all during the Lent term. Robinson was less stringent. In view of what she had "stood up to," a few inconsequential visits would make no difference. In addition, she anticipated a long separation from Austin as he was to depart on another African assignment. As she wrote Kahn, "Francie [Francis], understanding my position very well, used all her influence to persuade him from scrapping it."[71] After she became acquainted with Kahn, Robinson seems to have seen her life with Austin as poisoned by insincerity, dishonesty, and deception. She was deeply troubled by the fact that she was obliged to pretend to be what she was not. Although she did not put the matter in these terms, her profound dissatisfaction in the marriage lay in the fact that she could not follow the Goethean maxim, Become the person you are. As she wrote, "And these years it has never been Austin['s] sulking fits that have made me unhappy—it has been my own bitterness + self-pity. When I can lie him into superficial happiness I am more tempted to bitter hateful evil thoughts than when he is behaving badly."[72]

Robinson's more forthright assertions about Austin and her marriage were tied to an aspect of her personality that she cultivated and prized. She felt herself inhabited, and in her best moments inspired, by a being she called the imp. The Robinsonian imp was feisty, presumptuous, devilish, and above all impudent. In her scientific persona, the imp appeared in her contentious disposition and was perhaps most conspicuous in her polemical ruthlessness. The impish Robinson had a robust sense of her extraordinary singularity and intellectual superiority. In January 1939, the imp seems to have risen unimpaired and undaunted from the trauma of early October. It symbolized what freedom meant to Robinson — "to think + write + feel without fear." It was a freedom she believed she had lost in her complex relationship with Austin and Kahn. During her recovery, she regained it. As she wrote Kahn on January 2, "I have never felt the sweet sane calm delight of the imp so smoothly running thro' my veins as now" (RFF/13/90/1/210–15).

Just as Robinson behaved as if she were inhabited by a mischievous imp, so she ascribed a quite different persona to Kahn: a well-intentioned but ultimately destructive figure whom, perhaps following Lydia's name for Kahn, she called Alexander. In the course of their relationship during the 1930s, Robinson found Alexander endearing at first, then tiresome, and in the end intolerable. She was convinced that her freedom depended upon freeing Kahn, or perhaps persuading him to free himself, from Alexander. This called for the death of Alexander, in effect his murder at the hands of Kahn. Alexander represented a moralism that Robinson could no longer endure, an ill-defined collection of "old foolish irrelevant ideas that what is sweet to you must be a wicked crime against some one else." This someone else was Austin. Alexander's moralism lay in misplaced scruples, the mistaken belief that by enjoying Robinson he was depriving Austin of something that was rightfully his. Robinson unconditionally rejected this view of herself and her relationship with both men. She asked Kahn to "scatter Alexander's dust to the winds."[73]

Alexander was confused by the moral status of his desires. Since Robinson had written off her marriage, his scruples were based on a false assumption. They represented "fake soft pity and over-anxious protectiveness" of Austin, the "unworthy survivals" of a past that Robinson believed they had transcended.[74] This was 1932–38, a period in which their erotic life was governed by an Austinian creed: a belief that their feelings should not be consummated and Austin should be an unwitting partner in their relationship — a constant subject of interest, concern, and conversation. If Robinson had a tacit explanation of her breakdown, it lay in her inability to continue on these terms. By some point in autumn 1938, and certainly by the weekend of the breakdown, she and Kahn had abandoned the Austinian creed in favor of a new post-Alexandrian principle. Austin would be expelled from their relationship. His sentinel and champion Alexander would be dispatched and cast to the winds. On January 2, Robinson summed up her commitment to this new principle in the melodramatic and literary terms she sometimes favored:

As for the "flesh + the devil" what we so easily instinctively knew all along is now my complete conviction—it is only raw material, + the only wrong we ever did each other was to doubt that we had chosen the right way to deal with it. We've turned the flank of nature's messy mechanical contrivances, and felt the deep sweet poetry of the flesh. The fact that we had already got the problem solved that weekend [October 1–3] has done more to help me to survive these months than anything else. (RFK/13/90/3/210–15)

The world of the flesh and the devil was the erotic life. The post-Alexandrian principle dictated that Austin not only be dismissed from their lives but, to the extent possible, excised from their conversation. They would tolerate occasional references to him on Robinson's part since conventions required that they remain married. However, she chided Kahn for resurrecting "Alexander's ghost" and his "silly scruples" by indulging in pointless conversation about Austin, which she regarded as morally dishonest and an obstacle to her recovery. "One thing I must beg of you—spare me as much as you can talking about Austin. I will talk if I must for nothing is so important to me now as to have freedom + I can only free myself by freeing you. But if you can free yourself how much better." It was, she suggested, merely an intelligent application of the Benthamite calculus: "I will tell you what I must + you must spare me what you can."[75]

On January 19, Robinson saw two possibilities for Kahn's liberation from Alexander. Either she would free him from Alexander's scruples—presumably by persuading him that they were dishonest, silly, and an artifact of morally antiquated conventions. Or he would liberate himself, perhaps by arriving at the same conclusions. On January 2, however, she insisted that since Alexander was nothing more than an artifact of Kahn's mistaken sense that he had betrayed Austin, the question of how to eliminate Alexander was his problem. Apparently she had the same feelings the Thursday before her breakdown. As she wrote on January 2, 1939: "That scrap of paper I wrote you on Thursday 'that is your affair—do not ask me to solve your problem' still governs my attitude" (RFK/13/90/3/210–15).

Robinson resumed teaching in the Easter term of 1939. She and Austin continued to live together. At the beginning of September, Britain declared war on Germany, and in November Austin began war work in

Whitehall. She was not displeased by his absence, which was broken only by occasional weekends in Cambridge.[76] In November 1940, she wrote a more straightforward account of her erotic relationship with Kahn, who was also posted in London for war work. He had visited her on a Sunday in Cambridge:

Your letter did not come till this morning. No, my dear, you don't cause me to suffer. I was put out on Sunday because it is annoying always having to have a committee meeting beforehand + I thought just for once we had an unexpected stroke of luck. But, as you say, we do very well on the whole. I expected a great deal more trouble. My difficulty is that when I start persuading you I cease to want it—not out of female pride, but because one has to switch on to a different level—at least I do owing to not being able to behave like a bitch. The first time I was completely fed up by the time I had got your consent—but it doesn't matter because it all comes out in the wash. Anyway my dear all this is to me just as it were raw material for the really important thing—our confidence [in] each other. You know my slogan—friendship is more important than love. A friendship that can digest such episodes without a strain is something worth having. I am very proud of it because you know I like such odd combinations much more than commonplace success.[77]

2

The Making of *The Economics*
of Imperfect Competition

THE MARSHALLIAN GUILD

When Robinson began lecturing, her apprenticeship was formed by a culture that defined, in large measure, what it meant to be a Cambridge economist. More than twenty years after she began the long march to establish herself at Cambridge, she made the following observation: "When I came up to Cambridge, in 1922, and started reading economics, Marshall's *Principles* was the bible, and we knew little beyond it. [Stanley] Jevons, [Antoine Augustine] Cournot, even [David] Ricardo, were figures in the footnotes. We heard of 'Pareto's Law,' but nothing of the general equilibrium system. Sweden was represented by Cassel, America by Irving Fisher, Austria and Germany were scarcely known. Marshall was economics" (Robinson 1951, vii).

Although Robinson's reputation rested not least on a penchant for rhetorical excess, she cannot be faulted for exaggeration on this point. Marshall's teaching and writings dominated Cambridge economics during her undergraduate years and for more than a half century, from his appointment to the chair of political economy in 1885 through the civil wars of the Keynesian revolution in the 1930s.[1]

The Cambridge economics faculty of the 1920s and early 1930s can be understood as a guild, a network of professional and personal relations formed by intellectual, organizational, and proximal ties. Intellectual ties were based on the common Marshallian research tradition. Organizational ties that constituted the faculty as a self-governing collegium were established by membership on the Faculty Board of Economics and Politics and its various committees, which recommended appointments to lectureships, revised the curriculum, and evaluated the candidates for honors degrees who would reproduce the ethos of the guild. The secularized monastic residential college system, the distinctive social space of the ancient universities placed colleagues in close proximity during term time. The emoluments of a college fellowship included a small apartment or set of rooms, meals in the college dining hall, and the shared space of a clublike common room. All the men's colleges of this era were within a short walk of one another. Fellows met and entertained lecturers and fellows from other colleges in their rooms and at the college high table. The logistics of entertainment were managed by an elaborate staff of college servants who also operated an intercollege mail service. Messages circulated by servants, and the thrice-daily deliveries of the British post made it easy for the four academic generations of epistolary economists in residence at the beginning of the 1930s to correspond daily, often through several exchanges.

The basic structural component of this network was a set of intersecting and intergenerational master-apprentice relations. Pigou and Keynes, who learned their economics from Marshall, were the senior masters. Robertson and Shove attended Pigou's lectures on the principles of economics before the First World War. Keynes supervised both Robertson and Shove. Although Kahn was Keynes's protégé, he also attended Pigou's lectures on fundamentals. He heard Robertson on money, from whom he claimed to have gleaned little, and Shove on production, value, and distribution, from whom he drew ideas and lines of inquiry that were employed in his fellowship dissertation. Only Sraffa, an exceptional figure in many respects, stood outside this pedagogical lineage, in which everyone at Cambridge doing theoretical work was connected with everyone else.

The result was a pronounced exclusivity: restrictive, hermetic, and incestuous. Cambridge economists studied Marshall and Pigou. They read one another as well as the articles that appeared in the *Economic Journal*, edited by Keynes. By the standards of a cosmopolitan science, however, their training and theoretical perspectives were decidedly narrow. As Kahn observed with a mixture of incredulity and asperity, Shove went so far as to discourage his students from reading Harrod.[2] Kahn's tendentious reports on the state of economics at Chicago and Harvard marked him as a highly refined product of Cambridge arrogance. Outside opinions that failed to embrace Cambridge positions made little impact. *Wanderjahre* for Cambridge apprentices were neither expected nor encouraged. Students from the peripheries of the academic economic universe might spend a term or two at Cambridge to receive illumination; Harrod, Meade, and Abba Lerner spring to mind. However, the masters were in residence at King's and Trinity.

The masters of the guild were guardians of a culture of craftsmanship, the proper name for which is unquestionably Marshallian. As a rule, it may be an error to suppose that the origins of intellectual cultures lie in acts of foundation performed by dominant figures (Baehr 2002). If this supposition is indeed mistaken, Cambridge economics between the wars marks a significant exception. It cannot be detached from Marshall's ambitions, efforts, and scientific personality. The work that won Robinson recognition as a bona fide member of the Marshallian guild was *The Economics of Imperfect Competition*, a critique of Marshall's value theory that undertook to place its superstructure on new foundations. It was possible only on the basis of the institutional and theoretical transformations of Marshallian culture in the 1920s. Thus some remarks on what Marshall's followers at Cambridge made of his program for a science of economics are in order.

The Ethos of Discipleship

Marshall's *Principles*, lectures, and personal example were the objects of an ethos of discipleship at Cambridge that began before the First World War and was sustained into the 1920s. Its ultimate premise was piety: belief in his incontestable authority as the foremost economist of his time and a respect for his work that approximated veneration. In the early 1920s, Pigou, Keynes, and their students wrote as if Marshall had solved the basic problems of economic theory.[3] If further discussion of fundamentals was pointless, the only scientifically sensible course was to refine and extend his work.[4]

Pigou—"Marshall's favourite pupil" (Keynes 1951, 186)—was the high priest of the Marshallian brotherhood. In his presidential address to the Royal Economic Society in 1939, he recalled Marshall's august position in British economics: "Forty years ago, indeed down to the catastrophe of the War, economic thought in this country was dominated to a quite extraordinary degree by one man—Marshall. He was our leader, practically unchallenged. Edgeworth from Oxford explicitly acclaimed him as such. Not only for his former pupils in places of authority, but for the general body of economists in England he was 'the master'" (Pigou 1939, 219–20). In Pigou's view, Marshall's "moral dictatorship" produced immense benefits for students. Because he was acknowledged as the supreme grand theoretician, they were not tempted to begin their careers in vain attempts to "rebuild economic science from basement to roof." Instead they confined their efforts to issues more narrowly defined by Marshall's theoretical apparatus. The result was "a training which from tasks beyond our power we could not have obtained" (Pigou 1939, 219–20). The consequences of his dominance for economists who had completed their training were not so benign. Recognition of his preeminence as the artificer of a peerless engine of discovery condemned Marshall's followers to the condition of epigones, whose fate was to labor in the shadow of a great man. Pigou expressed this sense of inadequacy in comparing his own abilities with the theoretical powers he saw in Marshall. What was the point of beginning research in a new area if one knew that "in his head, if not his drawer, there was an analysis enormously superior to anything we could hope to accomplish?" (Pigou 1939, 220). Pigou had learned this lesson the hard way: "I remember, not once but many times, getting hold of some problem, and, after labouring over it with toil and pain, imagining proudly that I had made an original contribution to economic thought. I then turned to Marshall's *Principles*, and almost invariably in some obscure footnote there was half a clause, inside a parenthesis perhaps, which made it obvious that Marshall had solved this problem long ago but had not thought it worth while to write the answer down" (Pigou 1925, 85).

In the 1920s, Keynes also seems to have believed in Pigou's mantra that, in some sense, it's all in Marshall. In his long, masterful essay on Marshall, the centerpiece of his *Essays in Biography*, he made the following observation: "How often has it not happened even to those who have been brought up on the *Principles*, lighting upon what seems a new problem or a new solution, to go back to it and to find, after all, that the problem and a better solution have been always there, yet quite escaping notice! It needs much study and independent thought on the reader's own part before he can know the half of what is contained in the concealed crevices of that rounded globe of knowledge which is Marshall's *Principles of Economics*" (Keynes 1951, 190–92). Harrod, who spent a year at Cambridge in 1925–26, recalled that in the 1920s Keynes's Marshallian credentials were impeccable. Because Marshall had settled the major theoretical problems, progress in economics could be achieved only by applying the existing body of theory. "His recipe for the young economist," Harrod wrote, "was to know Marshall thoroughly and read his *Times* every day carefully, and without bothering too much about the large mass of contemporary publication in book form. He was careful to add that one must read one's Pigou and anything that came from the pens of the chosen few. His own reading after 1914 was probably not much more extensive" (Harrod 1951, 324). In the 1920s, Keynes identified the chosen few as "orthodox members of the Cambridge School of Economics": students of Marshall together with their students (Robertson 1952, vi).

The Radicalization of Immanent Critique:
Parameters of Criticism in the 1920s

In light of Marshall's Olympian status, it is not surprising that public criticism of his thought was slow to develop at Cambridge. However, the guild was not oblivious to weaknesses in the *Principles*. As Keynes observed in 1924, its analysis of time, although innovative, was a source of serious problems (in Keynes 1951, 185). One aspect of this analysis, Marshall's discussion of the laws of returns, was precisely the point at which immanent critique—criticism of Marshall within the limits of his own theoretical framework—entered the guild. Cambridge economists who had reached a dead end in applying Marshall's theories to solve empirical problems concluded that his methods were defective. Marshallian philology and exegesis—the practice of studying, teaching, and discussing the *Principles* down to the arcana of its footnotes—revealed logical and conceptual difficulties in Marshall's formulation of the laws of returns. Remapping the *Principles* by excavating and reexcavating the text exposed its limits.[5]

Although Cambridge economists had discovered conceptual difficulties in the laws of returns as early as Pigou's undergraduate years around the turn of the century (Pigou 1922, 458), they rarely challenged Marshall in print. The silence at Cambridge on the merits of Marshall's analysis of the laws of returns was decisively broken in 1922 by Clapham. In his article "Of Empty Economic Boxes," he argued that the Pigouvian restatement of the laws of returns was defective. A box on the shelves of a hat shop contains concrete items: hats or socks. The theoretical box of the laws of returns in the economist's mind, on the other hand, is empty because Marshall provided no criteria for identifying a unit of a resource, a commodity, or an industry. Even if the requisite criteria were at hand and the box could be filled, it would be useless for devising policy because the contents are inconsistent with the facts of economic life.

Clapham's critique marked a turn in the development of the guild, and the public airing of lapses or fallacies in Marshall's thought became a legitimate and standard guild practice.[6] It was also the beginning of the twilight of the idols. In 1925, Sraffa published a seminal critique of Marshall in Italian that attacked the foundations of his theory of value. Francis Edgeworth, Keynes's coeditor at the *Economic Journal*, was much impressed. On his recommendation, Keynes invited Sraffa to write a version of his paper in English for the journal. "The Laws of Returns under Competitive Conditions," published in December 1926, radicalized the Cambridge critique of Marshall.[7] Sraffa argued that Marshall's attempt to imbed the classical laws of returns in his neoclassical theory of value was a failure, producing an internal theoretical inconsistency. In order to analyze the equilibrium price of a single commodity, Marshall assumed ceteris paribus conditions: the demand for a commodity and its supply were independent of one another and also independent of demand and supply conditions for all other commodities. Sraffa demonstrated that these conditions are met only under constant returns to scale. The consequence for Marshall's position was devastating: demand plays no role in determining the equilibrium value of a particular commodity. Sraffa suggested some alternatives: "A simple way of approaching the problem of competitive value" was to use the "old and now obsolete" classical theory, which neglected the role of demand in price determination. As a first approximation to reality, this approach was "as important as it is useful." However, Sraffa did not seem interested in first approximations. In order to improve the empirical accuracy of a theory of competitive value, it was necessary to abandon the partial-equilibrium assumption. In principle, interdependence among industries could be analyzed by employing a system of simultaneous equations. However, the complexity of a general-equilibrium approach made it barren, "at least in the present state of our knowledge" (Sraffa 1926, 541).

There was a more attractive theoretical alternative that could rescue the long-period theory of value if economists were willing "to abandon the path of free competition" in favor of monopoly. Sraffa offered a rough outline of an alternative—later called imperfect competition at Cambridge—that took into account important realities. Because many firms operate under conditions of increasing returns that result from internal economies, a realistic theory of value would begin by treating increasing returns as a matter of fact. Such economies do not lead to monopoly. A firm's capacity for expansion is limited by its ability to sell increased output without lowering its price. It suspends production of additional output whenever a price reduction is no longer profitable. Firm size, Sraffa argued, is limited by demand, not costs (Sraffa 1926, 542–43).

Why is the market for a product segmented into smaller markets, each firm exercising monopoly power in its own submarket? Consumers prefer the product of a particular firm because of brand consciousness, custom, personal relations with the seller, product quality and design, familiarity with the product, or the ability to purchase on credit. These grounds of preference allow firms to sell their products at higher prices. Although each firm can dominate its own segment, attempts to extend operations beyond this sphere entail heavy marketing expenses (Sraffa 1926, 544–45).

In 1926, the Cambridge theory of monopoly was used only to analyze firms that enjoyed exceptional and incontestable market power, such as public utilities and railroad companies. Sraffa's challenge to abandon free competition and turn to monopoly was a potentially revolutionary proposal. On January 25, 1927, Keynes sent Sraffa his congratulations: "Your article in the December *Journal* has been very much liked over here. Everyone I have spoken to agrees that it puts you in the front rank of the younger economists" (quoted in Potier 1987, 30). That same year, Sraffa accepted a lectureship at Cambridge, and between 1928 and 1930 he lectured for five terms on the advanced theory of value (Marcuzzo 2001). Recall Harrod's remarks on Keynes's judgment concerning the state of Cambridge economics in the mid-1920s: members of the guild could be confident of the professional quality of their work if they studied Marshall with care, devoted the same attention to the daily *Times*, and stayed up to date on the work of his disciples. By 1929, when Kahn was writing his fellowship dissertation, this judgment was dead.

As a consequence of Sraffa's apparent demolition of Marshall's theory of value, the critique of Marshall by Cambridge economists was regarded as indispensable to the development of economic theory. This shift in the parameters of acceptable criticism proved to be a crucial factor at the beginning of Robinson's career. By 1930, institutionalization of immanent criticism had intersected with the recognition that a theory of imperfect competition in the long period was an important lacuna in Cambridge economics, an embarrassment that had been acknowledged but not addressed. Several economists at Cambridge were eminently qualified to develop such a theory. For a variety of reasons, none of them did so.

Although Pigou reconsidered his position in two articles (Pigou 1927, 1928), he did not follow the path Sraffa suggested. Instead, he modified the theory of competitive value so that it would no longer be vulnerable to the charge of internal inconsistency. Subsequently, he did not tackle imperfect competition beyond the occasional article. In the reprint of his *Economics of Welfare* (1952), he noted that the first comprehensive investigation of imperfect competition had been undertaken by Robinson and Chamberlin in the early 1930s. He understood that their work called for revisions in his arguments: "But Mrs. Robinson and Professor Chamberlin came on the scene too late to help me and I had not the vision to help myself" (Pigou 1952, 833).

Despite his criticisms of the Marshallian laws of returns in 1924, Robertson had no intention of abandoning Marshall's theory of value. His contribution to the symposium of 1930 on increasing returns in the *Economic Journal* was an unsuccessful attempt to retain some of Marshall's concepts as both "fruitful" and "indispensable" (Robertson 1930, 80). A loyal student of Marshall, he regarded the competitive theory of value as the main weapon in the arsenal of economics (Robertson 1930, 87). In light of his position, it is not surprising that he showed little interest in developing a theory of imperfect competition.[8]

Shove believed that free competition did not exist outside the imagination of Cambridge economists. This made him a good prospect for writing a book on imperfect competition. As he told his readers in 1930, he had been "engaged for some years" in writing an "unpublished study of the relations between cost and output" (Shove 1930, 94). At the time, however, it was not clear to his Cambridge colleagues or to Shove himself whether he would complete this manuscript. He was slow to publish, in some measure because of his reluctance to abstract from the empirical complexity of real economic life.

Although capable, Austin was not a plausible contender to fill the theoretical space created by Sraffa. In the first few years after his return from India, he was occupied with lecturing and supervision, teaching more than a standard lecturer's load. In addition, he had an "immensely industrious devotion to administration" (Cairncross 1993, 166). In 1931, he published *The Structure of Competitive Industry*, which demonstrated his sympathies with Sraffa's conception of competition. Although he announced an intention to publish a "volume dealing with the problem of Monopoly" (Robinson 1931, 6), his book *Monopoly* did not appear until ten years later. Letters from Robinson to Kahn show that theoretical work was not Austin's chief priority.[9]

Kahn had stellar qualifications for writing a book on imperfect competition. He had done a superb fellowship thesis with a solid basis in the subject, and he was well trained in mathematics. He also enjoyed the support of senior members of the guild: Keynes, Sraffa, Pigou, and Shove. And yet, he seems to have taken no interest in pursuing the project. After his election to King's, he began to revise his dissertation for publication, a task on which he worked fitfully for several years before finally abandoning it. When he began to replace Robertson as Keynes's chief theoretical interlocutor, his research time was often at Keynes's disposal. As Keynes began work on the ideas that became *The General Theory*, Kahn became his indispensable assistant.[10] And even if Keynes had not made extravagant demands on his energies, it is clear that Kahn would not have stood in Robinson's way. Once she decided to write her book, he was dedicated to her success.

Sraffa had discovered fatal defects in Marshall's theory of value and sketched an alternative approach. Why did he not exploit his own ideas? The answer lies in the rapid changes in his thinking on imperfect competition. In his Italian article of 1925, he demonstrated that the Marshallian premises of competition and partial equilibrium were compatible only on the assumption of constant returns to scale. By June 1926, he had outlined a theory of imperfect competition, which he preferred to both classical theory and a general-equilibrium framework. By late 1927, however, he had lost interest in imperfect competition (Cavalieri 2001, 102). At a time when neither Kahn's dissertation nor Robinson's book had even been imagined, Sraffa was at work on the outlines of a multisector model of the economy in which relative prices are determined independently of demand or changes in the volume of production. By 1930, when he was firing salvos at Robertson for clinging to the Marshallian representative firm, his rejection of Marshall's framework was complete: "In the circumstances, I think it is Marshall's theory that should be discarded" (Sraffa 1930b, 93).[11]

To establish herself in the Marshallian guild, Robinson had to prove her qualifications to the economic theorists at Cambridge. In view of her record as an undergraduate and the barriers to entry faced by women at Cambridge, at a minimum she needed to publish an ambitious piece of research that would serve in place of a successful fellowship dissertation. *The Economics of Imperfect Competition* was this work.

The chief credential that the guild required of apprentices was a capacity for temperate innovation: originality within the limits of theoretical soundness. Kahn's dissertation is a good example of the kind of performance that was called for. A standard practice for a young economist at Cambridge was to write a fellowship thesis that demonstrated mastery of preferred tools and analyses as well as an appropriate level of originality. Kahn explained what was required in the preface to his dissertation by citing the regulations of King's College: "The Candidate has to provide a general statement of 'the sources from which his information is taken, the extent to which he has availed himself of the work of others, and the portions of the dissertation which he claims to be original'" (Kahn 1989, viii). The expectations that the guild imposed on apprentices were not unreasonably taxing: mastery of the fundamentals of Marshallian economics and evidence of promise in advancing its theoretical program—either by building on its foundations, refining its apparatus, or discovering weaknesses in Marshall's analysis and showing how they could be corrected. Work at this level by younger economists would strengthen Cambridge orthodoxy by demonstrating that it was not a collection of rigid dogmas but a progressive and self-correcting research tradition.

Robinson's initiation into Cambridge economics occurred at a pregnant moment in the development of Marshallian culture. By 1930, the year she began work on the theory of value, Cambridge economists had made various attempts to come to terms with Sraffa's critique. For the reasons sketched above, no one followed Sraffa into the theoretical space he had opened and mapped out. How could a long-period analysis of value be developed along his proposed lines? This question remained largely untouched. It would have been risky for a novice to enter territory that an established member of the guild claimed as his special preserve, as Robinson later discovered when her lectures on applications of monetary theory led to internecine disputes and bitterness. In accepting Sraffa's challenge, she entered an open field with no significant competition. How did she pursue this opportunity?

RESEARCH AS DIALOGUE

By the late 1920s, research in conversation or correspondence with other members of the guild was a standard practice at Cambridge.[12] Suitable occasions for research were decided informally and sometimes serendipitously. There was no clear or hard distinction between the times and sites of academic and personal life. A research opportunity was any place or time at which dialogues on the problems of economics might be held. Participation and status as an interlocutor were independent of academic rank as well as disciplinary power and prestige. Interlocutors included both colleagues and pupils. The result was a pronounced, spirited sociability of research that moved easily from lecture halls, the Marshall Society, and Keynes's Monday Night Club to college high tables and common rooms, the rooms of fellows, walks in Cambridge, and correspondence.

Dialogue was a research tool, a way to achieve work of high quality, a convention of academic interaction, and a collegial ritual that had its own intrinsic value. For all these reasons, it was a mode of the conduct of life in Cambridge economics and a distinctive practice of the Marshallian guild.[13] Research as dialogue was grounded in the Cambridge pedagogy of tutorial supervisions and a common body of disciplinary skills and assumptions. Cambridge economists had been trained in the conversational pedagogy of the supervision, both as pupils and as supervisors. They also shared a broad theoretical and methodological background. As a result, guild members could generally exchange views on complex research problems without confusion or the risk of creating deeper, more intractable disagreements over fundamentals. Colleagues shared their ideas and drafts with interlocutors, who might enter a conversation in various ways: suggesting minor revisions, proposing alternative ideas or methods, developing counterarguments, or even drafting full-scale analyses and in effect becoming joint authors. Roles as commentators and authors were freely exchanged. In the 1920s, Robertson assisted Keynes with his work in progress, and Keynes returned the favor. In 1935, Robinson gave Keynes her comments on the proofs of *The General Theory*. The following year they switched roles as Keynes worked on the proofs of her *Essays in the Theory of Employment*. For various reasons, the Cambridge dialogue was not essentially Socratic. It was not typically agonistic, a contest in which the objective of one participant was to defeat the other by refuting his positions and analyses. The Marshallian heritage of the guild limited conflicts on theoretical grounds and its craft etiquette of intraguild civility sublimated them on cultural grounds. More often than not, dialogues were cooperative or collaborative ventures. Interlocutors worked together, even as they might disagree, with the joint aim of solving a problem or securing a draft from damaging objections. Participants did not invariably change their positions in view of what they learned from one another. Dialogues might harden all positions by achieving higher levels of clarity, precision, and technical refinement. In debates, interlocutors might discover new and more powerful arguments that had previously eluded them, strengthening their own positions or revealing weaknesses in counterpositions.

Perhaps the significance of dialogues in the production of Cambridge economics can best be appreciated by examining the experience of Kahn, who in early 1933 visited academic sites where he did not enjoy the sociality of the Marshallian guild. At that point, he was in the United States, chiefly at Chicago and Harvard. In struggling to enter the life of the economics departments at both universities, he was disillusioned—or was he delighted?—to discover that the intellectual life he knew at Cambridge did not exist there.

Kahn found academic life at Chicago hectic. Relations among colleagues seemed to reproduce the commercialism of American culture. He saw no informal exchanges of work in progress or a sense of their importance. The organizational basis of intellectual exchange was also primitive. He attended no departmental seminars comparable to the Marshall Society or the Keynes Club, only tea parties and informal meetings on monetary questions for graduate students and junior lecturers.[14] Instead of the easy informality between senior and junior colleagues that made Kahn so comfortable at Cambridge, he found a repressive academic regime imposed by two senior professors: Henry Schultz and Jacob Viner. The basis of their power was control over the stipends of graduate students, who worked as their menials—performing staff work, drawing charts, and doing calculations. Advanced students who demonstrated evidence of independent thought placed themselves in jeopardy. Undergraduates were regarded with contempt, and there were no close relations between faculty and undergraduates, a tradition at Cambridge. Kahn found virtually no one who could explain to him how undergraduates at Chicago were educated. "The pundits" taught only graduate students, and "the idea of explaining what marginal cost means to an undergraduate is regarded with scorn."[15]

Kahn found conditions only marginally better at Harvard, where he attended Schumpeter's seminar and lunched with colleagues at the faculty club. Chamberlin was a young member of the faculty about to publish a substantial revision of his doctoral dissertation. This was *The Theory of Monopolistic Competition*, which appeared some three months before Robinson's book. Although Chamberlin had been at work on this project for years, neither his colleagues nor his research assistants had any idea of what it might contain. Kahn saw this indifference as evidence of an abysmal scientific culture. "The pursuit of learning," he wrote, "is regarded as a business, to be discussed with underlings at 'conferences,' rather than a social act which pervades one's whole life."[16] As a result, he found it difficult to take Schumpeter seriously. He was "the main character in a musical comedy," a clown or a con man "sitting at his desk, with his legs up just like a big business man, having a 'conference' with his two research assistants."[17] If science was conducted as a business, it is understandable that Kahn did not have the relaxed, extended conversations with Schultz, Viner, or Schumpeter that he enjoyed with senior fellows at King's. At Cambridge, senior economists followed his work with paternal care and enthusiasm, offering suggestions and encouragement. At Chicago and Harvard, the economics establishment seemed to show little interest in what he was doing.

Kahn believed that three factors were paramount in discouraging a spontaneous exchange of ideas. The "grubbiness" of academic existence was pervasive. The pace was furious and inhospitable. Common meals, the place of so many Cambridge dialogues, were revolting. Reporting on a weekly dinner party at a Harvard dining hall, he found the meal "foul and hurried." His companions had the appearance of "shop assistants." The speaker for the evening "looked like a pork butcher." "As I swallow the revolting food that is served up in their halls and clubs," Kahn mused, "my mind turns insistently to the theme of *A Room of One's Own*. Even

Schumpeter's light is very definitely dimmed by the conditions in which he has to live." Schumpeter's Viennese sophistication could not overcome the social banality and gastronomic poverty of lunch at the Harvard faculty club: "The squalid conditions are too much for him."[18] The theme of *A Room of One's Own* to which Kahn alluded is Woolf's idea that the "rich yellow flame of rational intercourse" rests on gastronomic presuppositions. The quality of food, talk, and thought are integrated. Because "a good dinner is of great importance to good talk," one cannot think well unless one has dined well. Nor can one love or sleep well. The quality of dinner, it seems, is a measure of the value of all things.[19] Dinners at Harvard were "foul" and "revolting." Therefore the quality of intellectual exchange could be no better.

American competitiveness, the necessity of making a career by honing skills of self-presentation and impression management, was also an obstacle to dialogue. The imperatives of producing oneself as a commodity for sale on the academic market—"the terrible business of career hunting"—encouraged not only professional jealousy but also "the fear of saying the wrong thing (even though genuinely believed)."[20]

Finally, any intellectual culture produces a type of humanity: a specific sensibility characterized by a receptivity to its values. For Kahn, this was the fundamental consideration. The species of *Homo academicus* he found at Chicago and Harvard did not measure up to the moral, aesthetic, and intellectual expectations of Cantabrigian discursive culture. "These people," Kahn pronounced, "are incapable of the kind of social life we value."[21] At Harvard there was "an almost complete absence of talent." The undergraduates were "poor, mealy-mouthed, pimply (yeast tablets appear regularly on the menu), scraggy, hobbledehoys, extremely uncouth and uncertain of themselves." As for the faculty: "The senior people are not much better. (You ought to see their taste in ties.)"[22]

Kahn, miserable at Chicago, languishing at Harvard, and contemptuous of the United States and its denizens—"If I stayed here very much longer I should completely lose faith in myself"—longed to return to his rooms at King's. The easy civility among colleagues, the cuisine and wines of the King's high table, the pleasures of informal *conversazione*—all this, it seems, was best appreciated at a great distance, in the Cambridge of the west: "After watching the struggles of these wretched people I shall for the first time realize my good fortune in being a member of the King's High Table, and take more pleasure in its society than I have in the past."[23]

Research as dialogue was a practice of Cambridge economics that Robinson embraced with considerable enthusiasm and mastered quickly. It was critical to the development of her first research program and a resource without which she could not have written *The Economics of Imperfect Competition*. In the end, Robinson's book was a product of several intersecting dialogues. We turn to some of their key episodes.

Dialogues with Kahn

THE ARDENT TUTOR In Austin's recollections of the origins of *The Economics of Imperfect Competition*, Kahn's role was modest, limited to examining and correcting Robinson's "bright ideas." She framed the questions and took the initiatives in answering them (Robinson 1994, 8). In Robinson's assessment, Kahn had a more substantial role. The foreword to *The Economics of Imperfect Competition* begins and ends with "Mr R. F. Kahn," on whom the author relied for "constant assistance" and whose criticism entered "at every stage of the work from its inception," saving her from "innumerable errors" (1933d, v, viii). Kahn thought this appreciation excessive. On finishing the first complete set of proofs of the book in February 1933, he summed up his sense of Robinson's achievement as follows: "I have finished your book, and feel that I might be allowed to write to you. . . . It is an engaging piece of work. I find that I usually take it for granted, but whenever I stop to think about it I just can't believe it's true. Do you by any chance realise what you have done? in the course of two years of your long life?"[24] On March 30, he scolded Robinson for including in the foreword an appreciation of his contributions that he regarded as unreasonable and embarrassing. In his view, he had done little more than read her drafts. In addition, most of his ideas on theoretical problems had led to dead ends, which left Robinson to work out her own solutions. He pressed her to reconsider: "I suppose I ought to feel touched—and it *is* very sweet of you—but I only feel angry. Why must you take advantage of my absence to go on in this kind of way? You are saying very much more than would be justifiable on any kind of basis, and it just looks foolish. Please be reasonable and tone it down."[25]

Modesty, friendship, or affection may explain Kahn's self-deprecatory assessment of his role in *The Economics of Imperfect Competition*. However, both archival and published sources demonstrate that his contributions were more significant than Austin, Robinson, or Kahn acknowledged.

From late July 1930, months before Robinson considered writing a book, until April 1933, a few weeks before it was published, Kahn advised Robinson on what to read and how to understand it. He constructed paradoxes that he often solved himself or worked out with the help of other Cambridge economists.[26] He developed critical mathematical analyses and proofs that she employed. And he provided data from his own unpublished work for a book that, by Cambridge standards, was written on an uncommonly high level of abstraction: "I should rather like to suggest that you put in a spot of realism—just to show that it is not all a parlour game and nothing more."[27]

For Robinson, the months between autumn 1930 and spring 1931 were a period of intensive postgraduate education in theory and technique. Kahn was her tutor and set the agenda for their work: how does monopoly output compare to output produced in competitive markets? She was able to arrive at a diagrammatic answer to this question under a highly restrictive set of conditions that assumed linear demand curves and constant costs. Additional complexity exceeded her competence. Consider Kahn's long, two-part mathematical appendix of March 1931, in which he used elementary trigonometry to show that in more complex cases the answer to this question depends on a ratio—he called it "adjusted concavity"—that measures the curvature of demand and cost functions.[28] His reasoning was clear and methodical—moving from the general to the particular, breaking down the longer problem into several simpler parts, and explaining every step of his analysis. Yet Robinson found the appendix daunting: "I don't understand a good deal of it, but I will try to learn some trigonometry so as to master it."[29] As late as April, she was still trying to make sense of the appendix and sent him "a number of questions which I am too stupid to answer for myself." These questions had a common thread. Mathematically, she could grasp linear functions and graphs but not much else. "If you know a marginal curve," she wrote, "is there anything you can say about the average curve? If it is a straight line you can draw it at once. Is there any law connecting the concavity of the marginal curve with the average curve?" And what did "the marginal curve to a constant elasticity curve look like?" Robinson suspected that the answer to this question would enable her to derive average utility from the demand curve, which could have important applications in welfare economics.[30] Kahn was patient in educating Robinson on these matters and much more: "To know the height of the average curve at any point it is, as we know, necessary to know the *whole* of the marginal curve up to that point." However, he was doubtful about the theoretical payoff of establishing a relationship between the concavities of average and marginal curves. Instead of worrying over average and marginal utilities, Robinson would be better advised to consider Pigou's concept of average productivity. The relationship between a marginal curve and a constant elasticity curve was "another constant elasticity curve of the same elasticity." The relationship of average value, marginal value, and elasticity (E) could be stated in the following formula:

$$\text{Average value} / \text{Marginal value} = \text{E}/(\text{E}-1).$$

Given any two variables, the third could easily be calculated.[31] Kahn was not always ready with answers to her questions. In their discussions of 1930–31, however, it was generally Kahn who detected errors and refined concepts.[32]

The correspondence between Robinson and Kahn documents the time, effort, and theoretical powers he devoted to her work. The letter from Keynes to Lydia on February 1, 1932, quoted above shows that even before Austin left for Africa, the two were meeting in Kahn's rooms at King's (JMK/PP/45/190/5). There were long sessions at the Robinsons' flat as well: "Can you spare me the whole of Tuesday? Come here in the morning and have lunch here anyway."[33] Problems raised by marginal cost curves under monopsony were worked out in part on a long rainy day. Kahn to Robinson: "You will remember that we read through [Erich] Schneider's solution while it was raining all day and decided that though he had done it all wrong, it was an important problem to be attacked."[34]

The correspondence also documents Robinson's increasing proficiency in economic theory. By September 1931, Kahn was no longer devising problems for her to solve. Although he remained her indispensable helpmate, their paths had diverged. Robinson was developing analyses for her book and had definite ideas concerning its structure and substance. Kahn was reworking his thesis. He became less certain about his grasp of their joint problems at the same time that she became a much more confident interlocutor. Because she refused to learn more mathematics, he continued to derive mathematical relations on which her analyses depended. By this point, however, she was requesting solutions to specific problems entailed by her work on the book.[35] Robinson's progressive facility in solving economic problems independently can be credited in part to Kahn, who devised technical exercises for her instruction, requiring her to disentangle kinks in arguments he had generally unraveled himself. His letter to her circa September 17 is quite telling in this regard. "I think now I can see my way through this tangle, but I leave what I have written as I think it is an instructive muddle to have been in" (RFK/16/1/116–20).

By the end of March 1932, Robinson had substantially drafted the book. In rewriting her chapters on the demand and physical productivity of labor, the comparative analysis of demand for labor under monopolistic and competitive conditions, and the relationship between monopoly and the exploitation of labor, she reported her progress to Kahn, thanking him on March 31 for his help with the analysis of physical productivity (RFK/13/90/1/7–8). Writing again the same day, she claimed that she now understood the functional relationship between imperfect markets and exploitation (RFK/13/90/1/9–10). There is a break in the correspondence—the period of Austin's work in Africa—that includes only one letter. With Austin out of residence, it is reasonable to suppose that face-to-face conversation replaced correspondence. However, there is some evidence on the collaboration between the two in Robinson's letters to her husband. In August 1932, she was working with Kahn on price discrimination.[36] The manuscript accompanied Robinson to Austria, where she enjoyed a mountaineering vacation with Kahn and Guillebaud. Max Newman was also mountaineering in Austria and was drafted to help with the mathematics of price discrimination. As a result, "I have at last got that awful chapter done," she wrote on August 25. "It is full of very high class results, that no one will be able to understand" (EAGR/Box 9/2/1/17/276–77). Robinson persevered with revisions until the end of October. On November 7, she wrote her husband that she had "dumped the MSS on Macmillans after ten days of working like an ox to get it revised" (EAGR/Box 9/2/1/17/289–92).

By late December, Robinson was at work on galleys, and Kahn had sailed for the United States, and their dialogue continued in correspondence. On Christmas Day, she sent him the first batch of corrected galleys, comprising chapters 1 and 2, for his suggestions (RFK/13/90/1/22–23). Five days later, she sent more proofs, noting that she was especially interested in his views on the organization of Book III on competitive equilibrium.[37] Kahn had set an ambitious schedule for his American visit:

meetings with leading figures in the business and financial establishment in New York, Chicago, and Washington for which Keynes had liberally supplied him with letters of introduction, discussions with academic economists at several universities, lectures, and revision of his fellowship dissertation. In spite of this demanding agenda, he spent considerable time on Robinson's proofs and was delighted to do so. He seems to have worked on her material whenever the opportunity arose, using his free hours or occasional days without appointments. After receiving two packages of proofs, he wrote on January 24, 1933, "I will get onto Books IV, V, VI (the rest of the earlier books go off with this letter) but I can't quite say when they will be done. . . . I was fortunately able to make most of the day free and had a perfectly lovely time. I hope I got enough diagrams done to give you something to go on and that the cable was intelligible. I feel so much better after then. I think the pictures [diagrams] look splendid. They seem beautifully clear."[38]

On February 18, Robinson wrote that she was sending the last batch of her first set of corrected proofs to Macmillan and put Kahn on notice that he could expect the second set soon. The urgency of her note is evidence of the importance she ascribed to his work on the book. Could he send his corrections to the second set in time to meet Macmillan's production schedule? If not, she would insert his revisions directly into the page proofs. In addition, she wanted him to review the changes she had made in Book III (RFK/13/90/1/123–26). Kahn was apparently able to correct the second set in spite of the constraints of his schedule. On February 23, she thanked him for changes he had suggested to her footnote on the falling supply curve of labor, which she inserted in place of her own remarks. Although she now saw her error in analyzing a reduction in average productivity—she had confused daily wages with piece rates—she was convinced this matter called for further investigation and encouraged Kahn to clear up the chief issues in his own book (RFK/13/90/1/139–46). Robinson, therefore, saw her book and his as-yet-unwritten manuscript as companion volumes, contributions to the same research program and analyses based on the same ideas and methods.

In her foreword, Robinson made note of her debt to Marshall and Pigou; they had laid the foundations for her arguments (1933d, v.). Austin's work on the optimum firm was acknowledged as the basis of her account of competitive equilibrium and an influence on the discussion of increasing and diminishing returns in the appendix. Shove received a generous appreciation, and Sraffa was named as the intellectual godfather of the book (Robinson 1933d, v). However, she did not mention Kahn's dissertation. This seems anomalous. In order to execute the conceptual transition from competitive to imperfect markets, she required a manual to translate the Marshallian language of free competition into the new theoretical language that would be indispensable to her book. Kahn's thesis was her translation manual, the map that led her from Marshall and Pigou to *The Economics of Imperfect Competition*. Several explanations for her failure to mention his work come to mind. Most obviously, she may not have read it by that point. This is immaterial. There is more than one way to learn a text, one of which is to converse with its author. Robinson's dialogues with Kahn in correspondence as well as much of her book presuppose her knowledge of his dissertation. Perhaps she believed that his thesis was largely irrelevant to her work. If so, she was mistaken. At this point, it will be useful to survey several of Kahn's contributions that are not acknowledged by either Robinson or the secondary literature on *The Economics of Imperfect Competition*. This discussion also offers evidence that Robinson was engaged in an unacknowledged dialogue with Kahn's dissertation.

SCHOLARSHIP In order to pass muster as a serious piece of scholarship, a book is generally expected to exhibit certain features that professionals in the field will recognize as marks of expertise. One such feature is documentation that the author has covered the pertinent literature in the area of her work. In 1930–32, Robinson was not a professional scholar. Her knowledge of academic literature in economics was cursory at best and often superficial. It was also limited to sources then under discussion at Cambridge, where a myopic view of the scope of the discipline prevailed: economics was what Cambridge economists did. Her understanding of the theory of value was based on a quite narrow collection of sources—chiefly Marshall's *Principles*, Pigou's *The Economics of Welfare*, Sraffa's article of 1926, the symposium in 1930, and Austin's book, *The Structure of Competitive Industry* (1931). The references in *The Economics of Imperfect Competition*, however, extend beyond the confines of Cambridge or even Oxford and London, lending it a patina of scholarly sophistication. Consider her references to various independent discoverers of the marginal revenue curve. She owed many of these references to Kahn, whose scholarly skills and knowledge of the literature in the area of her research far exceeded her own. Writing on January 15, 1933, he noted that the curve had been introduced into Chicago economics some years earlier by "a young man called Yntema (see Journal of Pol. Econ., Dec. 1928) in a paper on dumping."[39] Viner was also acquainted with both the geometric and analytical relations between average and marginal curves: "He made out that he had discovered it [the marginal revenue curve] but I have since had reason to suspect that he got it from a young research student called Coe."[40] On reading Yntema's paper, Robinson concluded that footnotes to his work were called for as was an explanation of why his essay had been neglected in the recent literature. She also introduced a question on the ethics of footnoting, asking Kahn whether Yntema was "a nice man who ought to be flattered or the reverse." Based on his account of Yntema, she concluded that he was not "a nice man" and decided to be "a bit spiteful."[41] On February 17, Kahn wrote that he identified two additional discoverers of the curve: "Chamberlin I have already mentioned; and now I find that your Oxford man, [Arthur] Smithies, must be added to the list (unpublished, like Gifford and [P. A.] Sloan). I am including both these in the complete list I shall give in my article."[42] Robinson used Kahn's sources in her book (1933d, vi–vii).[43]

MARKET STRUCTURE AND LONG-PERIOD EQUILIBRIUM Kahn was the first economist at Cambridge to spell out the definitive conditions of perfect competition.[44] He argued that simple or perfect competition required the satisfaction of three independent conditions (it is not clear whether he regarded these conditions as necessary, sufficient, or both): (1) The number of firms in an industry is large enough to render each firm's output small compared to the total output of the industry. (2) Firms do not act collusively to control the size of aggregate output. (3) The market in which industry output is sold is perfect in the sense that differences in prices for the same product are ephemeral; if one firm increases the price of a good, either its sales drop to zero or other firms increase their prices for this good to the same level (Kahn 1989, 12–13). Robinson appropriated Kahn's analysis without revision (1933d 18, 89).

Kahn also classified market imperfections under the headings of preference and transport imperfections (Kahn 1989, 90), anticipating Shove (1930) by a few months. In deleting marketing costs from his analysis, he finessed Sraffa's argument that these costs make supply and demand interdependent (see Marcuzzo 2001, 91). Robinson followed him on this point as well, adding the stipulation that marketing costs incurred to increase sales are analytically equivalent to a price reduction that has the same effect (Robinson 1933d, 21, 89–90).

Kahn's dissertation did not address the conditions for long-period equilibrium in imperfectly competitive industries. In her article of December 1932, a response to the symposium, Robinson published the first Cambridge analysis of long-period equilibrium in such industries. She argued that equilibrium requires satisfaction of a "double condition": "Marginal revenue must be equal to marginal cost, and price must be equal to average cost" (Robinson 1932b, 547). As she informed the reader in a footnote, she owed this analysis to Kahn, "who, in turn, derived it by pursuing Mr. Sraffa's argument to its necessary conclusion" (Robinson 1932b, 547, n. 2). The double condition argument reappears in her book without attribution (1933d, 94).

THE IRRELEVANCE OF FIXED COSTS In his dissertation, Kahn repeatedly stressed that fixed costs were irrelevant to short-period equilibrium, and he occasionally chastised businessmen who failed to grasp this point.[45] *The Economics of Imperfect Competition* treats the irrelevance of fixed or overhead costs as a general rule, a point Robinson made in discussing monopoly equilibrium and the shape of the marginal cost curve. She rejected as a "false deduction" the position that a fall in average cost necessarily reduces prices: If average cost falls, it does not follow that marginal cost also falls. In any economic exchange, it is marginal cost that determines output and price (1933d, 49). Her evidence for the empirical validity of a constant marginal cost was also drawn from Kahn's work, again without attribution. His dissertation was based on an empirical investigation of the British cotton industry and included a detailed account of various ways of accommodating a decline in demand. For example, all machinery can be operated for fewer hours throughout the entire workweek, or some machinery can be operated full time but only on a few days of the workweek (Kahn 1989, 46). In her book, Robinson used Kahn's ideas and empirical work to argue that in the short period the marginal cost of plant operation at less than full capacity is often constant. Although she had done no research on the British cotton industry, she considered a cotton mill working with idle capacity because of a decline in demand, repeating the main lines of Kahn's analysis. Either all machinery in a mill may be operated for part of the workweek, in which case an increase in output is not followed by an increase in marginal cost; or some machines may be employed full time while others are left idle. Assuming uniform quality of machinery, an increase in output produces no increase in marginal cost (Robinson 1933d, 49).

THE KINKED DEMAND CURVE The discovery of the kinked demand curve is generally attributed to Robert Hall and C. J. Hitch (1939) and Paul M. Sweezy (1939). Kahn anticipated their work by ten years. His dissertation describes a possible market composed of more than two firms producing the same item at the same price, which is higher than each firm's cost of production. Under what conditions could the price of the item rise or fall? If a firm cuts its price, its competitors will respond by taking the same measure, thereby reducing the firm's revenue. And if the firm increases its price, its output will fall to zero. Because the firm knows what its marketing practices are, both an increase and a decrease in price seem to be out of the question: "But if the price can move neither downwards nor upwards, it must remain where it is. The equilibrium price is any and every price; and the price is where it is for no other reason than it happens to be so" (Kahn 1989, 103). This is the kinked demand curve, which he later characterized as a "quandary" and a "terrible tangle." Although he could see that it would not pay either to raise or lower prices, he had no idea how the position of the kink on the curve was determined. Could Robinson devote some thought to these difficulties?[46] Although she did not answer Kahn's question, Robinson introduced his idea of the kinked demand curve in considering whether a tax will increase a firm's prices. In what she called the extreme case—a firm with a kinked demand curve—she claimed that a tax might leave prices unchanged: "If the change in slope of the demand curve is so rapid that it contains a kink, there will be a discontinuity in the marginal revenue curve; and if the old and new marginal cost curves both cut the marginal revenue curve vertically below the kink in the demand curve, there will be no change in price" (Robinson 1933d, 81). As an example of such a demand curve, she considered the relationship between a monopolistic firm and its potential competitors. Although rivals operate with higher costs, this disadvantage might vanish if the monopoly increases its price above a certain level. Once the monopolist exceeds this critical price level, above which other firms can compete at a profit, potential rivals will enter the market as real competitors. It follows that the demand curve of the monopolist becomes quite elastic once the critical price is exceeded; and "even when his costs are augmented by the tax he will not find it worth while to raise his price above this critical level, provided that his rivals are not also subject to the tax" (Robinson 1933d, 81).

Although Kahn persevered for several years in preparing his dissertation for publication, he eventually abandoned the effort. It was finally published as a historical artifact more than fifty years after he submitted it to King's.[47] Within three years of Kahn's appointment to his fellowship, Robinson had produced a book based in large measure on his unpublished work. Thus she received credit for some of his original research.

Dialogues with Pigou

In her article of December 1932, Robinson took an important step in validating her credentials at Cambridge. Imperfect competition was regarded as an exciting new field and appeared to hold the promise of a significant research program. Equally important, it had stimulated path-breaking work by three members of the guild: Sraffa, Shove, and Kahn. In refining some of the arguments presented in the symposium, she demonstrated her sophistication in teasing out nuances of Marshallian value theory. She also called into question received wisdom of the guild on a significant theoretical issue. Finally, she offered a preview of the analyses that would shortly appear in *The Economics of Imperfect Competition*.

After explaining how market imperfections are created, Robinson considered the circumstances under which a firm could arrive at profit-maximizing levels of output and price in the long period. Firms could achieve this maximum if marginal revenue would equal marginal cost, and the price would just cover the cost of producing the average unit. The latter requirement is called the "tangency condition." The equality of price and average cost ensures that existing firms make normal profits, eliminating incentives for other firms to enter their market.

An increase in demand for a product enables existing firms to charge higher prices and reap above-normal profits. But abnormal profits are ephemeral; finding this market attractive, other firms enter, thereby reducing an individual firm's demand and profits. Entry ceases at a new equilibrium, where demand and cost curves are tangent once again. At the new equilibrium, costs lie below their old equilibrium levels. According to Robinson, the symposiasts assumed that the cost savings would be passed on to consumers as lower prices. She argued otherwise: in imperfect markets, there is no theoretically determinate connection between an increase in demand for a product and its price. Depending on how demand curves change, the new equilibrium price might exceed the old price, fall below it, or remain unchanged: "Some kinds of increase in demand will lower price, and some will not" (Robinson 1932b, 552).

Pigou was quite impressed by Robinson's article, judging it "extremely good and ingenious." In an undated letter written in early December 1932, he told her, "Besides having got some very good stuff, you've made it most uncommonly lucid and readable" (JVR/vii/347/16). However, he believed that revisions were needed if she intended to incorporate the paper into her book. Why, for example, did she assume that an increase in demand for a product would be followed by entry of new firms into the market? He asked her to consider a single grain monopoly that experiences increased demand. If the monopolist can meet the new demand, there is no basis for the entry of new firms. Why should the same conditions not hold in imperfectly competitive markets? Like the single monopolist, each producer—a local monopoly—would satisfy the new demand in its own market. Increased demand was more likely to stimulate entry in areas remote from local monopolies. Robinson's paper included no discussion of the conditions under which entry of new firms takes place. In Pigou's view, the mere fact that an industry is controlled by a plurality of monopolies and not one was not a satisfactory basis for her position. Robinson seems to have acted on Pigou's criticism. *The Economics of Imperfect Competition* identifies circumstances under which his supposition holds. Increased demand is not followed by entry of new firms. Existing firms enjoy abnormal profits because they sell patented products or hold a restricted number of licenses granted by a public agency (Robinson 1933d, 93).

On the same day, Pigou raised a more serious objection.[48] Suppose that the demand for a product increases. Firms begin to charge higher prices and make above-normal profits. According to Robinson, higher profits enjoyed by existing firms should lure other firms to the market. Entry continues until a new equilibrium is reached—the point of tangency between demand and average cost curves. Pigou maintained that the new Robinsonian equilibrium might be nothing more than a random and theoretically meaningless event. Suppose that the number of new firms necessary for equilibrium is N. Pigou held that Robinson's argument lacked a mathematical proof that tangency of the two curves would invariably be established by N, and only N, number of firms.

The dialogue on this issue began in a telephone call from Pigou to Robinson on January 13. He had discovered a fundamental weakness in her article. Would she like to hear it without delay so that she could make the appropriate revisions in her book? When she and Austin met him for tea the same day, he raised his objection by posing the following question: How could she demonstrate tangency in view of the fact that her analysis was based on two independent equations and only one unknown? Since her argument was mathematically overdetermined, a proof of her position was impossible on purely formal grounds. Robinson, who had only an elementary understanding of mathematics, was initially upset by this conversation and bewildered by the formal simplicity with which Pigou framed his objection. As she complained in a letter to Kahn—who was in Chicago and unavailable for tutorials on the problems her article had created—Pigou had a very "stilted" way of making his point. However, she quickly convinced herself that she grasped his objection and its source. On her interpretation, his criticism conveniently entailed no damaging consequences for her analysis. Although her response to Pigou does not seem to be extant, she gave Kahn an account. Pigou, she supposed, imagined a market with a small number of firms. Entry of one new firm would significantly reduce demand for existing ones. As she put it, demand would "jump down." If the entry or exit of a single firm substantially affected demand, equilibrium would become an incalculable and theoretically indeterminate event, a "fluke." She acknowledged that this was "a curious + interesting point" but believed it was irrelevant to her article, presumably because she assumed a market with a large number of firms.[49]

Pigou's reply convinced Robinson that her benign interpretation of his objection was erroneous. She assumed that the demand curve would shift continuously as the cost curve remained stable. Eventually the two curves would have to become tangent, establishing a new equilibrium. Pigou noted that on her assumption, the demand curve was free to move in all possible positions: "Because the curve moves about by continuous motion, it *must*, in one of its positions, become tangential." She was mistaken. "My point," Pigou stressed, "is that, since each of its possible positions is determined by the number of firms, it is *not* free to move about like that." In which case, how could the demand curve ever become tangent to the cost curve? On the assumptions of Robinson's analysis, this possibility seemed to be a theoretically insignificant and contingent event. Firms entering the market shift individual demand curves downward, making their slopes flatter. Robinson had no proof that there is some number of entrée firms—N—that produces tangency. A proof was necessary, he argued, in order to defeat the "adverse presumption" against tangency. Without it, her analysis was not merely incomplete but intuitively implausible and formally invalid.[50]

Robinson's report to Kahn on the above exchange, written on January 16, shows that she still did not see the point of Pigou's objection. "I think," she wrote, "it is all a fuss about nothing." Instead of coming to terms with Pigou's argument, she introduced the surprising speculation that his real worry was the "ragged-edge" problem. Entry of each additional firm into an imperfect market depresses individual demand curves by a discrete amount: "Therefore if you have one firm too few the demand curve may be a bit above the cost curve,—if one too many it may be a bit below, + never exactly tangential." Although price may be incrementally higher or lower than average cost, the two values would be equal only by chance. This was Pigou's fluke, a theoretically inexplicable event. Robinson told Kahn she had sent Pigou the following solution: add to the normal profit the above-normal profit that results when there is one firm too few. Then the two curves will be tangent.[51]

Although Robinson found her exchanges with Pigou stimulating, they were an occasion for some anxiety on her part. She hoped he would be convinced by her solution, not least because he had begun to use the mathematics employed in her article in his own work. As she wrote Kahn, "I want to restore his confidence."[52] Since Pigou's intervention held the promise of both risks and rewards, her anxiety was not misplaced. Endorsement of her work by the Professor would qualify her as a bona fide member of the guild by its most senior gatekeeper, arguably one of two Cambridge economists whose judgment carried substantial weight with all other members of the guild. He was charmed by her article. If his enthusiasm could be sustained, she would enjoy an advantage in competing for the next lectureship.

But what could Robinson expect if she failed to persuade Pigou? He now had insight into the quality of her thinking that he could not easily achieve independent of their dialogue. If his understanding of the logic underpinning her article persuaded him of fundamental weaknesses that otherwise would have escaped him, this deeper knowledge of her research would work to her disadvantage, perhaps convincing him that it did not, after all, measure up to Cambridge standards. Dialogue gave senior

Cambridge economists a means of tracking the work and assessing the merit of their apprentices. Thus it had an institutional function in the Marshallian guild that was independent of its uses as a tool for research. In January 1933, it was not clear what results her dialogue with Pigou would achieve for Robinson's career chances. She knew she was on dangerous ground. In prodding her to develop a mathematical proof of the conditions under which the tangency requirement could be satisfied, he had unwittingly posed precisely the sort of challenge she was least able to meet. In view of her deficiencies in mathematics, her complaint to Kahn is not surprising: Pigou was "nice to argue with," but he had "such a peculiar formal way of looking at things" that it was difficult "to meet him on his own ground."[53]

Pigou was not satisfied with Robinson's ad hoc solution to his problem. After making the obvious mathematical point that the ragged-edge problem was not peculiar to imperfectly competitive markets but arose whenever calculus was used to analyze finite changes, he repeated that the issue at stake concerned a formal flaw in her argument. What he wanted was a "*proof* that the number of equations in the problem was equal to the number of unknowns. Unless this can be proved the thing's not mathematically watertight."[54]

Robinson was in luck. Musing over the problem in bed one night, Pigou himself discovered a method for producing a proof. Moreover his formal solution was perfectly general, valid not only for the special case she had considered in her article—entry into markets of equal-size firms—but for all possible cases. He promised to send her his solution, which he claimed would include many equations, when he had written it out. The position she had taken on the tangency condition, he found, was correct. But it was far from obvious, and she had not proven it. In view of his bedtime discovery, he urged her to formalize her argument in a mathematically acceptable fashion by including a proof—he did not insist on his own announced but thus far unwritten demonstration—of how tangency could be met.[55]

Pigou's news left Robinson confused but also relieved and ultimately triumphant. She finally grasped what Pigou found objectionable in her article, although she still did not understand the objection itself or its importance. "It was," she wrote Kahn, "just the formal difficulty" of two equations and one unknown. She found this circumstance "quite fantastic" and proposed to consult Newman, the mathematician at St. John's

College who was her other tutor on mathematical problems. Although the discovery that her position was sound was due to Pigou, she celebrated the result somewhat surprisingly as her own victory. Claiming that "the day is won" in her exchange with Pigou over the ragged-edge problem, she paradoxically congratulated herself on the fact that she had "driven him to admit that there is no difference in this respect between perfect + imperfect competition, which is a great advance."[56] But it was Pigou who had pointed out to her that the ragged-edge problem was irrelevant to degrees of competition. Therefore her indulgence in one-upmanship seems peculiar.

Robinson consulted Newman, and his advice was blunt and unsparing:

> I must confess I don't blame the professor for not following. Why don't you learn some mathematics? The professor + I + everyone who will read your book will have to spend a lot of time disentangling what you really mean because you won't learn the language, on which a lot of thought has been spent, if you place it end to end, + which really contains fewer unnecessary frills than you think. You could learn all you want in two months (now your book is finished). I can't understand how you like to remain in a state where [a] 2nd year math[ematica]l. undergraduate can say in a superior tone that your analysis is rather shaky, + you will have to take it sitting, knowing that he knows nothing about it.[57]

Newman's vision of a Robinson minimally competent in the mathematics employed in the economics curricula of the time was not to be. She persisted in writing unregenerate nonmathematical economics, turning to others for help when she could not escape problems of formal analysis.

After two days elapsed without news from Pigou, Robinson concluded that no proof would be forthcoming. The Professor, she wrote Kahn, "was just being incredibly silly."[58] When his mathematical analysis arrived on January 23, 1933, however, she was singing a new song: "I take it all back about the Professor. After going thro' all these contortions he has ended by producing a very elegant algebraical version of my article, which is to appear as a note in the E[conomic] J[ournal] of March. It doesn't add anything, but it is very beautiful. I can put a footnote referring to it + that's that."[59] Kahn was pleased to learn that Pigou had placed himself at Robinson's disposal: "It is very good to hear the Professor acting as your mathematical handyman. It is magnificent how he has taken to you."[60] By February 20, Robinson had a copy of Pigou's note, which would appear in the *Economic Journal* for March. As she wrote Kahn, "The Prof's algebra is introduced by a most touching tribute ending 'This note attempts only the subordinate task of imposing, on a rather bleak ice-wall, a staircase which has already been made + ascended.' So that I don't do so badly on the whole."[61]

Pigou's characteristically self-effacing style and his understatement of the significance of his contribution to Robinson's analysis were marks of an older mode of intellectual self-presentation at Cambridge that had perhaps become archaic. In the Edwardian intellectual culture that prevailed before the First World War, academic rhetoric of self-promotion was bad form. On one important point his mountaineering metaphor was quite misleading, suggesting that in her article Robinson had achieved more than she had in fact done. The bleak ice wall was her account of imperfect competition, demand, average cost, and price. The staircase was his algebraic formalization of this account. The claim that she had already built and ascended the staircase, leaving Pigou with the purely menial function of placing it against the bleak ice wall, implied that Robinson herself had produced his proof and used it in order to arrive at her conclusions. He had merely clarified the mathematical analysis of the tangency problem that she had developed and used in her article. But of course Robinson had not performed Pigou's mathematical analysis, a task that exceeded her competence. In fact she seemed unable to understand the importance of the problem that moved him to devise a formal demonstration of her conditions for equilibrium. Pigou's metaphor seemed to confirm Robinson's self-congratulatory comment to Kahn: although his proof was an elegant translation of her account into algebra, it added nothing to her paper. Most important, the proof and the modest scientific rhetoric in which it was cast provided a happy solution to the difficulty that his original objection created. And they did so without suggesting that her paper was deficient in any respect. Thus Robinson had good reason to celebrate the results of her dialogues with Pigou. In responding to her letter of February 20, Kahn gave her additional reasons to be inordinately pleased with herself. He interpreted Pigou's introductory note—which Robinson characterized as a tribute—by inflating the importance of her work and the status Pigou ascribed to her. His metaphor "really does endorse his admiration, particularly when one reflects on such a metaphor being applied to a woman—by the Professor of all people."[62] "You are now definitely in the Marshall-Edgeworth class, or rather superior to them both for though you use all the latest gadgets, like Edgeworth, you reach your goal, like Marshall, with hands untorn and regularly debonair (only the loss of a button or two testifying to the difficulties of the ascent.)."[63]

Kahn's elevation of the twenty-nine-year-old author of a brief article to the pantheon of Edgeworth and Marshall was excessive. However, he did not exaggerate the importance of Pigou's endorsement. Publication of a paper that won the admiration of the most senior and prolific scholar of the guild was an important step toward accumulating credentials that would enable her to compete for a lectureship on the same level as candidates with conventional qualifications.

Robinson's circumstances called for a careful weighing of tactics, above all in her choice of research projects and the manner of their execution. "Imperfect Competition and Falling Supply Price" proved to be an inspired choice. The article entered the Cambridge debate on value theory, the theory of the firm, and imperfectly competitive markets that had engaged the guild since the reception of Sraffa's paper in 1926. It considered an issue in this complex of problems that the guild had treated as uncontroversial and settled: the relationship between increased demand and price. In assuming a variable relationship between the two, Robinson took a position designed to correct the thinking of the guild. The mode of analysis she employed demonstrated theoretical creativity on an important issue, but within acceptable limits. Since it was a variation on methods currently under discussion at Cambridge, it could hardly be regarded as a heretical or otherwise dangerous innovation. Finally, it was set out in a lucid, facile, and unornamented prose, economic writing of a clarity and simplicity unmatched by that of any member of the guild, including the author of *The Economic Consequences of the Peace*.

The article was a success at Cambridge, winning over Pigou as a de facto collaborator who was inspired to investigate formal problems it created but did not consider. This was an ironic reversal of the usual division of labor between junior and senior scientists, which called for the junior scholar to assume the subordinate role of performing mathematical analyses needed to formalize the theories of the more senior scholar. Robinson could not claim she had produced a "mathematically watertight" analysis. But she could claim that Pigou had performed this service for her. Since his note was published before her book, she was able to add the following footnote to her analysis of increasing demand and price in *The Economics of Imperfect Competition*: "Professor Pigou has published a confirmation and generalization of these results, in analytical form, in the *Economics Journal* [*sic*], March 1933 (pp. 108–112)" (Robinson 1933d, 110, n. 1).

From the standpoint of career production at Cambridge, Robinson's dialogues with Pigou achieved impressive results. A renowned economist who would later judge her qualifications for a lectureship published a formal proof and generalization of a thesis in her book some three months before it appeared. Her efforts to restore Pigou's confidence in her had clearly paid off, even if in an unintended fashion. If his confidence in her analysis was at stake, it was reestablished not through Robinson's labors but by the Professor himself. In a letter to Robinson after the publication of her book, he praised it as "a very fine effort," noting that it "should give you a very strong claim to the next lectureship that we have going."[64] Although she was not appointed to the next lectureship—Hicks was the successful candidate—Pigou played an important role in the eventual award of her lectureship in 1938.

KAHN AND ROBINSON IN AMERICA
An Outpost of Civilization

Kahn, anointed as Keynes's favorite pupil, took a First in Part II of the Economics Tripos after only one year of study. Following an additional year of research and writing, he completed an exceptionally successful book-length fellowship dissertation. Robertson declared it path-breaking. Pigou judged it quite astonishing and encouraged early publication.[65] Even before Kahn finished his dissertation, Keynes treated him as a theoretically sophisticated younger colleague. As early as summer 1929, he gave Kahn proofs of the *Treatise* for his suggestions (Marcuzzo 2002, 425, n. 7). When the Circus began to dissect the *Treatise*, Kahn was selected as the "messenger angel," ascending to Keynes with explanations and returning with his responses.[66] Thus when he sailed for the United States on December 21, 1932, he had abundant reasons for professional satisfaction and was confident that he had mastered Cambridge economics. At the time of his departure, Cambridge economists were engaged in research that he believed would produce exciting breakthroughs: the theory of imperfect competition and Keynes's post-*Treatise* work. Kahn himself had made original contributions in both areas. Rockefeller Foundation fellowships funded studies by foreign scholars in the United States. Kahn had a larger conception of his American visit. Important truths had recently been discovered at Cambridge, the center of the universe in economics. He would bring them to the periphery, where American economists—badly trained, intellectually shallow, and comparatively illiterate—labored in darkness. Kahn was largely ignorant of American economic theory. But why should he not have been? To know what was worth knowing in economics, it was hardly necessary to leave the precincts of Cambridge or even the grounds of King's and Trinity. As events quickly proved, his conception of his American visit was naïve and presumptuous in the extreme.

Kahn's first stop was Cincinnati, where the annual meeting of the American Statistical Association was held. On December 30, he presented a version of his article of 1931 on the multiplier under a new title, "Public Works and Inflation."[67] Although the paper was well received, he was astonished to discover that Americans had little interest in the progress Keynes had made since the *Treatise*. They were still committed to "the most doctrinaire sort of nonsense," such as the quantity theory of money, which Keynes and his followers had recently discarded. A "young monetary theorist" had not even heard of Keynes. Kahn's observations in Cincinnati left him with the impression that American economists "live in the Dark Ages."[68] More troubling surprises awaited him at the University of Chicago, where he spent the month of January.

Arrogance at Chicago:
The Problem of Schultz and Viner

Kahn's first discussions at Chicago were with the resident theoreticians Henry Schultz, for whom he had a letter of introduction from Keynes, and Jacob Viner. The results could hardly have been more demoralizing. "At the very outset," he wrote Robinson, "they made it clear to me that nothing being done at Cambridge would be of any interest to them." He encountered "a peculiarly self-satisfying kind of deceit"—a contempt for Cambridge economists and their works. Viner claimed he never allowed himself more than an hour to read the *Economic Journal*. Schultz maintained that he never read it. Indeed, he seemed to regard it as a mark of scientific connoisseurship that he had only glanced at the *Treatise*. Viner also feigned pride in claiming only a passing knowledge of a few pages of the book.[69] And what of the theory of imperfect competition? It was derivative and passé. Either it had been worked out by Cournot or others decades earlier, or Chicago people "had done it all themselves long ago." Viner claimed he had discovered the relationships between average and marginal cost curves that Kahn used in his dissertation, the same apparatus that would bear much analytical weight in Robinson's book. And the symposium of 1930 on increasing returns celebrated at Cambridge as a major event in research on imperfect competition? Viner had not bothered to finish it.[70] As a result, Kahn's conception of his role as emissary of Cambridge theoretical culture to the territory of the barbarians was quickly punctured. If Schultz and Viner regarded Keynes as a figure of minor importance and refused to take his work seriously, Kahn would have no success enlightening them about the advances made in the proto–*General Theory*. If they had already developed methods for analyzing imperfect competition that he and his Cambridge colleagues believed they had discovered, he would have nothing of originality to offer them.

With his initial vision of his American mission in shambles, Kahn began to improvise in an effort to fashion a more credible role for himself. His problem was to devise tactics to fight a battle he had not anticipated—to make a case for the importance of Cambridge economics against the view that it was outdated and irrelevant. In making this case, Kahn employed several tactics. He attempted to outflank Schultz and Viner by enrolling support from graduate students in economics, from whom the next generation of American theorists would be recruited. He also targeted faculty in the graduate school of business, who trained students in practical problems of managing businesses. And he took Chicago economists by surprise, defending Cambridge by using research that was new to them. The Cambridge artifacts that were at his disposal for this purpose were Robinson's work on imperfect competition: her article of December 1932 and the proofs of her book. Thus Kahn's support for Cambridge at Chicago intersected with advance marketing of her book. If he could convince graduate students in the economics department and faculty in the business school that her work on imperfect competition was important, his visit to Chicago would be a success.

Writing to Robinson shortly after his dispiriting talks with Schultz and Viner, Kahn discussed her place in his new plan: "It suddenly came home to me a couple of days ago that if it were not for your book Cambridge would be making a pretty bad showing and my position here would be untenable." After learning that several Chicago economists were pleased with her article, he asked Robinson for reprints, which he intended to circulate, also suggesting she send one to Viner with her "personal compliments."[71] Further conversations convinced him that, with the exception of Schultz and Viner, all the Chicago readers of her article who had an interest in imperfect competition were "highly impressed." Her methodological pamphlet was also being read, and there was some discussion of ordering copies for the university bookstore. Although Kahn found the intransigence of Schultz and Viner an obstacle, he was confident that her book would be a great success at Chicago.[72]

In defending Cambridge by promoting Robinson, Kahn found a receptive ear in V. F. Coe, a research student in economics who was supported by a fellowship renewable on a quarterly basis at the discretion of Schultz and Viner. After working for roughly a year in Schultz's statistics laboratory, he was studying cost curves and had made considerable progress analyzing average and marginal relationships. Kahn claimed he had "quite fired" Coe's imagination: "[Coe] went to Viner to suggest that somebody here ought to work on imperfect competition. (He meant that he would like to take it up himself but research students are not supposed to show signs of getting out of hand.) Viner made it pretty clear that it was a silly idea. The problem was of no particular interest, it all depended on what assumptions you made, and (I suspect) if he couldn't do it nobody else could. Coe did not improve his case by revealing that his mind had been stirred by talking to me about the work being done at Cambridge."[73]

By January 20, Coe was spreading the news of Robinson's work in the business school. This is surely not an idea that would have occurred to Kahn, who had no experience of graduate schools of business. He gave Robinson the following report on the efforts of his new recruit:

There is a man called [Simon H.] Nerlove in the Business School here who thinks that this kind of thing is the most important thing that has happened to economics in the last 40 years. And all that is derived from reading your article, reading your pamphlet (Coe showed it to him) and hearing Coe speak about his conversations with me and about your proofs (I hope you don't mind. I am allowing Coe to see your proofs. It seems such shocking waste to keep him waiting until publication and the book will be out in plenty of time to enable him to make proper acknowledgment.)[74] This kind of source—actually engaged in teaching men how to rear businesses—is worth a dozen Schultzes and Viners. And there are several others like him (I am talking of Nerlove, not Coe). (RFK/13/90/1/67–72)

Kahn later added that Coe anticipated "a great future" for Robinson's book at Chicago. The economics students would see to that: "He thinks that Viner will be forced to take it up by his lecture class, just as their money man was forced to read the *Treatise*."[75]

Robinson was pleased with the exposure she was receiving at Chicago.[76] She was also unimpressed by the dismissive response of Schultz and Viner to the belated Cambridge discovery of the marginal revenue curve and the promise she and Kahn saw in the possibilities of a marginal analysis of imperfect competition. Answering Kahn, she suggested that if there was some sense in which Chicago economists had anticipated marginal revenue before it was known at Cambridge, this might be "an amusing point" that he could include in the historical account of discoverers of the curve he was preparing for his Harvard paper. However, the matter of genuine importance was not mere acquaintance with the curve but a demonstration of how to use it in solving theoretical problems: "If Viner + Co[mpany] boast of knowing it all along they are giving themselves away badly for they ought to have produced my book in 1930."[77]

As Kahn explained to her, Coe was finishing his doctoral dissertation. With the help of Robinson's proofs, his analysis could be pushed in the direction she and Kahn were taking. Coe would be "eternally grateful." More important, his thesis would become "an instrument for approaching Viner and others at Chicago."[78] Robinson sent Coe a complete set of page proofs around March 25.[79] His belated letter of thanks, dated April 22, suggests that Kahn's revised Chicago strategy had met with some success. Coe was persuaded that her book would receive a warm reception in the United States. Viner would "make much use of it in his Theory courses," and Coe had learned it would be adopted as a text in the business school. Since the book was unpublished, this decision was certainly due to Kahn's campaign. Although Coe found her article brilliant, on a first reading he could not accept her unorthodox and surprising conclusion concerning decreasing costs. But in studying the essay more carefully, he discovered a footnote that exposed his own error, "for which there was of course no basis, except that it crept into my head to help and resist a new conclusion." Before Kahn's visit to Chicago, Coe had completed an analysis of the relations of cost curves, at least part of which he believed was new. On reading Robinson's proofs, he saw that she had "done the thing better and pushed the analysis much further."[80] Coe was singing from a score composed by Kahn for a chorus of male voices, his hymn to Robinson and the glories of Cambridge economics to be performed by University of Chicago economists.

Harvard

After his reception at Chicago, Kahn's spirit of Cambridge triumphalism was much dampened. His Chicago strategy would also be called for at Harvard. Instead of proclaiming the magnificence of Cambridge economics, he would defend it against skeptics and adversaries. And he would mount this defense not by an appeal to Keynes's new ideas but by promoting Robinson's recent and forthcoming work. The circumstances at Harvard that dictated this strategy differed from those he faced at Chicago. The strategic field on which he operated was defined chiefly by the presence of two men. Schumpeter had been persuaded to leave his professorship at Bonn and join the Harvard faculty in autumn 1932. In 1927, Chamberlin had defended his Harvard doctoral dissertation on monopolistic competition. After some six years of further work, publication of his book on the subject was imminent.

THE SCHUMPETER SEMINAR In October 1931, Schumpeter delivered three lectures at Cambridge, the occasion on which he met Kahn and Robinson (Allen 1994a, 280). When Keynes wrote letters of introduction for Kahn to open doors in the United States, he included no letters for Harvard because Kahn and Schumpeter were already acquainted. Schumpeter's correspondence shows that he was quite impressed with both Kahn and Robinson. On February 25, 1933, he wrote Ragnar Frisch, "We have now the visit of Richard Kahn of King's College, Cambridge, the favorite pupil of Keynes, who is a very good man. In fact when his book comes out I do think he will prove another candidate for Fellowship [in the newly established Econometrics Society, in which Frisch and Schumpeter played leading roles]" (RF/NBO Brevs. 761A). In a conversation during Kahn's visit, Schumpeter expressed "the profoundest admiration" for Robinson, calling her "one of our best men."[81]

None of these predilections disposed Schumpeter in favor of a Keynesian gospel, old or new. In his most famous anecdote, he claimed he had three ambitions in life: to become the world's greatest economist, lover, and horseman. Keynes did not compete in the last sphere. From Schumpeter's perspective, Keynes's ambivalent sexuality would disqualify him in the second. However, he stood in the path of Schumpeter's first ambition.[82] On Kahn's arrival at Harvard, he attended a party for Schumpeter's fiftieth birthday. Shortly thereafter, he wrote Robinson: "I fully realised the terrible depths of darkness in which he, and far more the others, are thinking on these questions. He is on the point of finishing a book all about velocities of circulation, and just can't see my point. The conversation turned to inflation. It was terrible—all about inactive deposits and increasing the circulation. I felt an awful chill of isolation." In Schumpeter's lectures, Kahn watched him tear to bits one of Keynes's analyses in the *Treatise*, passages of which he quoted "in a slightly mocking tone." To Kahn, Schumpeter's critique was a violation of "rudimentary canons of commonsense" and an "intellectually abominable performance." Although he contained himself during the lecture, his response to Robinson was livid.[83] Kahn's sense of his marginal status and alienation, first at Chicago and then at Harvard, led him to a characteristically extravagant conclusion: "I am now fully aware that there is not a single person on this continent with whom I could carry on a reasonably intelligent conversation on these matters."[84]

How could Kahn defend Cambridge at Harvard? Keynes's post-*Treatise* work remained unpublished and had been shared only with a select few. As he revised the proofs of *The General Theory*, Keynes was reluctant to discuss his new ideas with Cambridge outsiders. In September 1935, he received a request from Frisch, who was preparing his lectures on monetary theory for the upcoming Oslo term. Frisch had read the *Treatise* and was aware that Keynes was writing a new book on monetary theory. Uncertain as to whether it had been published, he asked Keynes for a few remarks on the evolution of his thinking in order to bring his lectures up to date. Keynes demurred: "I would very much rather, if it is possible, that you should wait until my new book is out before you inflict my opinions on your students. The new book makes a considerable difference, and I think they might lose their time if they were to go in any great detail into my previously published theory."[85] At Cambridge, the *Treatise* had been analyzed, criticized, and incorporated into the theoretical tradition that descended from Marshall. Locally, there is a sense in which it was a part of the theoretical canon. In the United States, it apparently remained "new and unexplored territory."[86]

In spite of Kahn's unhappy introduction to Harvard monetary theory, he was generally pleased with his circumstances at the university, at least early in his visit. There was "an air of real grace about the place," quite unlike the ambience at Chicago. His accommodations were "a very good imitation of College"—with the exception of a "horrible thing, a shower instead of a bath." Two young instructors attended to his needs, and he participated in Schumpeter's seminar, where he defended Cambridge economics by introducing Robinson's work. In celebrating the virtues of her research, he argued that Cambridge was in the forefront of innovation and rigorous analysis. If Schumpeter could be persuaded that her work was important, he would discuss it in his lectures and seminars. Harvard graduate students and instructors would follow the lead of their new principal theoretician. Cambridge ideas would be exported to Harvard, where they might take root. Theoretical tools forged at Cambridge would also be used at Harvard. In this manner the dominance of Cambridge economics, at least as Kahn understood it, would be extended to one of the most prestigious centers of American research and graduate study.[87]

Pleading the case for Cambridge by making use of Robinson was an intelligent move on Kahn's part. In Schumpeter, he found a receptive listener. Robinson was an attractive young woman—"the Beautiful Mrs. R." as Pigou called her—not one of the men of Schumpeter's generation, with whom he sometimes had diffident or competitive relations. Schumpeter took an active and generous interest in younger economists that seems to have been genuinely collegial. He also presented himself as a bon vivant and connoisseur of women. Although he could not match the conquests of Don Giovanni that Leporello recited to Donna Elvira, like the Don he boasted of his success in several countries—not in Italy or Spain but in Austria, Germany, England, and the United States.[88] But what did he know of Robinson's work before Kahn arrived at Harvard? Apparently very little. After she sent him an offprint of her article, he responded politely but without reference to its content or to her pamphlet, which she had also sent. Either it was misplaced or it never arrived. As Schumpeter wrote her, he hoped to become acquainted with the details of her work through Kahn.[89] Within a few days of Kahn's arrival, Schumpeter had read her article, and they were discussing it. Shortly after one of their first conversations, Kahn reported to Robinson: "He was effusive in praising the lucidity of your article, and gave me to understand that you are one of the best of the younger economists. He did not omit to mention some of your more unprofessional traits that make you so likeable. I was pleased—he was being quite sincere, so far as one can tell—but

I succeeded in maintaining a sober demeanor."[90] These conversations spilled into Schumpeter's seminar. Near the end of one session, he asked Kahn to reproduce the diagram of the kinked demand curve, which would shortly appear in Robinson's book. Schumpeter was "most impressed" and asked when publication could be expected.[91] He was also "very struck" with the average productivity curve, another tool Kahn and Robinson had developed: "We spent a good part of the hour at his seminar discussing it this morning. He told his class that they must familiarize themselves with it. 'It is not a question of believing it: it is a new tool capable of doing very useful work.'"[92]

THE CHAMBERLIN INCIDENT From the standpoint of Robinson's interests, Kahn arrived at Harvard at an opportune moment—just a few days before Chamberlin's book appeared.[93] Because Chamberlin and Robinson were covering the same ground and he was publishing first, Kahn quickly began to work on her behalf. In his discussions with Schumpeter as well as graduate students and younger economists, his objective was to make a preemptive case that her research was more sophisticated methodologically and promised more significant theoretical payoffs. As Kahn and Robinson understood, these efforts were important in supporting her claims to credit. If it were generally acknowledged that much of her analysis had been published by Chamberlin, her book might fall stillborn from the press. And if her work were not recognized as original, it would have little value in establishing her professional identity at Cambridge. Kahn's task was to make a plausible argument in a difficult situation. The obstinate and disagreeable fact was that Chamberlin's book would be read as the first attempt to develop a theory of monopolistic competition at a time when Robinson was correcting proofs. Although he enjoyed the conventional advantage of prior publication, was there an unconventional but overriding sense in which she could claim priority? In her competition with Chamberlin, the gods that decide success in scientific careers smiled on Robinson. At least three factors worked in her favor:

(1) Chamberlin claimed he had begun serious work on his doctoral dissertation in 1924 (Chamberlin 1961, 520).[94] Thus his research had been under way for some six years before Robinson's. However, she enjoyed a signal advantage. Her article was an early sketch of the basic arguments of her book. Chamberlin had no comparable preliminary publications. His article from 1929 "Duopoly: Value Where Sellers Are Few"

announced his forthcoming book on monopolistic competition; the article, he claimed, was only a fragment of this more ambitious study. But "Duopoly" merely synthesized and refined traditional literature on the subject: Cournot, Bertrand, Edgeworth, Marshall, and Pigou.[95] On this score, Chamberlin made a serious tactical error. By reserving his novel analysis for the book, he gave his competition opportunity to anticipate him and achieve priority. In the institutional allocation of credit, this was the significance of Robinson's article. Because Chamberlin lingered, she was able to exploit an opening he had left undefended. He did not understand that he was creating an opportunity for competitors. She did not know that publication of her article would give her an advantage. However, the absence of intentions and knowledge does not alter the outcome of the distribution of credit.

(2) Imperfect competition was high on the research agenda at Cambridge in the early 1930s. By March 1933, Sraffa, Shove, Robertson, Kahn, and Pigou had all published in the area. Not so at Harvard, where Chamberlin wrote in theoretical isolation. Robinson quickly mastered the Cambridge practice of collective research production. Kahn, Austin, Sraffa, Guillebaud, Newman, and even Keynes—whose work was quite remote from imperfect competition—all took a hand in her book. Only a few days before Chamberlin's book appeared, no one at Harvard seemed able to give an account of it.[96]

(3) Although Chamberlin was one of several independent discoverers of marginal revenue, he had little confidence in its analytical power, preferring instead Marshallian aggregate measures of revenues and costs. Except for a passing reference to marginal demand price, the concept of marginal revenue did not appear in his thesis (Reinwald 1977, 527). Although his book introduced the idea under the category of marginal receipts, he used it on only three occasions.[97] He also wrote at some length to impress upon readers his sense of the modest explanatory value of the curve.[98] Robinson's knowledge of marginal revenue was acquired by accident and through no effort on her part. However, she used the curve systematically as her most important methodological tool. In the disciplinary assessment of the two books during the 1930s, Robinson's innovative work in exploring a new technique and examining its implications gave her a significant advantage she would not have enjoyed had Chamberlin exploited his discovery.

In the final days before Chamberlin's book appeared, Kahn read a paper to a meeting of the Graduate Economics Club, an organization of lecturers and graduate students. His subject: new Cambridge techniques in the analysis of imperfect competition. From the standpoint of priority claims, Robinson and Chamberlin had approximately the same status on the day of his lecture: they were both authors of forthcoming books in the same area. By his account, Kahn lectured to an audience of more than one hundred. He was in an excellent position to advance an argument for Robinson's originality and the superiority of Cambridge methods. In Kahn's report, the event began in an auspicious fashion; the chairman opened the meeting by quoting Robinson's doctrine that economics is neither more nor less than its technique. Discussion of his lecture led to what Kahn called "a rather tragic scene." Debate was dominated by Chamberlin's objections to the marginal revenue curve. Kahn raised several counterarguments but to no effect. Because Chamberlin could not be moved, Kahn wrote, "rather cruelly I flung down a challenge." If the elasticity of demand remains constant, how can the effect of a change in demand or price be expressed in terms of average cost? He gave Robinson's solution to Chamberlin and asked him to translate it into his analytical language. "It was then," he wrote, "that the awful fact transpired that Chamberlin was unaware that an increase in demand could *under any circumstances* lead to a fall in price." The audience grasped the consequence. Chamberlin was refuted on the basis of his own premises. Or, in Kahn's more colorful language, he "stood competed out of his own mouth." Marshall did not apply marginal analysis to monopolistic markets. In his confrontation with Kahn in February 1933, Chamberlin remained true to the older Cambridge method. Kahn believed that this exchange settled any contest over priority in Robinson's favor. In light of Chamberlin's failure to meet his challenge, it was abundantly clear that Robinson had nothing to fear. More than one hundred young Harvard economists had taken in the result: Chamberlin had assisted Kahn in demonstrating the superiority of Robinson's new Cambridge method of analysis.[99]

Robinson's article on imperfect competition and falling supply price, which Chamberlin had not read until Kahn brought it to his attention, played a significant role in the above incident. In this paper, as we noted, Robinson had argued that under conditions of imperfect competition an increase in demand would lower costs but not necessarily prices. This was the result that left Chamberlin baffled and embarrassed. The argument of her article—obviously not mentioned in Chamberlin's book because he had not read it—was employed in *The Economics of Imperfect Competition*. In Kahn's view, this consideration was sufficient to give her what he called "technical priority" over Chamberlin, and she could "ignore him with an easy conscience."[100] Even though Chamberlin's book would be published first, *The Economics of Imperfect Competition* was based on an article from 1932. In judging priority technically—on the basis of first publication of the original elements of the theory of imperfect competition—Robinson would take precedence.

Because Chamberlin had told Kahn he intended to send Robinson a copy of his book, the question of how she should handle it in the revision of her proofs remained. Kahn coached her on tactics. If she did not have the book before she delivered her final set of revised page proofs to Macmillan, a studied silence was the best course. But if she received a copy in a timely fashion, a brief disclaimer was in order: the book had arrived too late for comment. In either case, readers of the two books would see them as instances of independent and simultaneous discovery. Thus Kahn was pleased that the problems created by Chamberlin's book would be easily resolved in Robinson's favor. Because Chamberlin had failed to take advantage of the theoretical potential of the marginal revenue curve, the outlines of which she had already published, her claim to priority could not be compromised by his book. Although comparisons and joint reviews of the two books were inevitable, they would work to her advantage. Robinson was quite happy with Kahn's conclusions. But in spite of his advice that she abstain from provoking premature controversy by maintaining a judicious silence until her book was published, she seemed ready for combat. As she wrote on March 2, 1933, "I feel a viscious [*sic*] pleasure at hearing that Chamberlin is no good. I should just put in a note that I had not read him until my stuff was completed. I might get [D. H.] Macgregor [assistant editor of the *Economic Journal* at the time] to let me review him—no on second thought that would be bad. But I can deal with him sometime after I am out" (RFK/13/90/1/155–61).

In early March, Robinson received a complimentary copy of *The Theory of Monopolistic Competition* and compared the extent of overlap with her work. The larger the overlap, the greater the difficulty in sustaining a claim for the originality of her book. If the overlap was modest, her prospects would be better. In her estimate, roughly one-third of his book covered territory she had explored. Only one-fourth of her book overlapped with his.[101] If Chamberlin had used the marginal revenue curve, the overlap would have been much greater, weakening her claims to originality. However, the temptation to do battle with Chamberlin, even if vicariously, and to demonstrate that she had bested him was too great. The following week, she suggested that Kahn introduce criticism of Chamberlin into his book: "I think you ought to put in some references to Chamberlin—and you might take the opportunity to criticise his idiotic way of talking about the 'elements of monopoly + competition' in a situation. It is only a verbal point but I have a suspicion that it leads him into actual error at times. He had so nearly got there—it seems queer that he should not have seen the proper way of looking at it."[102] This suggestion does not seem to have been an offhand remark but rather a calculated move by Robinson to weaken Chamberlin's position and strengthen her own in a potential competition for priority and credit. On March 30, she returned to the critique of Chamberlin: "Tell me if you have read Chamberlin. If so I will send you some comments" (RFK/13/90/1/215–16).

As Kahn predicted, the two books were widely compared and reviewed together. A roundtable organized for the American Economic Association meeting on December 27, 1933, was a telling indication of the early disciplinary consensus on their comparative merits (Schumpeter et al. 1934). The title of the roundtable was "Imperfect Competition." The gatekeepers of American economic theory adopted Robinson's concept and not Chamberlin's to identify the new research area. Although Robinson was not present at the roundtable, *The Economics of Imperfect Competition* was. The discussants were Chamberlin himself and A. J. Nichol. The chair was Schumpeter, who wrote a long, generally laudatory review of Robinson's book for the *Journal of Political Economy*.[103]

In December 1933, Schumpeter advised Kahn on German economics journals that might review *The Economics of Imperfect Competition* (Schumpeter 2000, 260). In May 1934, he wrote Abraham Flexner, director of the Institute for Advanced Study at Princeton, recommending Robinson for an appointment: "I rate her very high and if you plan to have, say, yearly guests, I strongly plead to invite her for a year at least in order to look at her" (Schumpeter 2000, 262). In December 1936, Schumpeter responded to a request from the president of Harvard, James B. Conant, asking for recommendations regarding "Promising Young Men to be Called to Harvard from Outside." After recommending Oskar Lange, Nicholas Gerogescu-Roegen, and Arthur Smithies, he noted that in making these suggestions he had "submitted to the apparently invincible Harvard prejudice against women." But: "Mrs. Joan Robinson of Cambridge, England, an economist of international fame, would be an extremely good acquisition and could be had for $4000 or a little more. I may add that if there were any wish to break that anti-feminist tradition, which to me seems, frankly, to be somewhat reactionary, her appointment would afford an excellent opportunity" (Schumpeter 2000, 287–88).

At the meeting of the American Economic Association in January 1944, Schumpeter chaired the committee formed to recommend foreign economists for honorary membership. Among others, the committee proposed Frisch, F. A. Hayek, Hicks, Gunnar Myrdal, Bertil Ohlin, Robbins, and Robinson. Schumpeter seems to have been the prime mover behind the choice of Robinson. In his report to the association as chair of the committee, he wrote the following: "I know I shall be considered out of order if in this anti-feminist country, I suggest honoring a woman, but Mrs. Joan Robinson had a well-earned international success with her book on the *Economics of Imperfect Competition* in 1933. By virtue of it she holds a leading position in one of the most popular lines of advance [of economic theory]" (quoted in Allen 1994b, 149).

Career Production at a Distance

Kahn's visit to the United States afforded Robinson an extraordinary opportunity to enhance her professional identity by proxy. Both she and Kahn took advantage of the possibilities, placing in circulation claims to the merits of her work in progress that he was able to substantiate. At Chicago, he distributed her article and the proofs of her book to good effect. At Harvard, he discussed the article with Schumpeter and his students, and in his lecture he was able to face down Chamberlin by using an analysis drawn from her book. When Kahn arrived in the United States, Robinson was a professional novice. Yet at both Chicago and Harvard, he was able to celebrate her research as the next big thing in economics. Initially thrown off balance when his early conception of his American visit as a mission of enlightenment to an academic backwater was shattered, he quickly found a new strategy. In defending Cambridge economics by means of Robinson's work, he assisted in the promotion of her nascent reputation, at that point barely visible outside a small circle of English economists.

The Cambridge Ethos

In one of the more arresting footnotes to his *History of Economic Analysis*, Schumpeter considered Kahn and Shove as exemplars of the cultural distinctiveness of Cambridge economics. He wrote, "Both are scholars of a type that Cambridge produces much more readily than do other centers of scientific economics or rather of science in general. They throw their ideas into a common pool. By critical and positive suggestion they help other people's ideas into definite existence. And they exert anonymous influence—influence as leaders—far beyond anything that can be credited to them from their publications" (Schumpeter 1954, 1152). Economists who cast their ideas into a common pool of artifacts that are undifferentiated as to their provenance make no claim to proprietary rights over what they produce. Schumpeter's scholars of anonymous influence are comparable to writers and masters of the European Middle Ages, known only by what they made or where they made it. Producing works that they did not sign and for which they expected no mundane credit, they made no claims to ownership. Schumpeter's metaphor detached Cambridge economics from the world of scientific careerism, where methods for distinguishing contributions according to authorship are indispensable because of the importance of bases for allocating rewards and markers for determining success. In the Cambridge of the Schumpeterian imagination, the question of who developed an idea is irrelevant, and the concept of the ownership of ideas makes no sense. It follows that claims to priority for scientific work, competition for credit, and conflicts over their attribution are not to be expected; these practices presuppose proprietary rights in ideas and an interest in asserting them, conditions that his account rules out.

Schumpeter's metaphor is worth taking seriously if for no other reason than the fact that Cambridge was its source. Kahn subscribed to this conception of Cambridge economics in his scathing observations on conditions at Chicago and Harvard. He attributed the intellectual emptiness he experienced there to the pursuit of higher learning as a business. Because of the ethics of "the terrible business of career hunting," his hosts at both universities were "incapable of the kind of social life we value." The scientific life of the Cambridge economist was a higher conversation, "a social act which pervades one's whole life," not a series of commercial ventures in which dialogue has no role and research is undertaken for its payoff in an academic career strategy.[104] In 1930, Goldsworthy Lowes Dickinson, the generalist in the moral sciences at King's, suggested that scholarship as the selfless and disinterested quest for knowledge, remote from the calculations and compromises of a career, was a distinctive feature of Cambridge intellectuality generally. The Cambridge man was unworldly and unambitious but not lacking in energy and initiative: "Through good reports and ill such men work on, following the light of truth as they see it" (in Keynes 1951, 245).[105] Did Schumpeter light upon a happy metaphor? What conclusions can be drawn from the making of *The Economics of Imperfect Competition* concerning the appositeness of his image of the common pool? Does research on imperfect competition at Cambridge during the early 1930s suggest that the Marshallian guild was a community of scientists committed to the investigation of the truth, irrespective of priority and credit?

At Harvard, Kahn was aggressive in pressing for recognition of the priority, originality, and superior analytical power of Robinson's work over Chamberlin's. The two books were in competition and would be read and reviewed accordingly. This meant there were rewards to compete over, scarce scientific goods the distribution of which would depend on judgments of priority. Robinson's concerns about overlaps and her encouragement of Kahn to attack Chamberlin on the basis of arguments she was assembling show that she saw their books in the same terms: she and Chamberlin were engaged in an unanticipated contest that she was determined to win. However, it was a competition between Robinson and Chamberlin, not between two members of the Marshallian guild. From Kahn's perspective, it was also a rivalry between Cambridge and Harvard—and American economics generally—for ascendancy in contemporary economic theory. Perhaps the common pool did not extend across the Atlantic? Were conditions more placid and companionable on the banks of the Cam? Although Cambridge economists competed for credit with outsiders, did competition have no place in the practice of economic science within the walls at Cambridge?

At the time of the gestation of *The Economics of Imperfect Competition*, two other Cambridge economists had a substantial investment in the field of imperfect competition. They were Schumpeter's paradigm cases of disinterested, collaborative research: Kahn and Shove, the models of a Cambridge culture in which the struggle for priority and credit had no place. It was clear to Kahn that he and Robinson had competing priority claims.

They were settled amicably if somewhat disingenuously by employing a tactic of selective disattention. There was a pretense not to notice certain issues, candid discussion of which might prove embarrassing or divisive. Shove seems to have been traumatized by anxieties over the damage that early publication of Robinson's book would inflict on his work in progress. The tensions and the conflicts they caused were worrisome to Robinson, relatively intractable, and the subject of tedious and inconclusive negotiations over credit claims.

Robinson and Kahn:
The Consensual Determination of Priority

Robinson and Kahn were intimate friends, whose research cannot easily be disentangled from their personal lives. They enjoyed a remarkably close working relationship, routinely sharing ideas and producing joint solutions to theoretical problems. However, they published no formally coauthored papers, and credit was assumed and claimed individually. This arrangement called for nice distinctions and a careful management of credit attribution, not least because a paper begun by Kahn was finished by Robinson.[106] It is not surprising that intimate collaboration without joint publication led to problems of credit allocation.

Consider Kahn's paper "Imperfect Competition and the Marginal Principle," written as a lecture for delivery at Harvard and then submitted to the *Quarterly Journal of Economics*. The paper drew on his fellowship dissertation and discussions with Robinson. Although he supposed it would be accepted, publication could not be expected before May, when the next issue of the journal was scheduled to appear. This was a generous estimate of the paper's importance: the editor of the journal would not only accept it but publish it as soon as possible. At this point, Kahn was under the impression that Robinson's book would appear before May. They had collaborated closely for more than three years. They shared a background in Marshallian economics and the lessons on its limits that they had learned from Sraffa and Shove. They employed the same theoretical premises and modes of economic analysis, which in some measure they developed together. Unsurprisingly, parts of Kahn's article intersected with arguments of Robinson's book. It was under these circumstances that he wrote Robinson about the paper on February 20, raising "a rather thorny problem of precedence":

I think you will agree that it would be rather stupid to make the thing appear as though it had been written after your book has appeared. The time would be all wrong and it would be necessary to show a lot of references. What I want to try to do, if Taussig is willing,[107] is to make clear that it was written as a lecture, delivered before your book had appeared, and just to insert in square brackets in the footnote that the book has since appeared. What do you think? Please let me know as I may be getting embroiled with Taussig over the matter, for all I know. The best thing would be if he refused to accept. I don't feel it ought to be published. And let me know the name of your book, so that I can refer to it correctly. (RFK/13/90/1/131–38)

Kahn's letter raises several questions. In view of his friendship with Robinson, it does so in a remarkably oblique fashion.

What was his chief worry? It was not the impression that his article had been written after her book appeared. Suppose that an article by one author was published shortly after a book by another author written along the same lines. This supposition provides no basis for inferences concerning which manuscript was written first. Kahn's article could have been written years before Robinson's book or, on the other hand, after its publication. Thus the "stupid" appearance that troubled him vanishes. His real difficulty was quite simple. Her book would be published before his paper. Unless he could claim that his article had been delivered as a lecture before the publication of her book, he would have no basis for a priority claim. His article would be perceived as a derivative artifact of questionable value, especially in comparison with her much more elaborate book.

In what sense was the problem thorny? Was it challenging or uncommonly difficult to resolve? Hardly. Kahn himself proposed a simple solution. The difficulty was not so much thorny as urgent. He expected the May issue of the journal to include his article. If the problem was not addressed before the issue went to press, any priority claim made on behalf of his article would be difficult to sustain.

What did it mean to say that "the time would be all wrong"? It would be wrong for Kahn because the impression that his paper was written after her book was published would make it difficult for him to claim credit for any argument in her book.

Finally, why would inclusion of numerous references to Robinson's book be so laborious? If she enjoyed legitimate priority because she was first in publishing arguments that they both employed, this would seem to be the only honest course. Considered purely as a matter of proper scholarly form, it would be obligatory. Kahn's other articles of the time were richly embellished with references and footnotes. Why were full references in this case so awkward? Again the answer turns on priority. Given their respective publication schedules as he understood them at that juncture, complete references to sources would substantially weaken any claim for the priority of his paper.

On March 2, Robinson informed Kahn that there was a good chance her book would not be out as early as she had anticipated. If it were published by May, she proposed that he employ his simple solution to the problem of priority: "You must just put in a footnote saying that your article was a lecture given at such + such a date" (RFK/13/90/1/155–61). Would a note that did not mention her book but merely stated that his article was delivered as a lecture in February settle all questions about priority? Robinson seemed to think so. Was it necessary for Kahn to include references to her book? She seemed to think it was not and gave him no help with the problem of the extent to which he should cite her forthcoming work. In handling the matter of citations, he employed a method of improvisatory and selective footnoting, omitting references to her book at points where they were called for. "I fear I sadly overdid the causal touch," he wrote. "I was so afraid of the opposite. It is very difficult to hit it off right. It would be so much easier to tell the truth, but I fear your academic reputation has to suffer in the interests of polite lying. But I feel I was too ruthless, and might have been more truthful."[108]

The exchange between Robinson and Kahn on the ethics of footnoting shows that they subordinated the question of proper scientific and scholarly practice in crediting sources to tactical calculations.[109] Robinson agreed that Kahn's tactic was a good one but also pointed out a potentially embarrassing oversight: his disposition to use her phrasing and diction: "You certainly don't need to say anymore about me than you do. The only point that I think is too much of a good thing is the *verbal* similarity between your monopoly tucked way in a watertight section of the text book + the corresponding passage in my introduction" (RFK/13/90/1/173–79).[110] Kahn agreed that this sort of unconscious plagiarism was dangerous: "I see that I shall have to be very careful about this sort of thing when I come to my book."[111]

In the end, Kahn's thorny problem disappeared, although not in a way he anticipated. He had suggested that the matter would best be resolved if the journal rejected his paper, a peculiar observation in view of his efforts to secure publication and credit.[112] On March 3, his wish was granted. His submission was rejected, another sharp and unexpected blow to his sense of preeminence over the Americans. Kahn's paper included ideas he had developed independently as well as results of his work with Robinson. Her book was based on ideas she had taken from Kahn and products of their collaborative efforts. Because of the rejection of his paper and publication of her book, from the standpoint of the allocation of credit his essay had become a scientific nullity. *The Economics of Imperfect Competition* would credit Robinson for her own work, their joint efforts, and some of Kahn's ideas. In employing parts of his unpublished article, her book deprived them of originality, rendering them unpublishable elsewhere. In working with Robinson, therefore, Kahn lost credit for some of the work for which he was responsible.

Although Robinson did not seem unduly distressed by Kahn's rejection notice, she attempted to console him with suggestions designed to make the best of a disappointing result. He could elaborate on his discussions of the irrelevance of overhead costs by including cases in which businessmen did not take them into account in setting prices. Although his paper discussed the latter point, he had interviewed a few more businessmen in the United States and intended to incorporate the results into his revised manuscript. This material could be published independently. "The rest of the article," she wrote, "will not be very pointful when I am out." However, it might be broken down into a few publishable notes. His history of independent discoveries of the marginal revenue curve could also be published, but not until "after I have been reviewed"; otherwise it might create an impression in the minds of reviewers that her book had not covered the relevant professional literature.[113] In sum: she offered advice on how to extract residual credit from his rejected article in ways that would not jeopardize her claims to precedence.

Robinson and Shove: Negotiating Credit Claims

In summer 1931, Robinson was working on her book and her first series of lectures, a short course on the pure theory of monopoly scheduled for the coming Michaelmas term. Both the lectures and the book would intersect with Shove's lectures on production, values, and distribution as well as a book he was planning on the subject. In Shove's mind this intersection portended a conflict over credit.[114] If he had published his lectures of the late 1920s, when Robinson was beginning her informal postgraduate studies, she could not have posed a threat. However, he was not quick to commit his work to the finality of print, a diffidence nicely captured more than a half century later in Kahn's eulogy of Shove: "He wrote much but published little. It is a great misfortune that in his Will he left instructions that all his manuscripts were to be destroyed. His determination not to publish anything until it seemed to say exactly what he meant—just that, and not another thing—sprang ultimately from a deep, indeed religious, fealty to truth" (Kahn 1987, 327–28).

Because Shove was hardly indifferent to recognition by the scientific community, his reluctance to publish was inconvenient. A ludicrous incident in 1933 makes this clear. When he saw Robinson's article in the *Economic Journal* of December 1932—a discussion that commented on some of his ideas—he decided to respond by writing a note (1933b). Keynes allowed Robinson a brief reply and sent her Shove's note. At this point, Shove seriously considered withdrawing from publication. On February 18, Robinson wrote Kahn, "I went to chat with Maynard about it + he was very amiable. He says Gerald has been giving him an awful time over it, + M finally got it out of him by saying that if he withdrew it he would encourage everyone to pinch all Gerald's ideas + never make any acknowledgement" (RFK/13/90/1/123–26). Keynes's clever manipulation of Shove's proprietary interest in his ideas settled the matter, and the note was published in March 1933.

As she was writing in summer 1931, Robinson "pinched" several Shovian ideas that were critical to her research at the time—above all his analysis of diminishing and increasing returns, cost curves, and rent. Shove received news of this fact somewhat awkwardly—not from Robinson herself but from Kahn, the "messenger angel" with whom he shared the high table at King's. On October 24, shortly after she had begun to lecture on the theory of monopoly, Shove wrote a preemptive note designed to ensure that any use she made of his work would receive proper acknowledgment: "I am delighted that any of my ideas or methods of exposition should bear fruit in this way, but may I say that I think some acknowledgement should be made of their source? I am sure that you will agree with me; but past experience has taught me that it is best to make one's feelings on these matters quite plain from the first—so I hope you will forgive me for writing" (JVR/vii/412/3–4).

Robinson was not revising the proofs of a book. She did not even have a text. She was writing the first draft of a manuscript Shove had not seen, and his information was based on conversations with a third person. How did he know that Kahn's account was accurate? How did he know that he had understood Kahn correctly? Even if Robinson's current draft employed some of his ideas, how did he know they would survive successive revisions? Shove's letter exhibits remarkable audacity and impertinence. It presumes that if he did not instruct Robinson on how to meet her scholarly obligations—or if Kahn had not played his role as Shove's informant—Robinson would publish his work as her own.

Robinson's letters to Shove have not survived. However, his letter of October 22 shows that she responded with uncharacteristic restraint, assuring him that she intended to make the conventional acknowledgments. He now claimed to be ashamed he had raised the matter at all: "I really felt sure all along that you intended to acknowledge anything you might owe to me." Really? In that case, why did he inquire into Robinson's lectures and the extent to which they might draw on his work? Shove's letters are calculated to give the impression that his chief worry was a matter of pedagogy: he had been "feeling a little uneasy about the possible overlap" in their lectures on the analysis of increasing and decreasing returns. However, he failed badly in sustaining this impression, unwittingly translating the issue of overlap between their lectures into a quite different and darker concern: her appropriation of his work. Again basing his speculations on conversations with Kahn, who had not given him a full account of the matter, he supposed that Robinson's lectures might follow the line he had already taken. Because her lectures were a book in progress, he concluded that they would appear in her book in some fashion. In documenting his priority in the investigation of diminishing and increasing returns, he mentioned his publications, Cambridge lectures, and even his supervisions as possible sources from which she might have drawn ideas. In view of these possibilities, which seemed to cover all conceivable intellectual performances with the exception of informal conversations, he proposed to send her "some short notes" on how he intended to begin his Michaelmas lectures. He suggested that if she advised him on the extent of similar or parallel treatments of common problems in their courses, he would revise his material in order to eliminate any redundancies.[115]

More than a month passed, and Shove did not send his short notes. However, he remained persistent in trying to discover how much of his work Robinson was using in her course. In writing her on December 2, his explanation was still the apparently innocent pedagogical concern. Unlike Robinson, he lectured on the theory of value over all three terms of the academic year. For this reason, he claimed, it would be "a great help to me in preparing my course for next term to know how much of my stuff you have covered in your lectures." Instead of sending her his lecture notes, he listed some of the topics he intended to cover during the following term, asking her to write yes or no beside each to indicate whether she had lectured on that issue. He added that he had not attempted to frame his various points "fully or accurately," informing Robinson only concerning the areas he proposed to discuss but not what he would say about them. "All I want to know," he reiterated, "is how much of the field I intended to cover you have covered already + how far you have dealt with it on the lines which I have been accustomed to follow" (JVR/vii/412/8–9).

This explanation is difficult to credit. Consider the fact that Shove lectured on the theory of value for three terms, Robinson only for one. Suppose there was a one-to-one correspondence in the topics they covered and the mode of analysis they employed. Even if this were the case, it is not reasonable to assume that the analysis of rent, for example, on which Robinson might lecture for a week would reproduce an analysis to which he would devote some three weeks. If his real worry was pedagogical redundancy, why did he fail to mention other areas in which their lectures were likely to overlap: their common background in Marshall's theory of value, Sraffa's critique, or the symposium? Shove was concerned with the extent to which she had taken his work and made it her own. If he did not want to lose proprietary control over his ideas, it makes sense that his résumé did not give a full account of the territory of his lectures.

Shove wrote again six days later. Robinson had complied with his request, and he appears to have been satisfied with the result. There was little indication she was using his work. Did this end his worries? Robinson had apparently mentioned that her lectures included a typology of four cost curves. In a pedantically detailed exegesis of one of his essays, Shove tried to make the case that he had already developed the theoretical concept on which three of her curves were based. In this letter, Shove abandoned even a feigned interest in the subject matter of lectures and addressed the issue of priority directly and unequivocally:

As regards the cost-curves, may I point out that in my first article in the [*Economic*] *Journal* (June 1928 p 264), I distinguish between

(1) average cost including rent

(2) average cost excluding rent

(3) final trade cost (there defined as the increase in aggregate cost, other than rent, accompanying a unit increase in output, or more properly, the ratio of this increase to the increase in output): (+ in the footnote 4) on page 259, I indicated the treatment of cost + rent which I proposed to substitute for Marshall[']s. I also allude on p 264 to the variation of these 3 costs with variations in output.

So far as I can understand, these are 3 of your 4 curves (I didn't know the curves, but that is simply a mechanical process when once the concepts are defined).

Shove added that two of Robinson's cost curves seem to have been taken from Kahn's work. From the standpoint of the distribution of credit, therefore, what was the result? "I don't want to claim more than I have contributed to the common pool, + perhaps I have misunderstood the nature of Kahn's curves. I certainly thought from what he said to me that they were based on the various senses of 'cost' which I distinguish in the passage I have referred to. But perhaps I was mistaken."[116] Although the rhetoric of Shove's letter was polite and reserved, its implications for Robinson's typology were devastating. She had employed four curves. Three of them, Shove claimed, could be found in his article from 1928. Thus her typology disappeared, leaving her with only one curve for which she could claim credit. Although the curves themselves were new to Shove, he regarded this fact as insignificant. He had developed the concepts without drawing the diagrams. Once the concepts were in place and clarified, producing the diagrams was a mechanical and intellectually trivial exercise. Robinson had merely drawn the diagrams, performing a useful but menial piece of scientific labor.

Shove's metaphor of the common pool is quite remote from Schumpeter's. Ideas cast into a Shovian pool are labeled with the names of their contributors, to be used only with appropriate attributions. Ideas cast into a Schumpeterian pool have no names attached; because ideas are not private property, the obligation—or even the practice—of crediting innovators has no place. Thus Shove was hardly a paragon of a putative Cambridge indifference to credit and priority.

Seemingly consumed by worries that Robinson might be gaining control over his unpublished but easily accessible work, Shove read for a second time her response to his request for yes and no answers and wrote her again the next day. "This really shall be the last time," he incautiously apologized. Perhaps there were other areas in which she had drawn on his work. For example, did she, following Shove, assume that factors of production were heterogeneous: some workers are more productive than others, some parcels of land more fertile than others, and so on? Shove wrote, "It would help me very much in thinking how full to make my treatment if you would tell me whether you did this in my way." Again, he ignored a wide range of possible overlaps in their lectures. What mattered was only what she might have taken from him. In spite of repeated queries and what appeared to be decidedly uncollegial insinuations of scientific theft, Shove stressed that he was "most anxious that this business should not cause any misunderstanding between us." In order to arrive at a mutual understanding on "the whole thing" without exchanging long explanations, he suggested they meet at King's for tea and conversation at an early date.[117] But if "this business" extended no further than a comparison of lecture notes, what was the cause for anxiety? In his vague but illuminating reference to "the whole thing," Shove again revealed that his worries were not over pedagogical minutiae. He and Robinson met sometime before December 19. By this point it was clear that his game of questioning a potential intellectual felon who was expected to respond to his interrogatories had become something quite different. Each party was now engaged in a contest with the other, attempting to preemptively establish priority for specific ideas and deprive the opponent of credit. Robinson had developed an analysis of exploitation under conditions of imperfect competition. She apparently knew that Shove had done no significant work on this issue. This was an opportunity to confirm her own originality. She succeeded: He admitted that he had done no work on this subject meriting recognition.[118]

Shove became quiescent for almost six months. However, in June 1932, with the tripos season ending and the long reprieve from lecturing and supervision in sight, he was ready to resume work on his book. Perhaps more important, he had new information from Kahn that Robinson was undertaking an extensive revision of her manuscript. What did her revisions entail for differences between their analyses of diminishing returns on which she had reported in December? Her book would certainly be published before his. If her account now approximated his more closely, his priority on a major theoretical problem would be threatened. Shove returned to the field in a letter of June 9, noting that he was making plans to revise his work on value and distribution. In order to eliminate material that would be covered in her book, he needed an account of her revisions. Although he wanted to know whether she had changed her position on the question of the homogeneity of factors of production, he also raised a much more general consideration: "I am assuming that you have not altered your treatment so as to make it still more like mine either in these matters or as regards the various elaborations I have been putting into my lectures. Is this all right?" (JVR/vii/412/20–21). On this occasion, Shove put the question not in his usual oblique fashion but directly: had Robinson appropriated his work on any of the points covered in his lectures? This letter ended Robinson's season of forbearance. She replied with some asperity, writing Shove twice before he finally responded on June 21. She was not pleased with his suggestion that she would—in language he quoted from one of her replies—"cross-examine young men" who had attended his lectures in order to get ideas for her book. When Shove finally answered, he made a desperate effort at damage control. He began badly, insisting that he was not opposed to Robinson's use of his work "with such acknowledgement as you think suitable." At the same time, he registered a complaint he had harbored for almost a year without mentioning: her failure to inform him during the previous summer that she was writing a manuscript on diminishing returns that was very similar to his ideas, a text intended not only for her lectures but for publication. He pummeled her alternately with an iron fist and a velvet glove: "But that is all past and done with + I did not, + do not, intend to say anymore about it."[119]

Shove found Robinson's silence concerning her invasion of what he clearly regarded as his privileged domain quite galling, "especially after you [Robinson] had Dennis' letter." Was this a letter from Robertson instructing her on proper conduct in such a case? or perhaps informing her of Shove's unhappiness and suggesting how it might be alleviated? Regardless of Shove's view of its contents, the letter did not exist, as he admitted a few days later. It seems there was some conversation between Robinson and Robertson on intersecting research plans at Cambridge.[120] Shove's remark suggests that messages concerning research transmitted between members of the guild were sometimes filtered through hints, innuendos, and fragments of conversation with third persons.

Although Shove denied that he had accused Robinson of using supervisions to appropriate his ideas, his explanation was weak, seeming to confirm that this is precisely what he suspected. Kahn again entered the drama as his source of information about the progress of Robinson's work: "Kahn told me some time ago that he had heard that you were revising your work a good deal + I thought you might be able to tell me, from what you had gathered in the ordinary way in supervision or from [illegible names]'s notes or from the sketch I sent you of my proposed treatment of rent in the individual firm + D[iminishing] R[eturns] whether your revision was along the same lines as my further elaborations."[121] It was not clear to Robinson how she could have drawn any conclusions "in the ordinary way in supervision" without steering her supervisory sessions to Shove's lectures and posing questions to students in order to learn more about his most recent work. In this exchange, Robinson offered to delay publication of her book until Shove's work had appeared. This would allay his concerns over credit by ceding priority to him. Shove responded, "It's very kind and generous of you to offer to postpone publication, but *please* don't. I shall probably never publish + anyhow I should have to keep you back."[122] This does not seem to have been a genuine offer of heroic generosity but rather a pseudo-magnanimous gesture made on the assumption that it would not, and perhaps could not, be accepted.

It is true that Shove did not relish the prospect of seeing Robinson grind his ideas into fertilizer for her publications. His response to *Economics Is a Serious Subject* made this quite clear. When Shove received his copy, he discovered that he had made an appearance in the text. Following Robinson's classification of economists as either optimistic and analytical or pessimistic and methodological, she further distinguished the pessimists as fundamental, methodological, or English—all this without further explanation. English pessimists were said to be pure or logical, and Shove fell under this heading. She even designated him as the leading figure in this group, which "challenged the optimists by proposing new sets of assumptions just too hard for the existing technique and meanwhile, by their own methods, prospects for more complicated techniques adapted to realistic problems" (Robinson 1932a, 12). Shove was not amused. He was irritated to find himself relegated to an inferior status, a subaltern figure in the economic establishment who generated problems but not solutions. As he wrote her on October 19, 1932, "I can't help feeling a little—shall I say hurt at being publicly relegated to the duty of suggesting 'fresh problems' for you to solve" (JVR/vii/412/30–31). However, acceptance of Robinson's offer to defer publication would have been an act of reputational suicide on Shove's part. By mid-1932, it was known in the small research community of the Marshallian guild that she was an ambitious and aggressive scholar, just as it was known that he was not. Shove did not want to discourage Robinson from publishing. But he insisted that she credit him for unpublished work he regarded as his property. In this way, he would achieve quasi-priority through her references to his ideas. Even if he published little, he would still be read in her book as an innovator in the theory of value. Shove understood that in science a claim to credit is a claim to precedence, institutionally determined by priority of publication. He also understood that he would be defeated in a short-term priority contest with Robinson, a race for precedence in publishing a post-Sraffian Cambridge analysis of price theory. But could he win a longer-term contest by imposing restrictions on her book? Could he extract concessions by persuading her to acknowledge use of ideas for which he claimed proprietary rights even though they were not published? If he was successful, he might win priority by proxy.

Although proof of precedence may have been irrelevant to the value of Shove's ideas and the extent to which they were used by other economists, it was decisive in allocating credit.[123] If the number of problems recognized as significant issues in a scientific discipline is smaller than the number of researchers at work on these problems, competition is inevitable. Production of ideas that the scientific establishment certifies as meritorious may be somewhat loosely connected to recognition, reputation, and success in a scientific career. The development of original scientific ideas and the validation of claims to credit for these ideas are independent projects. There seems to be no essential connection between the skills needed to do original thinking in science and those required for success in validating claims to credit for original thinking. Economists like Shove, who are gifted in developing new ideas, might fail miserably in producing accounts of their ideas that establish claims to priority. If Kahn's judgment on Shove was sound—he would not publish a text until it seemed to say precisely what he meant to say—this placed him at a disadvantage to Robinson: a quick thinker, an astute scientific networker, and a nimble writer. The question of whether the originality and depth of her ideas matched his played no role in the validation of claims to credit for these ideas. Shove seems to have grasped an important consequence of these considerations: scientists may do work for which they receive little or no credit.

The vision of the Cambridge economics faculty that emerges from Shove's interrogations of Robinson is not attractive. The Marshallian guild of the Shovian imagination was driven by an obsession over intellectual property rights. Cambridge economists were operators of small-scale intelligence networks that exercised surveillance over colleagues and extracted intellectual resources that could be employed to advantage. It was an intensely competitive little world in which members could be expected to use all means at their disposal to acquire intellectual capital: lectures of colleagues, third-person reports or rumors about the contents of these lectures, and conversations with third persons about other conversations. Students who appeared for supervision might also be useful sources of intelligence for adroit economists who knew how to pose clever questions that would elicit information about new ideas on which their colleagues were lecturing. In order to survive in this world, constant vigilance was called for and a readiness to take measures that might be required to deter theft of intellectual property. The tone of intraguild interactions was thus defined by jealousy, envy, spite, suspicion, anxiety, and mistrust.

The Cambridge Ethos Reconsidered

So much for Schumpeter's metaphor of the common pool. Shove, Kahn, and Robinson, the Cambridge economists working in the area of price theory and imperfect competition, were hardly indifferent to proprietary rights in ideas. The making of *The Economics of Imperfect Competition* offers no support for the view of the guild as a secular knighthood of the grail of science, a collectivity committed to the disinterested pursuit of truth.

In "Science as a Vocation," a classic examination of the cultural significance of scientific and scholarly work, Max Weber distinguishes science as a career from science as a calling. Institutionally, science is grounded in the economic conditions of academic life, the division of labor in university faculties, and the social organization of teaching and research. The institutions of science operate as social selection mechanisms that recruit candidates for scientific work and place some of them in career paths of varying promise and prestige; others it eliminates. Ethically, science is a set of values commitment to which differentiates candidates who have a genuine calling for science from those who, as Weber puts it, "should do something else." Conceived as a vocation, science is defined by the categorical imperatives of the scientific calling: clarity, intellectual integrity, and the project of fashioning the world as a "cosmos of truths" based on empirical and logical reasoning (Weber 1946, 129–56). Science as a vocation is about research. The question of who is credited for a discovery is of no importance. Science as a career is about priority for research. The question of who is credited for a discovery is more important than the discovery itself. To pursue science as a vocation is to live for science. To pursue science as a career is to live off science. The Cambridge Apostles of the early twentieth century wrote as if an unconditional commitment to intellectual integrity and the pursuit of truth for its own sake were ultimate axioms of the higher culture their little society embodied. Lowes Dickinson, Bertrand Russell, Leonard Woolf, and their friends generalized these axioms as a Cambridge ethos. Schumpeter regarded it as a distinctive feature of Cambridge economics. During the years of the inception of *The Economics of Imperfect Competition*, Robinson, her indispensable collaborator Kahn, and her chief irritant, Shove, may have been convinced that as intellectuals they lived exclusively for science. As the above account shows, they also lived off science, using their research and its artifacts to establish proprietary rights over ideas.[124]

Postscript—Kahn and Shove:
Forestalling a Credit Conflict

In September 1934, when Kahn was drafting his article on ideal output, he began to worry over what he perceived as an impending conflict over precedence with Shove. David Champernowne, a student of King's, had discussed with Shove some ideas in this area that he had heard in Kahn's lectures. Following this discussion, Shove sent Kahn a set of notes on the same subject. Instead of reading them, Kahn wrote Keynes: "I find that Gerald has been striving to write something on the question of whether there are too many entrepreneurs. I feel rather dismayed, as I do not want to aggravate his persecution complex, though I felt I had to tell him that in my article I was leading up to the same topic (I have not quite got there yet)." Kahn's letter posed a problem of precedence. If both he and Shove wrote articles for the *Economic Journal* along the same lines and at the same time, his claim to priority would be weakened. However, he did not want to discourage Shove from publishing, especially since "he had obviously got quite thrilled about it."[125] In that event, how could the allocation of credit be managed? Kahn's solution was to share credit with Shove. In an effort to arrange publication of articles on the same questions by himself and Shove—at the time Kahn raised these concerns, neither he nor Shove had submitted or even drafted an article—he suggested to Keynes that both pieces be published as independent contributions in the same issue of the journal. The result would be understood as a case of simultaneous discovery. With Keynes's agreement, he left Shove's notes unread until his article was finished. It appeared in the March issue of the journal (Kahn 1935). He finally read Shove's notes late that month with results he found "rather horrifying." As he reported to Keynes, "There is very little of the latter part of my article which Gerald has not got hold of, and indicated in these notes, and in some respects he has gone far further than I have. In some ways the resemblance between our works is overwhelming."[126]

At this point Kahn's concerns shifted from protecting his credit claims—now guaranteed by publication—to the question of how Shove might receive credit for his article, which remained unwritten. He had advised Shove either to submit the current version of his notes with an addendum stating that they had been written long before Kahn's article was published, or to begin where Kahn's article ended and develop his own position. He also asked Keynes to support this suggestion by offering Shove an editorial invitation for a contribution on ideal output.[127] Kahn's plan assumed that neither he nor Shove was motivated by a pure passion for discovery irrespective of distribution of credit. Neither would anonymously cast his ideas into a Schumpeterian research pool of ideas undifferentiated by their provenance. Kahn's proposal was an arrangement to divide credit. In the end his concerns proved to be misplaced. Shove, it seems, had no plans for an early publication on ideal output. As Kahn wrote Keynes shortly after corresponding with Shove about his notes, the March article had caused no conflict over credit, and an editorial invitation to submit an article was now moot: "I have received an extremely kindly letter from Gerald replying to my comments on his notes. My article has done no harm. If it should provoke him into print, so much the better; but he expresses admiration rather than criticism, and I do not regard it now as important that he should be urged to publish something as I did when I wrote to you about it."[128]

Science and scholarship rest on economic presuppositions. On the whole, as Weber put it, the academic career is based on "plutocratic prerequisites": "It is extremely hazardous for a young scholar without funds to expose himself to the conditions of the academic career. He must be able to endure this condition for at least a number of years without knowing whether he will have the opportunity to move into a position that pays well enough for maintenance" (Weber 1946, 129–30). Robinson was not subject to the economic hazards of becoming a Cambridge economist. She lived an upper-middle-class life in Cambridge. Like the lilies of the field in the Gospels, she did not sow nor did she reap. But in the absence of a regular stipend, how was it possible for her to consume without producing and at the same time write her book? The answer is simple. She married Austin Robinson, who earned the income required for her life as an apprentice academic intellectual and liberally endowed her with the financial resources on which her early success rested. In the Robinsonian domestic polity and economy, three factors were especially important:

(1) As a young member of the Marshallian guild, Austin was a success. He had a stellar record as an undergraduate, moving from one prize and honor to another.[129] In 1916, he was awarded a scholarship in classics by Christ's College. Following two years in the Royal Naval Air Service during the First World War, he placed in the First Class in 1920. On the advice of his supervisor, Fay, and apparently after attending a lecture by Keynes on the economics of the Treaty of the Versailles, he switched to economics and took another First in Part II of the tripos in 1922. He won the Wrenbury scholarship and, on the advice of Keynes, sat for and won the Almeric Paget Studentship. With these credentials and funding to do postgraduate work, he was elected a fellow of Corpus Christi in 1923.

(2) As noted earlier, shortly after their marriage in summer 1926 the Robinsons sailed to India, where Austin had accepted a position as tutor to the ten-year-old maharajah of the State of Gwalior. The appointment seems to have been arranged through personal connections. One of Robinson's friends, Dorothea, was the daughter of Sir Theodore Morison, a former head of Osmania University in India with close contacts among officials of the State of Gwalior. When they approached him for

advice on an appropriate tutor for the maharajah, he interviewed Austin at his daughter's suggestion. It appears that Robinson brokered the appointment, a job for which, as Austin later put it, he received a "tax-free stipend higher than I have ever earned since" (in Cairncross 1993, 20). In India, the Robinsons occupied a villa staffed by fifteen servants, including kitchen help, housekeepers, maids, gardeners, and chauffeurs. Notwithstanding this style of life, Austin was able to save some £100 a month during their years in India. After his return to Cambridge as a fellow of Sydney Sussex College in 1929, he wrote *The Structure of Competitive Industry* (1931), a highly successful book based on his fellowship dissertation. His only other book was *Monopoly* (1941). Robinson doubted it would ever be completed. In early 1933, she wrote Kahn that Austin never mentioned it and suggested that it had "better be quietly forgotten."[130] In Cairncross's judgment, the book, unlike its predecessor, was derivative and appeared too late in the development of research on monopoly to achieve prominence.

On returning to Cambridge, Austin found his true academic vocation, which lay in administration. His "addiction to administration," according to his biographer, was perhaps the most striking feature of his career, and he was a model of a type of British academic that Annan has called "the don as administrator."[131] From May 1930 to February 1934, he was secretary of the faculty board. Pigou, chairman of the board at the time, had a pronounced distaste for administration and delegated many of his duties to Austin. During the 1930s, Austin was also an important contributor to the reform of the Economics Tripos and, at Pigou's request, assumed responsibility for creating and planning the Marshall Library as well as managing its relocation. Austin stepped down as secretary of the board in order to accept Keynes's offer of the assistant editorship of the *Economic Journal*. A letter to Lydia on February 11, 1934, shows that Keynes knew his man: "This afternoon I have been round to Austin Robinson to talk about his being assistant editor of the *Economic Journal*. He jumps at it gladly as I thought he would" (JMK/PP/45/190/5). Austin's responsibilities were to proofread galleys for all issues, serve as book review editor, and write short notes on new books (Robinson 1990, 166). He was compensated for all this work. Austin's letter of appointment from Keynes placed his annual stipend at £225 for the period June 1934 to June 1937 (EAGR/Box 9/2/1/17/73). His income also increased when he consulted on British economic affairs in Africa. In addition to his six-month research contract in 1933, he participated in the massive Africa Survey, produced under the direction of Lord Hailey. His chapter on labor and economic development consumed much of his Cambridge summer vacations in 1934–37.

(3) Although Austin could not be described as a feminist, from the perspective of his times, the academic culture in which he moved, and his position in it, he was a liberal and enlightened husband. Because his academic interests were more bureaucratic than theoretical, he did not compete with his wife for domestic research resources. There seems to have been no professional competitiveness or jealousy. Austin was proud of his wife's work, encouraged her to pursue it, helped her improve it, and disposed of marital assets that gave her the leisure she needed to do it. The table on the next page documents annual lecture loads and compensation figures for the Robinsons in 1930–39. In the years she worked on *The Economics of Imperfect Competition*, Robinson earned little and had no private income from her family. In 1918, her father had been dismissed from the British army during a widely publicized conflict with Prime Minister Lloyd George.[132] Aside from the meager £25 she received for a short course of lectures in Michaelmas 1932, her only source of income was student supervision. However, she had a reputation for insisting on choosing her own pupils. As Austin observed much later, it was not her intention to make a "heavy commitment to doing college teaching" (quoted in Turner 1989, 21).

Without a fellowship or lectureship, Robinson lacked the resources required for scientific production. Robinson had no room of her own in the expansive Virginia Woolfian sense — no control over the production and disposition of the necessities of life at Cambridge. The lease on the flat at 3 Trumpington Street, where she did her writing and which was only a short walk from the university library and the men's colleges, was paid from Austin's salary. His income also covered the wages of a housekeeper who performed chores, prepared meals, and even collected mail and delivered it to Robinson's room. She timed her first pregnancy to minimize interference with research, another decision supported by Austin.[133] After her first daughter was born, a nurse was added to the household staff. Even in later life it was said that Robinson was completely dependent on domestic help.[134] Perhaps these stories are not entirely apocryphal. In February 1933, she wrote Kahn that Robbins, who was visiting

LECTURES DELIVERED BY AUSTIN AND JOAN ROBINSON
AND THEIR RESPECTIVE STIPENDS, 1930–39

ACADEMIC YEAR	AUSTIN	ROBINSON	STIPENDS
1930–31	Economic Structure (M^a, L^b) Power Transport and Localization (M, L) Money, Banking, and International Trade (E^c)	None	Austin, £408 Robinson, 0
1931–32	Economic Structure (M, L) Current Economic Problems (L) Money, Banking, and International Trade (E)	Pure Theory of Monopoly (M) A short course at no pay (E)	Austin, £320 Robinson, £25
1932–33	Economic Structure (L, E) Money, Banking, and International Trade (E)	None	Austin, NA Robinson, None
1933–34	Economic Structure (M, L, E) Elementary Economic Theory (L)	Economics of Imperfect Competition (M, L)	Austin, £286 Robinson, NA
1934–35	Economic Structure (M, L, E) The Coalmining Industry (M, L)	Economics of Imperfect Competition (M) Applications of Monetary Theory (L)	Austin, £290 Robinson, £100
1935–36	Economic Structure (M, L, E) The Coalmining Industry (M, L)	Applications of Monetary Theory (M, L) Some Problems of Economic Theory (E)	Austin, £290 Robinson, £145
1936–37	Economic Structure (M, L, E) The Coalmining Industry (M, L)	Applications of Monetary Theory (M, L) Some Problems of Economic Theory (E)	Austin, £300 Robinson, £160
1937–38	Economic Structure (M, L, E) The Coalmining Industry (M, L)	Applications of Monetary Theory (L, E) Some Problems of Economic Theory (L)	Austin, £337 Robinson, £160
1938–39	Economic Structure (M, L, E) The Coalmining Industry (M, L)	Applications of Monetary Theory (E) Some Problems of Economic Theory (E) Discussion class (E)	Austin, £350 Robinson, £350

[a] M = Michaelmas (autumn), [b] L = Lent (winter), [c] E = Easter (spring)

SOURCES: Compiled from the Minutes of the Meetings of the Faculty Board of Economics and Politics and *Cambridge University Reporter*, various years.

Cambridge to deliver a lecture to the Marshall Society, would spend the night with the Robinsons. But "owing to my excellent Mary [the maid] being ill, we shall have to dine at the Union."[135]

In sum, during the critical years of her apprenticeship and early scientific production, Robinson had no financial responsibilities. She was not obliged to devote her time continuously or even intermittently to gainful employment. Free of the burden of making a living and the toils of housekeeping and child care, she spent much of her day on creative work. After her first child was born, her practice was to write from nine until noon each weekday (Turner 1989, 20), a schedule made possible by the household organization that Austin's income supported. Work during vacations and family holidays was part of her routine. On a family holiday in August 1936, Robinson—mother of a three-year-old child and hostess to relatives and friends—wrote Kahn of her success at maintaining a full work schedule. Perhaps unnecessarily she added, "I find intensive family life quite amusing, but I can see it wouldn't suit me for an occupation."[136] The occupation she chose rested on opportunities and economic underpinnings secured by her husband's position at Cambridge.

Joan Robinson. By permission of The Cambridgeshire Collection, Cambridge Central Library.

Austin Robinson. By permission of The Cambridgeshire Collection, Cambridge Central Library.

Richard Kahn. By permission of The Cambridgeshire Collection, Cambridge Central Library.

Arthur Cecil Pigou. By permission of The Cambridgeshire Collection, Cambridge Central Library.

John Maynard Keynes. By permission of The Cambridgeshire Collection, Cambridge Central Library.

3

†

Becoming a Keynesian

PROTÉGÉ WITHOUT A PATRON

Academic patronage—the investment of personal and institutional prestige, power, and intellectual capital in the career of a protégé—was one of
the methods Cambridge economists used to produce and reproduce the
culture of Marshallian economics. Perhaps it could be said that the guild
began with an act of patronage. Pigou's patron was Marshall himself. The
master of the guild managed the selection of his successor as Professor of
Political Economy by lobbying the electors to support his choice. Pigou,
then only thirty, was chosen over three more experienced men, including
Marshall's old friend H. S. Foxwell, who had a reasonable expectation for
the chair.[1] When Keynes's dissertation on the theory of probability was
rejected for a prize fellowship at King's, Pigou and Marshall cooperated
to arrange his appointment to a lectureship. Keynes in turn was Shove's
patron. His tenacious support for the election of his former student to a
fellowship at King's, notwithstanding a failed dissertation and a modest
record of publication, finally succeeded in 1926.[2]

Patronage lowered barriers of entry to the guild for protégés, endowing them with resources not available to other candidates. It eased the path to lectureships and fellowships for the favored few, at the same time enabling the guild to control access to membership on the basis of close personal acquaintance with aspirants for entry. The acquisition of a patron was more often than not a significant step in advancing the careers of Cambridge theoreticians in residence in 1930. As protégés, Pigou, Keynes, Shove, Sraffa, and Kahn all benefited from the power, generosity, and largesse of savvy patrons. In principle, the patron-protégé relationship could be initiated by either party. Patrons could choose promising students as protégés, or aspirants could make the first move in attempting to attract a patron. In fact, all Cambridge theoreticians of the 1920s who were beneficiaries of patronage had been among the chosen.

In 1930, no Cambridge economist had chosen Robinson as his protégé. Because she was not an attractive investment, she would have to take the initiative. What were her options? In the 1920s, no women had entered the circle of Cambridge theoreticians. Pigou was notorious for his reserve toward women. Although only fifty-three in 1930, he was regarded as being old by the younger fellows. Shove was moody, volatile, and uncertain of his abilities. Sraffa was not a political force on the faculty and by 1931 had withdrawn from lecturing (Marcuzzo 2005). Robertson was attempting to maintain his status as Keynes's most trusted client, a position he would soon lose to Kahn. If patronage requires a sure and confident hand in deploying valuable resources in the interest of a client, it is not surprising that Robinson chose Keynes. Among the senior economists at Cambridge, his skills in the arts of patronage were the most polished and practiced. Shove, Robertson, Sraffa, and Kahn as well as several Cambridge academics who were not economists had been his beneficiaries. However, Robinson faced daunting obstacles. Her early contacts with Keynes as Austin's wife and then as Kahn's special friend were not to her advantage. The first left her invisible.[3] The second represented her as a source of conflict and high risks, a party to a dangerous liaison with the protégé in whom Keynes had invested most and for whom he had the highest expectations. To acquire Keynes as a patron, she would develop new terms of engagement and give him reasons to accept her on these terms. One of her tactics was to define roles for herself that he found congenial and perform them to his satisfaction. Robinson would become the expositor, propagator, and propagandist of the Keynesian revolution, defending the hero of the new science against the slings and arrows of his adversaries and explaining and extending his doctrines. Several incidents gave Robinson opportunities to move in this direction and at the same time to move Keynes, first to qualified support and finally to active patronage. The results she achieved by managing these opportunities were dramatic. However, they were not produced quickly or without careful planning and laborious efforts on her part.[4]

THE HAYEK CONTROVERSY

Robinson's first successful attempt to refashion herself as a protégé of Keynes began in early 1932. The occasion was his controversy with Hayek: the gifted young Viennese economist, recently appointed professor at LSE, and author of a faultlessly civil but devastating review of the *Treatise*, an autopsy in vivo of its logical and conceptual weaknesses.[5] Hayek's attack left Keynes uncharacteristically stunned, bewildered, and resentful. Robinson was able to use the Hayek affair in order to make herself serviceable to Keynes in a matter to which he ascribed considerable importance. After her interventions on his behalf, he had reason to see her as one of the brighter young Cambridge economists whose services he might employ to good advantage. Robinson courted Keynes by volunteering to translate and refine the ideas he called his intuitions into theoretical models that could be expected to sustain criticism without suffering undue damage. Because the Hayek controversy proved to be a critical rite of passage in her efforts to acquire Keynes's patronage, some observations on Hayek's critique and Keynes's response are in order.

In his lengthy review, published in two parts in *Economica* (1931b, 1932), Hayek tossed Keynes bland compliments as he dismantled the underpinnings of the *Treatise* and cut its main ideas to shreds. He began with a telling observation: "The appearance of any work by Mr. J. M. Keynes must always be a matter of importance: and the publication of the *Treatise on Money* has long been awaited with intent interest by all economists" (Hayek 1931b, 270). Keynes had indeed announced publication of his theory of money with considerable fanfare. Seven years in the making, it was his first systematic effort at economic theory, a book that could be expected to establish his reputation as a grand theorist. It was not to be. The work was bound to disappoint, Hayek claimed, because the unfinished and experimental quality of the exposition made it painfully obvious that

Keynes's new line of analysis—based on the premise that the main problem of monetary theory was the rate of interest and its relation to saving and investment—was also new to him. The *Treatise* bore all too clearly the marks of a first draft, an initial attempt to integrate the analytical methods entailed by this premise into the traditional conceptual apparatus of Cambridge economics (Hayek 1931b, 270). However, what was new to Keynes was well-trodden ground to continental economists, who had been thoroughly trained in the works of Knut Wicksell and Eugen Böhm-Bawerk, the chief architects of the methodological strategy that he had recently and unwittingly rediscovered. Keynes assumed the improbable guise of the muddled pedant Mr. Casaubon in George Eliot's *Middlemarch*: vainly ambitious, self-important, and hopelessly confused, he labored for years and wrote at great length on problems that had been solved long before by continental scholars whose work he had either failed to read or misunderstood. Hayek pronounced the *Treatise* obscure and unsystematic, not only unfinished but "unintelligible" (Hayek 1931b, 271).

Hayek undermined Keynes's theoretical structure at several significant points. Unaccountably, Keynes's concept of money income did not include the profits of entrepreneurs. He assumed that total profits can increase only if the amount of money in circulation increases. He failed to recognize that output can be increased by changes in relative sectoral profits. His analysis of investment was weak since it included no account of the conditions under which it becomes more or less attractive, and his concept of investment seemed to be intolerably vague, varying from case to case as he moved from one problem to another. He attempted to analyze complex dynamic processes without providing an adequate static foundation. He failed to develop a comparative statics that would specify the requirements for maintaining capital intact or defining equilibrium conditions that obtained at specific savings rates. He appropriated the ideas of other economists, misinterpreted them, and built the misconceived ideas into his own theory. Perhaps most egregiously, he employed Wicksell's theory of interest rates but changed his definition of what the interest rate is. He also seemed to be ignorant of the basis of Wicksell's position in Böhm-Bawerk's theory of capital (Hayek 1931b, 273–80).[6]

In a brief rejoinder to the first part of the review, Keynes attempted to blunt the force of Hayek's criticisms by means of various denials and explanations. The results were not persuasive, betraying uncertainty on Keynes's part over what he had actually written in the *Treatise*. He denied that he subscribed to the view that the amount of money in circulation is the only factor that alters the balance between saving and investment. However, he acknowledged that he might be responsible for this confusion since other economists shared Hayek's impression. Some of Hayek's misinterpretations, he admitted, were a result of ill-formed analyses in the *Treatise*, produced by the circumstances in which the book was written. As he wrote the final two-volume version of the book, his thinking on the theory of money was in flux, a point Hayek had made at the beginning of his review. In the *Treatise*, Keynes finally abandoned his long-standing commitment to the quantity theory of money and embraced a new view. But he was unsure about the exact relation between his old and new positions and not altogether clear concerning which view he had defended (Keynes 1931, 389–90).

Were these concessions damaging? Remarkably, Keynes claimed they were not, although in making this assertion his usual sense of certitude was missing: "I think I can show that most of my alleged terminological inconsistencies are either non-existent or irrelevant to my central theme" (Keynes 1931, 391). This was a lame response. Hayek was not chiefly interested in terminological niceties. He argued that many of Keynes's most important positions were mistaken and his analyses of these positions invalid. He also questioned Keynes's standards of intellectual craftsmanship, suggesting that the *Treatise* was a product of shallow thinking and shoddy scholarship. And even if Keynes thought he could finesse Hayek's criticisms with cosmetic rhetorical concessions and debating tactics, what was the point? After all, he contended that Hayek's objections did not depend on questions of terminology at all. They were a consequence of irreconcilable worldviews. This meant that Hayek was "looking for trouble" (Keynes 1931, 388). As Keynes understood their differences, Hayek believed that an increase in voluntary saving would invariably be followed by higher rates of investment unless the banking system intervened with measures that distorted the quantitative equivalence of saving and investment. Keynes, on the other hand, argued that changes in the rate of saving or investment did not depend solely on monetary authorities. Decisions taken by economic actors could change these rates and create an imbalance between the two values. In the *Treatise*, there was no self-regulating mechanism that could reestablish the balance between saving and investment (Keynes 1931, 393).

Hayek addressed the decoupling of saving and investment in a reply to Keynes's rejoinder and also in the second part of his review (Hayek 1931c, 1932). He argued that Keynes's position was based on the peculiar and insupportable assumption that output in both consumption and investment goods sectors remains constant under all conditions. In fact, he claimed, an increase in discretionary or voluntary saving reduces the demand for consumption goods, making that sector less profitable and investment goods relatively more attractive. As a result, entrepreneurs in the consumption goods sector reduce their output, releasing factors of production that are then used to increase the output of investment goods. Keynes's assumption of fixed output in both sectors entailed that the quantity of factors of production in consumption goods remains constant notwithstanding steep declines in profitability. Hayek maintained that on this premise, new investment was impossible in principle. He charged Keynes with circular reasoning: "The most curious fact is that, from the outset, all of Mr Keynes's reasoning which aims at proving that an increase in savings will not lead to an increase in investment is based on the assumption that, in spite of the decrease in the demand for consumption goods, the available output is not reduced; this means, simply, that he assumes from the outset what he wants to prove" (Hayek 1932, 31).

Hayek had drawn blood, and Keynes knew he had been wounded, as his first lecture of the Easter term in 1932 shows. Entitled "Notes on Fundamental Terminology," it was defensive and at some points tart and captious. This was not the standard Keynes, who had a reputation for dazzling brilliance, logical virtuosity, and near invincibility in disputation. Bertrand Russell judged his mind "the sharpest and clearest that I have ever known. When I argued with him, I felt that I took my life in my hands, and I seldom emerged without feeling something of a fool" (Russell 1967, 88). The petulant tone of this first lecture makes sense only if it is read as a veiled rebuke of Hayek, who is not mentioned even though the second part of his review had appeared in February. The lecture considers three main issues: the logical status of theoretical definitions, the importance of precision in framing theories, and the extent to which theorists should anticipate and answer objections that might be raised by obtuse or unreasonable critics.

Keynes's discussion of the first issue was surprisingly perfunctory. After all, he had just been treated quite roughly by a critic whose objections, as Keynes represented them, were based on presumptive logical defects in his theoretical framework. He instructed his audience that if definitions are followed consistently, no set of theoretical concepts is logically preferable to any other. The choice between alternative definitions should be made on purely pragmatic grounds, by considering their utility for theory construction. He did not consider the possibility that a set of theoretical definitions might be internally inconsistent or that a single definition could be self-contradictory. In either case, definitions are incoherent on logical grounds alone and independent of pragmatic considerations. Although Keynes's discussion of the second issue was more extensive, his main point concerned not precision but a principle of scientific ethics that supports a high tolerance for vagueness. All definitions are vague in some respects, and it would be futile to strive for an unattainable ideal of precision. Such an attempt would be self-defeating since the author "may never perhaps reach the matter at hand and the reader certainly will not" (Keynes 1979, 36). He stressed that his method was based on a legitimate expectation of "intelligence and good will" on the part of professional readers of scientific works. Readers could not be taken seriously if they pursued the scientific enterprise in a morally perverse fashion, insisting on criteria for precision that do not apply to relevant theoretical issues and may even be unsatisfiable in principle. The theoretician who did not act on Keynes's expectation would quickly reach a dead end, finding himself compelled to "concoct a legal document which he is prepared to stand by literally and to suffer deprivation of rights if any case or contingency can be discovered for which he has failed to provide strictly and explicitly beforehand" (Keynes 1979, 37). In discussing the third issue, Keynes argued that economic theory is based on moral foundations. Theoretical work is possible only if economists act on a principle of charity that requires readers to follow arguments and understand them as they were intended. In the language of contemporary analytical historiography, economists have an obligation to grasp the illocutionary force of a theory—what the theoretician intended to do in taking the positions articulated in the theory. As Keynes put it, readers have an obligation "to catch the substance, what the writer is at" (Keynes 1979, 37). Self-indulgent quibbling over definitions that are largely arbitrary or an insistence on logical strictures and other purely formal requirements that have no place in economics violates this ethic. This is why it is pointless to anticipate and answer the objections of an irresponsible critic—"someone who has not really followed the argument or taken in the point," the reader "whose mind is really running on another track" (Keynes 1979, 37).

Who was the unnamed target of Keynes's lecture, the critic whose mind was "running on another track"? Who had violated the ethic of charity by withholding the good will required to understand Keynes's ideas on their own terms and as he intended them, thereby failing to grasp the substance of his arguments? It was Hayek, as Keynes made clear in notes he wrote on the first installment of Hayek's review: "Hayek has not read my book with that measure of 'goodwill' which an author is entitled to expect of a reader. Until he can do so, he will not see what I mean or know whether I am right. He evidently has a passion which leads him to pick on me, but I am left wondering what this passion is" (Keynes 1973a, 243).

Robinson saw the Keynes-Hayek controversy as an opportunity to change the basis of her relationship with Keynes. She had read Hayek's review and his exchange with Keynes, and she was in close contact with Kahn, on whose judgment Keynes relied in responding to Hayek.[7] It is reasonable to suppose that she knew Keynes had asked Sraffa to review Hayek's book *Prices and Production* (Hayek 1931a)—a crushing logical attack on its theoretical structure, the very point on which Hayek had hammered Keynes mercilessly (Sraffa 1932). Although Keynes's lectures in 1932 did not begin until April 25, he was discussing them with Kahn as early as February 11 (Moggridge in Keynes 1979, 35). It is likely that Robinson became acquainted with the lectures as he discussed them with Kahn. When Kahn was not on hand in the days immediately before the first lecture, the Robinsons seem to have taken his place. As Keynes noted to Lydia on April 24, "Yesterday I went to tea with Joan and Austin (Kahn is away at Passover) to talk high economics" (JMK/PP/45/190/5).

Thus as Keynes was writing his lectures for the Easter term, Robinson had an insider's perspective on the damage Hayek's review had inflicted. Her essay "A Parable on Saving and Investment"—which she playfully dubbed "Peas and Gold"—was redrafted against this background. An attempt to clarify and support the basic position Keynes had taken against Hayek, it was a résumé of some of the work done by the Circus in 1930–31 and represented her first published effort to establish her credentials as a Keynesian.[8] She was reworking the paper by March 31, 1932, when she asked Kahn for his comments before sending it to Keynes for his approval (RFK/13/90/1/9–10). As another letter to Kahn the same day shows, she was keen to share her examination of the Hayek matter with Keynes: "I have written to him [Keynes] mentioning the peas. I quite agree they must be reboiled before he sees them, but I thought I should open negociations [*sic*]. Also I have offered him the Nightmare for the Club" (RFK/13/90/1/7–8).[9]

Why the urgency to begin negotiations? And what was there to negotiate? Not the possibility of publishing her essay in the *Economic Journal*. Robinson had already decided on *Economica*, where Hayek's review and the Keynes-Hayek exchange had appeared. Could she have been anxious to gain Keynes's agreement to her decision? Hardly. As she wrote Kahn on May 6, "I can't get Miss Lane [typist] till tomorrow so the peas are delayed. I fear I may miss JMK. I will write to *Economica* and ask for space without sending the MS" (RFK/13/90/1/11–12). What about a discussion with Keynes on her exposition and critique of the *Treatise*? This explanation is also ruled out; at this point she intended only to inform him of the essay, not send a copy. Another possibility remains: Robinson's purpose was to transact an informal exchange, offering to perform a service for him, in return for which she would receive something she wanted. What could Robinson give Keynes at this point that he did not have? A more lucid analysis of the relations between changes in demand and prices in the consumer and investment goods industries than his account in the *Treatise*. More important, she would show that in spite of his various blunders, Keynes's views on the fundamental theoretical questions in his dispute with Hayek were sound. What did Robinson want from Keynes? Most immediately, acceptance of her offer to read a paper at his Monday Night Club. At this point in her development as an economist, when she was an occasional supervisor and lecturer with no scientific credentials, the Monday Night Club was an ideal forum for her work. Keynes selected speakers for this informal seminar, which met in his rooms at King's. Presentation of a paper was a mark of prestige at Cambridge. Although there is no reason to suspect that he intended such a move, acceptance of her offer would be tantamount to use of his power in breaking a barrier to her entry into this all-male gathering of the guild, where members established their credentials and gained recognition of their status. A chance to read her work in this setting would give Robinson a first public opportunity to demonstrate her theoretical strengths to Keynes in the company of other members of the economics faculty and a select audience of brighter undergraduates. Prima facie this speculation may seem improbable, not least because it presumes a rather crude quid pro quo tactical calculation on Robinson's part. However, it is the only explanation of her remark to Kahn on negotiations that is consistent with the facts; it is reasonable given her efforts to gain access to Keynes at this time; and, as the following account shows, it conforms to her career management program between 1932 and 1938: to achieve success at Cambridge by succeeding with Keynes.

By April 6, Robinson had Kahn's notes. Three days later she was assessing the paper in light of his comments: "Thanks so much for saving me from my headlong errors. But except for profits on gold I am prepared to defend myself. We must leave the other points until you come up [to Cambridge]. Meanwhile I will send this to JMK" (RFK/13/90/1/17–18). The same day, she sent the paper to Keynes with the following note:

> I hope you will like my green peas. If you have any suggestions perhaps you could send this back with notes. If not send me a post card saying O.K. and I will send another copy which I have by me to *Economica*.
>
> The argument is a bit thin in places as I have tried to make it extremely simple. In its present form I don't think it could stand up to cross examination by hostile counsel. But I didn't want to sacrifice the clarity of the outline by guarding myself at all points against crabbed objections. It's intended for people who don't know what to think, not for the ones who have their own answer for everything. (In Keynes 1973a, 268–69)

In the article, Robinson called her ideal reader the "ordinary muddle-headed reader of economics," to whom she addressed one central point in the controversy between Keynes and Hayek. Hayek maintained that increased voluntary saving necessarily led to increased investment. Keynes held that there was no mechanism that brought these two values to equality. Which position was correct? Robinson proposed to prove that notwithstanding Keynes's error of assuming that the total quantity of output in the consumption and capital goods industries was fixed, he was right on the essential issue of the dispute.

Suppose that voluntary saving increases, thereby reducing the demand for consumption goods. Suppose also that there is no hoarding, in which case additional savings cannot remain idle. Based on the discussions of the Circus, Robinson attempted to explain Keynes's argument in her parable of peas, or consumption goods, and gold, investment goods. Because consumption goods can be stored only briefly, their inventories are small. Increased demand for peas will quickly exhaust inventories and increase prices; in a period of declining demand, prices will drop because entrepreneurs cannot maintain larger inventories of peas. The capital goods industry follows a different economic logic. Compared to current output, inventories of gold are large. The pivotal role in the market is played by speculators, not producers. Suppose that voluntary saving increases and the demand for peas drops. In that case, the demand for securities—investment goods, or titles to the existing stock of gold—will increase. Given the absence of hoarding, if economic actors are not buying consumption goods, they must be buying investment goods. On Keynes's assumption that entrepreneurs in the consumption goods sector continue to produce the same level of output, they will begin to sell their inventories of gold to cover their losses. In that event, the increased demand for investment goods will be met by a larger supply of gold from existing inventories. What follows from these considerations is that neither the price nor the output of investment goods can be expected to increase.

On one point Robinson agreed with Hayek. In the face of losses, it was unrealistic to assume that the output of peas would remain constant. This is why the "simple minded reader" of the *Treatise* found it difficult to imagine "an acute slump with full employment, and a trade boom without any increase in output" (Robinson 1933a, 84). However, introduction of realistic premises into Keynes's arguments did not affect his conclusions. Faced with losses, producers of peas would lay off workers and reduce output rather than sell gold. At that point, unemployed workers would have two options. They might draw on their savings, expenditures that would offset the increased voluntary saving that initiated the process of unemployment. Or they might go on the dole, financed by a government issuing additional securities. In neither case would greater saving increase investment.

What did Keynes make of all this? As he wrote Robinson on April 14, the paper was excellent. Although he suggested minor revisions to some of her arguments and noted that she had perhaps treated him a bit roughly over the assumption of constant output, he speculated that readers would find her parable helpful in understanding the *Treatise* and the issues at stake in his dispute with Hayek. He was especially pleased by the fact that she had made a case for the main lines of his analysis: "My own general reaction to criticisms always is that of course my treatment is obscure and sometimes inaccurate, and always incomplete, since I was tackling completely unfamiliar ground, and had not got my own mind by any means clear on all sorts of points. But the real point is not whether all this is so, as of course it is, but whether this sort of way of thinking and arguing about the subject is right. And that is what I am grateful to you for defending and expounding" (Keynes 1973a, 270). Keynes did not grasp the importance of Robinson's major tactical initiative: the attempt to recruit allies among undecided or confused readers and people who did not know what to think. Keynes was intent on persuading his adversaries, who were generally established economists. Robinson was convinced that success depended on converting the uninitiated.

THE MANIFESTO OF THE TRUMPINGTON STREET SCHOOL

Although "A Parable on Saving and Investment" put Robinson on Keynes's map of Cambridge economists, it was not a piece of original thinking. Borrowing heavily from the work of the Circus as well as from Kahn's article "The Relation of Home Investment to Unemployment" (1931), its derivative character could hardly have escaped his notice. In spring 1932, *The Economics of Imperfect Competition* was still an incomplete manuscript. Even if the book were finished, there is no reason to suppose it would have made Robinson more appealing to Keynes. As editor, he published articles on imperfect competition in the *Economic Journal* because the idea had stimulated new theoretical work, not least at Cambridge. But as Robinson observed many years later, he did not take an active interest in this new research program (Robinson 1979, 5). She could expect to engage his attention only by moving into an area that attracted him—research that promised contributions to his current thinking. Although she would continue to work on her book for another year, Keynes's Easter term lectures in 1932 provided an occasion for this sort of reorientation on her part—an opportunity to present herself as a junior colleague he would find useful, someone who not only grasped his theoretical intuitions but was prepared to recast them in the technical language of economic analysis.

After his first lecture on April 25, Keynes wrote Lydia that Kahn, the Robinsons, and Sraffa had been on hand "to spy on me" (JMK/PP/45/190/5). Although he was pleased with this lecture, his second effort on May 2 left him annoyed and vexed with himself. Writing Lydia again: "I've moved into a cycle today; stammered at my lecture and gave a bad one (as Kahn agreed)" (JMK/PP/45/190/5). Why was Keynes displeased? In his second lecture, he attempted to construct a proof that an increase in investment also increases output. This correlation became an important step in the evolution of his thinking about the relationship between aggregate demand and employment, a central theme of *The General Theory*. But the proof was unsatisfactory. He was able to make only an empirical case that investment, output, and employment move in the same direction. A logically tight demonstration was beyond his reach, and in the lecture he made a point of considering exceptions that show they can move in opposite directions (Keynes 1979,41). Following this exposition, he challenged his audience to find other exceptions he might have overlooked. Kahn and the Robinsons took up this challenge with much enthusiasm and ingenuity. The result was "The Manifesto of the Trumpington Street School." This text responded to Keynes's charge by identifying counterexamples to his position that had escaped him. It also pursued a more ambitious course by reconstructing the logic on which the lecture of May 2 was based. The manifesto argued that although Keynes's conclusions were sound, his "method of formal logic" was unduly restrictive, and his proof was fallacious. Although Kahn, Austin, and Robinson all signed the manifesto, she assumed the role of correspondent with Keynes. This is not surprising in light of her interest in beginning a serious theoretical conversation in order to establish her credentials with him. The details of their exchanges need not be considered here (see Aslanbeigui and Oakes 2002). Their ceremonial qualities are significant in documenting the modest success she achieved in reducing the distance between them.

Robinson's exchange with Keynes over "A Parable on Saving and Investment" was essentially a petition for his endorsement followed by a gracious reply on his part. The manifesto gave her more proximate access for a brief but intensive dialogue that took place in early May. As correspondence shows, she used the manifesto to propose face-to-face conversations. After receiving his reply to the text, she apologized for its lack of clarity and added, "Could we have another word, perhaps during the weekend?" Among other matters, she hoped to persuade him that he had misunderstood his own argument in the second lecture: "I will leave that point in the hope of seeing you and having it out by word of mouth" (in Keynes 1979, 47).[10] In attempting to show Keynes that she could work on his level, Robinson experienced difficulties in self-presentation that became especially pronounced when she took issue with his views. In criticizing his thinking, she became tentative, apologetic, self-deprecatory, and deferential. In early May, she asked, "Please why are you allowed to talk about prime cost but we are not allowed to talk about short period supply price?"[11] In an undated letter in early May, she asked Keynes to forgive her if she seemed "pig-headed."[12] On May 10, she apologized for her "rough manners in controversy."[13] Finally on May 11, she felt "very much ashamed" that she had failed to spell out in exact detail the differences between the methodological strategies of the manifesto and Keynes's second lecture, a matter that he could presumably be left to resolve without instructions on her part. She closed "with apologies" (quoted in Keynes 1973a, 379).

In corresponding with Keynes, Robinson was trying to demonstrate her competence in an area of theoretical analysis that was important to him. However, she was uneasy about how to conduct herself. Did she have good grounds for uneasiness? If he took umbrage at her manners, she risked losing the ideal patron, who had much to offer or withhold. Robinson had good reasons to be apprehensive over engaging Keynes in debate. Although she was determined to prove her merits, she seems to have had little grasp of Keynes's conception of the etiquette appropriate to scientific controversy. Prior to publication of *The General Theory*, Keynesian scientific controversy was not primarily a contest in which dominance was demonstrated by destroying the position of an opponent. Although a serious theoretical exchange called for unsparing criticism, it was restrained by a highly refined civility that ruled out ad hominem attacks as vulgar and intellectually shallow. These standards were not idiosyncratically Keynesian. They were the norms of intellectual exchange that prevailed in the Society of the Apostles when he was an undergraduate and a young fellow of King's. As noted above, they were also the norms of the Marshallian guild. An etiquette that ritualizes a sphere of conduct also creates possibilities of transgressions within that sphere—violations that span the space between poor taste or bad form at one extreme and ceremonial profanations at the other. Was Robinson guilty of unintended lapses from the required ceremonial idiom? Had she perhaps committed acts of "ritual contempt" (Goffman 1956, 493–95), insulting Keynes and profaning the guild at the same time? She did not know, which was the source of her worries. Troubled by her ignorance, she feared she had carelessly stigmatized herself by failing to demonstrate the expected proprieties in debate. Thus her apologies for any unwitting infractions she might have committed. Robinson's role as rapporteur for the Trumpington Street School shows that her socialization as a Cambridge economist was deficient. Her exchanges with Keynes on the manifesto formed a chapter in her apprenticeship, an opportunity to acquire both intellectual and social skills.

Although the manifesto gave Robinson new access to Keynes, it seems that their exchanges brought her no closer to him. The manifesto was a collaboration. Keynes's letter of May 8 to Lydia is a telling indication of his judgment on her status in the Trumpington Street School: "Oh! I'm so tired—I've been arguing nearly all day on a theoretical-didactical point with Kahn and then with Kahn and his Joan. However we came to an amicable conclusion in the end" (JMK/PP/45/190/5). In Keynes's phrase, "his Joan" was not an independent thinker but Kahn's trinket and at best an emissary. Had he believed that she met his standards, no protracted discussions with Kahn would have been called for. And when Keynes did talk with Robinson, Kahn was on hand as well. In spring 1932, Keynes's view of Robinson was largely determined by his worries over her relationship with Kahn. Any move on his part that suggested encouragement of her efforts to establish herself at Cambridge was out of the question at this point.

THE SECTARIAN

With "A Parable on Saving and Investment," Robinson began her long career as an advocate of Keynes's ideas. As a supervisor, she was also a committed Keynesian—passionate, obstinate, and with a pronounced tendency to dogmatism. From the beginning, her conduct in this regard was an occasion for remark at Cambridge. As early as October 16, 1932, Tappan-Holland chided Robinson for her methods in supervising first-year students. Robinson, it seems, introduced freshmen to economics by employing Keynes's post-*Treatise* ideas as the theoretical basis of the science, arguing that this was the only acceptable alternative to feeding them "spoonfuls of the stuff in the books" (JVR/vii/208/12). Tappan-Holland reminded her that this practice contravened a ruling of the faculty board: serious study of economic principles should not begin until the second year. Robinson's supervisory approach also penalized weaker students—many of whom, Tappan-Holland claimed, were "well below the average of ability"—by compelling them to struggle with theory too early in their curriculum.[14] Finally, Keynes's most recent lectures on monetary theory were hardly the only alternative to teaching from textbooks. These objections did not move Robinson. Her pedagogical strategy was to teach the "freshers" Keynes's new ideas as if they constituted an exhaustive conception of the discipline, and to do so before they were exposed to alternative positions. Her objective was to ground economics in Keynesian thinking, making it difficult for students to distinguish economic theory from Keynesian theory. If her methods were successful, students would be able to understand alternative views only by translating them into Keynesian language. Robinson had no interest in weaker students. The future of economic theory and policy would be decided by students reading for the tripos. Her aim was to ensure that they believed in the new ideas.

Tappan-Holland was also unhappy with Robinson's assumption that Keynes's post-*Treatise* thinking constituted a "self-consistent system based on common sense." His ideas were new, largely untested, and a matter of controversy even at Cambridge. They were also in flux, with Keynes "constantly rebutting his own views and making new excursions." Under these circumstances, it was rash to suppose that his current work was systematic or internally consistent. Thus Tappan-Holland found Robinson's confident display of certitude misplaced. It was especially objectionable in propagating a "gospel view of economics." Robinson seemed to think that there was a single body of economic truth and a one-to-one correspondence between this system and economic reality. Keynes's recent lectures had the status of sacred texts. Any deviation from his position was not only mistaken but heretical. And who was the Messiah proclaiming the new gospel? Tappan-Holland had the impression that it was none other than Robinson herself, whom she compared to Robbins as "one awful example of the result of despising what has gone before and taking upon oneself the role of Messiah."[15]

Keynes saw his Cambridge lectures as instrumental, transitional performances. Their purpose was to solidify and clarify his thinking, providing material for discussion that would lead to better ideas. As he explained to Robinson, the real point was not whether he was right about details—he knew he was not—but whether his "way of thinking and arguing about the subject" was sound (Keynes 1973a, 270). However, Tappan-Holland seems to have been correct in thinking that Robinson treated his recent lectures as established theoretical wisdom. In January 1933, some three months after Tappan-Holland's admonitions, Robinson was considering how to incorporate into her book Keynes's arguments that there is no self-adjusting economic mechanism that reestablishes states of equilibrium at which labor is fully employed. By this point, he had concluded that even in a conceptually ideal state of competition, employment is a function of saving and investment. Should she cite the proto-*General Theory* as the source of this idea? She thought not. It would not be a good tactical move, as she wrote Kahn on January 18, 1933: "Ought I to mention J.M.K.? I think myself that it is smarter to regard it as the accepted theory" (RFK/13/90/1/57–58). Kahn agreed: "The right touch is attained by not mentioning J.M.K."[16] The relevant text in *The Economics of Imperfect Competition* includes no reference to Keynes. It states his speculative theoretical views as if they were facts: "It is not our present purpose to discuss how equilibrium would be attained. There is no natural tendency even under competition to maintain full employment, which depends upon the levels of saving and investment" (Robinson 1933d, 310).

Tappan-Holland was mistaken in thinking that Robinson had anointed herself the Messiah of the new gospel. Although she may have taken a messianic view of economics, in her eschatology the Anointed One was Keynes. Cambridge insiders characterized the local response to his new ideas in evangelical metaphors—some playfully, others with ominous seriousness. His new thinking was a gospel. Economists who were convinced that he had superseded the old dispensation of Marshallian thought had seen the light. Those who were not convinced remained children of darkness (Robinson 1947, 56–57; see also Robinson 1985). In this quasi-biblical interpretation of post-*Treatise* developments at Cambridge, Robinson played two roles. Like John the Baptist, she proclaimed the coming of the Messiah: the Word was indeed made flesh and dwelt among Cambridge economists in his rooms at King's. And like the Apostle Paul, she propagated the teachings of the Messiah to the uninitiated.

Although Robinson's response to Tappan-Holland is not known, it undoubtedly magnified her worries over Robinson's use of supervisory sessions as opportunities for proselytizing. Tappan-Holland also found Robinson's self-confessed zealotry quite troubling. She was "very much concerned that you shouldn't 'seriously' become the 'fanatic' you so lightly label yourself." She defended the guild etiquette of controversy as a frank but civil airing of views against the position she ascribed to Robinson— controversy as a struggle between a new and an old dispensation, the forces of light and the forces of darkness. She also switched metaphors, exchanging the rhetoric of salvation religion for that of armed combat: "Do the more recent developments of Cambridge economics require flag-waving or battle cries for those who are responsible for them to be assigned the role of gladiators?"[17] In October 1932, Tappan-Holland saw Robinson as a sectarian warrior, mounting the barricades or suiting up for a struggle to the death. More than three years before Keynes published *The General Theory*, she was identified as an intransigent propagandist for his ideas at a time when it was not clear even to Keynes himself precisely what these ideas were. What was his response to her enthusiasm for his work?

THE MACMILLAN REVIEW

In late October 1932, Robinson handed the manuscript of her book to Harold Macmillan, the Conservative MP and head of the family publishing house. Pigou seems to have been the source of the recommendation that she submit her book to Macmillan. As she wrote Austin on October 4, "The Prof via Kahn strongly advised me to offer my book to Macmillan. I will talk to Maynard about it" (EAGR/Box 8/1/13/117–19). Macmillan was Keynes's publisher, and on November 16 he asked Keynes for an opinion, albeit with some reluctance since he had doubts about the importance of the work. However, Macmillan had his reasons for publishing Robinson's book: General Maurice, her father, was a friend of the Macmillan family (JVR/vii/298).

In November, Keynes wrote an oddly dismissive endorsement of the manuscript. His recommendation—"I have no doubt that you ought to accept this book"—was followed by numerous caveats and qualifications. Keynes seemed to damn the book with the faintest of praise. Although he acknowledged that Robinson had made significant contributions to the theory of value, he was silent about what they were. The book included material that was "more or less new." But in the main it was a derivative and summary account of ideas that had been developed by other economists, work that by that point was "widely current not only for learned articles but in oral discussion at Cambridge and Oxford" (Keynes 1983, 866). Robinson had read the recent literature on the theory of value, listened to what her colleagues at Cambridge and Oxford were saying, and written a compendious exposition of these developments. This was her chief contribution. Because of the clarity of Robinson's writing, Keynes found the book easier to read than much of the literature on imperfect competition. Yet he admitted that he had not undertaken a critical assessment, a task which he claimed would be formidable. Why did he think he was justified in sparing himself this responsibility, which would seem indispensable in rendering an informed opinion? It was because Kahn had already performed it. As Robinson noted in her preface, Kahn had given her detailed and comprehensive criticism. Because of his contribution, Keynes was confident that the book would be reasonably free of errors. His review was a spirited encomium to "the most careful and accurate of all the younger economists" and "a long way the ablest and most reliable critic of this type of work now to be found" (Keynes 1983, 867). Robinson largely disappeared from his report. Had she not enjoyed Kahn's services as critic and editor or had his contribution been more peripheral, Keynes's confidence in the quality of the book would have been much diminished. This was not the strongest endorsement of its author. Keynes closed with a backhanded recommendation: "If, therefore, you are predisposed to accept the book through your old-established relations with the Maurice family, I think you should certainly not hesitate to accept this, which is a serious and valuable work" (Keynes 1983, 867).[18] If Macmillan had an interest in publishing the book based on the extrascientific motive of old family ties, Keynes assured him there were no grounds for worry over its quality, which Kahn had guaranteed. This conclusion twisted the knife. If the book was a genuinely "serious and valuable work," why base a recommendation on nepotistic connections between families of the British upper classes? In this manner Robinson's manuscript appeared between the covers of a book.[19]

In November 1932, Keynes represented Robinson as a clever textbook writer with a gift for exposition and synthesis, but not a thinker of the first class with important original ideas. The use he could make of her or the value she might have for his projects was not yet clear to him. Until he discovered these virtues, she would remain an anxious, determined petitioner for his attentions.

CREATING ACCESS

Between 1932 and 1935, Robinson's identity was transformed several times in Keynes's imagination: from the wife of a junior fellow and Kahn's inamorata to a competent if not brilliant Cambridge economist, and finally to a theoretical confidante on whose judgment he depended. Was there a point at which the terms of engagement that governed Robinson's relationship with Keynes took a pronounced turn, even if this occurred with reservations on his part? If so, when did this change take place? And what was the microsocial dynamic—the pattern of interpersonal and collegial interaction—that intersected with a shift in relations? Although the literature on Cambridge economics in the 1930s considers the first issue, it seems that the second and more interesting question has not been addressed.

Cristina Marcuzzo has considered the relations between Keynes and Robinson in the early 1930s—her participation in the Circus, their exchanges on the manifesto, his response to her early essays, and his report to Macmillan. She concludes that by spring 1932 they had developed a "warm relationship" (Marcuzzo 2003, 551). Are these episodes evidence of personal warmth on Keynes's part? Although Robinson was a member of the Circus, it is not clear what she contributed to its work.[20] When the Circus began to meet in autumn 1930, she was still a relative novice in economics. She had attended Sraffa's lectures and had begun work on imperfect competition but had made no serious study of other areas of economics since her undergraduate years. As her correspondence with Kahn shows, the *Treatise* was largely terra incognita to her until four years later, when she read the book carefully during the summer vacation of 1934. Under these circumstances, it is not apparent what she could have brought to an original analysis of a new, massive, and confusing book on monetary theory. Nor is there reason to suppose that Keynes credited her with any of the ideas generated by the Circus. We have considered Keynes's reaction to Robinson's work on the manifesto and his bland, equivocal report on her book. It is true he responded with enthusiasm to her two articles. In the case of "A Parable on Saving and Investment," her critique of Hayek, this was to be expected. The paper was an attempt to strengthen Keynes's position in a contest he seemed to be losing badly. Although "Imperfect Competition and Falling Supply Price" may have been a "most beautiful and lucid" essay, it was quite remote from his interests.[21] There is no evidence that his response to these articles demonstrated personal engagement or even a disposition to engage in theoretical dialogue.

As the above account shows, there was no close relationship between Keynes and Robinson in 1932. In view of his worries over her friendship with Kahn, there could not have been. Did he ever form a personal relationship with Robinson? It seems that Keynes did not allow their relationship to extend beyond joint scientific and professional interests. Above all it revolved around research—chiefly his own, which in some fashion or other was the subject of most of their correspondence. Robinson did not share the details of her life with Keynes. In her letters to him, there are no observations about family, vacations, entertainment, ambitions, or political views; no gossip about colleagues; no candid judgments about any extrascientific or nonacademic matters; no accounts of her emotional life—none of the personalia that filled her letters to Kahn and that she generally shared with friends. When she notified him of her first pregnancy in March 1934, she delivered the news in a cool and nonchalant fashion in a letter chiefly concerned with her lectures for the following year. She briefly mentioned that she was about to "produce" a baby, as if she were contemplating a new industrial enterprise.[22] Since she sought his approval, she delivered this news with some trepidation. Keynes did not reply. In view of these considerations, it seems more promising to analyze how the relationship between Keynes and Robinson actually developed. Robinson became a client of Keynes in the course of the 1930s. How was the tie between client and patron formed? Here the issue is not a hypothetical transformation from casual acquaintanceship to some version of intimacy but a change in Robinson's social status.

If there was a defining moment that marked Robinson's arrival in the Keynesian social firmament, it came not in spring 1932 but some three years later, in June 1935, when Keynes asked her to comment on the galleys of *The General Theory.* Yet Robinson had carefully laid the groundwork for this event in more than three years of effort to change his conception of her as an economist and reduce the socioprofessional distance between them. In 1932–34, expertise in Keynes's post-*Treatise* thinking was a very scarce commodity. Robinson trained herself in the new ideas and created and exploited opportunities to gain access to Keynes. Professional expertise and personal access were interdependent. Discussions with Keynes would give her insight into the development of his ideas, which were evolving rapidly. And a more sophisticated understanding of his thinking would improve her chances of access. These efforts were designed to convince Keynes that she was a valuable asset, ensuring that when he was finally ready to call on her, he would not be disappointed.

The distance Robinson had to traverse is nicely illustrated by two accounts of conversation over tea with Keynes at 3 Trumpington Street on January 23, 1933, while Kahn was in the United States. As Robinson wrote

Kahn, he "wanted to hear all about you, who you had met + so forth." A title for her book was also discussed. Keynes was not happy with her original choice. Austin proposed "The Economics of Imperfect Competition." Although this suggestion made little sense to Robinson, she acquiesced. Her preference was to retain the original title, "but Maynard won't let me."[23] Since the title was decided that afternoon, it was presumably an occasion of some significance for Robinson. What was Keynes's account of the same event? Why was he visiting the Robinsons? As he wrote Lydia, to "hear news of Kahn," who was then in Chicago and had had "a good success in Cincinnati where he read a paper to assembled economists" (JMK/PP/45/190/4). Robinson's success in finishing her book and their selection of its title were not mentioned.[24]

Robinson had an acute sense of the distance between herself and Keynes. She was also quite savvy at taking advantage of opportunities to reduce it by changing the tenor of their relationship. On occasion this called for measures to arrange an audience with Keynes that otherwise would not have taken place. Consider the brief furor over Shove's note on her article "Imperfect Competition and Falling Supply Price" (1932b). In part, this article was a critique of Shove's views. On February 15, 1933, an excited Robinson reported to Kahn that Shove had written a note for the *Economic Journal* (1933b) in response to her essay and had sent her the substance of his comments the previous day. Not disposed to place her teaching obligations above the imperatives of publication, she turned her "pupils from the door + told them to come another day" in order to compose a quick reply. She described her predicament to Kahn:

> I had a hectic day yesterday. Gerald sent me the proof of his note (except for the constructive suggestions at the end) by the first post. I rang up Maynard and asked if I was to reply. He said No, the E[conomic] J[ournal] was all standing in page champing its bit waiting for Gerald, was anyway too long already. Then he rang up again + said if I would decide there and then to do no more + no less than one page he would wire + keep a page for me. So I rashly agreed. You can imagine the horror of trying to reply to Gerald in 400 words + no time. You will see the prints of all this in the E[conomic] J[ournal]. I hope I haven't dropped any bricks. (RFK/13/90/1/119–22)

After she had written her one page, it was quickly typeset, and the galley was sent to Shove. On Sunday at 6:30, while Robinson was entertaining her "grand grown up relations"—a dinner party for her father and an aunt and uncle from India—Keynes telephoned. A bizarre episode ensued. Shove was in Keynes's rooms claiming that Robinson's reply misrepresented his note, and he insisted on writing an additional note to this effect. Although Keynes agreed with Robinson that Shove's conduct was "frightfully tiresome," a lengthy argument on the telephone between Robinson and Shove followed, punctuated on her end by questions from the dinner guests. Keynes finally cut in, reminding both authors that as editor he needed to know what to publish in the journal. Unable to reach agreement on the phone, she abandoned her guests and repaired to Keynes's rooms, where the three would decide what steps to take. On her arrival, arguments with Shove continued. In the end, as she wrote Kahn, "I had to sit in a corner + draft my version while G + M chattered away—and Gerald complains of the nervous strain."[25]

The flippant pose Robinson struck for Kahn in ridiculing "poor old Gerald, who takes it all so much to heart when it only makes me laugh," was not a position she could afford to act on.[26] In writing a reply to her article, Shove gave Robinson opportunities she would not otherwise have enjoyed. She used them cleverly. His response to her article increased its value by demonstrating that it merited comment from a senior member of the guild. As a result, she could exercise her right to respond and exhibit her skills at intellectual combat in print, gaining further exposure in the journal. In appealing to Keynes, Shove made it necessary for him to discuss the matter with Robinson, unwittingly giving her the proximity she hoped to achieve. His use of Keynes's willingness to intercede on his behalf made it possible for Robinson to gain an audience with Keynes, moving her, at least for the moment, from the periphery to the center of his attention. This was an opportunity for her to give a performance demonstrating the qualities he valued in an interlocutor: intellectual acuity and agility, candor and determination in controversy, and the ability and willingness to grasp adversarial positions as their authors intended them to be understood. Robinson seems to have understood all this quite well. As she wrote Kahn, "I think Gerald has made a fool of me, but it is all in a good cause." At the discussion in Keynes's rooms, she made concessions to Shove in the interest of maintaining comity. This gave the more obstreperous Shove certain advantages. In Robinson's view, her conciliatory position was a prudent move. It was "a triumph to have drawn him [Shove] into print at all." And she thought the incident moved her closer to Keynes, who was "an angel [calming] Gerald to prevent him from getting hysterical, + and telling me that anyway I ought to be pleased to get so much 'reaction' to my article."[27]

On February 18, Robinson used the occasion of the delivery of her reply to Shove to meet with Keynes again. Why meet? There were no further problems to resolve and her four-hundred-word note could easily have been posted. As an aspiring client, Robinson had few opportunities for face-to-face contact with Keynes. Their conversations were infrequent, significant events during which she could present herself as a promising theoretician and also learn in some detail exactly what problems Keynes was working on, how he understood them, and the difficulties he confronted. From this latter perspective, a meeting with Keynes was a fact-finding expedition, an opportunity to gather information on his research with a view to making herself useful. If he could be convinced that she could help solve his problems, he might begin to see her as a potentially valuable asset. The functions of face-to-face meetings as fact-finding missions and opportunities for self-presentation were linked. By using her meetings with Keynes as tutorials on his research, she could reorient her work in the same direction, making his problems her problems. This was the method she had used in writing "A Parable on Saving and Investment" during his controversy with Hayek. If she could persuade him of her value, her chances of representing herself as an attractive investment would be substantially improved. In the conversation of February 18, Robinson's intelligence-gathering tactic worked reasonably well. As she reported to Kahn, "Maynard has been trying to find out what the marginal productivity of capital means. He says no reputable writer ever uses it. But he hasn't made much progress with defining it as far as I can make out from his conversation." Once Robinson had this information, she apparently could make little use of it. Keynes showed no inclination to share his work with her, much less ask for her help in advancing it.[28] In view of Robinson's modest professional qualifications, she was in no position to propose herself as his critic or muse, a point Kahn impressed on her. But if he made an offer, he urged her to accept it: "If Maynard hints that he would like you to look at his stuff I do wish you would. I must confess I am a bit appalled at the prospect of having the sole responsibility thrust on to me after my return."[29]

In spite of Keynes's indifference to her attentions, Robinson continued to pursue opportunities that might enable her to prove herself as a disciple worthy of the master. On February 24, 1933, Robbins gave a lecture to the Marshall Society entitled "Some Addenda to the Cost Controversy." Shove and Sraffa, two of the 1930 symposiasts, both attended, and Robinson listened carefully. She was especially interested in an exchange between Robbins and Sraffa on increasing returns and roundaboutness.[30] Although we have not located a copy of Robbins's lecture, it is reasonable to suppose that he discussed roundaboutness along Austrian lines. Production technologies that rely on capital—roundabout methods of production—are more effective than alternatives. They are also more time-consuming, requiring a longer average period of production. Further extensions of this period, or roundaboutness, increase productivity at a diminishing rate. This is the phenomenon of the diminishing marginal productivity of capital, which was closely tied to Keynes's research problems at the time.

Since Robinson had no understanding of roundaboutness, how could she turn this knowledge to her advantage? By seeking illumination from Sraffa. Robinson wrote Kahn on March 3, "Piero came this afternoon (at my request of course) to take me for a walk + talk about Roundaboutness. I cleared up my ideas a lot" (RFK/13/90/1/168–72). The chief motive behind the walk with Sraffa and her new interest in roundaboutness was simple: the chance to contribute to Keynes's work should the occasion arise, even though this seemed improbable at the time: "Of course I should jump at an offer from Maynard to look at his stuff but he shows no signs of suggesting it. I embarked on my roundabout walk with Piero partly with a view of butting in on Maynard."[31] Two years and three months later, Robinson's roundabout tactic paid off. In June 1935, while assisting Keynes with revisions of *The General Theory*, she was able to put her modest education in the Austrian theory of capital to work, instructing him on the concept of roundaboutness and explaining Marshall's criticism of Böhm-Bawerk's theory of capital.[32]

THE ANONYMOUS REVIEW OF PIGOU'S *THEORY OF UNEMPLOYMENT*

When Kahn returned to Cambridge from the United States in May 1933, he was again at Keynes's disposal and prepared to resume work on the proto–*General Theory*. At that point, Keynes had no incentive to include Robinson in his theoretical dialogues. A few months later, he showered extravagant praise on Kahn as a critic: "There was never anyone in the history of the world to whom it was so helpful to submit one's stuff." The recipient of this remark was Robinson.[33] However, Kahn's return did not mean Robinson's access to Keynes was terminated. On the contrary, her information about his intentions and the progress of his work was much improved. What Keynes discussed with Kahn was also a subject of conversation between Kahn and Robinson. As a result, she became a vicarious participant in the dialogues that produced *The General Theory*. Just as Keynes had renewed access to Kahn, so did Robinson. She used it in part to relay her suggestions to Keynes—presumptuous though they may have been—on how to construct *The General Theory*. Through Kahn, therefore, she attempted to gain a voice in producing Keynes's work.

In summer 1933, moreover, Robinson performed a task for Keynes that required considerable delicacy: she wrote a review of Pigou's new book, *The Theory of Unemployment* (1933). At the time, Keynes regarded "the classics" as the most important readers of his work in progress. They were established economists, mostly trained before the First World War, steeped in classical doctrine, and committed to its basic premises. Theoreticians such as Hawtrey, Pigou, and Robertson were the masters of the classical citadel Keynes had recently abandoned and was attempting to destroy. His earliest rhetorical strategy in planning *The General Theory* was to persuade classical economists by engaging them in controversy. It was a minimalist strategy designed to narrow the concessions the classics would have to make in acknowledging his victory. The bloodless revolution would succeed if the classics agreed to two propositions: (1) the assumptions of classical economics were special cases, confusingly or mistakenly stated, of Keynes's more general assumptions, in much the same sense that Newton's laws of motion were special cases of Einsteinian mechanics; (2) public works projects supported by economists such as Pigou had no basis in classical theory, which held that the free play of supply and demand would eliminate involuntary unemployment; this meant that efforts by the state to erase unemployment were unnecessary, perhaps even pernicious. Keynes's post-*Treatise* thinking rejected the view that self-correcting market mechanisms would restore full employment. Thus it provided a coherent theoretical basis for state intervention in markets.

In her review of Pigou's book for the *New Statesman and Nation* of August 26, 1933, Robinson employed Keynes's rhetorical strategy. This operation required some tact. Pigou was an early and generous supporter of her work on imperfect competition. She had just received a note of warm congratulations from him, suggesting that publication of her work would place her in a strong position for the next university lectureship in economics.[34] Pigou's support was freely given; Robinson had not attempted to recruit him as an advocate. Unlike Keynes, Pigou took an active interest in her work. Also unlike Keynes, he did not have to be courted. A review that moved Pigou into the camp of the anti-Robinsonians would be foolhardy. However, Robinson had tied her interests and ambitions to Keynes and his new theoretical program. Thus her problem in the review was apparent: how should she employ Keynes's rhetorical strategy in discussing the work of the most distinguished and powerful classical economist at Cambridge without compromising his support? Tactically, this was a problem of determining how to maintain that Keynes was right and Pigou was wrong without giving offense and blocking her chances for a lectureship. Robinson developed a low-risk, high-reward solution to her problem. Employing arguments drawn from *Economics Is a Serious Subject*, she defended technical economic analysis conducted in a specialized theoretical language against public expectations that economic writing should be easy to understand. The review began and ended with a celebration of Pigou's virtues as a professional economist: the rigor and austerity of his work, its reliance on technical terminology, and its concentration on theory at the expense of questions of policy. If *The Theory of Unemployment* represented a serious challenge even to "the hardened students of economics," the lay reader was likely to be defeated by a text that made no concessions to nonspecialists.

Robinson had nothing to say about the main theses and analyses of the book, not even by way of summary. Instead, she made several points that followed Keynes's current line on how to convert the classics to his way of thinking. He had adopted and renamed Kahn's concept of the multiplier, arguing that expenditures on public works created both primary and secondary employment. In *The Theory of Unemployment*, Pigou seemed to reject the multiplier effect. Robinson argued that this was merely appearance. When the differences in how Keynes and Pigou conceived real wages and money wages were properly understood, the contradiction disappeared, and Pigou's position became a special case of Keynes's more general thesis. Although Robinson did not stress this point, she noted that both Keynes and Pigou advocated public borrowing to support public works in periods of high unemployment and had written to this effect in the pages of the *New Statesman and Nation*. Keynes had a theoretical rationale for this policy. Pigou did not, at least not unless his view was translated into Keynesian language. If it was, he could be right even if he was wrong in *The Theory of Unemployment*. Keynes, of course, was simply right. In this manner, Robinson executed Keynes's rhetorical strategy in handling the classics. At the same time she offered a gentle, muted, and decidedly un-Robinsonian critique of Pigou. Finally, she supplied herself with a safety net, publishing her review unsigned and making it unlikely that Pigou would be able to discover the identity of the reviewer even if he were interested in doing so.

On August 25, 1933, the day before the review was published, Keynes wrote Robinson, "I have seen a proof of your review of the Professor, and think it quite excellent. I agree that it had better be anonymous" (JVR/vii/240/6–7). How did Robinson, who did not have contacts with journals of political opinion, arrange to publish an anonymous review of a large, specialized, difficult book on economic theory in the *New Statesman and Nation*? Although the following considerations are speculative, they seem reasonable given the evidence. In 1923, Keynes became chairman of the board of directors of the *Nation*, a political and literary weekly and the intellectual voice of the Liberal Party. When the *New Statesman*, a competitor leaning to the left, acquired the *Nation* through a merger, he proposed Kingsley Martin as editor of the new magazine. Keynes had known him since Martin's undergraduate years at Magdalene College shortly after the war. After Martin's dissertation failed to win a fellowship at King's, Keynes recommended him for his first job in journalism (Skidelsky 1992, 134–39, 388). In light of these associations, consider two scenarios. The more probable in view of Keynes's connection with the *New Statesman and Nation*: Keynes selected Robinson, who understood the response he wanted to draw from classical economists, to write the review and send it to the editor with whom he had arranged publication. The less probable: Robinson, who knew what Keynes wanted to see in a review of Pigou, suggested the idea and Keynes handled publication. Robinson did not want her name in circulation as the author of the review. On the same day Keynes read the proof, she asked Kahn to notify him that Martin had made her look foolish by altering several words in the review. She also saw that his editorial mistakes held advantages since evidence of elementary incompetence on the part of the unknown reviewer would be useful in maintaining her anonymity (RFK/13/90/1/246–47). Most important to Robinson, Keynes was happy with the result. As she wrote

Kahn on September 12 (ironically she was visiting Buttermere in the Lake District, where Pigou's cottage was located): "Maynard sent me a note about my review. I was very pleased that he appreciated my low cunning" (RFK/13/90/1/249–51).

LEARNING MONETARY THEORY

During the Cambridge summer vacation of 1934, Robinson gave herself a quick course in monetary theory. Her immediate objective was to prepare lectures—applications of monetary theory—scheduled for the Lent term of 1935. A larger aim was to learn enough to contribute to Keynes's current research in the area and even to publish articles that she would write from a Keynesian perspective. Her first daughter had been born at the end of May. Vacationing with family near the coast of Cornwall in southwest England, she swam in the ocean, read Harrod, Hawtrey, and perhaps Wicksell, and wrote her lectures. In August, she began her first careful reading of the *Treatise*.[35] Kahn was with Keynes at Tilton working on *The General Theory*. Robinson shared her impressions in studying the *Treatise*, sometimes writing him more than once a day. Although she found volume 1 to be "an extraordinary combination of genius, confusion + sophistry," volume 2 was an important contribution to her education.[36] She also began an irreverent "Dictionary of the Treatise," which offered simple definitions of basic concepts for which Keynes had generally supplied elaborate, complex analyses. The "normal level of investment," for example, meant the "level you first thought of." "Overinvestment" was "more investment than before."[37] Although she worked in isolation from Keynes, she used her connection to Kahn to collaborate at a distance, asking him to make a case to Keynes in support of her proposals. For example, she anticipated that economists would find the new Keynesian doctrine on the equivalence of savings and investment counterintuitive. In order to forestall objections, she offered a suggestion: "Try to get Maynard to quote the Treatise to the effect that saving + investment are necessarily equal. He is going to get such a lot of trouble about it. P. 126 or 140 are suitable passages."[38] In reading the *Treatise*, she also made plans to develop rough drafts of analyses on selected problems, to be reworked as articles later.[39]

Cristina Marcuzzo and Claudio Sardoni maintain that the summer of 1934 marked a "change in the personal relationship" between Keynes and Robinson (Marcuzzo and Sardoni 2005, 176). As evidence they quote one sentence of a letter Robinson wrote Kahn on August 15. She noted that in closing a letter to her by typing "yours faithfully," Keynes had crossed this out in ink and had instead simply written "ever" (RFK/13/90/2/39–40). The full text of the letter shows that Robinson's worries over her relationship with Keynes remained. She had written a paper, "Indeterminacy," based on her reading of the *Treatise* and sent it to Keynes, hoping to gain his approval for publication in the *Review of Economic Studies*, where Lerner was one of the editors. She had also sent Keynes the proofs of her essay on Euler's Theorem, which would appear in the *Economic Journal* for September 1934. "Maynard," she wrote Kahn, "sends a curt note saying there's no objection to printing my Indeterminacy *as far as he is concerned*. But I put this down to toothache and I shall send it to Lerner as you approve of it. Maynard also says the proofs were all right. I see Maynard signed yours faithfully in type + crossed it out + put ever in ink so I can't really complain" (RFK/13/90/2/39–40). Robinson was still in doubt about Keynes's judgment of her, searching his letters for signs of her status and scrutinizing his phrases as if they were codes that might indicate her place in the Keynesian social and intellectual order. Was there some significance in the fact that his note was curt? In writing that her paper was unobjectionable as far as he was concerned, did this imply that it might be objectionable on other grounds? Or perhaps these locutions were not signals at all but merely a consequence of his toothache. After all, had he not struck out "yours faithfully" and added "ever" at the end of his note? Robinson's letter is not a mark of her confidence in her standing with Keynes. There seem to be no grounds on which an extraprofessional personal relationship can be ascribed to Keynes and Robinson in 1934 or at any other point. When she had questions to put to Keynes or suggestions to offer concerning his work, she usually approached Kahn, who had an established and comfortable relationship with him. If she was on terms with Keynes that could be characterized as personal, it seems odd that she delegated the announcement of the birth of her daughter to Kahn.[40] If Robinson could write Kahn on the birth of her daughter, why could she not write directly to Keynes?

Kahn and Robinson had a running joke on an imaginary request from Keynes: would she write a preface for his new book, showing how it draws on the *Treatise* but also departs from it? She would, of course, comply, and Keynes would include a generous acknowledgment in *The General Theory*, thanking her for helping him understand what he had failed to see. As she wrote Kahn on September 4, 1934, "Of course I would love to have a footnote from Maynard. 'Mrs. Robinson has pointed out to me that this definition appears in my Treatise'—but Maynard knows better than to put the family jokes in print (even when he sees them which isn't often)" (RFK/13/90/2/85–88). The next day she continued their little game: "Of course I am absolutely full of views about the Treatise. Would Maynard like me to write him a preface for the new work showing in what respects his ideas have altered?"[41] Missing the joke, Marcuzzo and Sardoni read the letter as a serious proposal to write a preface for *The General Theory*. This misunderstanding leads them to conclude that she had become "confident in her role as one of Keynes's interlocutors" (Marcuzzo and Sardoni 2005, 176). Quite the contrary. As the above considerations show, she remained on uneasy grounds with Keynes throughout 1934 and preoccupied with measures to win his confidence.

MICROPOLITICS

In early 1934, Robinson was appointed to a part-time probationary faculty lectureship. Her appointment quickly led to changes in the lecture list on money, which had been revised after considerable deliberation the year before. The terms of the appointment called for her to deliver one and one-half sets of lectures per year. Before 1934, she had supervised students and taught only occasionally on monopoly. This was standard practice in Cambridge economics; new lecturers taught relatively specialized courses on their research. Lectures that prepared students for the tripos were the responsibility of more senior faculty. In her first year as a probationary lecturer, however, she proposed to teach not only a short course of some five weeks on imperfect competition in the Michaelmas term of 1934 but also a new, full-term course in Lent 1935: applications of monetary theory, which was intended for second-year students who were preparing for Robertson's advanced course on money in their third year. This proposal would reverse the changes in the lecture list on money that had been introduced in 1932–33. A few remarks on the history of changes in the curriculum on money are in order at this point.

In February 1930, the faculty board revised requirements for the Economics Tripos. In order to pass the required paper on money, students would be expected to demonstrate some mastery of banking systems, currencies, price levels, trade, investment, and monetary theory—all of which would require analyses of a wide range of monetary phenomena and their causal relations.[42] To prepare students for these requirements, the board offered several sets of lectures in 1931–32. Part I students could attend Leonard Alston's lectures on money and banking. Part II students would sit in Guillebaud's three-term lectures on currency and banking in their second year. In their third and final year, Part II students would enroll in Robertson's three-term set of lectures on money supplemented by Keynes's eight lectures—delivered only once each year—on the pure theory of money in the Easter term, the last lectures before tripos questions were set. In 1932–33, the board had second thoughts about its new lecture list. Alston's lectures were eliminated. Instead, first-year students heard Guillebaud on currency and banking. Lectures on money were deleted from the second year, following which Robertson continued his lectures for third-year students. Keynes's eight lectures would be devoted to the monetary theory of production in 1932–33 and to his drafts of the proto–*General Theory* the following year. Robertson, therefore, taught the principal course on money for Part II students.

The board accepted Robinson's proposal, and she quickly began planning a syllabus. On March 26, 1934, she wrote Keynes, ostensibly seeking his advice on her preparations. The letter is a complex, multilayered text that expresses a variety of intentions, some stated clearly, others somewhat awkwardly veiled. Robinson had grandiose ambitions for her lectures, which she would use as a pedagogical weapon to advance the cause of Keynes's new ideas. She hoped to enlist him in this undertaking as her ally, advisor, and source of higher wisdom. She also wanted to inform him of an event that could be expected to complicate her professional agenda by limiting her ability to achieve such large objectives—her first pregnancy, which she announced with an insouciance that did not conceal some uncertainty:

My dear Maynard

I have not had time till now to write out my syllabus. Both versions are for your eye alone. When the time comes I will draw up a version suitable for the Lecture List Committee under your directions. I would very much like to be let loose on the Grand Scheme, but I quite see how it is. You must let me know how much you think I shall be able to get away with.

There's another point I think I ought to mention—I am expecting to produce a baby in the summer. I don't think myself that this ought to be considered relevant to the question of lecturing—but I quite see that there is another point of view.

I haven't told any of our colleagues except Kahn + Piero. Do you think it might be left to dawn on the others gradually or ought it to be mentioned when my Lectures are discussed?

I hope this news does not disconcert you too much. I think it is a good idea.

There is another point where it comes in—you see that I have rather a lot to do one way + another, so I ought to start on these Lectures as soon as possible. I would be very grateful for your private view as to what line to start on, without prejudice, of course, to the discussions of the Committee.

The Children have asked me to find out if the E[conomic] J[ournal] would give them favorable terms for an advertisement.[43] I don't see why it should not if you are still feeling tender towards them perhaps you might.

My salutations to Lydia

Yours

Joan

I am polishing up on my learned article. I will send it along shortly.

Note to J.M.K.

Of course there is a lot to be said against starting from this high + dry way. But it has some advantages of which the chief is that it makes it possible to avoid controversy entirely. The historical episodes can then be treated without any reference to conflicting interpretations. . . .

I have only given headings for the historical section to follow. They can be done straightforwardly if the theory is behind us. But see inferior scheme for details that will have to be brought out. (JMK/UA/5/3/124–30)

Robinson referred to two versions of her syllabus. The "Grand Scheme" was a plan for an unconventional and formidable set of lectures that would detach monetary theory from Marshallian foundations and reconstruct both theory and history by employing the emerging apparatus of *The General Theory*. Beginning "high and dry" with an austere presentation of theoretical abstractions, she envisioned a critique of political economy and a reinterpretation of modern economic theory from a Keynesian standpoint, all in the space of some two months. The more modest and conventional syllabus that she called the "inferior scheme" would dispense with general theoretical considerations. Instead, specific economic problems would be analyzed by employing Keynes's most recent ideas. The draft of the inferior scheme is not in the King's College archives, and the draft of the grand scheme is only a fragment. In the critique of political economy, which she placed under the general heading "Controversy," Robinson proposed to consider several versions of the quantity theory of money; the classical theory of the rate of interest and its relation to modern theory; the "Treasury view" of monetary economics as a "degenerate descendent" of classical theory; various writers, including Ricardo, Karl Marx, Marshall, and Ludwig von Mises; and more indeterminate matters that she placed under the headings "cranks" and "modern cranks." In her reconstruction of economic history, she planned to discuss the German inflation of the early 1920s, Great Britain on the gold standard in 1925–31, and the tract by Hubert Henderson and Keynes on this subject—*The Economic Consequences of Mr. Churchill* (1925), the crisis of the English pound, the New Deal ("The Roosevelt Experiment"), and other matters as well (JMK/UA/5/3/124–30).

Keynes quickly saw that this syllabus was tendentious, beyond the powers of second-year students, and impossible to execute in a short period. Robinson's lectures had been approved by the board as a prerequisite for the main lectures in this area delivered by Robertson; but her syllabus was more advanced than the course for which it was intended as a prerequisite. Finally, the grand scheme did not conform to Robertson's approach to the analysis of money. The inconsistencies between the two sets of lectures would inevitably confuse students, embarrass Robertson, and intensify dissension among the faculty, who were already forming opposing camps as a result of Keynes's new views. Thus Keynes's judgment on March 29, 1934: "The grand scheme is really out of the question." He approved her more modest plan: "By grouping your ideas round concrete problems, you avoid the strain of abstract treatment whilst really able to bring in the general sort of approach you want and can awaken their [the students'] curiosity in the right directions" (JMK/UA/5/3/131). An analysis of specific problems on Keynesian premises was a sound tactic for planting the principles and methods of the new economics in the minds of Cambridge students. A frontal assault would only end in disaster.

Did Keynes hope to dampen Robinson's enthusiasm for more aggressive revolutionary action at Cambridge, temper the conflict between her and Robertson, and neutralize her as a source of tension within the faculty generally? If so, his success was fleeting at best. Shortly after her appointment, the Appointments Committee of the board announced a new university lectureship, the position to begin in the Michaelmas term of 1935.[44] Robinson applied (Moggridge 1992, 599). On February 18, 1935, the committee—which included Fay, Keynes, and Robertson, who was the newly elected chairman of the board—recommended the young LSE economist Hicks.[45] Pigou then suggested to Keynes that Robinson be promoted to a full-time lectureship the following academic year, an appointment entailing three full courses of lectures.[46] Robinson used this opportunity to propose to the board that she teach applications of monetary theory over two terms, Michaelmas 1935 and Lent 1936. Keynes or Wynne Plumptre would complete the academic year with a third course on money in the Easter 1936 term.[47]

On March 1, 1935, the Lecture List Committee met to consider courses for the following academic year. The controversy generated by Robinson's proposal is best understood in the atmosphere of confusion, anxiety, suspicion, and revolutionary fervor surrounding Keynes's work on *The General Theory*. By this point, Robertson had seen drafts of Keynes's critique of classical economics. He rejected Keynes's account of classicism as preposterous and intellectually dishonest. He also found much of Keynes's new theoretical language to be "almost completely mumbo-jumbo" (in Keynes 1973a, 505–06). Robinson, on the other hand, was a dedicated Keynesian partisan who took pleasure in staking out a position and fighting for it. Some members of the guild saw in her partisanship a contemptuous disparagement of all pre-Keynesian monetary theory. The implications of her proposal to teach two full courses on money and enter Robertson's domain in a faculty that remained small and understaffed in relation to its growing number of students were not attractive to Keynesian skeptics. Was she suggesting that Robertson, who had published extensively on monetary theory and enjoyed an international reputation as a foremost authority in the area, was incompetent? Or were the Keynesians intent on marginalizing Robertson and dominating the tripos, in which case the next generation of Cambridge economists would be lost to Keynesian dogmaticians? Robinson's intervention fractured the uneasy peace in the faculty by forcing colleagues to take sides in the contentious atmosphere of 1935. Like revolutionary partisans generally, she was committed to clarity, precision, formalism, and unequivocal positions. This held true not only in her research, but also in the stands she took in the economics faculty. In the Marshallian guild, conflicts were generally resolved consensually. Issues likely to divide the faculty into factions based on conflicting positions concerning fundamental questions were not formulated with pristine clarity. In any case, the most important matters were not open to explicit formulations. As the unexpressed premises on which agreements were based, they were not possible objects of formal agreement. Because every formal understanding presupposed a background of tacit assumptions, not all assumptions could be formalized. Moreover, precision changed the import and practical significance of controversies and exacerbated conflicts by exposing their ultimate premises. Efforts to drive disagreements down to their foundations were immensely risky because the directions they might take could not be anticipated. A clarification of positions not only articulated differences but also formed them, and the reduction of ambiguity and imprecision in faculty deliberations generated disagreements that would not otherwise arise. It was better to resist precise definitions, refuse to make ultimate commitments, and forego interventions that revealed basic differences.[48] By exposing sources of opposition that otherwise would have remained latent, Robinson's proposal created mistrust, resentment, and bad feelings generally. It frayed the ties that loosely bound members of the guild together in a community of mutual trust, compromising a condition without which collective action by a small fellowship of academics would have been impossible.

Several factors are important in the response to Robinson's proposal. The conversion of her position to a full-time lectureship took some members of the board by surprise—among them Pigou, who had originally suggested the conversion to Keynes but forgot he had done so. Some members of the board were unaware that Robinson intended to deliver two sets of lectures on money. Robertson, the lecturer who would be most damaged by her proposal, was regarded by his colleagues as modest and self-effacing, perhaps to a fault. It was unlikely he would raise objections on his own behalf. Austin's membership on the board and his participation in the discussion made a frank appraisal of his wife's proposal and her credentials awkward at best. Finally, there was Keynes, who was on good terms with most of the faculty and legendary for his powers of persuasion. He enjoyed immense power and prestige outside Cambridge as well as an intimate knowledge of what were then called affairs—the world of Whitehall, the City, and the boardrooms of great banks, investment firms, and corporations in Britain and abroad. If he supported Robinson, others would find it more difficult to oppose her.

Fay was one of the board members vexed by Robinson's proposal. He had supposed that Pigou, as the professor of political economy and the most senior member of the faculty, would take the initiative in supporting Robertson. When this did not happen, he decided to act. Within hours of the committee meeting, he sent Robertson the following note:

You may think I have acted awkwardly, but I have written to Robinson and his wife, stating the apprehension which some people felt that her course would cramp the 3rd year money teaching and be rival rather than complementary, and hoping that it will not be so.

I shall in future speak openly at the [Appointments] Committee or the Board, whether Austin is present or not. I am a reader of senior standing and so are you; and if the Prof. does not take the lead it is our duty to step in, where the welfare of the Tripos is concerned, and I am ready to do so, without mincing matters.

My view of Keynes, and here again I shall mince no words in future, is that when he so desires he argues for a person, without regard to the principle. (DHR/B2/1)

The board had an obligation to support its chairman, and on the decision over Robinson's proposal it had failed do so. Fay had entered the meeting under the mistaken impression that Robertson and Pigou had conferred and reached an agreement on how to handle the Robinson matter. As he wrote Robertson, this was an error he did not intend to repeat: "I shall go more warily in the future and try to make sure that your hand is being in no way forced" (DHR/B2/1).

Although efforts to locate a copy of Fay's letter to the Robinsons have not succeeded, the grounds for his dissatisfaction are stated in a letter he circulated the following day to Pigou, Keynes, and Shove—old Kingsmen and colleagues of long standing to whom he felt he could write in complete candor. The letter is a rambling, confusing, repetitious document in which it is difficult to discern a coherent line of reasoning—further evidence that Robinson's adversaries had left the meeting the previous day in a state of puzzlement. Addressing "old friends at King's," Fay raised several matters that gave him special cause for worry. The meeting was held under "embarrassing circumstances" that made it difficult for the board to support its chairman. The source of the embarrassment was Austin, who did not recuse himself from deliberations on his wife's proposal. However, Fay did not hold Austin responsible for the result. On an earlier occasion when she was under discussion, the board assured him that he should feel free to take part in the meeting, and he did so. In this case, Fay surmised, perhaps Austin felt that "it was his duty to do his best for his wife's emphatic desire."[49] Fay also felt that no reason had been given for reinserting a course on money into the second-year lecture list, much less a two-term set of lectures by Robinson. The decision had no sound curricular basis. On the contrary, it was a result of coercive maneuvers. The previous evening, Fay had written as much to Austin "as an old friend and pupil"—as noted, it was Fay who had first encouraged Austin to become an academic. On the issue of subsequent board discussions of Robinson, Fay was not in favor of excluding Austin. Instead, he proposed an uncompromising and unrealistic standard of candor: "We must always speak of Mrs. Robinson exactly as we would if [Austin] Robinson were not present. Otherwise we will be guilty of a sort of favouritism." It was obvious to Fay that the syllabus Robinson presented to the board was not a prerequisite for Robertson's lectures. Her lectures would compete with his, very likely preempting his mode of analysis. The result would either dispose students against his approach or confuse them in their efforts to prepare for the tripos paper on money. In either case, the result would be a "disaster."[50]

Robinson's partisanship on behalf of Keynes's new ideas was an important issue in the controversy. As Fay understood him, Keynes now seemed to think that solutions to most problems in economic theory could be derived from the theory of money. If "the money people" were granted their own territory, they would impose "a sort of theoretical suzerainty" on the faculty. Because it would stratify the faculty along the lines of theoretical allegiances, this was a dangerous prospect: "On the one hand," Fay wrote, "the central theorists, and on the other hand the rest of us counting as frills." Fay envisioned a new Keynesian regime at Cambridge that would produce a radical shift in the balance of power in the faculty and realign the status of its members. For the first time in the history of the Marshallian guild, status would be decided on the basis of theoretical commitments. An elite of monetary theorists—Keynes and his followers—would be positioned at the top of this new order. Those who failed to demonstrate appropriate enthusiasm for their views would suffer a loss of prestige. In essence, a theoretical loyalty test would determine the career chances of Cambridge economists. Fay also feared that Keynesianism, at least in the lectures of Robinson, would become an economic theology at Cambridge. The golden age of the Marshallian guild and its liberal intellectual culture of debate and innovation within the capacious and vaguely defined boundaries of Marshall's *Principles* would be succeeded by a dark age of Keynesian dogmatism, sectarianism, and the prospect of internal ideological warfare. All this to accommodate the excessive ambitions of one well-connected and ill-mannered woman? Fay insisted that there was "no conceivable danger" of a Keynesian hegemony if Keynes himself delivered the tripos lectures on money—this "because of his vast experience in affairs." Robinson was not Keynes: "It would be altogether wrong to suggest to Mrs. Robinson that she is in any way capable of acting as his substitute here." In Fay's abysmal vision of Cambridge economics, Robinson, Kahn, and Hicks—the youngest members of the faculty, whom he represented as followers of Keynes and ignorant of the realities of economic life—would dominate the curriculum.[51] Fay's solution to the immediate problem created by Robinson's proposal was to restrict her to one set of second-year lectures on money in the Lent term that would equip students for Robertson's lecture in their third year. Would this deprive Robinson of a full-time job? Perhaps, but that did not trouble Fay: "This change in her status was sprung upon us, as has indeed every change from the time when she asked permission to give occasional lectures."[52] He concluded, perhaps somewhat sanctimoniously in light of his withering criticism of Robinson and her supporters, that his intention in writing at such length was "above all things to be loyal to our new Chairman."[53]

Keynes found Fay's letter both annoying and ominous. As he wrote Lydia on March 4, "The trouble between Joan and Dennis (which I thought I had settled) may crop up again. He's getting dangerously near to trying to prevent her from lecturing; and if he were to succeed, the state of rift between the older people and the younger would be dreadful. I shall have to exert my full force, and it would end in Dennis being frightfully upset. Why are all economists mad?" (quoted in Moggridge 1992, 600). Keynes's diagnosis of the Robinson affair makes several points. As his letter indicates, the difference between Robinson and Robertson did not begin with this incident. He assumed that Robertson was the prime mover behind Fay's letter. He also supposed that Robertson was responsible for the attempt to restrict Robinson's lectures, which he described as an effort to "prevent her from lecturing." Keynes saw the dispute as an intergenerational confrontation. Although this perception was largely true, it did not identify the definitive feature of the conflict. The schism was between followers of Keynes, most of whom were younger, and others he had stigmatized as classics, all of whom were older. He also failed to see that Robinson's incursion into Robertson's territory would inevitably intensify dissension regardless of the decision of the board or the direction in which he exercised his influence. A decision in favor of Robinson would damage Robertson. A decision in favor of Robertson would weaken the core of the revolutionary party at Cambridge. Finally, he seems to have forgotten that only a year before, he had told Robinson that the syllabus she called the Grand Scheme was unacceptable. Or had the constellation of powers and interests changed in the intervening months, causing Keynes to change his mind?

Keynes immediately began a counterinitiative to persuade Fay, Pigou, and Shove not to reopen the board's discussion of Robinson's lectures. In a letter of March 5 to Fay, he argued that a decision to veto Robinson's proposal would be an excessively severe and virtually unprecedented step. It was not a measure to take against a lecturer whose success with students had been amply demonstrated. In addition, a veto would give the unfortunate and mistaken impression that the board was censoring Robinson—preventing her from "preaching her own line of approach." This impression would suggest that Cambridge was becoming sectarian and moving in the direction of LSE, "where differences of doctrinal opinion are capable of coming into the picture."[54] Keynes also reminded Fay that in proposing to convert Robinson's lectureship to a full-time position, he was not taking the board by surprise. "I was," he explained, "simply reminding Pigou that he had previously expressed the opinion to me that, as she was rather unlucky in not getting a University Lectureship, we should at any rate make her a full-time assistant lecturer, if she wanted to be one." Keynes found this argument especially compelling, since Robinson's position on the faculty did not match her scholarly accomplishments. If an entirely new set of lecturers were appointed, he asked, would not her credentials be judged superior to the qualifications of some current occupants? Finally, Keynes argued that in view of the current proliferation of theories of money, representation of more than one position in the tripos lectures was not only proper but inevitable. This was a case for "some measure of duplication and even a possible overweighting."[55] Regardless of the intentions behind this argument, it afforded him a convenient rationale for putting his most combative and unrestrained polemicist in place as a counterweight to Robertson, who was now an adversary.

On the same day, Keynes wrote Shove along the same lines but much more briefly.[56] Although it is not clear whether he also wrote Pigou—correspondence between them on this matter has not survived—the Professor's views can easily be reconstructed. It was Pigou who was impressed with *The Economics of Imperfect Competition* and suggested that the book would make Robinson a strong contender for the next lectureship.[57] And it was Pigou who made the original suggestion to promote her to a full-time position. Finally, a much later piece of evidence indicates that he supported Robinson's proposal not because he agreed with her approach to economics but on the basis of the fundamental premise of intellectual liberalism: academic freedom.[58]

In the end Fay relented, insisting on two conditions. If the board accepted Robinson's lectures as she proposed them, it would have to take measures to spare Robertson the embarrassment its decision would cause. In its next meeting, could Keynes offer a brief rationale to the board for this departure from the lecture list? He also called on the board to reject the assumption that Robinson or Kahn could replace Keynes in the curriculum. This was out of the question given Keynes's "superb knowledge of affairs," which he claimed was "the greatest single asset of our Tripos" and precisely the area in which Keynes's followers were deficient. Fay had no reservations about Robinson's competence, and he knew she was respected at LSE and Oxford. However, he objected in strong terms to her abrasive style of self-presentation, which he regarded as crude and boorish. As he complained to Keynes, "It is an awful pity she is so bloody rude."[59] Notwithstanding Fay's reservations, in the March meeting of the board, Robinson's triumph was absolute. Her proposal to teach two courses on money in the coming academic year was approved, and she was permitted to continue her current lectures into the summer. With Keynes's help, Pigou's backing, her husband's support, and her opponents' confusion, disarray, and tolerance, she was able to implement the "Grand Scheme" Keynes had rejected the year before.

READING THE PROOFS OF
THE GENERAL THEORY

Keynes's position in the dispute over Robinson's lecture program was perhaps his first act of patronage on her behalf, the first occasion on which he employed his social and intellectual capital to advance her career. Both the import and the timing of the event were of some significance for the patron. In the controversy of March 1935, Keynes made several choices; some were explicit and intentional, others perhaps tacit and unwitting. He supported Robinson's freedom to lecture according to her own lights against arguments that would restrict this freedom. He advocated a pluralist pedagogy in the theory of money, an academic policy that might result in conflicting and dueling lecturers, leaving students uncertain as to how they should approach tripos questions. He rejected a unified pedagogy designed for consistency and ease of comprehension because it did not conform to the fluid state of research on monetary theory. In a conflict between Robertson and Robinson, he took a strong stance in favor of his new advocate and against his old friend. It was Robertson, he thought, who was getting "dangerously near" to preventing her from lecturing. He was prepared to use all his resources and exercise his "full force" to see that this did not happen, even if his opposition caused Robertson to become "frightfully upset." He supported younger members of the faculty over his contemporaries and older students. This meant supporting Robinson, Austin, and Kahn against Fay, Robertson, and Shove. It also meant supporting Keynesian faculty against the classics, acting on behalf of proponents of his new theoretical program and against those he hoped to convert. And although he could not have been expected to see this at the time, it meant supporting the nascent party of the revolution against Robertson, who would become the most intransigent Cambridge counterrevolutionary.

Some two months before the Robinson controversy, Keynes began to take advice on revising *The General Theory* by sending galleys to Robertson. The theoretical strategy of the book was underpinned by a rhetorical strategy. Keynes hoped to persuade economists to "re-examine critically certain of their basic presumptions" (Keynes 1936, vi). In conducting this reexamination, his readers would conclude that if their assumptions were employed to understand the economy, the results would be not only mistaken but "disastrous" (Keynes 1936, iii). He seems to have conceived *The General Theory* as an extended set of arguments the logic of which did not differ substantially from his *Essays in Persuasion*. His ideal readers were economists who felt secure in the magnificent edifice of the classical citadel. Their thinking would be reoriented by a combination of abstract argument and controversy. He would reformulate the basic elements of classical economics and expose its fundamental premises. Then he would demonstrate that they were vulnerable to fatal objections and show how his theory could solve the problems these objections posed. When he had completed his arguments, economists would be ready to abandon their intellectual fortress, convinced by his analysis that the impressive super-structure of classicism rested on irreparably flawed foundations.

During his years of work on the *Treatise*, Keynes regarded Robertson as his most valuable aide on theoretical questions. And with good reason. Robertson was an expert in the area of Keynes's research on monetary theory. They agreed on basic theoretical assumptions, a requirement of scientific dialogue that Keynes regarded as indispensable. Discussion pre-supposes what is beyond discussion, a bedrock of assumptions that are not open to question. Unless interlocutors accept this requirement and agree on their fundamental assumptions, the conditions for a Keynesian scientific discussion are not met. Robertson was a sympathetic reader ea-ger to grasp Keynes's insights. He possessed to a high degree a quality Keynes did not find in Hayek during their exchanges in 1930–31: good will, the determination to understand a writer's ideas as he intended them to be taken. Robertson made suggestions that were designed to strengthen Keynes's reasoning. He also developed analyses that translated Keynes's speculative insights into arguments, the detailed work of proof for which Keynes had little patience and which he regarded as subordinate to the more challenging work of discovering new lines of inquiry. Finally, Robertson was open to persuasion. Within the limits of the assumptions they shared, he could be convinced that Keynes was on the right track con-cerning the basic problems of economic theory and how to tackle them. By March 1935, Robertson was no longer Keynes's ideal interlocutor, as Robertson himself recognized. Their discussion of the galleys during the first ten weeks of the year had not been successful. At first he was skeptical of Keynes's ideas. As Keynes proved unwilling to budge on fundamentals, making it clear that it was the critic and not the author who was expected to change his thinking, Robertson became more resolute. He rejected Keynes's account of orthodox economics as a bad parody, historically pre-posterous, and intellectually dishonest. Keynes's reconstruction of classi-cism was irresponsible in the extreme, and his treatment of Marshall was a travesty. These abominations, as Robertson saw them, destroyed much of their common ground. He also found Keynes's new theoretical language not merely wanting in clarity but unintelligible (in Keynes 1973a, 505–06). On February 10, he warned Keynes, "I'm afraid you'll feel the general tenor of my comments (which seems almost to have reached the dimensions of a book) rather hostile" (in Keynes 1973a, 506).[60] He remained defiant until March, when he concluded that their dialogue was futile. Keynes agreed. He had failed to move Robertson on the basic issues that separated them, and on March 14 their exchange was terminated (Keynes 1973a, 522–23).[61]

Thus a few days after Keynes's expression of support for Robinson in the board, his discussion with Robertson collapsed, giving him the first serious indication that his rhetorical strategy might be misguided. In spring 1931, Robinson had begun her ambitious project of socioprofessional self-formation, writing on Keynes's new ideas and preparing herself to carry out his commissions when he was finally ready to call on her. Some three months after the exchange between Keynes and Robertson lapsed, her efforts paid off. On June 8, Keynes wrote that he was sending Robinson the available galleys of the book in two installments. He would be "extremely grateful for any criticisms of form or substance." The tone of this letter differed markedly from his previous correspondence with Robinson, which was correct but cool and sometimes perfunctory. The letter included an invitation to dinner and a concert: "Could you and Austin dine with Lydia and me in King's on Thursday (June 13) at 8:0, and then come with us to the Handel afterwards?" (Keynes 1973a, 638). Robinson had finally arrived.

What had changed since the previous summer, when Robinson was offering suggestions on *The General Theory* to Kahn in the hope that they might be relayed to Keynes? In spring 1935, Keynes faced a new strategic predicament. A draft of the book was now complete and being set in galleys. He needed assurances that it would indeed initiate a revolution in economic thought. Because of his failure to persuade Robertson, the problem that had bedeviled him in his controversy with Hayek arose once again, but in a more acute fashion. In order to revise the manuscript he had written with Kahn's assistance, he needed to be satisfied that it was free of the kinds of embarrassing conceptual and theoretical errors Hayek had found in the *Treatise*. For this purpose, he needed a reader with the requisite logical and theoretical sophistication, someone who had followed the direction of his post-*Treatise* thinking, a critic of good will who was sympathetic to his new approach and could be expected to strengthen it by pointing out errors that he and Kahn had missed. By June 1935, Keynes believed Robinson was that reader. At this point, her

Keynesian self-education and efforts at self-presentation intersected with changes in his strategic position. Before the disappointing exchange with Robertson, he had no reason to see her as an attractive resource. Now he did. Given Keynes's ambitions, limitations, and expectations, she could be useful, perhaps even valuable, in finishing the book. As in so many instances, events proved Keynes's judgment sound even if not precisely in the way he anticipated. Within four days of receiving the second set of galleys, Robinson sent him an extensive and detailed set of comments as well as her general impressions of the book (Keynes 1973a, 638–45). How was this extraordinarily swift and thorough response possible? Keynes sent Harrod the galleys on June 5 but did not hear from him until July 31 (see Keynes 1973a, 526–27). Hawtrey's set was sent on June 12, and he replied by the end of the month (1973a, 567). In four days, how could Robinson read a difficult and confusing book, digest it, and write elaborate and carefully crafted suggestions, many of which Keynes adopted?

In addressing Keynes's request so quickly, she profited from her long-term investment in the study of Keynesian thought. In 1930–31, she was present at the meetings of the Circus when the building blocks of *The General Theory* were constructed. In spring 1932, she worked with Austin and Kahn on the manifesto and debated its merits with Keynes. Thereafter she kept in touch with changes in his thinking through frequent discussions with Kahn, an important part of her professional routine. She also spoke more occasionally with Sraffa, who met with Keynes regularly to discuss their current research. And she decided to lecture on applications of monetary theory, which called for a self-taught crash course on the theory of money during the summer vacation of 1934. Her principal text was the *Treatise*. Robinson's facility in commenting on Keynes's galleys was also due to the stunning simplicity of her understanding of the field of monetary theory. Theories of money were either true, approximations of the truth, misconceived, or false. Put another way, they fell into one of four categories: Keynes's current views, positions that approximated them more or less closely, or positions that were either irrelevant to his views or inconsistent with them. Theories in the last two categories were either uninteresting or wrong. In either case, they did not merit serious study. Unlike Robinson, Robertson, Harrod, and Hawtrey were veterans in the field. Their reading of Keynes was informed by their own theoretical views and many years of work on the literature and its complexities. They were positioned in a tradition of thought about monetary questions and responded to Keynes from the standpoint of their location in this tradition. This meant that they read *The General Theory* not as revealed truth but from the standpoint of the place it occupied in the history of monetary thought. Because they knew more than Robinson, they were able to see more—chiefly more problems posed by Keynes's theoretical language, assumptions, mode of analysis, and scholarship. Not so Robinson, an enthusiast whose convictions did not recognize tradition as an authoritative source of knowledge. If serious work on monetary theory began with Keynes, other authors, to the extent they were worthy of consideration, could be routinely dispatched by reading them from the perspective of their consistency with his ideas. In this respect, Robinson was an ideal revolutionary activist. The founding text of the revolution could be fully inscribed as scientific truth in the relatively empty space of her mind, where it did not face competition from opposing positions. In *The Economics of Imperfect Competition*, she confessed with peculiar hauteur that she was almost completely innocent of mathematics. She was also innocent of much economic literature. To see *The General Theory* as the first genuinely significant contribution to monetary theory was to read Keynes independently of other work in this area. Criticism would necessarily be limited to immanent critique—criticism that presupposed his assumptions and their boundaries. In this regard, the narrow scope and relative superficiality of Robinson's professional training were quite useful to an author seeking grounds for confidence that his analyses were sound.

Robinson's letter of June 16 reproduces the time-honored idioms of client-patron relations. She offered effusive praise but not the false applause of the lackey. Lavish compliments were tempered by carefully considered suggestions, for which she made no claim to originality or even authorship. Keynes was assured that her proposals would have occurred to him in any event. Indeed, he might already have considered them and drawn his own conclusions, in which case Robinson's gentle criticisms were implicitly ascribed to Keynes as original insights into his own work. Robinson began by apologizing for possible impertinence in expressing her delight with the book, as if it might be bad form on her part to offer an opinion, even though this is precisely what Keynes had asked her to do. Excesses of flattery followed. The book made "an impression of great power and coherence." It was "the most *readable* book of its weight ever," a view that generations of his readers would find difficult to credit. There were "eloquent passages" that appeared at just the right point to keep the reader engaged. Because of the clarity and cogency of his analysis, it would be "extremely difficult to attack" (in Keynes 1973a, 638). Keynes's correspondence with Robertson had given him reason to suspect that her last judgment was quite far off the mark, and the responses of Harrod and Hawtrey would strengthen this impression. Robinson did not seem to grasp Keynes's fundamental rhetorical objective. His purpose was not to achieve immunity from attack by means of arguments that would generally be regarded as the last word on economic theory. Although he was convinced that his general line of analysis was sound, he knew his arguments were unclear, fragmentary, and inconclusive. *The General Theory* was the beginning of the assault on classicism, not the final, victorious battle. His aim was to invite counterattacks by stimulating controversy. Robinson saw the book as a finished system, sufficiently free of flaws that criticism would be seen as frivolous and harmless, even laughable, with the result that critics would damage not Keynes but themselves (in Keynes 1973a, 638).

In the Robinsonian hermeneutic, *The General Theory* was self-interpreting. A clear understanding of its meaning flowed smoothly from the lucidity, internal consistency, and force of Keynes's arguments. Its only errors lay in matters of detail. Because the book was a self-contained and transparent system, they could be corrected on the basis of its own logic. Keynes's meta-interpretation was quite remote from Robinson's. In his response to Harrod's worry that his account of classical economics would gratuitously raise a "storm of dust" by indulging in criticisms that were ill-founded and easy to refute, he replied that his critique of economic orthodoxy was essential to the intelligibility of the book. It was necessary to raise a storm of dust because "it is only out of the controversy that will arise that what I am saying will get understood" (Keynes 1973a, 548). If Keynes's assault on the classics was sharp enough, they would be compelled to respond, and the import of his own theory would emerge in the ensuing controversy. Otherwise it would be misunderstood or perhaps not understood at all. On this view, *The General Theory* cannot be understood immanently. Moreover, it could not be understood in summer 1935, when it had not yet been published and subjected to the classical counterattack. This meant that it could not be understood by sympathetic readers of the galleys such as Harrod, a point Keynes attempted to impress on him. Nor could it be understood by a partisan reader like

Robinson, a consequence of his hermeneutic that Keynes did not consider. Because a proper understanding of *The General Theory* depended on adversarial dialogue, his attacks on classical economics were not merely an exercise in scientific polemics. They had a strategic function that was indispensable to his purpose. A harmonious or pacific reception would show that the book had failed in its objective of initiating a revolution in economic thought. Thus Keynes's sharp and tendentious criticisms, the postpublication controversy, and achievement of his purpose were all tightly connected.

As Robinson's letter of June 16 shows, she saw herself as Keynes's comrade in arms, engaged in a scientific offensive that she conceived as a quasi-military operation. In *The General Theory*, he had succeeded in securing all the flanks of the revolutionary forces. As a result the movement could "push ahead" without fear of damaging counterattacks (in Keynes 1973a, 638). Keynes was pleased with Robinson's comments and especially interested in the difficulty she encountered in reading chapter 17, "The Essential Properties of Interest and Money." As he wrote on June 18, he was not troubled by possible errors in details or problems concerning specific concepts. His only worry was the coherence of the general analysis employed in the chapter. If that proved "fully intelligible in the long run," he would be satisfied. For Keynes, the General Theory was not the book but how its ideas—unfamiliar and obscure not only to the reader but to the author as well—would be understood once they were in circulation and contested. Robinson sought, and in many respects supposed she had found, certainty in the text itself. This was not Keynes's expectation. Clarity in all respects was not merely improbable but impossible in principle without discussion of his ideas. If his strategy was sound, errors or sources of confusion would be cleared up to his advantage in subsequent controversy (Keynes 1973a, 645).

Keynes's invitation to correspond on the proofs and his appreciation of Robinson's comments seem to have strengthened her self-confidence. In responding to his remarks on chapter 17, she told him that his difficulties lay in advice he had taken from Kahn. She and Kahn had argued over the chapter and concluded that she was right and he was mistaken.[62] She did not regard it as unacceptably presumptuous to instruct Keynes concerning his new concept of liquidity preference. Although he discussed liquidity and used the idea, he never specified with any precision the economic behavior that the concept was meant to designate. On this point, Robinson moved beyond the task of offering comments and wrote a text that she invited Keynes to appropriate.[63] She also asked to see the outstanding galleys once they were available. Keynes seems to have accepted Robinson's new self-representation. On September 3, he sent her the remaining galleys, suggestions to facilitate her reading, requests for advice, and explanations of the current state of his revisions. He also put her on notice that she could expect to receive his revised versions of Books I and II. He had completely rewritten Book II in the weeks since she had seen the first set of galleys, with the result that "practically not a word of the version you had read has been left standing." Her letter of September 7, which concerns dinner at her flat, makes it clear that she wanted him to know she was fully at his disposal: "Thursday at 8:00 will be fine. It is possible Austin may have to be away, but I won't ask anyone in, in case you would like to talk about the book" (in Keynes 1973a, 651).[64] Personal access to Keynes began to deliver small benefits. On October 21, Robinson read a paper to his Political Economy Club, and Kahn celebrated the occasion by giving a dinner before the meeting. Keynes attended both events, finding her paper "crystal clear and extremely interesting" (Keynes 1973a, 652).[65] At the same time, he sent the first sixty-four page proofs for her scrutiny, promising further installments as they became available.

On November 20, Robinson accepted a more difficult assignment: a final settlement of Keynes's accounts with Hawtrey over their differences concerning the book. From the standpoint of his original strategy, Hawtrey was one of the more important members of the cohort of economists to whom he had addressed *The General Theory*: a Cambridge contemporary and an old friend, in Keynes's view the most sophisticated economist at the Treasury, and a proponent of Cambridge classicism. When Hawtrey began to read the galleys in June, he answered with long memoranda-like letters covering an extensive range of issues. An attempt to respond to Hawtrey's memoranda point by point at the same time that Keynes was handling comments from Harrod, Kahn, and Robinson and rewriting much of the book was out of the question. Yet he was determined to persuade Hawtrey to execute a paradigm shift. After struggling through some five months of exchanges in an attempt to woo Hawtrey from his commitment to the orthodoxy they had shared, Keynes concluded that he would not be moved. On some points Keynes had not been able to offer a satisfactory explanation of his new views, which Hawtrey still did not understand. In addition, his arguments were cast in a new theoretical language. Hawtrey had misunderstood too many of these arguments because he had translated them into the language of orthodox theory, the premises of which rendered Keynes's ideas either counterintuitive or nonsensical. He regarded most of Hawtrey's objections as of minor importance. His main objective was to get Hawtrey to see the problems of economics in a new way by persuading him to think about them in his new language. If he succeeded, any outstanding problems would eventually be resolved in his favor since they would be articulated in a language in which classical assumptions had no place. Keynes concluded that he had failed in this larger effort. Why did so many issues still divide them? Because, as he wrote Hawtrey shortly after he had sent his book to the printer: "So many points are still seen through your spectacles and not through mine!" (Keynes 1973a, 627).

On November 29, Keynes delegated the Hawtrey problem to Robinson: "Unless it would bore you, I would be rather grateful if you would look through this voluminous correspondence with Hawtrey. I have arranged it in chronological order. By the time you have got to the end of it, you will see that we are recurring over and over again to two or three points where I am indisposed to give way. My final letter to him, with today's date on it, has not yet been dispatched. I should rather like to know whether, looking at it impartially, you feel that there are any further concessions which he can justly claim from me" (Keynes 1973a, 612). In sending the entire correspondence to her instead of first asking whether he might impose on her time, Keynes evidently assumed she would respond as he expected. He was not disappointed. And as he surely knew, her answer to his question would not be impartial. Writing on December 2, Robinson compared Keynes's handling of Hawtrey to the conduct of a higher moral being: "I don't think an archangel could have taken more trouble to be fair and clear." Like Robertson, Hawtrey had not "gotten" or "taken in" Keynes: he had not understood Keynes's analysis as he intended it to be read. This was Hawtrey's failure, not Keynes's. Until he had properly read *The General Theory*, it was useless to argue with him. Additional concessions were not called for, and there was nothing further to be said (in Keynes 1973a, 612–13). On December 27, Keynes wrote Robinson a warm letter of appreciation, acknowledging his "great debt of gratitude" for her work on his proofs. He also confided his feelings at the end of five years of labor on a book from which he expected so much. "Author's melancholy" had set in, and in his final reading of the proofs he found the book "flat and stale." Although the support of Kahn and Robinson had cheered him, Hawtrey's final prepublication letter convinced Keynes he had failed utterly to change the thinking of an economist shaped by the orthodoxy of the time. Hawtrey's letter now seemed "more heart-breaking than ever" (JVR/vii/240/9–10).

If Hawtrey's letter was heartbreaking, the intransigence of Robertson was surely even more painful. He spent much of the summer of 1936 studying *The General Theory*, but with no change of mind. "It's no use pretending," he wrote Keynes on September 28, that "I like it much better or that I don't agree more or less with most of the Prof's review, including the first section" (in Keynes 1979, 163). The review in question was Pigou's blistering critique of *The General Theory* published in *Economica* for May 1936, which Keynes declared "most dreadful" and "profoundly frivolous."[66] In writing Robertson on September 20, he defended his polemical account of classical economics, which Harrod, Hawtrey, Pigou, and Robertson all saw as an irresponsible caricature. At the same time he understood that his rhetorical strategy had not succeeded: "What some of you think my excessively controversial method is really due to the extent that I am bound in thought to my own past opinions and to those of my teachers and earlier pupils; which makes me want to emphasise and bring to a head all the differences of opinion. But I evidently make a mistake in this, not having realized either that the old ones would be merely irritated, or that to the young ones, who have been, apparently, so badly brought up as to believe nothing in particular, the controversy with older views would mean practically nothing" (Keynes 1973b, 87). Keynes's theoretical language was novel, confusing—especially when it used orthodox terms in new ways—and either inconsistent with classical doctrines or untranslatable into its theoretical language. In view of the epistemological and professional investment in orthodoxy made by his contemporaries, the expectations that Keynes imposed on them were unreasonably costly. In his metaphor of classicism as a military fortification, Hawtrey, Pigou, and Robertson surveyed the territory of economic theory from within its walls. He had given them no reason to believe that their fortress was insecure. It was naïve in the extreme to suppose they would abandon a position they had occupied with confidence for many years in favor of a blueprint they regarded as defective and in large measure incomprehensible. In the revolutionary wars of the 1930s, classical economists were not likely to find Keynes's book convincing. And it is not plausible to suppose they would welcome a competitive dialogue that would drive the revolution to a successful conclusion: a debate in which *The General Theory* set the issues and the terms of the dispute.

Some three years before Keynes concluded that his strategy for engaging his contemporaries was flawed, Robinson had seen that revolutionary ideas would be least attractive to economists who knew what they thought and were heavily invested in orthodoxy. The ideal readership of her article "A Parable on Saving and Investment" comprised individuals who had made no theoretical investments and did not know what to think (in Keynes 1973a, 268–69). It followed that Keynes's neglect of the revolutionary potential of the younger generation was a mistake. Because he believed that their scientific education was seriously deficient—they had been brought up so badly that they believed "nothing in particular"—he concluded that his efforts to undermine the foundations of orthodoxy would have no significance for them. Robinson saw their theoretical innocence as an advantage in revolutionary recruitment. Precisely because of their ignorance of established theories, younger economists had made no professional commitments. Ideally, initiation into Keynes's ideas would occur at the beginning of training. Students would learn economics on Keynesian premises and translate all economic positions into his theoretical language. An appreciation of Keynes's struggle with his academic apprenticeship and his attack on classicism would have no place in this discussion. From the standpoint of the revolutionary movement, however, this was not a deficit. The architect of the revolution believed that its success depended on settling accounts with the past. Robinson, who would become the chief propagandist of the revolution, saw that success depended on forming young economists who would decide the future. Keynes's ideas would show young people what to think by providing a basis for research programs, the production of scientific credentials, and the formation of professional identities. Wittingly or unwittingly, the work of the next generation would constitute an assault on the established order.

Robinson concluded that it was necessary to educate students in the doctrines of the revolution by designing new curricula and syllabi, writing lectures and examination questions, and planning supervisions to achieve the proper quality and level of indoctrination. Students could not be expected to join the great debate Keynes anticipated. Because they were "uncontaminated" by knowledge of the discipline, they lacked the qualifications to participate. But because of their innocence, they were ideal recruits for the astute revolutionary lecturer. Both Robinson and Robertson were much more savvy than Keynes in grasping the importance of teaching as a decisive factor in the conflict between classicism and Keynesianism at Cambridge. Because most Cambridge economists were products of the Economics Tripos, Robinson and Robertson had good reason to think that the successors of the faculty of the 1930s were being trained in their lectures. Robinson seemed to have a firm grasp of the revolutionary tactic to which Keynes was apparently oblivious: if students were introduced to economics under her tutelage, she had a good chance of forming them into the Keynesians of the future.

THE REVOLUTIONARY PROPAGANDIST

While Keynes was writing *The General Theory*, Robinson was already at work on articles intended to extend its scope and increase its explanatory power. As early as August 1934, she drafted a paper entitled "Indeterminacy" that received his approval.[67] In March 1936, only a month after *The General Theory* appeared, she published "The Long-Period Theory of Employment" (1936b). Keynes's assumptions were restricted to the short period. By attempting to show how *The General Theory* could be generalized to analyze long-term conditions, she made the case that his arguments were more powerful than his book suggested. In June 1936, her article "Disguised Unemployment" appeared (1936a). In discussing employment, Keynes considered conditions under which insufficient demand left workers completely idle—a state of open unemployment. Robinson argued that when workers are laid off they take less productive jobs in order to survive even if they are reduced to selling matches on street corners. Although they are formally employed, their output is negligible. This was disguised unemployment. Robinson was able to move so quickly by closely following the development of Keynes's thought as he drafted and revised *The General Theory*. In September 1934, when she was preparing her lectures on applications of monetary theory, her plan was to write rough drafts on Keynesian themes and problems that she would later prepare for publication. This idea marked the beginning of more ambitious efforts to demonstrate to academic economists—and perhaps to Keynes himself—how *The General Theory* could be exploited.

Promoting *The General Theory*:
Essays in the Theory of Employment

In 1936, Robinson decided to publish a collection of papers that would employ the analytical tools of *The General Theory* to investigate problems it had not explored. This collection became her second book: *Essays in the Theory of Employment* (1937a). Between September and November of 1936, the proofs of this book were the subject of a spirited correspondence with Keynes that numbers twenty-two letters. This dialogue is of considerable interest, not least because of its marked contrast to their exchange on the manifesto in May 1932. By 1936, Robinson had acquired the theoretical knowledge and socioprofessional skills that were expected of a member of the Cambridge guild, competence she did not possess in 1932. Confident of her mastery of the protocols and techniques of scientific debate, she was no longer spellbound by the Keynesian aura. Her standing with Keynes had also been transformed. The appendage of Kahn had become an ally and critic on whom Keynes depended. The correspondence of 1936 also exhibits a reversal in the roles taken by Keynes and Robinson. In 1935, she had moved closer to Keynes by working on his proofs. It was Keynes, the author and senior partner in the dialogue, who initiated the exchange. In 1936, she was the author, and Keynes was the reader and critic. It was Robinson who initiated the exchange by sending him proofs for comment. Although the master had not become the apprentice, Robinson behaved as if her years of apprenticeship had ended. On the whole, she conducted her side of the debate as a dialogue between equals. She was still the junior partner and performed ritual acts of deference to his authority. However, they were made in her acknowledgment of appreciation for his help after the dialogue had ended, not in the debate itself. Discussion of her proofs promised obvious benefits for Robinson. Yet there were advantages for Keynes as well. He was determined to begin an intensive disciplinary controversy over his book. The terms of engagement were scientific polemics—a war of words in which classicists, once lured into combat, would be defeated by Keynesian arguments. Robinson was the most dedicated, fearless, and aggressive polemicist at his disposal. If a dialogue on her proofs would give him a voice in shaping her arguments along lines he regarded as most favorable to the grand debate, so much the better. Given their interests, both parties played their parts well.

Keynes took his role as commentator seriously, pointing out passages he regarded as factually mistaken, theoretically misguided, or logically fallacious. He tempered criticism with encouragement, praise, and his personal endorsement, which Robinson prized above all other marks of approbation. The tone of his remarks was not dogmatic or didactic, and there is no evidence here of the "attitude of omniscience on all topics" that Robert Skidelsky sees in the Keynes of late 1939 (Skidelsky 2000, 60). His observations were self-deprecatory and reserved, displaying one side of his fabled persuasive skills. The reader of this exchange does not find the world's most famous economist addressing an acolyte from Olympian heights but two like-minded, antiorthodox Cambridge theoreticians attempting to correct weaknesses in papers written by one of them. When he was convinced that Robinson was in danger of committing a damaging error, he could be firm and insistent. Otherwise, he was often tentative, encouraging Robinson to enlighten him. Her boldness in arguing with Keynes over his theories is striking, demonstrating her version of discipleship, the extent to which his ideas had become hers, and the poise she had achieved in the relationship.

Most of Keynes's reservations concerned two of the essays: "Mobility of Labour" and "The Foreign Exchanges." In *The General Theory*, Keynes analyzed involuntary unemployment caused by a drop in aggregate expenditure. Although he recognized the existence of frictional unemployment, it was not central to his analysis. In the first essay, Robinson considered frictional unemployment, caused by adventitious and ephemeral forces that rule out continuous full employment. She was chiefly interested in showing that frictional unemployment and aggregate expenditure were interdependent. In a recession, for example, it is difficult for workers who quit their jobs to find other work because of the decline in aggregate expenditure. In "The Foreign Exchanges," she argued that there was no unique equilibrium exchange rate. The exchange rate, the interest rate, the level of effective demand, and the level of money wages were mutually interdependent: it was impossible to determine the value of any one of these factors unless the other values were known. *The General Theory* was based on the assumption of a closed national economy. Because Keynes bracketed all extradomestic economic relations, he did not address problems posed by exchange rates.

Keynes found it difficult to comment on "Mobility of Labour" because he could not understand Robinson's arguments. At several points, he could identify no logic at all in her reasoning, leading him to conclude that the main theses of the paper were probably mistaken. As he wrote on October 15, "Will you think it over again and enlighten my darkness if I am simply misunderstanding it all" (Keynes 1973b, 138). The following day, Robinson sent him a new version of the objectionable passages. But she, too, was dissatisfied with her analysis and recognized that it was vulnerable to criticism. "Perhaps," she asked Keynes, "you could help me to clear it up—but the first step is to see if my argument is correct." This was a new move on Robinson's part. Not only did she ask Keynes for help with her work, she told him how to go about it. She also suggested that if he was free, they meet over the weekend to discuss this paper (in Keynes 1973b, 139). Shortly thereafter, Robinson notified Keynes that she was performing a "drastic overhaul" of the essay in an effort to clarify her argument and eliminate the grounds of their disagreement. When the new version was ready, she would send a copy (in Keynes 1973b, 140). She cheerfully assumed he was prepared to reserve part of his time at Cambridge, on which there were many demands, to read successive drafts of her essays, write comments, and argue out contested points. She was not mistaken. On November 6, she thanked him for further comments, noting that she would make most of the changes he had suggested. But in spite of his objections to the "general line" of her analysis, she intended to retain the current structure of her argument (in Keynes 1973b, 143). In this exchange, it seems, Keynes was not always recognized as the ultimate authority on Keynesian economics.[68]

In 1936, Robinson's dialogue with Keynes on her *Essays* also exposed a fundamental difference in their conceptions of economic theory. On September 17, he commented on her paper on foreign exchanges, noting "the extraordinary artificiality" of her position (Keynes 1973b, 136). On October 5, after he and Lydia had returned from Sweden, he wrote Robinson that during this trip he had read her first set of proofs, which included the essays "Full Employment" and "Certain Proposed Remedies for Unemployment." Although he praised the first paper, he noted the "formal and abstract" character of her argument in the second. This struck him as "a little unreal," especially in an essay devoted to policy proposals that were obviously intended to be empirically realistic and feasible (Keynes 1973b, 137). In comments written on November 4, he returned to her essay on foreign exchanges and the dangers of her method as he understood it. Robinson had begun the paper by assuming conditions of neutral equilibrium that are a consequence of absolute liquidity preference. In his view, these conditions could not be expected to conform to real economic behavior. His chief objection, though, concerned not her counterfactual assumption but how she used it: to make deductions that she then applied to actual economic affairs in which liquidity preference is not absolute. As he laconically observed, this method of argument was "unsafe and not likely to lead to reliable conclusions" (Keynes 1973b, 141). Robinson sympathized with Keynes's impression that her argument was indeed "very queer." She too had been quite surprised when she discovered the consequences that followed from her assumptions. But she was steadfast. If her reasoning was valid, the conclusions she reached did indeed follow and must be accepted as true even though they were counterintuitive and "a bit disconcerting" (in Keynes 1973b, 142). If Keynes's theoretical inferences contradicted his intuitions and failed to conform to economic facts as he understood them, he reexamined his theory to locate the problematic assumptions. If his results were unreasonable or implausible, the defects must lie in his theory, which required revision. Robinson, on the other hand, held fast to the philosophy of economic science she had sketched in *Economics Is a Serious Subject* in 1932. If her assumptions were "tractable"—amenable to current techniques of economic analysis—then inconsistencies between the consequences of these assumptions and the facts were not worrisome. Tractable assumptions took precedence over facts. Economic theory was an axiomatic and deductive project. Assumptions were not selected on grounds of empirical plausibility or even verifiability but by reference to their conformity with the existing apparatus of analysis. In choosing assumptions, the decisive question was always whether available methods could be employed to best advantage. The issue of whether the assumptions or their consequences were consistent with economic facts was irrelevant.

The home of this philosophy of economic science was not Cambridge but Vienna; its author was Carl Menger, not Alfred Marshall. Both before and after *The General Theory*, Keynes conceived economics as a moral science in the sense in which Marshall and Pigou understood this concept. In the final analysis, economics was defined teleologically. Its purpose was to advance human welfare by solving real economic problems. This meant that the chief desideratum in economics cannot be method. If the bedrock of economic science were constituted by methodological principles, economic theory would be reduced to a sterile intellectual game. In making theoretical assumptions, the decisive criterion was ethical and political: What premises were required to address the most serious and persistent economic problems of the time? For Keynes, economics remained political economy: an investigation of the economic conditions on which policies for enhancing human well-being can be pursued with the best prospect of success. Given the contingencies of human affairs, these conditions can be expected to change. It follows that economic theory as a universal set of doctrines that remained valid at all times and under all circumstances was out of the question. Although he stressed his break with orthodoxy and his struggle to free himself from the tradition in which he was trained, in these respects *The General Theory* remained a Marshallian text. Its purpose was to construct a new engine of discovery and analysis that would improve human life.

Keynes's conception of human well-being was indebted to G. E. Moore's salon ethic of exquisite emotional and intellectual sensibilities. However, Moore's *Principia Ethica* says nothing about the conditions that make possible a social world in which human beings can pursue intimate friendships, aesthetic delights, and the contemplation of knowledge as the highest goods (Moore 1903). The earlier Victorian moral fervor of human betterment that burned in Henry Sidgwick and Marshall also animated the work of Keynes. It is expressed in the toast he offered at a dinner given in February 1945 to celebrate his retirement as editor of the *Economic Journal*: "To economists, who are the trustees, not of civilisation, but of the possibility of civilisation" (in Skidelsky 2000, 168). Civilized life rests on a complex, fragile network of institutions that is possible only under special economic conditions. The final test of an economic theory is its contribution to the investigation of these conditions. Hypothetical and empirically arbitrary axioms that are detached from economic realities cannot pass this test. This is the ultimate reason Keynes rejected axiomatization and formalism as intrinsically important values in economics. A theory that pursued rigor for its own sake could not be expected to achieve the most powerful analysis of the economic underpinnings of civilization.

In her *Essays*, Robinson wrote as a model builder who made occasional pro forma and ad hoc gestures of deference to Cambridge moral science. Methodological refinements of theory were her primary consideration. Yet she was determined to become the most authentic of all Keynesians and the purest of the revolutionaries. On her interpretation, this meant absolute fidelity to Keynes's intentions in *The General Theory*. Robinson was not one of the younger generation of economists so badly educated that she did not know what to believe. She believed in the ideas of *The General Theory*. But in what sense was she committed to Keynes's ideas? Keynes wrote theory as strategy, designed to address the main economic problems of his age. Although he was persuaded that the fundamentals of his book were sound, much remained doubtful to him even as he published it. He wrote on the understanding that his ideas would require substantial reconsideration and revision. Robinson interpreted Keynes's ideas as doctrinal truths to be translated and systematized into the analytical language of a postrevolutionary system of economic science and packaged for consumption by economists. This was the work of the chief ideologist and propagandist of the revolution, a post she created and reserved for herself. Circa 1936, her conception of economics had no theoretical space for grandiose civilizational visions or moral objectives. As a body of economic truths, *The General Theory* was incomplete only in a formal sense: its assumptions had not been systematically stated, and their consequences had not been spelled out and analyzed. In light of her deviations from the spirit of Keynes's thinking, Robinson's acid criticisms of IS-LM formalizations of *The General Theory* are not without irony. They suggest that notwithstanding her apparent zeal in pursuit of ideological purity, Robinson herself was perhaps the first "bastard Keynesian."

Keynes had little sense of these departures from the fundamentals of his thought and Robinson none at all. The significance of their metatheoretical disagreements seems to have remained opaque to them both and proved to be no obstacle to the pursuit of their respective agendas. Keynes needed allies to prosecute the war he had declared on orthodoxy. Doctrinal purity was immaterial to his cause. In recruiting supporters, he followed a latitudinarian principle not generally associated with leaders of revolutionary movements. Endorsement of the main lines of his analysis seems to have been the sole qualification, and he took a relaxed view of disagreement among his supporters. Since he was convinced that much remained unclear and probably mistaken as well, a liberal principle of recruitment that tolerated divergent readings of *The General Theory* made good sense. Disputes among the initiated that did not touch basic issues were largely insignificant. However, Robinson's abstract formalism seemed to transgress even these permissive limits. Because it detached economics from economic reality, making any attempt to develop policy a theoretically arbitrary undertaking, the Robinsonian analytical economics of her

Essays was opposed to Keynes's conception of economic theory and its aims. Nevertheless, Keynes's objections remained marginal, and Robinson was able to "become a Keynesian," believing in her fidelity to his intentions and promoting *The General Theory* to the economics profession with remarkable success. At the same time, she pursued a methodological program he had rejected as inconsistent with the objectives of the revolution.

In the end, Keynes gave the book his qualified blessing. The essays were uneven, as she knew. But on the whole he judged the results "splendid, full of originality and interest" (Keynes 1973b, 147). In 1932, his ambivalent evaluation of *The Economics of Imperfect Competition* was based largely on his judgment that the book lacked innovative ideas. It would be difficult to make a case that the *Essays* was a more original work. As Pigou observed, *The Economics of Imperfect Competition* developed and clarified an analytical apparatus that could not be found in the recent literature. In her first book, Robinson proved to be more of a toolmaker than a tool user. In the *Essays*, she employed Keynes's tools. Both in intention and execution, the book was derivative. Theoretical premises and modes of analysis were drawn from *The General Theory*. Her aim was to make a case for Keynes's new program by showing economists how it could be used to analyze specific questions in economic theory. Given Keynes's ambitions, his judgment of the two books is perhaps not surprising. He had no interest in becoming the leader of a movement to promote the investigation of imperfect competition. In an oblique reference to the sharp polemics of the *Essays*, he speculated that Robinson's fierceness might not be well received by some readers. But he was pleased with her more polemical arguments, which were developed against his enemies, and did not encourage a more temperate rhetoric (Keynes 1973b, 147). In view of Keynes's efforts on Robinson's behalf, is it surprising that her preface includes no acknowledgment of his help? She rightly supposed he would not relish public recognition of his work on her proofs (in Keynes 1973b, 148). The propaganda value of the *Essays* could only have been diminished by the impression that Keynes himself had taken a hand in writing it.

The Children's Tale: *Introduction to the Theory of Employment*

Waiting for the page proofs of the *Essays* to arrive, Robinson was already contemplating a second Keynesian book. In the *Essays*, her audience was the economics profession. She made a case for *The General Theory* by showing academic economists how to refine and extend it. Only four days after sending him a final note of thanks for his help, Robinson tried to interest Keynes in a plan to reach a much larger audience. Her idea was to write what she dismissively called a "told to the children" version of *The General Theory*, a textbook that could be assigned to complement introductory lectures in economics. The scope of *The General Theory* would be reduced to its basic principles. Analyses would be simplified to meet the needs of beginning students, who had no knowledge of the theoretical background against which Keynes was writing. In an elementary textbook, much of *The General Theory* would necessarily disappear. "I would," Robinson explained to Keynes, "be as uncontroversial as possible and treat everything in the straightforward way that one can with an uncontaminated audience" (in Keynes 1979, 184–85). Because Keynes's critique of classicism would be incomprehensible to beginning students, his criticisms of orthodoxy and orthodoxy itself would disappear. Or rather Keynes's ideas, which were new and controversial, would be presented as if they constituted orthodoxy. Oblivious of alternatives, new students would be taught Keynesian economics, suitably translated and simplified, as if it were the only conception of how economics could be done. Although Robinson had already drafted some material, she did not want to proceed without Keynes's approval. Was he interested (in Keynes 1979, 184–85)?

Initially, Keynes was not. Waiting a week without a response, Robinson wrote again on November 25, asking for a meeting over the weekend when he would be in Cambridge. After they met, he wrote on December 2, explaining his reservations about her proposal. He had two main worries. He was wary of any publication that would represent *The General Theory* as established doctrine. Convinced that the broad outlines of his analysis were acceptable, he had doubts about some of his conclusions and the methods he used in reaching them. Correspondence and reviews had persuaded him that the book was not a success in all respects. To what extent and in exactly what respects? Only subsequent controversy would tell. He was intent on keeping his ear tuned to responses of his critics: to "what raises difficulties and catches people's attention—in which there are a good many surprises" (Keynes 1979, 185). What was and was not sound in *The General Theory*? Because of surprises hidden in controversies that were only beginning, this question could not be answered in December

1936. Nor was it possible to anticipate the criticisms that were indispensable in arriving at an answer. The book represented Keynes's views as of December 1935. Because he believed that further progress depended on extensive debate, he suspended revisions in order to initiate this conversation. However, publication did not suspend Keynes's thinking on the problems of the book, which proceeded apace and without significant interruption. Moreover, his ideas on the merits of particular analyses could change quite quickly as he responded to the impressions of his correspondents. *The General Theory* was written in response to objections and suggestions posed by the critics of the *Treatise*. In autumn 1936, Keynes was apparently thinking along similar lines. A new theoretical work would be needed to address the problems posed by critics of *The General Theory*. Criticism was already under way. Thus Keynes was against a simplified version of a book that was, in a sense, already dated. He was in favor of waiting, reflecting, and "gestation" (Keynes 1979, 186). Independent of these considerations, Keynes had no clear sense of how a popular version of *The General Theory* should be written. Although this was a matter to which he had devoted some thought, at that point he had reached no conclusions. He was skeptical of any reduction of his book to lessons in economic policy. This would encourage applications of his ideas to current economic problems on the part of readers who did not have the training to grasp his formal theory (Keynes 1979, 186). Robinson assured Keynes that her children's book would not be an exercise in popularization. She did not propose to bowdlerize his ideas and encourage readers to apply them to questions of policy. She had conceived a work of a quite different genre—a basic textbook that would reconstruct economics on Keynesian foundations and with Keynesian tools. The question of how such a book should best be written was a difficult matter. Her idea was to prepare a manuscript and test it on students that she, Austin, and Kahn supervised. Here the matter rested until March 6, 1937, when she wrote Keynes that her test marketing had demonstrated a "strong demand" for the manuscript. In addition, she was convinced that students in the Workers' Educational Association—a charity founded in 1903 to educate adult workers—were "thirsting for *The General Theory*, and scorn tutors who serve up the old stuff." Because of the knowledge of economics that Keynes presupposed, they found his book puzzling (in Keynes 1973b, 148–49). Thus the need for her textbook. In December, Keynes had explained that in the interest of making progress with his theoretical work, he was against "crystallising" his thinking on the basis of what he had published in *The General Theory* (Keynes 1979, 185). Robinson agreed with the wisdom of "not crystallising too soon." But she did not regard his prudence in resisting premature closure on unsettled issues as an obstacle to her project, which would cover only basic principles. At this point she left Cambridge for a vacation in Syria and Palestine.

While she was away, Keynes reconsidered and reversed himself. On March 25, he sent a letter to her Cambridge address approving the project. Although he maintained that the best elementary exposition of *The General Theory* would depart from the original more substantially than Robinson's text had done, he had no suggestions as to how such an exposition might be written. Thus his advice: "By all means get on with this" (Keynes 1973b, 149). In early April, Robinson, still in Syria, had not received Keynes's letter but only news from Austin in Cambridge that Keynes had written "rather hesitantly" about her book—a peculiar reading of his encouragement. As was her habit, Robinson attempted to press Kahn into service to intercede with Keynes on her behalf. Concerning the book, she wrote on April 7, "I think you could have a heart to heart with him." And yet she also insisted that she had no interest in whether she completed the book: "It is for you chaps to say if you need it" (RFK/13/90/2/173–74). This last remark hardly rings true. Robinson pushed herself to produce manuscripts and publish them. Between 1931 and 1937, she moved swiftly from one project to another in spite of deficits in professional training, pregnancy and motherhood, and the difficulties presented by her relationships with Austin and Kahn. She was persistent in her efforts to gain Keynes's benediction. She had written a manuscript and revised it, based on assessments of its use at Cambridge. When she returned to Cambridge, Keynes wrote again. He did "not really feel the least objection in the world" to her text and agreed that it would be valuable (Keynes 1973b, 150). The book was published later that year.

In several respects, the dialogue between Keynes and Robinson on the merits of her textbook reproduces the positions they took in their exchanges on her *Essays*. Keynes saw *The General Theory* as a work in progress subject to further clarification and revision. How should the theses of *The General Theory* be understood? Which of its claims were promising and which should be discarded? Answers to these questions would emerge from a grand disciplinary symposium. In order to initiate hostilities, a declaration of war—*The General Theory*—was needed to mark off contested territory, specify terms of engagement, and place potential combatants on notice. Although Keynes was confident of ultimate victory, the question of how exactly his enemies would be vanquished could be decided only in the conduct of the war itself. On this matter, he took a Clausewitzian view of the contingencies of scientific warfare. Because every war has its own surprises, it was necessary to remain flexible and alert to the kinds of criticisms readers raised. This meant that the project of *The General Theory*—as opposed to the text of *The General Theory*—was a strategic enterprise in which adventitious opportunities were paramount. It was driven not by its own immanent logic but by interventions of economists in the great debate and by how Keynes and his supporters responded to them. Although it was impossible to predict the dynamics and consequences of this debate, Keynes was certain it would change his thinking and complete the work he could not have done as he was writing the book. Thus the dangers of crystallizing ideas prematurely, before the debate had run its course. In *The General Theory*, Keynes took the advice he gave economists in his essay on Marshall and followed the path he claimed Marshall did not take. He was prepared "to cast his half-baked bread on the waters," trusting "in the efficacy of the co-operation of many minds" and allowing "the big world to draw from him what sustenance it could." Like Jevons's *Political Economy*, *The General Theory* was "no more than a brilliant brochure." Like Jevons, Keynes was willing to "spill his ideas, to flick them at the world." Leaving to Adam Smith, John Stuart Mill, and Marshall "the glory of the Quarto," Keynes acted on his own imperative: "Write always *sub species temporis*" (Keynes 1951, 173–74).

This was not Robinson's conception of *The General Theory*. Unlike other work in economics, it should be read *sub species aeternitatis*. Keynes had discovered a body of economic truths that could be applied to resolve economic problems and provide the basis for a new pedagogy. Robinson had no doubts about what these truths were and how they should be understood. Doubts were inconsistent with her agenda. They would forestall her plan to indoctrinate beginning students, "uncontaminated" by training in economics. They would also compromise her own Keynesian research program. After publishing her first book, Robinson invested in Keynes. If his new ideas were quickly superseded by even newer developments in his thought, *The General Theory* might share the fate of the *Treatise*. In that case, it would be regarded not as his masterwork but as a flawed and transitional effort, overshadowed by the thinking that was apparently germinating in autumn of 1936 and about which Robinson knew nothing. Suppose the canonical text of the revolution turned out to be not *The General Theory* but an as-yet-unwritten work. In that case, Robinson's turn from imperfect competition to *The General Theory* might prove to be a disappointing investment. In order to retain her status as a leader of revolutionary elite, she would face the prospect of yet another investment, this time in Keynes's post–*General Theory* work. And if the *Treatise* had been succeeded by *The General Theory*, which would be superseded by another new work, was there any reason to believe that this unwritten work would not be replaced by yet another batch of new ideas, leavened by Keynes's creative but restless brilliance? If one set of half-baked analyses was followed by another *ad seriatim*, could Robinson expect to arrive at settled doctrines she could believe in, market to economists, and exploit in her own research? These uncertainties dictated a commitment to the solidity of *The General Theory*. As regards fundamentals, Robinson wrote confidently that "we know near enough where we are" (in Keynes 1973b, 149). Confirmation of basic Keynesian truths did not depend on the controversy produced by a general conflagration in economics. These truths were revealed hermetically through personal contact with the master and his intimates. The qualification for understanding *The General Theory* was not participation in a disciplinary dialogue but membership in a charismatic set of the chosen, the privileged experience of being one of the Cambridge illuminati—"we happy few in Cambridge . . . we and Maynard," as Robert Solow characterized the gnostic ethos of Keynes's disciples in the 1930s (1989, 545).

Robinson's understanding of *The General Theory* as revealed truth entailed a distinctive conception of the dynamics of the Keynesian revolution. The lapsarian classical age of darkness was transformed into a new enlightened Keynesian age of grace. The revolution was a cataclysmic event, a scientific "ten days that shook the world," following which economics would settle into a new normality grounded in secure principles. This was not Keynes's position. He saw the revolution not as a single shattering event but as a process of continuous reconsideration, revision, and renovation. This is why it was essential to maintain theoretical flexibility and reject any apotheosis of his current ideas into a pseudocanon. For the near term, the only period he was prepared to consider, Keynes saw not the pacification of economics but implacable struggle, a condition that would approximate Trotsky's state of permanent revolution: much controversy, persistent argument over fundamentals, and no consensus or stability. A new state of normality was not on the horizon. Keynes, his mind in motion and his ideas in transition, would continue to stoke the fires that fueled the revolution.

THE LECTURE LIST DISPUTE

In October 1933, Kahn was appointed to a part-time university lectureship for a three-year term. On May 25, 1936, the faculty board recommended him for a full-time lectureship to the General Board of the Faculties (FB/Min.V.118). As a part-time lecturer, he delivered two sets of lectures on the short period in the Lent and Easter terms to students in their final year of Part II of the tripos. On a full-time appointment, he would be responsible for an additional set of lectures. He decided on the title "Some Current Economic Problems," which would include monetary theory. This meant that four lecturers would teach money in Part II of the tripos. Robinson's lectures on applications of monetary theory covered the second year in Michaelmas and Lent. Kahn, Keynes, and Robertson would teach third-year students. Robertson lectured on money in Michaelmas, Lent, and Easter. Keynes planned to lecture on the subject "Footnotes to the General Theory of Employment, Interest, and Money" in Lent. And Kahn's new lectures would be added in Michaelmas.[69] Thus the Cambridge curriculum on money would be represented by Keynes, his two most ardent disciples, and Robertson, the sole orthodox dissenter.

Kahn's lecture proposal initiated a dispute in the economics faculty that centered on Robinson. Although not every piece of correspondence on this matter is available, its history can be reconstructed from extant documents. The discussion began in the Lecture List Committee, where the appropriate clientele for Kahn's lectures was considered. Someone— Kahn claimed it was not him—suggested opening his lectures to both second- and third-year students. The committee decided in favor of this suggestion should it be found "humanly possible." Kahn thought it was a good idea but at the same time declared: "The matter was not one on which I felt more than lukewarm."[70] This result seems to have caused consternation in the committee, chiefly on the part of Robertson, as his later correspondence with Keynes shows.[71] The general issue in the dispute was Robertson's sense that the Keynesians were attempting to dominate the curriculum in monetary theory and discredit orthodox views. He was especially unhappy with Robinson, "both the lecturer and the lectures," as Keynes later put it.[72] The specific issue was Robertson's mistaken impression that Kahn intended to require attendance in Robinson's lectures as a prerequisite for his course.

Kahn cleared up the mistake in a letter to Maurice Dobb, secretary of the faculty board, on June 2, using the occasion to indulge himself in a wicked parody of academic pedantry.[73] The difference between Robinson's lectures and his proposed lectures, as he explained it, was quite simple. She discussed examples of monetary issues in order to illuminate general theoretical principles. He would assume that his audience had covered the fundamentals of monetary theory and intended to discuss specific cases for their intrinsic interest. As a supervisor, he would advise his second-year pupils to attend her lectures, also informing them that "it was a matter of indifference whether they attended my lectures in their second or in their third year." This indifference left open the possibility that, schedules permitting, a student might attend the lectures of both Robinson and Kahn in the same term, in which case her lectures could not serve as a prerequisite of his. Feigning bewilderment and indulging in witticisms at the expense of his colleagues while scrupulously observing the amenities, he offered his deepest apologies to Dobb and the committee for the trouble he had unwittingly caused them: "I thought that in making what seemed to me a very simple suggestion I was raising a matter of pure routine. I had no idea that any point of principle was involved. What that point is I cannot pretend to know. But I must apologise for having unwittingly raised it" (JMK/UA/5/4/9/10–11).

On being shown this letter by Keynes, Robertson confessed that he had misunderstood Kahn's proposal. Robertson's response to Keynes is a tortured document. Hypersensitive, he perceived slights that were not intended and imagined conspiracies that did not exist. At the same time, he was punctilious on matters of form: "I should like to say that on reading Kahn's letter again I can see that I was wrong in questioning your interpretation of it, and did him injustice in suggesting that he was intimating to the Committee that he could regard it as objectionable to have at his Lectures men who had not attended Mrs. Robinson's Lectures. I realised that he did not say this in so many words, but it seemed to me that in effect that was what his letter came to. I can see now that I was wrong."[74] After admitting his error, Robertson apologized to virtually everyone in sight: Keynes, the entire Lecture List Committee, and indirectly, Kahn:

"I cannot well apologise to Kahn for something of which he is in ignorance. But I hope that if on his return word reaches him of our discussion, word will also reach him of this letter."[75] No apology was extended to Robinson.

In this fashion, the contretemps over Kahn's lecture proposal seems to have been put to rest. Not so Robinson's lectures to second-year students, which remained a source of disagreement. As a general rule, the second year of the economics curriculum was the first year of Part II of the tripos. Students who had read economics in their first year would have heard Pigou's lectures on elementary principles, a paradigmatic exposition of classical economics by one of its most creative and influential contemporary exponents. Students who had been instructed by Pigou in classical principles were not likely to find Robinson's caricature of classical economics convincing or even plausible. However, students arriving from Part I of the tripos of other fields to receive their baptism in the fundamentals of economics from Robinson were in a quite different position. In view of her provocative approach to teaching, their initial exposure to economics might well be disastrous for their receptivity to classicism and to Robertson's lectures in particular.

In March 1935, the question of Robinson's appointment as a full-time assistant lecturer and her proposal to deliver two terms of lectures on applications of monetary theory for second-year students had been a subject of bitter contention in the faculty. At the end of that dispute, Robinson won everything she wanted: the lectureship, the two-term course, and her tendentious syllabus. Her adversaries walked away with nothing. In 1936, Robertson, still the chairman of the board, raised objections to Robinson's second-year lectures on money. He had two fundamental complaints. It was unacceptable to offer a narrow and tendentious set of lectures to students who had read no economics. As he wrote Keynes, "I *don't* think it is good that people coming over from other subjects [into Part II of the Economics Tripos] should get their first introduction to this whole range of very controversial topics from someone who seems to think that everything that has been said and thought about it is 'moth-eaten' rubbish except one book—and that, whatever its merits, a very difficult one!" (quoted in Moggridge 1992, 600). In addition, he maintained that Robinson's conduct, and perhaps the behavior of her supporters, posed a threat to the liberal culture of the Marshallian guild by introducing dogmatic, ideological premises into disputes over academic and scientific questions. Robertson regarded this as a dangerous innovation. As he wrote Keynes, "Over this business [concerning Robinson's lectures] there is an atmosphere of dogmatism and proselytisation about into which our socialists and communists have never landed us + which is new and un-Cambridge-y" (quoted in Moggridge 1992, 600).

Keynes responded by taking Robinson's part. His letter to Robertson was measured and diplomatic. He wrote not as a partisan but as an impartial judge, full of good will for all parties. In his view, there were four serious weaknesses in Robertson's position: (1) Perhaps most troublesome, Robertson's intervention—essentially an attempt to force Robinson to change the content and perspective of her lectures—would set an unfortunate precedent. Keynes made it clear that Robertson was not the only guardian of the Cambridge tradition of intellectual liberalism and *Lehrfreiheit*. On the assumption that they covered the required territory, Keynes argued, it was understood that university lecturers had the right to follow their own lights. "It would have been a dangerous thing," he warned, "for the Chairman of the Board to have used more than a very modest pressure to interfere with the lecturer's strong wishes." (2) Because of Robertson's objections to both the lectures and the lecturer, his opposition would have left "a sense of persecution" in the minds of some colleagues. Keynes wanted to avoid this result. In opposing Robertson and supporting Robinson, he claimed that his sole motive was "to prevent a very unpleasant personal situation from arising." (3) Robertson had also failed to consider that monetary theory was in a state of disarray and the subject of considerable controversy. Using the argument for a pluralistic pedagogy in the field of money that he had employed in 1935, Keynes held that areas of the curriculum that were subjects of substantial theoretical conflict required a laissez-faire pedagogy, not centralized planning by the board or the committee. In matters of university teaching, apparently, classicism was still valid. (4) Finally, Keynes was persuaded that university lectures would make little difference, either in the long run or even in the short run, in deciding the controversy sparked by *The General Theory*. The great debate over Keynes's ideas would be settled elsewhere.[76]

On September 28, Robertson conceded defeat but with little grace. He accepted the current lecture list as "the least bad in the circumstances." At that point, nothing could be achieved by further argument. As he wrote Keynes, "I realise it's no use at present our trying to see eye to eye about this: and also that the position is complicated by my inability, after years of effort for Austin's sake, to preserve personally cordial relations with Mrs. R." (quoted in Moggridge 1992, 600).

ANTICLIMAX:
THE UNIVERSITY LECTURESHIP

Robinson's appointment as assistant lecturer would expire in September 1938. The main source of evidence concerning her appointment to a university lectureship is a report that Kahn sent Keynes in a long letter written over February 14–18, 1938. Kahn maintained that the board recommended her appointment without enthusiasm, some members taking the view that her original part-time appointment had been a mistake. Keynes was not happy with the "wretches" on the board who had refused to acknowledge her merits. However, he responded to Kahn's news with some relief: "For if it [the appointment] had fallen through, it would really have been a cause for armed insurrection."[77] In light of Kahn's report and the minutes of the board meeting, what can be said concerning the circumstances of Robinson's appointment?

Kahn speculated that faculty thinking on the appointment began with Pigou. Toward the end of Michaelmas 1937, he met with Robertson to discuss what to do about Robinson's position on the faculty. From the outset, the two seem to have assumed that she should be advanced to a university lectureship.[78] The issue concerned the best way to secure the appointment. They concluded that the Appointments Committee of the board should recommend her for a lectureship on the assumption that the university would fund the position. The board, following standard procedure, would then petition the General Board of the Faculties to establish a lectureship in economics, which would be offered to Robinson. The committee was composed of the university vice chancellor as chair, Pigou, Keynes, Robertson, Fay, and two noneconomists appointed as representatives of the general board. Pigou and Robertson shared their thinking informally with at least one member of the Appointments Committee, who was not in favor of reserving the position for an inside candidate: on principle it should be filled only after a search governed by open competition. This view did not prevail, and the committee followed the Pigou-Robertson plan.

As chairman of the board, Robertson prepared a draft on the appointment that was discussed in its meeting of January 24—"the curious draft report, prepared by Dennis," as Kahn called it. It seems Robertson made a case for Robinson's appointment without taking note of her qualifications for the job. His rationale was that a current university lecturer in economics, W. S. Thatcher, was leaving economics for geography. This meant that a lectureship in economics was about to be vacated and should be filled. The board quickly rejected this draft. As Kahn observed, one of the general board representatives "told us at once—as was indeed obvious—that the Thatcher device was too thin to take in the G[eneral]. B[oard]." Kahn proposed that the board, like other such boards at Cambridge, support the appointment on the basis of increased enrollments and sound pedagogy: although the number of undergraduates in economics had risen sharply, the size of the economics faculty had remained stable, reducing the lecturer/student ratio. Appealing to the "Thatcher device" without making an independent argument for the appointment, Kahn claimed, would weaken the board's case. Presumably he expected the general board to conclude that if the economists employed such a transparently weak argument for the position, they had no strong argument. However, Kahn's proposal was roundly criticized and rejected.

At that point in the meeting, Shove finally introduced Robinson's name into the discussion, suggesting that his colleagues be frank about their intentions. If they wanted not merely a lectureship but Robinson, they should say so. This prompted one member to introduce such a proposal, which would call for a letter petitioning the general board to create a lectureship for Robinson. The board rejected this proposal as well, at least initially. It apparently escaped the board that its own Appointments Committee had already made precisely the proposal they were rejecting. This lapse is especially surprising since three members of the board—Pigou, Robertson, and Fay—served on the committee. Faced with a deadline governing decisions on university lectureships and the possibility of an embarrassing conflict with its committee, the board reversed itself after a fashion. Shove was delegated to revise Robertson's draft for the general board. All members of the board signed the revised letter, which did not mention Robinson. Noting the expiration of the term of the assistant lectureship, the letter, in Kahn's words, "left it studiously doubtful who would be appointed to a new lectureship (the present Assistant Lecturer or someone else)."[79]

The general board responded on February 10. A new lectureship would be created on the proviso that the assistant lectureship about to expire would remain unfilled. As its language indicated, the general board seems to have assumed that the current assistant lecturer would occupy the new position: "That such a lectureship should be established on the understanding that the Faculty Assistant Lectureship *so vacated* should not for the present be filled."[80] The assistant lectureship would be vacated because the current occupant would fill the new position. As a result of this decision, the Appointments Committee quickly convened and unanimously recommended Robinson's appointment to a university lectureship in the event the position was created. The board met the next day and unanimously endorsed the committee's recommendation. In this manner, Robinson became a university lecturer. When the board recommended Kahn for a full-time lectureship, its decision was "based on the importance attached by the Board to the retention of Mr Kahn's services as a lecturer."[81] Not so the recommendation to appoint Robinson, which fell far short of a ringing endorsement. The minutes of the board meeting of February 14 recommending her appointment read as follows:

A discussion took place on a reply from the General Board concerning the Report on the Lectureship in the Faculty at present occupied by Mr. Thatcher. The following resolution was moved by Professor Pigou & was agreed to unanimously: "The Faculty Board of Economics & Politics learn that the Appointments Committee of the Faculty have agreed to appoint Mrs. J. V. Robinson to a University Lectureship for an initial period of three years in the event of the University deciding to establish such a lectureship. The Faculty Board accordingly agree to the proposal of the General Board in their letter of February 10: 'That such a Lectureship should be established on the understanding that the Faculty Assistant Lectureship so vacated should not for the present be filled.[']" (FB/Min.V.118)

Kahn's account of the result was embittered by his sense that the board made Robinson the object of a degradation ceremony even as it approved her appointment. Although unanimous, the decision "could not conceivably have been more grudging." Robinson's record of scientific achievement was passed over in silence. Since her probationary appointment in 1934, she had published two books and several important articles. The board made no case for either the intrinsic importance or influence of this work. Neither the broad disciplinary reputation she had achieved nor her success as a supervisor was discussed. The only rationale for the appointment was an argument based on "legitimate expectations": failure to make the appointment would have been a departure from the standard practice of granting regular lectureships to assistant lecturers whose performance proved satisfactory. As a result, "it certainly seemed to transpire that it was a great mistake to have taken Joan on in the first place." Moreover, the board approved the appointment only in the sense that it accepted "the situation forced on them by the G.B." Because of the rationale employed in the board's original proposal to create the lectureship, the general board approved the new position only on the condition that Robinson's assistant lectureship be vacated—left open by her move into the new position. As Kahn read the decision, this gave the board no choice in naming the candidate. In his view, Robinson became a university lecturer by default.[82]

"Who Is
Joan Robinson?"

TWO HISTORIOGRAPHIES

In the main, the literature on Joan Robinson and Cambridge economics in the 1930s is devoted to the analysis of ideas and the explication of texts, several of which are now considered classics. The chief desideratum is to understand her economic thought, identify the economists who influenced her, and show how her work was tied to the main currents in Cambridge economics of the time. This historiography—the story of economic theory as an immanent history of ideas—begins and ends with books and essays and traces their relationships to other books and essays. It is situated in a grand tradition of writing on the history of science, from Edwin A. Burtt (1926) and Herbert Butterfield (1957) to Alexander Koyré (1957) and E. J. Dijksterhuis (1961). As Richard Westfall's masterful work on Isaac Newton shows (1981), this tradition maintained its force and vitality into the late twentieth century.

This book takes a different course. We analyze Robinson's early work on economics, but we do so in order to explore her early career, examining her ideas only to understand how she established herself at Cambridge.

We consider how she understood imperfect competition and Keynes's work but do so in offering an account of the formation and development of her professional identity. We are less concerned with how her thinking was tied to the Marshallian tradition or to Sraffa or Keynes than with the question of how she operated in the Marshallian guild—how she employed its resources as she moved from marginality to apprenticeship and, by 1935, to a position of power in the revolutionary cadre that transformed the guild. In considering *The Economics of Imperfect Competition*, our concern is not principally what she wrote but the social process of composition. We are less interested in the precise sense in which she was a Keynesian than in the social dynamics of her acceptance and endorsement by Keynes. We do not consider the respects in which her analyses may be valid and her conclusions true but the circumstances under which her writings were acknowledged as valuable contributions to Cambridge economics. During the 1930s, Robinson became a success at Cambridge. We analyze the conditions under which her success was achieved, how it was managed, and the resources on which it depended.

In sum, the foregoing account abandons the path of the standard historiography on the young Robinson in order to investigate the institutional and strategic foundations of her early career. The institutional strand of the analysis examines the rapidly changing social and intellectual resources that the Marshallian guild placed at her disposal. The strategic strand considers how these resources were mobilized and deployed on her behalf—generally by Robinson herself, sometimes by her advocates, and occasionally, in self-defeating fashion, by her adversaries, in all cases with consequences that worked to her advantage. Robinson's integration of theoretical work, professional identity formation, and career production seems to approximate an ideal type of the scientist as strategist in the "actor-network theory" of Bruno Latour and his collaborators. On this view, science is a battleground on which actors compete for sponsors, allies, and resources in an effort to achieve mastery over the organization and practice of a scientific field. The objective of theorists is to gain leverage by establishing strong networks of support. Combatants on the scientific battleground can succeed only by becoming Archimedean "macro-actors" who gain access to powerful networks.[1] This was Robinson's position by the end of 1935, after she had commented on the proofs of *The General Theory* and Keynes's correspondence with Hawtrey. Once leverage is achieved, relatively small-scale efforts by a scientist can achieve consequences of considerable significance, as her Keynesian textbook shows.

In November 1952, apparently after Robinson experienced a psychiatric breakdown (less severe than her illness of 1938), she offered a retrospective explanation of her success. Writing Kahn, she observed: "I think the reason I have done so much more with a much weaker brain than any of us is because of my extremely simple minded attitude."[2] Putting aside the question of whom she might have meant by "any of us," Robinson's career in the 1930s cannot be understood this easily, even if her account of her "attitude" is accepted without a demurrer. In 1930, she was a faculty wife. By 1937–38, she was a power in the economics faculty and an internationally respected theoretician. How did this happen? We stress the respects in which she achieved success by leveraging herself into positions that served her purposes. During the 1930s, Robinson assembled a formidable strategic tool kit, linking herself to the interests of others, connecting them to her ambitions, and in the case of Keynes making herself a resource for the project of a powerful sponsor. In showing how she surmounted, dismantled, or evaded the various barriers to entry in her path, it is useful to see Robinson as equipped with several assets, some of which we consider in the ensuing.

STRATEGIC SAVVY

Robinson consistently demonstrated an acute sensibility in recognizing contingencies as opportunities that could be exploited with substantial payoffs. In her first research program, she was perceptive in seeing imperfect competition as a new field that would excite interest. Quick to identify a well-defined but empty theoretical space, she did not hesitate to fill it with a technically innovative book. In doing so, she appropriated Cambridge resources that were on hand and easily accessible. In this regard, the collaboration between Robinson and Kahn is quite instructive. When Kahn made his availability clear to her, she took advantage of his liberality in placing his time and skills at her disposal. Kahn was a resource she used for a variety of purposes as he helped draft, revise, edit, proofread, and promote her book.[3] The Cambridge reception of *The Economics of Imperfect Competition* was secured in part by the method of the book's production. In both research and writing, Robinson was adept in the uses of dialogue. Her colleagues proved willing interlocutors. Pigou, Keynes, Sraffa, and

Kahn all took some part in the work and had a stake in the result. Moreover, as we observe above, Robinson's relationship with Robertson did not begin in a poisonous manner. In Michaelmas 1928, when Austin had given her the task of inquiring into possible fellowships and lectureships for him at Cambridge, the "charming" and winsome "Dennis" was her main contact with the faculty board.[4] And when *The Economics of Imperfect Competition* was still at an early stage of composition, she tried to interest him in writing a preface, hoping to appropriate his reputation in order to smooth her path to a publisher. The book appeared without a preface or blessing from Robertson. However, in 1938, Robinson wrote Austin that long ago she had discovered that good reviews could always be secured by an appropriately congratulatory preface.[5]

Kahn's efforts at Chicago on Robinson's behalf seem to have paid off handsomely in the reception of the book outside Cambridge. Some three months after publication, Viner sent her a glowing letter of congratulations from London, noting that she had succeeded in improving analytical technique and advancing the investigation of problems further than he had done:

I had hoped to find time before leaving England to read your book, but could not manage it. I am ordering a copy sent to me to Geneva, however, and will have time before long to go through it with the care it deserves. In the few minutes of turning its pages in Hicks' study, I saw that you had the same type of discriminating monopoly solution as mine, but that you had apparently succeeded in going further than I could, since you appear to have a general mode of treatment of curves. Given any set of curves, I could solve the problem, but I was not able to find the criteria which led to the alternative types of results, except for straight lines.

I wonder if you have looked into the problem where the two markets are not wholly independent of each other, and where they cannot be served at identical cost to the seller — both conditions likely to prevail. Perhaps you have dealt with them and solved them in your book! I saw enough of it to see that it is an important contribution.[6]

A letter of January 1935 from Paul Douglas, an economist at the University of Chicago, is evidence that *The Economics of Imperfect Competition* was being read as Robinson intended, indicating that she had succeeded in marking her identity as an innovator in a new theoretical field. Douglas stressed the originality of the book and its contribution to analyses of value and distribution:

I am taking the liberty of writing you to tell you how much I have gained personally from your splendid book *The Economics of Imperfect Competition*. I have been working through it off and on for a number of months, and find it admirable in all respects. Your introduction of the marginal revenue curve gives us a most powerful weapon in the analysis of monopoly price and as you well bring out alters greatly the discussion of the problem of distribution. If I were rewriting my book on *The Theory of Wages*, I would certainly include another chapter discussing the effect of monopoly and of imperfect competition upon the shares of the factors. And it would, of course, be very largely based upon your work.[7]

Robinson's second research program did not begin so easily. When Keynes was writing *The General Theory*, she was in no position to serve as midwife at the birth of the Keynesian revolution. Until August 1934, she had not even undertaken a careful reading of the *Treatise*. By that point, Keynes's new ideas and the scaffolding of his conceptual apparatus were in place and drafting was under way. After the birth of her first child, however, she wasted little time in closing gaps in her training. In preparing to lecture on applications of monetary theory, she made a thorough study of the *Treatise*, and, in conversations with Kahn and Sraffa, she kept abreast of changes in Keynes's post-*Treatise* thinking. After reading the proofs of *The General Theory*, she saw the problems posed for revolutionary propaganda by his conceptual and terminological innovations and the introduction of analyses that were both counterintuitive and inconsistent with received economic doctrine. Other genres of economic writing would be needed to consummate the revolution he had begun. *The General Theory* required translation, adaptation, and extension—a reorchestration of the new economic score for audiences Keynes had not addressed. Because Robinson had made herself into a Keynesian as he was writing *The General Theory*, she was able to publish both her *Essays* and the *Introduction* the year after his book appeared. These works refashioned her identity, distinguishing her as the leading Keynesian expositor of the day. The results of her efforts are nicely documented in a letter of congratulations on the *Introduction* from Evin Durbin, a lecturer at LSE at the time. Although his theoretical sympathies were remote from Keynes's ideas, he saw virtues in the *Introduction* she had not anticipated, suggesting that the book had exceeded her expectations:

Since I have returned from America I have read your little book "The Introduction to the Theory of Employment". I should like to say, if I may, how very much

I have enjoyed it. It seems to me to be one of the most brilliantly lucid books that I have ever read. You say that it is not addressed to your fellow economists; but I cannot help feeling that most of us, however professional we may be, will feel that great light has been thrown upon Mr. Keynes' contributions to monetary theory by your own exposition of them. I am not sure that students will find the book quite as easy as I think you expect them to do. Rigid clarity is not always what the beginner can understand; but I have certainly profited. I expect I am a beginner.

I am sure you will understand that I do not pretend to be a convert to these views. Indeed, at some time in the future I must write you a long letter to explain why I still am not a convert. But it was a real intellectual pleasure to find a perfect statement, even of views with which one does not agree.[8]

Keynes's patronage certified Robinson as an influential member of the most powerful network of economists at Cambridge, at the same time strengthening her position in her conflicts with Robertson during 1935–38. Robertson not only refused to enroll in the Keynesian movement but became its most persistent and intransigent Cambridge critic. In opposing the Keynesians and failing to form a countervailing faction, he diminished his power to resolve differences with Robinson in his favor. As he became weaker by attacking *The General Theory*, she became stronger by performing as the ideal Keynesian critic—combining sympathy with the author, agreement on fundamentals, and logical acuity in correcting errors. After *The General Theory* was published, she acquired Keynes as a commentator on her proofs while Robertson languished, worrying over whether his long personal and professional friendship with Keynes was disintegrating. In this manner, the predicament of Robinson's nemesis became increasingly uncertain as her position became more stable. By the Michaelmas term of 1938, she was a university lecturer, and Robertson was leaving Cambridge for a professorship in London, abandoning the intramural battle with the Keynesians and conceding defeat over the future of Cambridge economics (Aslanbeigui and Oakes 2002).

IMPRESSION MANAGEMENT

When circumstances seemed to warrant it, Robinson could produce carefully calibrated impressions for key Cambridge colleagues. In her dialogues with Pigou on her article of December 1932, she was not prepared to admit she had failed to understand his mathematical objection. Instead of confessing at that point her relative ignorance of mathematics to the professor of political economy, she continued the conversation, keeping Pigou engaged, sustaining his enthusiasm, and giving him time to solve his own problem. When he had done so, the results worked to her advantage. In her exchanges with Shove over credit attribution and priority, Robinson resisted his attempts to eviscerate her claims to credit for work that would appear in her book. She was firm but also wary of his tendency to petulance and jealousy. As a result, she achieved her objective without antagonizing an old friend of Keynes and a member of the faculty board who would have influence on her career. She demonstrated the same interpersonal management skills when Shove responded to her critique of the symposium of 1930. On this occasion, she represented herself as a model of reasonableness and an ally of Keynes in pacifying Shove.

In handling the assignment of commenting on the proofs of *The General Theory*, Robinson balanced the roles of champion and critic. On basic premises, she showered Keynes with praise. On details, her corrections were careful and moderately useful even if innocuous from the standpoint of the general program of the book. Unlike Hayek in 1930–31 and Robertson and Hawtrey in 1935, her performance satisfied the only audience that mattered: Keynes, whose conception of scientific controversy depended on acute criticism of specifics within a framework of assumptions that were shared by both author and critic and were closed to debate. In considering Robinson's efforts to form Keynes's conception of her as a reliable and effective ally in the months following publication of *The General Theory*, Hubert Henderson's lecture to the Marshall Society is instructive. When she published her article "The Long-Period Theory of Employment," she sent Henderson a copy. Because his distaste for Keynes's new analytical framework was well known in Cambridge, she surely anticipated objections on his part. In responding, Henderson did not conceal his vexation over *The General Theory*: "I'm afraid that, as you probably know, I'm unsympathetic to the point of acute exasperation with the whole method of approach of Maynard's book, which your article follows."[9] Although Robinson's reply has not been located, it is clear she did not change Henderson's position. He remained, as he put it, "violently dissenting."[10] Some three weeks later, he read a paper to the Marshall Society that set out the grounds for his dissent. Robinson attended, and on May 3, Keynes gave Lydia an account of the event:

Hubert came to the Marshall Society yesterday, with Dennis in the Chair, to read his paper against my book. I was astonished at the violence of his emotion against it; he thinks it a poisonous book; yet when it came to the debate there was very little of the argument which he was really prepared to oppose. He came off badly in the debate with Joan and Alexander and myself barking round him. The undergraduates enjoyed the cock fight outrageously. One got the impression that he was not really much interested in pure economic theory, but much dislikes for emotional or political reasons some of the practical conclusions to which my arguments seemed to point. As a theoretical attack there was almost nothing to answer. (JMK/PP/45/190/7)

Robinson had succeeded in representing herself as a valuable member of the revolutionary cadre, acting in concert with Keynes and his adjutant in defending *The General Theory* against an early enemy—a classical economist and precisely the sort of adversary Keynes was determined either to convert or defeat.

SIMPLICITY AS A TACTIC

On March 23, 1938, Robinson advised Keynes to rewrite a rejoinder he had drafted on a note that Robertson had submitted to the *Economic Journal*: "Abandon D.H.R. [Robertson] as hopeless and write as tho' for a 2nd year man who is hoping to get a II2 [Second Class in Part II of the Economics Tripos]. You want the reader, merging dazed from D.H.R., to feel that you represent simplicity and commonsense" (in Keynes 1979, 169). Throughout the 1930s, Robinson wrote for academic economists as if they were Cambridge students. Writing economics, even her most abstract and demanding work, was not in principle distinguishable from teaching it. As she explained in a memorandum she prepared for Schumpeter in early 1933 on how economics should be taught, economic "Laws and Doctrines can be divested of mysticism and turned into what they really are—simple but useful mental gadgets" (JVR/vii/2/1–9). Robinson reduced complex problems to simpler issues that could be explained by familiar examples or analogies. She did not indulge in the scholastic subtleties that attracted some of her colleagues, and she was ruthless in wielding Occam's razor, introducing new analytical apparatus only when there seemed to be compelling reasons to do so and elucidating technical jargon in everyday language. In writing economics, she adopted the principle that even the most recondite problems could be analyzed by mundane reasoning and in lucid prose. One result of theoretical demystification was a facile and eminently accessible style of writing high theory. It differentiated her work from the writings of her contemporaries and was recognized as distinctively Robinsonian.

The basis of Robinson's project of theoretical simplification was her methodological position: economics is its technique. The technique of her day, she insisted, was too unsophisticated to investigate the complexities of economic reality. Equipped with her box of tools, the analytical economist would find the facts of economic life intractable. In her metaphor, "the knives are of bone and the hammers of wood, only capable of cutting paper and driving pins into cardboard" (Robinson 1933d, 327). The *hiatus irrationalis* between method and reality called for "very severe simplifying measures" (Robinson 1933d, 327). Economists were instructed to abstract from the complexity of real problems and consider instead simplified hypothetical issues that were framed to demonstrate the power and limits of available methods. The theoretical assumptions required by Robinson's methodology—"set out in all their naked unreality" (Robinson 1933d, 8)—created imaginary buyers and sellers, firms, industries, and commodities that were amenable to analysis but, precisely for that reason, remote from the facts of real economies. The path to economic reality lay in the development of more powerful techniques, the prolegomenon for any future economics. In the 1930s, however, Robinson was determined to follow the logic of her methodology and its theoretical simplifications. Faced with a choice between sacrificing a "charming diagram" or attempting to match the complexity of empirical reality, her decision was unequivocal (Aslanbeigui and Oakes 2006, 424). She arrived at this position in 1932 and maintained it through the 1930s, as the exchanges with Keynes on her *Essays in the Theory of Employment* make clear.

However, Robinson's commitment to simplicity as a tactic was also based on rhetorical considerations. Early drafts of *The Economics of Imperfect Competition* show that it was originally composed in a somewhat colloquial manner, as if the author were lecturing to students. Following Keynes's advice, she deleted many of these passages, at the same time taking measures to make the book readable. She provided instructions for technically unsophisticated readers, including cautionary footnotes advising novices to skip certain passages or even entire chapters in the interest of understanding fundamentals. Deficiencies in technical skills, she argued, were not impediments to following economic reasoning. Thus she saw no professional stigma in the declaration she made in the book that she was "almost entirely innocent of mathematics" (Robinson 1933d, 12). Although Kahn and Newman—and, in one case, Pigou—supplied her with formal proofs, she insisted that mathematical demonstrations were never essential to her arguments. They were instruments of precision, devices for restating more exactly conclusions she had discovered by using "unsophisticated methods" based on "purely economic reasoning," the concept of elasticity, and "one or two theorems from the book on triangles in a school geometry" (Robinson 1933d, 12).

Evidence considered above on the reception of Robinson's work in the 1930s shows that in this respect she achieved a brilliant success.[11] Douglas underscored the pedagogical value of *The Economics of Imperfect Competition*, which he had been using in his classes. "You must be interested to know," he wrote, "that introduction of your analysis into class work interested the students very much, and I notice on their part a far keener and more vivid interest than when I used a more antiquated type of analysis." The type of analysis Douglas had employed presumably did not include Robinson's suggestions to readers or her method of elucidating the logic of theoretical discovery by showing in a step-by-step fashion how her arguments were constructed. Douglas was immensely impressed: "I wish to extend not only my congratulations but my personal appreciation for the good work which you have done and say that you have put us all in your debt."[12]

The aims of theoretical demystification were both analytical and expository. An analysis would succeed in solving a problem only if it were clear. The solution would be grasped by readers only if it were explained in language that was plain and simple. These aims were not universally understood. On April 6, 1934, Frank Taussig, the editor of the *Quarterly Journal of Economics* at Harvard, wrote Robinson that he was pleased to accept her article "What Is Perfect Competition?" However, he suggested revisions that did not conform to her conception of how economic analysis should be written: "The first half of the paper, say as far as page 13, seems to be addressed to a somewhat younger audience and perhaps a more miscellaneous group than that which we ordinarily try to reach. Some of your illustrations—say, the 'cherries' and the 'barkeeper'—are appropriate in an address, but less so when stated in cold print to the scientific reader" (JVR/vii/442/1–3). Taussig did not grasp the point of Robinson's expository methods. Commonplace examples clarified and simplified complex arguments. They were no less essential to an article than to a lecture. From Robinson's perspective, the distinction between more and less professionalized readerships had no place in writing economics. In their efforts to understand new solutions to problems, all economists were students. Even in "cold print," it was impossible to see that a position was sound unless it was stated with requisite clarity. And clarity could be achieved only by writing in a straightforward style and using everyday illustrations. In this respect, there was no difference between the theoretically sophisticated—Taussig's conception of the readership of the *Quarterly Journal of Economics*—and readers whose technical facility was relatively modest.

Robinson's integration of scientific and scholarly writing with teaching was perhaps tied to the pleasure she took in teaching at Cambridge, especially when she was spurred by the influence of her imp.[13] She enjoyed pleading with students, in the sense of making a case for a position.[14] In making economic theory simple and sensible, listening to the voice of the imp by lecturing with a polemical edge, and taking definitive positions on basic issues instead of leaving students to decide controversial matters on their own, Robinson became a successful teacher and a pedagogical asset to the Cambridge faculty. When Fay attempted to prevent her from extending her one-term set of lectures on applications in monetary theory to two terms, Keynes responded with arguments that were based in part on her success as a lecturer. There was no question, he said, "as to the quality and popularity of the lectures." From what he had heard, they were "exceedingly good and amongst the most successful with the young men."[15]

"Who is Joan *Robinson*?" the young Viennese economist Gottfried Haberler asked Kahn shortly after reading the *Economic Journal* for December 1932. He had recently received an offprint of "Imperfect Competition and Falling Supply Price" from the author, whose name he did not recognize: "The Christian name sounds like a woman's, but the article seems to me much too clever for a woman."[16] Robinson apparently had comparable questions about her professional identity before she wrote *The Economics of Imperfect Competition*. Shortly after recovering from an extremely stressful period of writing in October 1932, she wrote Austin in Africa that she had experienced a transformation comparable to a religious conversion: "The thing is that all these years I have suffered from the inferiority complex of an intelligent woman + the emotional conflicts of a hermaphrodite. But now I have (almost finished writing) written one damn good book." How did the experience of writing the book change Robinson's conception of herself? "I feel absolutely differently now when J.M.K. sends for me to try out his new theory of interest, or Max [Newman] explains to me quite earnestly about the 'axiomatic method' in pure mathematics. I used to think 'what a joke for them to take a handsome young woman seriously on their own ground.' Now it just seems quite natural, + as I am self-confident instead of merely conceited I can admire the great + suffer fools gladly + admit I have a conscience + generally behave in a perfectly grown up manner."[17] In fashioning her career in the 1930s, Robinson took steps that ensured no economist of Haberler's stature would have occasion to raise questions about her identity again or to commit the Haberler fallacy of conflating cleverness in economic analysis with masculinity.

† NOTES †

COLLAGE WITH WOMAN IN FOREGROUND

1   See special issues of the *Cambridge Journal of Economics* 1983, and *Review of Political Economy* 2003; Feiwel 1989a, 1989b; Turner 1989; Rima 1991; Harcourt 1995; Marcuzzo et al. 1996; Kerr and Harcourt 2002; and Gibson 2005.

2   For a survey of the major debates in this controversy, see Harcourt 1972.

3   Letter from Pigou to Robinson, circa June-July 1933, JVR/vii/347/6.

4   Letter from Pigou to Robinson, circa June-July 1933, JVR/vii/347/27–28.

5   Letter from Austin to Robinson, circa October-November 1932, JVR/vii/378/135.

6   Letter from Fay to Pigou, Keynes, and Shove, 3/2/35, JMK/UA/5/31/137–38.

7   Letter from Fay to Keynes, 3/6/35, JMK/UA/5/4/31–32.

8   See also Bruno Latour on the strategic and tactical logic at work in the career of Louis Pasteur (Latour 1988) and the physicist Frédéric Joliot (Latour 1999). We also follow the path taken by Guy Oakes and Arthur Vidich (1999) in their analysis of the strategies employed by C. Wright Mills, who used his close relationship and collaboration with Hans Gerth to establish his professional identity as one of the first American Weberian sociologists.

9   On the case for a geography of science, see also Ophir and Shapin 1991 and Shapin 1998. Historically rich investigations of the role of local scientific cultures in the conception and production of research programs, the constitution of scientific identities, and the socialization of scientific workers include Olesko 1991; Rudwick 1985; Shapin 1994; Shapin and Schaffer 1985; Traweek 1988; Warwick 2003.

10 The reliability of our account depends in part on our efforts to decipher handwritten notes and letters exchanged by Cambridge economists: chiefly Austin and Joan Robinson, Kahn, Pigou, Shove, and, to a more limited extent, Keynes. On the whole, we are confident of the results, even in the case of Pigou, whose barely legible scrawl often defeated his friends, colleagues, typists, and publishers. With the exception of punctuation, which we have added to avoid confusion, we have remained faithful to archival sources. In

Robinson's letters, for example, sentences are generally separated by spaces instead of periods, and apostrophes are rare. Where needed, we have added the appropriate punctuation without using brackets, the sheer number of which would have proved distracting. We have been able to supply exact or approximate dates for some undated letters. This was possible by cross-checking dates of letters written by different correspondents on the same matter and by examining the lecture lists in economics published in the *Cambridge University Reporter* (1930–39), contemporaneous newspaper articles, and calendars for the years in question.

11　E. Roy Weintraub sketches some provocative historiographic issues posed by the premise that the period of apprenticeship or professional identity formation—the years of early adulthood between twenty-three and thirty-four—are crucial in defining the "life scripts" produced by economists. See Weintraub 2005.

12　For recent scholarship on Sraffa's life and work, see special issues of the *Review of Political Economy* (2005) and the *European Journal of the History of Economic Thought* (2005) as well as Kurz (2008).

I THE IMPROBABLE THEORETICIAN

1　The university lectureship sealed Robinson's career at Cambridge. She had received an appointment as part-time assistant lecturer in autumn 1934 and was promoted to a full-time assistant lectureship a year later (5/7/34, FB/ Min.V.117; 5/4/35, FB/Min.V.118). However, the latter position was not a permanency; nor was it even a sure path to a university lectureship, as we see in the ensuing. Assistant lecturers were also called probationary lecturers, and for good reason. Their selection for university lectureships depended on an assessment of satisfactory performance. Robinson was a contentious figure and a persistent source of conflict in the economics faculty. It is not surprising that her candidacy was a matter of considerable dispute. Recommendations for appointments to university lectureships in economics were made to the General Board of the Faculties by the Faculty Board of Economics and Politics. She faced opposition from several members of the faculty board, one of whom was its chairman at the time her appointment to a university lectureship was considered.

2　Letter from Kahn to Keynes, circa mid-February 1938, JMK/L/K/89–93.

3　Letter from Keynes to Kahn, 2/19/38, JMK/L/K/94–96.

4　Although Austin Robinson had exhibited great promise as a theorist in *The Structure of Competitive Industry* (1931), he had shown greater interest in university administration as well as work in applied economics.

5　*Cambridge University Reporter*, 4/19/30, 917.

6　On Kahn's life and work, see the special issue of *Cambridge Journal of Economics*, 1994. On his contributions to imperfect competition and *The General Theory*, see O'Shaughnessy 1994, Marcuzzo 1994, and Harcourt 1994.

7 On the history of IS-LM interpretations of *The General Theory*, see Warren Young (1987).

8 JVR/vii/268/2. In fact, the letter included twenty signatures.

9 Letter from Robinson to Kahn, 9/4/34, RFK/13/90/85–88.

10 See Harrod 1936, 1937a. Robinson seems to have taken these criticisms seriously. Following the Second World War, the measurement of capital and development of a dynamic theoretical analysis were central themes of her work.

11 Unless otherwise specified, the biographical information that follows is based on Aslanbeigui 2002; Collard 1990; Dennison and Presley 1992; Fletcher 2000; Harcourt 1994; Kahn 1987; Moggridge 1992; Potier 1987; Saltmarsh and Wilkinson 1960; and Skidelsky 1983.

12 Wittgenstein 1953, x (our translation). On the intellectual exchange between Sraffa and Wittgenstein, see Marion 2005.

13 On the events of May 1897, see McWilliams Tullberg (1998) and Deslandes (2005). In the Cambridge Union debate of May 11, the rooms of the Union were opened to all male members of the university. Women spectators were excluded from their customary places in the galleries. Attendance at the debate matched the advanced publicity of the meeting, and hundreds of men were turned away. All male undergraduates, regardless of whether they were members of the Union, were given an opportunity to air their views. After several hours of speeches, rejection of the proposal by those present was overwhelmingly endorsed by a vote of 1,083 to 138 (Deslandes 2005, 206–7). On the carnival-like polling day of May 21, graduates with master's degrees arrived to vote, and effigies of female students were prominently displayed outside the University Senate House. The M.A.'s defeated the proposal 1,707 to 661. An independent nonbinding undergraduate vote was more decisively opposed: 2,137 to 298. Following the results of the vote, some 200 undergraduates marched on Newnham (Deslandes 2005, 208–9). For an insider's account of these events, see Phyllis Deane's biography of John Neville Keynes 2001.

14 On Marshall's views concerning higher education for women, see Sutherland 1992 and McWilliams Tullberg 1990, 1995, 1998. On Victorian conceptions of the relations between higher education and the condition of women, see Burstyn 1984 and Dyhause 1995.

15 On the vote of October 20, 1921, see McWilliams Tullberg 1998, 98–118, 163–65, 176. At least some of the leading Cambridge economists seem to have taken a more progressive stance than the majority of their colleagues. T. E. B. Howarth claims that Pigou, Keynes, and the economic historians J. H. Clapham and Fay all supported the more liberal grace of 1921 that would have granted degrees to qualified women (Howarth 1978, 76). In 1923, Parliament was considering the Universities Bill, which would have substantially equalized the status of men and women in British universities. Robertson published an article in the *Nation and Athenaeum* criticizing

the conservative position as pedagogically unsound, blatantly unjust, and doomed to failure. He urged Parliament to put the affairs of the university in order by ending "what has become a rather tedious and ridiculous situation" (Robertson 1923,447).

16 The secularized institution of the Cambridge purdah produced striking contradictions. Jane Harrison, the most influential woman in the history of classical scholarship, was a fellow of Newnham from 1898 to 1922. Although she was a regular interlocutor with Francis Cornford and James Frazer in their discussions on the esoterica of early Greek religion, regulations prohibited her from borrowing books from the university library. See Beard 2000, 207.

17 Joan Robinson and Marjorie Robinson were friends in the 1930s, a relationship that ended with the early death of Marjorie in 1939. In his touching eulogy, Henderson observed that domesticity, not science and scholarship, took first place in her life (Henderson 1940, 161–62). Thus for several reasons she was not a possible model for the formation of Joan Robinson's professional identity.

18 3/10/32, JMK/PP/45/190/5. It is evident from the Robinson-Kahn correspondence of the 1930s that neither held Tappan-Holland in high regard. In addition, Tappan-Holland and Robinson clashed on their approach to teaching first-year students.

19 See Virginia Woolf's famous account of a sumptuous, leisurely lunch prepared by cooks of one of the Cambridge men's colleges and served in the rooms of a fellow, followed the same evening by an unappetizing and perfunctory dinner at one of the women's colleges (Woolf 1993, 9–16). As Claude Lévi-Strauss later observed, certain foods are good to think and others are not (Lévi-Strauss 1983). In "A Room of One's Own," the cuisine served at the wealthy men's colleges was good for thinking and cultivation of the good life generally. The cuisine of the less well endowed women's colleges was not.

20 Circa 9/22–26/28, EAGR/Box 8/2/1/13/34–44.

21 Letter from Robinson to Austin, 10/8/28, EAGR/Box 8/2/1/13/58–59.

22 Robinson's preface does not seem to have survived in the published report. The general foreword is written by another author. Although part 2 begins with a brief introduction (The Directorate 1929, 135–37), it includes constitutional and diplomatic matters that lie outside Robinson's competence.

23 Letter from Robinson to Austin, 10/3/28, EAGR/Box 8/2/1/13/26–32.

24 Letter from Robinson to Austin, 11/13/28, EAGR/Box 8/2/1/13/78–81. See The Directorate 1929, 197–201 ("The Salt Monopoly") and 201–05 ("Railways").

25 Letter from Robinson to Austin, circa 9/22–26/28, EAGR/Box 8/2/1/13/34–44.

26 Circa 9/22–26/28, EAGR/Box 8/2/1/13/33–34.

27 Letter from Robinson to Austin, 10/18/28, EAGR/Box 8/2/1/13/64–67.

28 Letter from Robinson to Austin, 11/3–6/28, EAGR/Box 8/2/1/13/26–32.

29 Circa April 1930, JVR/vii/378/42–45.

30 The rate of unemployment for insured workers reached 14.6 percent by the end of 1930, 3.6 percent higher than the rate in 1929. By the end of 1931, the rate had climbed to 21.5 percent (Mitchell 1978, 66, 69).

31 The Modern Archives, King's College, Cambridge University contain a carbon copy of a three-page, single-spaced manuscript with the title "A Passage from the Autobiography of an Analytical Economist" (RFK/16/2/134–39, hereinafter "Autobiography"). Robinson's initials are typed at the end of the document, which is dated October 1932. The Autobiography is reproduced in Aslanbeigui and Oakes 2006, on which we draw in the ensuing.

32 Marcuzzo seems to be mistaken in supposing that Robinson attended Sraffa's lectures in Michaelmas 1928 (2005, 430). During this term, when Austin was still in India, she was based at the London flat of her parents, working on the Indian report, reestablishing contacts with friends, and acting on Austin's behalf to explore prospects of a lectureship or fellowship for him at Cambridge. Sraffa, whose name she misspelled in a letter of October 18—"The erratic Straffa"—was an item only in the sense that his malperformance as a lecturer might improve Austin's chances for a lectureship (letter to Austin, EAGR/Box 8/2/1/13/64–67). In Robinson's letters to Austin during Michaelmas 1928, there is no evidence that she attended Sraffa's lectures that term.

33 For a discussion of Sraffa's lectures, see Marcuzzo 2001 and Signorino 2005.

34 Autobiography, in Aslanbeigui and Oakes 2006, 423.

35 Letter from Robinson to Kahn, 1/23/33, RFK/13/90/1/73–77.

36 Letter from Pigou to Kahn, circa spring 1930, RFK/2/8/18–19.

37 The Autobiography was apparently drafted in October 1932. The typescript in Modern Archives, which seems to be the only extant copy, was not made until some months later. In a letter of March 2, 1933, to Robinson, Kahn suggested that she add a new section to her text (RFK/13/90/1/162–67). She replied somewhat mysteriously, alluding to a superstitious reluctance to having it typed but admitting that eventually it would have to be done (3/23/33, RFK/13/90/1/205–208). Since the carbon copy refers to page 275 of her book, the Autobiography was not typed until she had seen the final set of page proofs, and perhaps not until the book had appeared. The Autobiography also shows that she had drafted "The Theory of Money and the Analysis of Output," published in the *Review of Economic Studies* for October 1933. Thus there is no doubt she revised the October 1932 text before finally handing it to a typist. Robinson's correspondence with Kahn shows that she was interested in publishing the "secret document." Although Austin advised against it, his reasons remain obscure (letter from Robinson to Kahn, 1/31/33, RFK/13/90/1/84–87).

38 Aslanbeigui and Oakes 2006, 423; see also Robinson 1933d, vi.

39 See Annalisa Roselli's illuminating essay on the correspondence of Robinson and Kahn (2005a), which seems to treat Austin's story as historical fact. Are there lessons here? Consider the inconsistencies between Robinson's laconic account in the foreword and the Autobiography and Austin's more colorful reminiscences, which call to mind C. P. Snow's novels on life in a Cambridge college of the 1930s. When Robinson was writing, she was present at the creation. Austin was writing at a distance of six decades. Robinson could hardly be expected to falsify her account. Both the Autobiography and the foreword were read by Austin and Kahn, the two men who knew most about her research. If Austin's account was accurate, why did he fail to correct the Autobiography and the foreword? If his version of events was true in 1990, it was also true in 1933. These considerations are grounds for skepticism concerning Austin's narrative. At a minimum they show that it should not be elevated to the status of an authoritative chronology.

40 Autobiography, in Aslanbeigui and Oakes 2006, 424.

41 Ibid.

42 Note that at this point Robinson shifts her criterion for genius from a mistakenly titled and misconceived book to a misnamed and misunderstood theory.

43 Letter from Robinson to Kahn, 9/4/34, RFK/13/90/2/76–83.

44 Autobiography, in Aslanbeigui and Oakes 2006, 425.

45 As Robinson understood, the originality of the economic genius and the profundity of his errors are commensurate. Deep misconceptions require many more years to clarify than less fundamental mistakes. The project of asking questions of Marshall's technique, learning from its answers, and finally reconfiguring the *Principles* on a new set of assumptions required some fifty years. In the case of the *Treatise*, this project was executed in roughly a week. As Robinson surveyed the pantheon of economic genius in 1932–33, Marshall stood in first place, with Pigou a distant second. The "Fundamental Equations" of the *Treatise*, however, were "to be congratulated on Mr Keynes' progress" (Autobiography, in Aslanbeigui and Oakes 2006, 425).

46 Letter from Robinson to Kahn, 10/30/32, RFK/13/90/I/19.

47 See Raffaelli (2007) for a discussion of Marshall's methodological metaphors.

48 Although the pamphlet was written in a playful manner, this should not give the impression that Robinson regarded it as a frivolous exercise. Several members of the economics faculty at Cambridge received copies, each with a pithy and sometimes cryptic dedication (for the dedications and their recipients, see Harcourt 1990, 425). Robinson expected a review of the pamphlet in the *Economic Journal* and was disappointed when none appeared (letter from Robinson to Kahn, 3/3/33, RFK/13/90/I/168–72).

49 The pamphlet is dedicated "To The Fundamental Pessimist." This was Sraffa.

50　Robinson recognized no differences in the national economic traditions of Austria, Germany, Italy, Sweden, and Switzerland, which all fall indifferently under the heading of "Continental" economics.

51　Here we part company with Harcourt on one point. He states that Robinson abandoned much of the pamphlet almost immediately, so quickly that very little of its argument remains in the methodological introduction to *The Economics of Imperfect Competition* (Harcourt 1990, 412–13, 424). We find no evidence for Harcourt's thesis, in either his paper or Robinson's book. Quite the contrary: (1) Harcourt supposes that Robinson wrote her book the year after she published the pamphlet. This is not the case. She delivered a complete manuscript of the book to Macmillan in October 1932, the month the pamphlet was printed. If the book is inconsistent with the pamphlet, it is not because Robinson abandoned her earlier views—the two texts were contemporaneous—but because she contradicted herself. (2) The Autobiography, which sketches in abridged fashion the methodology of the pamphlet, was not finally revised and typed before spring 1933, after Robinson had seen the page proofs of her book. Again, any inconsistency cannot be explained by the thesis that Robinson later discarded in her book views she had embraced in the Autobiography. Considered from the standpoint of compositional history, the typescript of the Autobiography is a later text than *The Economics of Imperfect Competition*. (3) Finally, Harcourt's own discussion of the relationship between the pamphlet and the book supports the view that the pamphlet reproduced the argument of the book (see Harcourt 1990, 424).

52　Autobiography, in Aslanbeigui and Oakes 2006, 424.

53　Ibid., 425. Lionel Robbins published *An Essay on the Nature & Significance of Economics Science* (1932) only a few months before Robinson's pamphlet appeared. Did she see *Economics Is a Serious Subject* as a Cambridge alternative to the Viennese metatheory of the time, imported by Robbins to LSE and distilled in his essay? If so, the pamphlet was a peculiar response. It approximates much more closely than Robbins's essay the orthodox Viennese commitment to axiomatics and deductive methods. The basic premise of Robbins's book is a distinction between the subject matter of economics and its method. For Robinson, this is not a possible distinction; the subject matter of economics is its method. Robbins disclaimed philosophical pretensions and any attempt "to elaborate, out of the void, a theory of what Economics should become" (Robbins 1932, ix). He made no claims to originality, insisting that he was merely stating views that qualified as "the common property of most modern economists" (Robbins 1932, ix). Robinson proposed to delimit the sphere of analytical economics *de novo* and instruct economists on the conclusions they should draw from her conception of the discipline. Finally, in contrast to the methods of Robinsonian economics, which give only "unreal answers to unreal questions," Robbins stressed the empirical basis of the postulates of abstract economic theory.

Read in the light of Robbins's essay, Robinson's pamphlet is a more radical departure from the methodological traditions of Cambridge economics. On the British origins of Robbins's essay, see Howson 2004.

54 See Robinson's notes, not dated, RFK/16/1/1, and Kahn's response, 7/29/30, RFK/16/1/2–4.

55 See, for example, graphs and notes by Kahn, RFK/16/1/27, RFK/16/1/29–30, RFK/16/1/31–32 and RFK/16/1/52; and graphs and notes by Robinson, RFK/16/1/28 and RFK/16/1/53–55.

56 Letter from Robinson to Kahn, 3/30/31, RFK/16/1/59–62.

57 Letter from Robinson to Kahn, 3/31–4/2/31, RFK/16/1/63–64.

58 See the table of contents Robinson drew up in a few days (RFK/16/1/5) as well as her letter to Kahn on 3/30/31 (RFK/16/1/59–62).

59 Letter from Robinson to Kahn, 3/31–4/2/31, RFK/16/1/63–64.

60 Ibid.

61 Ibid. This was the famous multiplier article, a preliminary draft of which had been employed by Keynes in September–October 1930 at meetings of the Committee of the Economists in order to make a case for government spending to increase employment. Kahn was a secretary of the committee (see Moggridge 1992, 497–500). The article was published in the journal in June 1931.

62 Letter from Robinson to Kahn, 3/31–4/2/31, RFK/16/1/63–64.

63 Letter from Robinson to Robertson, circa late September 1931, RFK/16/1/92–93. In the table of contents she sent Robertson, Austin had disappeared and Kahn remained as the author of the "mathematical appendix."

64 Letter from Robinson to Kahn, 9/17/31, RFK/16/1/94–99; letter from Kahn to Robinson, circa 9/18/31, RFK/16/1/116–20.

65 Letter from Robinson to Austin, 10/11/32, EAGR/Box 8/2/1/13/120–22.

66 Letter from Robinson to Austin, circa mid-October 1932, EAGR/Box 8/2/1/13/123.

67 Letter from Robinson to Austin, 10/11/32, EAGR/Box 8/2/1/13/120–22.

68 Ibid.

69 Ibid.

70 Letter from Robinson to Austin, 10/16/32, EAGR/Box 8/2/1/13/124–26.

71 Letter from Robinson to Austin, 10/20/32, EAGR/Box 8/2/1/13/127–30.

72 Letter from Robinson to Austin, 10/25/32, EAGR/Box 8/2/1/13/131.

73 Letter from Robinson to Austin, 11/7/32, EAGR/Box 9/2/1/17/289–92.

EXCURSUS

1 Letter from Kahn to M. Ignatieff, 8/18/83, quoted in Marcuzzo 2003, 546.

2 Robinson was also friendly with Richard Braithwaite, another young fellow of King's. It was an excess of Richards among the acquaintances of the Keyneses that caused Lydia Keynes to christen Kahn "Alexander."

3 Letter from Robinson to Kahn, 3/21/30, RFK/13/90/1/3–4.

4 Letter from Robinson to Kahn, 3/31–4/2/31, RFK/16/1/63–64.
5 At the time, this was the title of Robinson's book.
6 Letter from Keynes to Lydia, 2/1/32, JMK/PP/45/190/5.
7 If Keynes's worries revolved around the professional hazards of a "desperate affair" for his protégé, his anxieties were not misplaced. He was well acquainted with the William Empson matter at Cambridge in 1929, less than three years before Keynes surprised the pair in Kahn's rooms. Empson, who would later distinguish himself as a literary scholar, was elected to a Magdalene fellowship and appointed junior fellow of the college. Some seven weeks thereafter, the fellowship election was nullified and he was "sent down." Empson's offense was that he had occasionally entertained a woman for overnight visits in his rooms at a college hostel, a fact he made no effort to conceal from students and servants in the house. In moving Empson's things into his new rooms in Magdalene, a college servant found contraceptives—a "French letter" in the quaint language of the time—in a drawer with his belongings. The servant gossiped, and the story made the rounds of the university and the town. The fellows of Magdalene could not revoke Empson's degree. However, they performed an official degradation ceremony by exacting the most severe penalties at their disposal for sexual misconduct. Empson's tutorial file and even his name were expunged from college records, and his right to reside in the town of Cambridge was rescinded. As the historian Frank Salter, one of the more liberal fellows of Magdalene, wrote Empson's mentor, I. A. Richards, "What has to be remembered is that sexual misconduct is a University offence & that when detected in an undergraduate, it leads almost invariably to expulsion; as long as this is so, it is not unreasonable to expect senior members of a College to conform, or for us to find it a bit difficult to continue an offender in residence" (in Haffenden 2005, 245). The difficulty, as Salter explained to Richards, was not the act of sexual misconduct as defined by university regulations. This was commonplace and might be passed over in silence if done with discretion. Empson's recklessness had led to gossip, publicity, and the danger of scandal. Empson wrote Richards that he had been guilty of "criminal carelessness" in leaving contraceptives where they could easily be found. Indulging in gallows humor at his own expense, he reported the sentence passed on him by the master of Magdalene: "Anybody who had ever touched a French letter no matter when or why, could ever again be allowed safely in the company of young men, because he was sure in some subtle way, however little, he himself wished it, to pollute their innocence" (in Haffenden 2005, 250). The biochemist J. B. S. Haldane wrote Keynes concerning the details of the case in the hope he would help find Empson a job. In 1925, Haldane himself had been deprived of his university readership on grounds of "gross immorality" when he acknowledged that he was a correspondent in a divorce case. Although Haldane successfully appealed the decision on his readership, it seems he was not electable as a fellow of

any college, and he left Cambridge in 1932 (Hafenden 2005, 258–59). In light of Keynes's knowledge of positions taken by the Cambridge faculty on the relationship between sexual conduct and academic ethics, his concern over the tryst he observed between Robinson and Kahn does not seem unreasonable.

8   Letter from Robinson to Kahn, 3/31/32, RFK/13/90/1/9–10.

9   Cairncross holds that even a separation would have been difficult in view of Cambridge ethics on conjugal matters. He notes that a similar case at Caius College (which he does not otherwise identify) ended the career of the fellow implicated (Cairncross 1993, 172).

10   Letter from Keynes to Lydia, 5/12/32, JMK/PP/45/190/5.

11   Letter from Robinson to Kahn, 6/30/32, RFK/13/90/2/117–20.

12   In mid-August 1932, Robinson and Kahn traveled to Austria to spend a few weeks with Guillebaud and do some mountaineering on their own. See letters from Robinson to Austin, 8/6–8/32, EAGR/Box 9/2/17/266–71; circa 8/16/32, EAGR/Box 9/2/1/17/276–77; 9/16/32, EAGR/Box 8/2/1/13/111–12; and 9/20/32, EAGR/Box 8/2/1/13/113–16.

13   Letter from Robinson to Kahn, 7/10/32, RFK/13/90/2/132–33.

14   Letter from Robinson to Kahn, 7/8/32, RFK/13/90/2/128–31. In a postscript to a letter from Keynes to Robinson concerning the renewal of Austin's lectureship, Lydia apologized for not responding to this invitation. In return, she asked her to spend a weekend with them (EAGR/Box 9/2/1/17/284–85). On September 20, Robinson wrote Austin that she was going to Tilton in a few days, "but I shan't say any more about it unless Maynard mentions it" (EAGR/Box 8/2/1/13/113–16). There is no evidence as to whether she did in fact spend the weekend with the Keyneses.

15   Letter from Robinson to Kahn, 3/3/32, RFK/13/90/1/9–10.

16   Letter from Kahn to Robinson, 2/24/33, RFK/13/90/1/147–54.

17   Letter from Robinson to Kahn, 3/8/33, RFK/13/90/1/173–79.

18   Letter from Kahn to Robinson, 1/4–8/33, RFK/13/90/1/33–40.

19   See letters from Robinson to Kahn, 1/6/33, RFK/13/90/1/28–33; 1/7/33, RFK/13/90/1/31–32; and 1/23–26/33, RFK/13/90/1/73–77.

20   Letter from Kahn to Robinson, 1/20–24/33, RFK/13/90/1/67–72.

21   1/4–8/33, RFK/13/90/1/33–40. See also letter from Kahn to Robinson, 2/7–9/33, RFK/13/90/1/95–100.

22   For Robinson's replies to Kahn's questions, see 2/23/33, RFK/13/90/1/139–46; 3/16/33, RFK/13/90/1/191–97; and 4/2/33, RFK/13/90/1/217–18.

23   Letter from Kahn to Robinson, 2/10–13/33, RFK/13/90/1/105–14.

24   Letter from Kahn to Robinson, 1/20–24/33, RFK/13/90/1/67–72. Kahn borrowed the verse from the minor metaphysical poet John Hoskyns (1566–1638). In *Absence, Hear thou my Protestations*, a poem of twenty-four lines, Hoskyns found virtues in the separation of lovers, an argument that spoke to Kahn's feelings as he wrote Robinson from Chicago. The pertinent verses read as follows:

Absence, hear thou my protestation
　　Against thy strength,
　　Distance and length:
Do what thou canst for alteration;
　　For hearts of truest mettle
Absence doth join, and time doth settle.
Who loves a mistress of such quality,
　　He soon hath found
　　Affection's ground
Beyond time, place, and all mortality,
　　To hearts that cannot vary
　　Absence is present, time doth tarry.
(University of Toronto Library 2002)

25　Letter from Kahn to Robinson, 2/10–13/33, RFK/13/90/1/105–14.

26　Letter from Kahn to Robinson, 3/12–15/33, RFK/13/90/1/184–88.

27　Letter from Kahn to Robinson, 3/28–30/33; RFK/13/90/1/209–12.

28　Letter from Robinson to Kahn, 4/24/33, RFK/13/90/1/230–32.

29　Letter from Robinson to Kahn, 4/19/33, RFK/13/90/1/235–36.

30　Letter from Keynes to Lydia, 10/13/33, JMK/PP/45/190/4.

31　See letters from Robinson to Kahn, 9/12/33, RFK/13/90/1/249–51; 9/19/33, RFK/13/90/1/259–60; and 11/2/33, RFK/13/90/1/265–66.

32　In autumn 1932, the couple had decided to delay having a family for a year so that she could further develop her ideas on imperfect competition (see letter from Robinson to Austin, 10/16/32, EAGR/Box 8/2/1/13/124–26 and letter from Austin to Robinson, circa October-November 1932, JVR/vii/378/135).

33　Letter from Robinson to Kahn, 5/29/33, RFK/13/90/2/17–19.

34　Letter from Robinson to Kahn, 9/16/34, RFK/13/90/2/89–92.

35　Letter from Robinson to Kahn, 8/22/38, RFK/13/90/3/14–15.

36　The Maurice family home in London was located in Kensington Park Gardens.

37　Gilbert and Gott 1963, 126–28; Robbins 1968, 223–25. The interpretations of Robinson's psychiatric collapse by Kahn, Austin, and Keynes are tied to the war panic of autumn 1938 in Britain. In the absence of commentary on the political background of the correspondence, the exchanges on Robinson's breakdown make little sense. Hence the ensuing account of the Czech crisis and negotiations between Chamberlain and Hitler.

38　The following account draws on Robbins 1968, 262–82. On the Czech crisis and its resolution, see also Douglas 1983; Evans 2005; Kershaw 2000.

39　Letter from Robinson to Sraffa, 9/27/38, RFK/13/90/3/30–31.

40　Ibid. Robinson's perception of a British public united against appeasement and demanding a military defense of Czechoslovakia was mistaken. The Czech crisis of September 1938 was the most divisive British foreign policy issue of the interwar years. It split social classes, political parties, and even families. The conflicts within her own family should have shattered Robinson's illusion of unity on this issue. Her father supported appeasement, and her sister supported the revolt in the Conservative Party against Chamberlain. Austin seems to have been against a war irrespective of consequences. And Robinson took an aggressive anti-German position. In addition, British public opinion on the crisis was fickle, varying with the apparent success or failure of Chamberlain's efforts (see Madge and Harrison 1939).

41 Letter from Austin Robinson to Keynes, 10/4/38, JMK/L/K/100–105. We thank Cristina Marcuzzo for pointing out this letter to us.

42 Anonymous 1948; Milner 1954.

43 Letter from Kahn to Keynes, 10/3/38, JMK/L/K/98–99.

44 Letter from Austin to Keynes, 10/4/38, JMK/L/K/100–105.

45 Letter from Austin to Kahn, 10/6/38, RFK/13/90/3/107–13.

46 Letter from Kahn to Austin, 10/6/38, EAGR/Box 9/2/1/17/66–67.

47 Letter from Kahn to Keynes, 10/3/38, JMK/L/K/98–99. In his letter to Keynes, Kahn drew a parallel between Robinson's "frenzy" of October 1–3 and her state of mind in autumn 1932, when she wrote *Economics Is a Serious Subject*, apparently in a state of considerable excitement. In 1932, Keynes had compared her psychological condition to that Samuel Taylor Coleridge described in his account of the circumstances under which he composed his poem "Kubla Khan." Coleridge wrote that in 1797, "in consequence of a slight indisposition"—dysentery—he took two grains of opium. He maintained that during some three hours of deep sleep, he had composed two to three hundred lines of verse. On awakening, he seemed to remember the whole and began to write. However, an interruption of more than an hour by a visitor left him only "a vague and dim memory of the general purport of the vision." The result of his reverie was a composition of fifty-four lines. Coleridge referred to the verses of his dream as well as the poem he wrote as his vision (see Sisman 2006, 193–96). In October 1932, Robinson described her new conception of what she had achieved in *The Economics of Imperfect Competition* as a sudden revelation and a vision and claimed she had written her methodological essay in a trance (Letters from Robinson to Austin, 10/11/32, EAGR/Box 8/2/1/13/120–22; 10/16/32, EAGR/Box 8/2/1/13/124–26; 10/20/32, EAGR/Box 8/2/1/13/127–30). Kahn saw Coleridge in 1797 and Robinson in 1932 and 1938 as cases of absolute and surreal confidence on the part of persons who were beyond the limits of self-consciousness. Coleridge had a trancelike dream, an effect of disease and opium. Robinson's state of mind in 1938 was due to extreme sleep deprivation and fixation on a conviction or vision that enabled her to escape the nightmare of political reality.

48 Keynes does not seem to have understood the chronic nature and severity of Woolf's psychiatric problems. See especially his use of the past tense. The most recent account of these problems, written from the perspective of her husband and chief caregiver, Leonard, is Glendinning (2006).

49 Keynes followed a Victorian socio-gynecology according to which a woman cannot combine childbearing and strenuous intellectual enterprises without seriously damaging her health. On this view, see Burstyn 1984.

50 Until his break with David Lloyd George near the end of the First World War, Robinson's father spent his life as an army officer. Maurice (1871–1951) was educated at St. Paul's School, where Joan Maurice later attended the day school for girls, and the Royal Military College at Sandhurst. At the beginning of the war, he was an instructor at the Army Staff College. In 1914, he served in France at the headquarters of the 3rd Army Division and was promoted to head its general staff during the British retreat from Mons. When Sir William Robertson became chief of the Imperial General Staff in December 1915, he promoted Maurice to major-general and brought him to the War Office as director of military operations. Maurice's ascent in rank and responsibility ended precipitously in spring 1918. In March, a massive German attack in the west broke the British lines and threatened to drive its armies back to their embarkation points on the channel ports. This was uncomfortably close to the decisive offensive in the west envisioned by German Field Marshall Erich Lueddendorf and his strategists, a breakthrough that would end the stalemate of more than two years of futile trench warfare and set the stage for a German victory. The government of Lloyd George was held responsible for this defeat by withholding conscripted troops in England and failing to act on Robertson's warnings of a German spring offensive. Lloyd George responded to attacks on his government in the House of Commons and the press by claiming that Field Marshall Douglas Haig's army was considerably stronger in January 1918 than it had been a year earlier. Because of his senior position in the War Office, Maurice, who had been knighted at the beginning of the year, knew that this claim was false. On May 7, he published a letter in London newspapers charging the government with deception concerning the strength of British forces and the length of the British line on the western front. Two days later in the debate on Maurice's letter in the House of Commons, Lloyd George defended himself and easily defeated an opposition motion that would have censored him and led to the collapse of his government. The incident ended the military career of Maurice, who was immediately retired for breach of discipline without benefit of an investigation or a court martial. Thereafter, he returned to writing and university teaching and administration. From 1922 to 1933, he was principal of the Working Men's College in London that his grandfather Frederick Denison Maurice helped found, and in 1927 he became professor of military studies at London University. Joan Maurice was then preparing for her Economics Tripos in 1925, her father was a lecturer at Trinity College. The year after she received her degree, he was awarded an honorary doctorate by Cambridge (Kennedy 1951–60).

51 By the mid-1930s, some officials of the British Legion had developed ties to the National Socialist regime. Hitler declared himself "most appreciative of

the initiative of the British Legion, whose activities he has always followed and supported with great sympathy." In 1935, a legion delegation visited Hitler, enjoyed a family dinner with Heinrich Himmler, chief of the SS, and received a guided tour of the concentration camp at Dachau arranged by Joachim von Ribbonstrop of the German foreign office. The delegation returned to Britain convinced of the peaceful intent of the Nazi government and its explanation of concentration camps as repositories for subversives, sociopaths, and irredeemable criminals (Peace Pledge Union 2005).

52 See the biography of Spears by Egremont (1997, 134–42).

53 Letter from Austin Robinson to Keynes, 10/4/38, JMK/L/K/100–105.

54 Letter from Austin Robinson to Kahn, 10/4/38, RFK/13/90/3/103–104.

55 Letter from Kahn to Austin, 10/6/38, EAGR/Box 9/2/1/17/66–67.

56 Letter from Austin Robinson to Kahn, 10/6/38, RFK/13/90/3/107–13.

57 Ibid.

58 In spite of Austin's instruction not to respond, Kahn answered his letter. However, Kahn's intention was not to invite further correspondence on their future but to persuade Austin not to hold himself and his views on appeasement and the war responsible for Robinson's breakdown (letter from Kahn to Austin, 10/7/38, EAGR/Box 9/2/1/17/68–69).

59 Letter from Austin Robinson to Kahn, 10/6/38, RFK/13/90/3/107–13.

60 Letter from Austin Robinson to Keynes, 10/4/38, JMK/L/K/100–105

61 See letter from Stephen to Kahn, 10/10/38, RFK/13/90/3/114–17, a response to a letter from Kahn.

62 Letter from Stephen to Kahn, 10/10/38, RFK/13/90/3/114–17.

63 Robinson's expenses at Brooke House for the period October 3, 1938–January 1, 1939—which did not include the entire duration of her stay—amounted to some £165 (EAGR/Box 9/2/1/21/14–18). This exceeded her Cambridge stipend of £160 in 1937–38 and was almost half of Austin's £337 stipend.

64 Letter from Kahn to Keynes, 10/12/38, JMK/L/K/106–107.

65 Ibid. We have no evidence that Keynes offered this loan. Robinson continued to be paid a lectureship stipend during her illness (10/26/38; GB/Box 3011). On November 7, 1938, the faculty board recommended "the payment of a Fellowship Allowance of £150 per annum to Mrs. J. V. Robinson as part of her pensionable salary" (FB/Min.V. 119).

66 Letter from Chennell to Kahn, 11/4/38, RFK/13/90/30/129–31. When Chennell wrote Austin the next day, it was not to convey his wife's worries over him or to ask for reassurances but to relay her request for clothes so that she could stroll the grounds of the clinic (11/5/38, EAGR/Box 9/2/1/21/9–10). During the Christmas holidays, he took a skiing vacation in Switzerland while Robinson remained hospitalized in Brooke House (letter from Robinson to Austin, 12/22/38, EAGR/Box 9/2/1/21/20–28).

67 Letter from Robinson to Kahn, 12/13/38, RFK/13/90/3/152–53.

68 Ibid.

69 Ibid.
70 Letter from Robinson to Kahn, 1/2/39, RFK/13/90/3/210–15.
71 Letter from Robinson to Kahn, 1/18/39, RFK/13/90/3/264–70.
72 Ibid.
73 Letter from Robinson to Kahn, 1/2/39, RFK/13/90/3/210–15.
74 Ibid.
75 Letter from Robinson to Kahn, 1/19/39, RFK/13/90/3/264–70.
76 Letter from Robinson to Kahn, 12/15/39, RFK/13/90/3/328–31; Cairncross 1993, 172.
77 Letter from Robinson to Kahn, 11/20/40, RFK/13/90/4/354–55.

2 THE ECONOMICS OF IMPERFECT COMPETITION

1 A précis of the analysis in this part of the book was published in Aslanbeigui and Oakes 2007.
2 See letter from Kahn to Robinson, 3/28–30/33, RFK/13/90/1/209–12.
3 See Pigou 1925, 85; 1939, 219–20; Keynes 1951, 190–92; Harrod 1951, 324; Robertson 1952, vi.
4 The early work of Maurice Dobb documents Marshall's preeminent status at Cambridge in the early 1920s. Dobb was an anomalous figure among the Cambridge Marshallians. An active member of the Communist Party since 1921, he achieved a First in both parts of the Economics Tripos in 1922 and then wrote a doctoral dissertation with Edwin Cannan of LSE. In 1925, he published *Capitalist Enterprise and Social Progress* and returned to Cambridge to accept a university lectureship. Dobb's position on Marshallian economics was not influenced by communist polemics of the day, nor did he attempt to destroy Marshall's system by employing a Marxist critique. Instead, he translated Marxist economics into conventional British economic parlance using the *Principles* as a translation manual. On Dobb's view, Marx had proven he was the greatest classical economist by transcending the works of Smith and Ricardo. However, his system could be reconstructed for a bourgeois readership by using the tools developed by the greatest capitalist economist of the era: Marshall. According to his British Academy biography, Dobb had an intriguing Buñuel-like dream in which a fellow of St. John's held a sherry party in an attic room above the college chapel for the purpose of introducing Marx to Marshall: "The party was apparently a great success: the two old men were talking together with tremendous animation and in perfect amity" (Meek 1977, 343).
5 Immanent critique of the laws of returns was not limited to interventions by Cambridge economists. Certain attacks on Marshallian analysis launched from outside the walls were too damaging to pass over in silence. In their efforts to repair the edifice of the *Principles*, members of the guild writing in defense of Marshall sometimes embraced elements of the rival positions to which they were responding. See, for example, Allyn Young's criticism

of Pigou's transposition of the laws of returns into welfare economics (1913) and Pigou's acceptance of his point (Pigou 1924, 194). Examples of immanent critique outside Cambridge include Knight 1924 and Robbins 1928. For other types of criticism concerning Marshallian laws of returns, see Young 1928 and Schumpeter 1928.

6   See Pigou 1922, 1927, 1928; Robertson 1924, 1930; Sraffa 1926, 1930a, 1930b; and Shove 1928, 1930.

7   For comparisons of Sraffa's articles of 1925 and 1926, see Maneschi 1986 and Mongiovi 1996.

8   See Sraffa's destructive criticism of Robertson's position (Sraffa 1930a).

9   See letters from Robinson to Kahn, 1/28/33, RFK/13/90/I/78–83; 12/25/33, RFK/13/90/I/270–71.

10   On the close collaboration between Keynes and Kahn, see Marcuzzo 2002.

11   On Sraffa's contributions to economics, see Nisticò and Rodano 2005. Several scholars have offered explanations for Sraffa's abandonment of the Marshallian theoretical framework and rediscovery of classical economics. See, for example, Cavalieri 2001, 100–106; Dardi 2001; Kurz and Salvadori 2005; Marchionatti 2001, 75; Marcuzzo 2001, 89–92; and Signorino 2005. On the timing of Sraffa's conversion to classical economics, see Garegnani 2005; Naldi 2005; and Rosselli 2005b.

12   The ensuing is based in part on Aslanbeigui and Oakes 2008.

13   Distinctive does not imply unique. See, for example, Kadish (1982) and Lee (1981) on forums of collaborative research at Oxford in the late nineteenth century and the 1930s, respectively.

14   Letter from Kahn to Robinson, 1/4–8/33, RFK/12/90/I/33–40. Kahn's judgment of Chicago economics is perhaps due to superficial impressions of a relatively disengaged visitor with little understanding of the changing institutional structure and culture occurring at the time of his visit. For alternative perspectives on Chicago economics, the changes taking place in the department and the university following the arrival of Robert Maynard Hutchins as its fifth president, and the level of interaction among students and faculty, see Emmett 1998; Kitch 1983; and Reder 1982.

15   Letter from Kahn to Robinson, 1/15/33, RFK/13/90/I/44–57, quoted in Aslanbeigui and Oakes 2008.

16   Letter from Kahn to Robinson, 2/15–21/33, RFK/13/90/I/131–38, quoted in Aslanbeigui and Oakes 2008.

17   Letter from Kahn to Robinson, 2/7–9/33, RFK/13/90/I/95–100, quoted in Aslanbeigui and Oakes 2008. Schumpeter's corruption by American ways must have been remarkably swift. He assumed his professorship at Harvard only the semester before Kahn's arrival. It is instructive to compare Kahn's perception of the quality of life in the Harvard Economics Department with the account given by Schumpeter's most recent biographer. During his first few years at Harvard, Schumpeter had lunch and dinner most days with students and members of the economics faculty. The va-

riety of dining companions is impressive, ranging from undergraduates to full professors. As faculty advisor to the Graduate Economics Club, he also organized informal seminars at which papers were read and discussed. Schumpeter established at least three such discussion groups: the Chance, Love, and Logic Society; the Cournot Group; and the Group of Seven Wise Men. Members included Chamberlin, Gottfried Haberler, Seymour Harris, Wassily Leontief, and Edward Mason. Meetings were held once or twice a month, generally for dinner at one of the better Boston restaurants, "where the wine flowed freely and the talk often continued past midnight" (McGraw 2007, 212–13). On Schumpeter's impression of the high quality of economics students and younger faculty at Harvard in the late 1920s and early 1930s, see McGraw 2007, 187–89, 195–96; Allen 1994a, 242, 245–48.

18 Letter from Kahn to Robinson, 2/15–21/33, RFK/13/90/1/131–38, quoted in Aslanbeigui and Oakes 2008.

19 Woolf 1993, 10, 16, 21.

20 Letter from Kahn to Robinson, 2/15–21/33, RFK/13/90/1/131–38, quoted in Aslanbeigui and Oakes 2008.

21 Ibid.

22 Letter from Kahn to Robinson, 3/2–6/33, RFK/13/90/1/162–67, quoted in Aslanbeigui and Oakes, 2008.

23 Letter from Kahn to Robinson, 2/24/33, RFK/13/90/1/147–54, quoted in Aslanbeigui and Oakes 2008. Kahn's complaints and his sense of deprivation—at Harvard, of all places—betray an insensitivity to Robinson's circumstances. His correspondence devotes many pages to comparisons of Harvard and Cambridge as academic societies. As a fellow of King's and a Rockefeller Foundation fellow, he had the good fortune to be a member of both. As he knew, Robinson was unable to enjoy the excellence of the discourse, the cuisine, or the cellar of King's or any other male college. Nor was she in a position to indulge in comparisons of the quality of life at Cambridge, Chicago, and Harvard. In winter 1933, when she was reading Kahn's letters, she had no access to the academic culture he took for granted. Kahn's withering observations on Harvard gastronomy also express a remarkable obtuseness, especially on the part of a social scientist trained in economics. The collapse of the capitalist economy, the failure of thousands of American banks before President Franklin D. Roosevelt declared a "bank holiday" during Kahn's visit to the United States, and the possibility that these events might reduce funds available for the operation of the Harvard faculty club did not seem to register in his consciousness. The entrenched class stratification of British society—which entailed a relative indifference of the upper classes to the suffering of those not so well situated—enabled Cambridge academics to continue their privileged lives as if there were no depression. Kahn's complaints were based on the assumption that the absence of this political ethos in the United States was yet another defect of American society.

24 Letter from Kahn to Robinson, 2/7–9/33, RFK/13/90/I/95–100.

25 Ibid., quoted in Aslanbeigui and Oakes 2008.

26 Letter from Robinson to Kahn, 3/31–4/2/31, RFK/16/I/63–64. See letter from Kahn to Robinson, 7/29/30, RFK/16/I/2–4, in which he tells her he has consulted Shove on the issue of joint supply. See also letters and notes from Pigou to Kahn, circa late 1930–early 1931, in which Pigou discusses Kahn's paradoxes on monopoly (RFK/13/I/39–51).

27 Letter from Kahn to Robinson, 9/16/31, RFK/16/I/72–75, quoted in Aslanbeigui and Oakes 2008.

28 Circa March 1931, RFK/16/I/121–27, and RFK/16/I/131–34. Kahn later showed that adjusted concavity was important in determining whether a discriminating monopolist—who charged different prices for the same product—produced more than a monopolist who charged uniform prices (not dated, RFK/16/I/29–30). Robinson appropriated both the concept and the mathematical derivation but credited Kahn only for the derivation (Robinson 1933d, 40–41, n. 3; 193–94, n. 2).

29 Letter from Robinson to Kahn, 3/30/31, RFK/16/I/59–60.

30 See letter, notes, and questions from Robinson to Kahn, 3/31–4/2/31, RFK/16/I/63–64, RFK/16/I/28, and RFK/16/I/100–101.

31 Kahn's Answers to Robinson's questions, circa early April 1931, RFK/16/I/102–05. For Robinson's use of this formula without attribution, see *The Economics of Imperfect Competition* (1933d), 36, 54.

32 See notes by Kahn on price discrimination, not dated, RFK/16/I/29–30, and Kahn's Answers to Robinson's questions, circa early April 1931, RFK/16/I/102–05.

33 Letter from Robinson to Kahn, circa mid-September 1931, RFK/16/I/109–10, quoted in Aslanbeigui and Oakes 2008.

34 See letter from Kahn to Robinson, 2/24/33 (RFK/13/90/I/147–54, quoted in Aslanbeigui and Oakes 2008), in which Kahn remembers the episode.

35 See, for example, her postcard to Kahn (9/15/31, RFK/16/I/70–71). "I now can't see any reason to expect the multiplication of A[verage] + M[arginal] curves to give an A + M result. But there must be some definite relation between the resultant curves. Let me have it if it is not anything complicated. It doesn't matter in itself so don't bother if it is difficult. I should like the result of the other point (whether a rising supply curve of capital destroys our relationship for the average net curve) as it comes into the next bit that I have to write. Send me a line to say whether it is all right or not. I have got into a mess over the maxima of the three curves, but hope for a prosperous issue."

36 Letter from Robinson to Austin, 8/8/32, EAGR/Box 9/2/I/17/266–71.

37 Letter from Robinson to Kahn, 12/30/32, RFK/13/90/I/24–25. *The Economics of Imperfect Competition* includes ten books numbered I–X. The books are divided into short chapters numbered 1–27.

38 RFK/13/90/1/67–72, quoted in Aslanbeigui and Oakes 2008. The book was scheduled to appear in late May or early June, leaving little time for further work. Meeting Robinson's deadlines meant occasional communication via telegram, a costly affair for Kahn, who was pressed for funds generally, in debt to Keynes, and traveling on a fellowship stipend. "Would you be an angel," she wrote on January 6, "+ cable if you find the figures passable (with the corrections I have marked) as I want to send them back as soon as possible. 'Robinson Cambridge 2248 correct' will do. Otherwise I will keep them until you write." However, she was not oblivious of the expense, adding a footnote that "if 20 words at a weekend is cheaper so much the better" (RFK/13/90/1/28–30). The expense of dialogue by cable does not seem to have posed an obstacle to Kahn. By January 26, Robinson was thanking him for his cabled revisions and noting that he had identified many errors she had failed to note (RFK/13/90/1/73–77). Again on January 31: "Many thanks for 2 cables which arrived yesterday + to-day. I was delighted to have them. I am glad you are pleased with the figures on the whole" (RFK/13/90/1/84–87).

39 This is a telling mark of Cambridge complacency. In 1930, Kahn and Robinson knew about Yntema's 1928 article through Gifford's supervisory essay. Yet before Kahn's deflationary experience at Chicago, they had neither read it, nor did they even remember his name.

40 RFK/13/90/1/44–51, quoted in Aslanbeigui and Oakes 2008.

41 Letter from Robinson to Kahn, 2/3/33, RFK/13/90/1/88–93, quoted in Aslanbeigui and Oakes 2008.

42 RFK/13/90/1/131–38, quoted in Aslanbeigui and Oakes 2008.

43 The article to which Kahn referred was the lecture on imperfect competition and the marginal principle that he delivered at Harvard.

44 See, for example, Pigou's treatment 1929, 215.

45 Kahn 1989, 15–16; see also chapter 11.

46 Letter from Kahn to Robinson, 2/24/33, RFK/13/90/1/147–54, quoted in Aslanbeigui and Oakes 2008.

47 *The Economics of the Short Period* was first published in Italian with an introduction by Marco Dardi. Marcuzzo and Harcourt played an important part in arranging its publication in English in 1989 (see Kahn 1989, x). Kahn published papers drawn from the dissertation. For example, his article on duopoly (1937) is a substantially revised version of chapter 7.

48 On December 7, 1932, Robinson expressed her delight in receiving Pigou's letters: "But I am getting in the harvest of my efforts. Pigou wrote me a letter about my article in the E[conomic] J[ournal] which was not only very warm but full of a lot of economics." Later on the same day: "Another letter from the Prof. It is really a great thing that he is taking an interest in the modern economics — I was afraid he was going to be bored by it" (letter from Robinson to Austin, EAGR/Box 8/2/1/13/132–35).

49 Letter from Robinson to Kahn, 1/14–16/33, RFK/13/90/1/52–54, quoted in Aslanbeigui and Oakes 2008.

50 Letter from Pigou to Robinson, circa mid-January, 1933, JVR/vii/347/10–12, quoted in Aslanbeigui and Oakes 2008.

51 Letter from Robinson to Kahn, 1/14–16/33, RFK/13/90/1/52–54, quoted in Aslanbeigui and Oakes 2008.

52 Ibid.

53 Ibid.

54 Letter from Pigou to Robinson, circa mid-January, 1933, JVR/vii/347/13, quoted in Aslanbeigui and Oakes 2008.

55 Letter from Pigou to Robinson, circa mid-January, 1933, JVR/vii/347/13.

56 Letter from Robinson to Kahn, 1/14–16/33, RFK/13/90/1/52–54, quoted in Aslanbeigui and Oakes 2008.

57 Letter from Newman to Robinson, circa January 1933, JVR/vii/314/7–11, quoted in Aslanbeigui and Oakes 2008.

58 Letter from Robinson to Kahn, 1/18/33, RFK 13/90/1/57–58, quoted in Aslanbeigui and Oakes 2008.

59 Letter from Robinson to Kahn, 1/23/33, RFK/13/90/1/73–77, quoted in Aslanbeigui and Oakes 2008.

60 Letter from Kahn to Robinson, 2/10–13/33, RFK/13/90/1/105–14.

61 RFK/13/90/1/127–30, quoted in Aslanbeigui and Oakes 2008.

62 Pigou had a reputation for being austerely reserved toward women. Historians of economic thought have interpreted his attitude as misogyny. See Aslanbeigui 1997.

63 Letter from Kahn to Robinson, 3/2–6/33, RFK/13/90/1/162–67, quoted in Aslanbeigui and Oakes 2008.

64 Circa June 1933, JVR/vii/347/6, quoted in Aslanbeigui and Oakes 2008.

65 For evaluations of Kahn's fellowship thesis, see RFK/2/8.

66 James Meade, quoted in Keynes 1973a, 339.

67 This paper argued that public works financed by borrowing boost aggregate demand, national output, and employment. Because an increase in public works employment stimulates consumption, employment in other sectors will also rise. Using Keynes's ideas but not mentioning his name, Kahn instructed his audience that prices are determined not by the quantity of money, the received view, but by the shape of the aggregate supply curve. In a depression, significant unemployed resources permit the economy to increase production substantially without raising prices. A change in the quantity of money does not affect the level of output. Causation operates in the other direction: as consumers spend more, they also hold more money.

68 Letter from Kahn to Robinson, 1/4–8/33, RFK/13/90/1/33–40.

69 Letter from Kahn to Robinson, 1/15/33, RFK/13/90/1/44–51.

70 Ibid.

71 Letter from Kahn to Robinson, 1/4–8/33, RFK/13/90/1/33–40. On January 20, Robinson asked Kahn if he had received enough reprints and noted that she would send one to Viner (RFK/13/90/1/64–66).

72 Letter from Kahn to Robinson, 1/15/33, RFK/13/90/1/44–51.

73 Ibid.

74 Kahn added a footnote to this statement: "Since I wrote this Coe has told me how frightfully impressed he is with what he sees" (RFK/13/90/1/67–72).

75 Letter from Kahn to Robinson, 2/7–9/33, RFK/13/90/1/95–100.

76 See letter from Robinson to Kahn, 2/3/33; RFK/13/90/1/88–93.

77 Letter from Robinson to Kahn, 2/11–13/33, RFK/13/90/1/115–18.

78 Letter from Robinson to Kahn, 2/15–21/33, RFK/13/90/1/131–38.

79 Letter from Robinson to Kahn, 3/23–25/33, RFK/13/90/1/205–08.

80 Letter from Coe to Robinson, 4/22/33; JVR/vii/108/1–2.

81 Letter from Kahn to Robinson, 2/10–13/33, RFK/13/90/1/105–14.

82 See Swedberg 1991, 12. Schumpeter allowed that he had not become the world's greatest horseman.

83 Letter from Kahn to Robinson, 2/10–13/33, RFK/13/90/1/105–14. Schumpeter, who was also at work on a theory of money, took a quite different tone in writing Keynes after reading the *Treatise*: "This is truly a Ricardian *tour de force*, and must cause you the most intense satisfaction. I believe it will ever stand as a landmark in its field" (Schumpeter 2000, 180–81). His judgment in a letter to the Viennese economist Haberler was more temperate: "Certainly a splendid achievement by an immensely gifted man, but nothing new in the general approach—although perhaps in many individual points" (Schumpeter 2000, 181–82, our translation). When *The General Theory* appeared in 1936, Schumpeter wrote a dismissive letter to Oskar Lange, condemning the book as "obviously bad workmanship," a book that "could have been written a hundred years ago and shirks all real problems." Keynes was the "dying voice of the bourgeois crying out in the wilderness for profits it does not dare to fight for" (Schumpeter 2000, 296). However, he envied Keynes's Cambridge network of collaborators, especially Kahn and Robinson. As he confided to his diary in the 1940s, "Why do I have only so few and characteristically useless followers—from [x] to [y] to [z]? Why not the splendid praetorians of Keynes?" (quoted in Allen 1994b, 160).

84 Letter from Kahn to Robinson, 2/10–13/33, RFK/13/90/1/105–14. Kahn's letters to Robinson are marked by the florid locutions and hyperbole of English upper-class speech in his day. They call to mind the parodistic dialogue of a Noël Coward play and read as if Kahn himself were one of Coward's characters. Keynes's achievement in the *Treatise* was a performance of "stupendous brilliance" (2/10–13/33, RFK/13/90/1/105–114). Coe was "frightfully impressed" with what he had seen of Robinson's proofs, which meant that it would be a "shocking waste" not to give him a full set (2/20–24/33,

RFK/13/90/I/67–72). Robinson was advised to send Schumpeter another copy of her pamphlet. An earlier mailing had apparently been misplaced or lost, and it would be "a tragedy" to deprive him of her inscription (2/15–21/33, RFK/13/90/I/131–38).

85 Letter from Keynes to Frisch, 10/1/35, RF/NBO Brevs. 761 A; see also the following letters in the Frisch Papers: Frisch to Kahn, 9/18/35, RF/NBO Brevs. 761 B, and Frisch to Keynes, 10/15/35, RF/NBO Bervs. 761 A.

86 Letter from Kahn to Robinson, 2/10–13/33, RFK/13/90/I/105–14.

87 Letter from Kahn to Robinson, 2/7–9/33, RFK/13/90/I/95–100.

88 Allen 1994a, 90, 233–34, 245–48; 1994b, 6.

89 Letter from Schumpeter to Robinson, 1/21/33, JVR/vii/400/1.

90 Letter from Kahn to Robinson, 2/7–9/33, RFK/13/90/I/95–100.

91 Letter from Kahn to Robinson, 2/10–13/33, RFK/13/90/I/105–14.

92 Ibid.

93 On February 9, Kahn wrote Robinson that he was about to meet with Chamberlin, whose book was expected to appear in two days (RFK/13/90/I/95–100).

94 Chamberlin's article of 1961 is a peculiar exercise. More than thirty years after submitting his dissertation, he indulged in a scholastic excavation of this text and an elaborate exegesis of subtle revisions that he introduced in his book. He also tilted at windmills, returning to imaginary scenes of battles with Robinson that she never fought. In attempting to demonstrate the derivative character of her book, he argued that his own work was strikingly innovative and without precedent. If Robinson saw far enough to write *The Economics of Imperfect Competition*, it was because she was standing on the shoulders of Marshall, Pigou, and Sraffa. He, on the other hand, was able to write *The Theory of Monopolistic Competition* not because he stood on the shoulders of giants or any other species of economist but simply because he saw further than others. Thus Chamberlin ascribed to himself the godlike power of thinking ex nihilo and creating something out of nothing (see Chamberlin 1961, 516, 532–33, 536–37). This self-assessment cannot withstand historiographic scrutiny. In modern science, research is performed against a disciplinary background. It is based on other work in the field and, in some fashion, responds to it. For a more balanced and intelligent account of Chamberlin's sources, see Blitch 1985.

95 The article introduced no new tools. Under the guise of marginal demand price, Chamberlin mentioned marginal revenue in a footnote, and it was implicit in his mathematical appendix. However, he did nothing with it.

96 Letter from Kahn to Robinson, 2/15–21/33, RFK/13/90/I/131–38.

97 Chamberlin 1933, 77; Reinwald 1977, 527.

98 On Chamberlin's strictures against marginal techniques generally and his aversion to marginal revenue, see Chamberlin 1933, 191–93, and Reinwald 1977. Reinwald argues that Chamberlin misunderstood and understated the significance of marginal revenue for his work (1977, 529).

99 Letter from Kahn to Robinson, 2/15–21/33, RFK/13/90/I/131–38. Later that month, Schumpeter gave Frisch his impressions of Kahn's lecture: "It is funny, and indeed a very hopeful sign, how the ideas of all of us move in the same line. When I look at the state of economic discussion and teaching and conclude that it is in a hopeless mess it is always this observation which comforts me. To give an instance: In an address here at Harvard, Kahn developed a formula (no great discovery but quite serviceable) linking up price and marginal cost under conditions of imperfect competition [$P = $ Marginal Cost $\times$ (E $+$ 1)/E], and on the very same day I read a paper which Schneider sent me and found therein, among other things, exactly the same expression" (2/25/33, RF/NBO Brevs. 761 A).

100 Letter from Kahn to Robinson, 2/15–21/33, RFK/13/90/I/131–38.

101 The foreword to *The Economics of Imperfect Competition* noted that Chamberlin's book "provides a crop of coincidences"—presumably closely parallel or intersecting claims—"but it appeared too late for me to notice them in detail" (Robinson 1933d, vii).

102 Letter from Robinson to Kahn, 3/8/33, RFK/13/90/I/173–79.

103 Schumpeter's endorsement of Robinson's book, although qualified by pointed criticisms, seems to have strained his relations with Chamberlin, who had been one of the young Schumpeterians during Schumpeter's visiting year at Harvard in 1927–28. See Allen 1994b, 64.

104 Letter from Kahn to Robinson, 2/15–21/33, RFK/13/90/I/131–38.

105 Lowes Dickinson was one of Pigou's teachers and a colleague of all the Cambridge economists of the 1920s. In Annan's account of "the ethos of Kings" during the early years of the twentieth century, the pursuit of success in a career is damned as a mark of shallowness and banality, perhaps even a vice (Annan 1999, 108–9). Austin was firm in insisting that property in ideas had no place in Cambridge economics during the 1920s and 1930s. He regarded questions about the distribution of credit for the work produced in the Marshallian guild as pointless and misguided. As he wrote about Keynes and his colleagues in the 1930s, the "whole concept of private property in ideas, subsequently bred by the Ph.D. thesis and competition for faculty promotion, was alien both to him and to most of his Cambridge contemporaries. At that moment we were more excited about what was happening to economics as a whole than about who might possibly claim responsibility for which brick" (Robinson 1963, 89; see also Robinson 1985, 54).

106 See Kahn's letter to Robinson, in which Kahn mentions "my article on Euler's theorem" followed by a sketch of its argument (2/10–13/33, RFK/13/90/I/105–114). Although Kahn did not publish on the theorem, Robinson did (Robinson 1934a).

107 Frank Taussig was the editor of the *Quarterly Journal of Economics*.

108 Letter from Kahn to Robinson, 2/24/43, RFK/13/90/I/147–54.

109 Robinson gave Kahn suggestions on how to inflict damage on Chamberlin by a judicious use of destructive footnotes on which they would collaborate

for his book. See letters from Robinson to Kahn, 3/8/33, RFK/13/90/1/173–79, and 3/30/33, RFK/13/90/1/215–16.

110 In *The Economics of Imperfect Competition*, Robinson stated that the older textbooks customarily "set out upon the analysis of value from the point of view of perfect competition. The whole scheme appeared almost homogeneous and it had some aesthetic charm. But somewhere, in an isolated chapter, the analysis of monopoly had to be introduced. This presented a hard, indigestible lump which the competitive analysis could never swallow" (1933d, 3).

111 Letter from Kahn to Robinson, 3/22–24/33, RFK/13/90/1/201–04.

112 Letter from Kahn to Robinson, 2/15–21/33, RFK/13/90/1/131–38.

113 Letter from Robinson to Kahn, 3/16–18/33, RFK/13/90/1/191–97.

114 See Rosselli (2005c, 356–64) for a similar interpretation. The most sophisticated literature on the institutional construction, attribution, and allocation of credit and priority in science has been produced by Robert K. Merton, his students, and followers—christened the Merton School in the science studies literature. See Barber 1990; Cole 1992; Merton 1957, 1968, 1973, 1979; Mulkay 1991; Storer 1966; Zuckerman 1977.

115 Letter from Shove to Robinson, 10/27/31, JVR/vii/412/5–7.

116 Letter from Shove to Robinson, 12/8/31, JVR/vii/412/10–12.

117 Letter from Shove to Robinson, 12/9/31, JVR/vii/412/14–15.

118 Letter from Shove to Robinson, 12/19/31, JVR/vii/412/16.

119 Letter from Shove to Robinson, 6/17–21/32, JVR/vii/412/22–25.

120 Letter from Shove to Robinson, 6/23/32, JVR/vii/412/26–28.

121 Letter from Shove to Robinson, 6/17–21/32, JVR/vii/412/22–25.

122 Ibid.

123 On the distinction between the use of research and distribution of credit for research, see Hull 1988.

124 On the preeminent status ascribed to the disinterested pursuit of truth, the repudiation of knowledge as private property, and the ethical denigration of careerist intellectuality, see Dickinson 1973; Forster 1907, 13–14, and 1934, 66; Russell 1967, 67–90; Woolf 1960, 129–30. On the Cambridge Apostles, see Levy 1981.

125 Letter from Kahn to Keynes, 9/16/34, JMK/L/K/78–79.

126 Letter from Kahn to Keynes, 3/25/34, JMK/L/K/84.

127 Ibid.

128 Letter from Kahn to Keynes, 3/28/34, JMK/L/K/85–86.

129 This account of Austin's early Cambridge career is drawn from Cairncross 1993.

130 Letter from Robinson to Kahn, 1/28/33, RFK/13/90/1/78–83.

131 Cairncross 1993, 166; see also Annan 1999, 256–77.

132 On General Maurice's financial predicament following his dismissal from the army, see Kennedy 1951–60, 721–22.

133 Letter from Austin to Robinson, circa late autumn 1932, JVR/vii/378/135; see also letter from Austin, circa late autumn 1932, JVR/vii/378/142–44.

134 See Sylvia Hewlette in Turner 1989, 201.

135 Letter from Robinson to Kahn, 2/23–24/33, RFK/13/90/1/139–46.

136 Letter from Robinson to Kahn, 8/11/36, RFK/13/90/3/6–7.

3   BECOMING A KEYNESIAN

1 On Marshall's manipulation of the election, see Coase, 1972; Coats 1968, 1972; Jones 1978; and Groenewegen 1995, 622–27.

2 Skidelsky 1983, 183–85, 213–14.

3 See letters from Keynes to Lydia on 3/12/30 and 5/4/31 (JMK/PP/45/190/4).

4 Late in life, Robinson maintained that she became a Keynesian for political and ethical reasons: his research program held out promise of significant improvements in the economic conditions of human life (Robinson 1979, x). We find no evidence of this motive in the archival sources of the 1930s. However, our account of Robinson's early history as a Keynesian does not rule out her account. We show how she acquired Keynes's patronage. We do not argue that she became a Keynesian in order to become a client of Keynes. The preferred site for research on patronage and science has been early modern science, the period before the rise of research institutes, professional scientific associations and communities, and the research university. See, for example, Lux 1989; Moran 1991; Smith 1994. Have the autonomous reward structures, prestige hierarchies, and career paths of modern science eliminated the functions and payoffs of patronage by tying the scientific career to performance criteria that are internal to science? Are scientific careers formed by different cultural and social systems that operate in different historical periods—the patronage system of early modern science and the professionalized institutions of modern science? As the history of the Marshallian guild suggests, the interests of many parties inside social networks of scientific institutions ensure an important place for patronage in the development of modern scientific careers. Typical patrons have changed, from ecclesiastical and secular princes and their advisors to senior scientists and scientific administrators. The functions and effects of patronage remain: allocation of positions in the scientific establishment and the determination of socioprofessional status, the distribution of prestige, control over resources for research, and power to influence attribution of priority and credit. Early modern scientists worked in a culture of princely patronage. The natural philosopher was one among many court ornaments (Biagioli 1993). Following the development of relatively independent scientific institutions, modern scientists performed in a disciplinary and academic culture in which patronage practiced by masters of these institutions smoothed the path to a successful career. In the literature

on patronage and scientific careers, Dorinda Outram's study of the French naturalist Georges Cuvier (1984) is noteworthy. Outram does not posit a pair of linked dichotomies: a historical dichotomy of early modern science and modern science and a sociological dichotomy of the authority of princely patronage and the authority of scientific institutions. On the contrary, modern scientific institutions are understood as social selection mechanisms in which careers are made and sustained by patronage networks. As Biagioli notes (1993, 14, n. 8), breaking down these dichotomies indicates a continuity in the structural underpinnings of career formation from early modern to modern science.

5 See Caldwell 2005, for an intellectual biography of Hayek. See Hayek 1995 for a history of the debates between Hayek and Keynes.

6 As Hayek noted in the second part of his review, Keynes failed to grasp Wicksell's point that although increases in saving may not affect prices, they can change inventories. This means that any act of saving is also an act of investment, a conclusion that contradicts the basic thesis of the *Treatise*.

7 In a letter of February 1, 1932, referring to his correspondence with Hayek, Keynes asked Kahn: "What is the next Move?" (RFK/13/57/9).

8 Robinson drafted the article in summer 1931, after the meetings of the Circus concluded (Kahn 1985, 49). However, she did not submit this draft for publication. It was Kahn who told Robinson about Hayek's "rather silly review of the Treatise in the August Economica" (two-part letter from Kahn to Robinson, 9/16/31, RFK/16/1/72–75 and RFK/16/1/76–77).

9 The "Nightmare" was the name Robinson used among Cambridge insiders for the work that would become *The Economics of Imperfect Competition*.

10 When Robinson sent her "peas and gold" manuscript to Keynes on April 9, 1932, she signed herself "Joan Robinson." Although she used the same signature on the cover letter to the manifesto (in Keynes 1973a,269, 376), this formal mode of address was dropped quite early in the correspondence. In her second letter, she had become "Joan" (Keynes 1979, 47).

11 Letter from Robinson to Keynes, circa early May, quoted in Keynes 1973a, 376.

12 Letter from Robinson to Keynes, circa early May, quoted in Keynes 1979, 47.

13 Letter from Robinson to Keynes, 5/10/32, quoted in Keynes 1973a, 378.

14 Letter from Tappan-Holland to Robinson, 10/23/32, JVR/vii/208/3.

15 Letter from Tappan-Holland to Robinson, 10/16/32, JVR/vii/208/12.

16 Letter from Kahn to Robinson, 2/13/33, RFK/13/90/1/105–14.

17 Letter from Tappan-Holland to Robinson, 10/23/32, JVR/vii/208/3.

18 The connection between Robinson's father and the Macmillan family suggests that she may have benefited by her membership in a multigenerational network of upper-middle-class British families that Noel Annan christened "the intellectual aristocracy" (Annan 1999, 304–51). Her maternal grandfather, Frederick Howard Marsh, was professor of surgery and master of

Downing College, Cambridge. Her uncle Edward Marsh, a graduate of Cambridge and an art collector, was Winston Churchill's chief of staff, amanuensis, and ghostwriter during his Liberal period. Her maternal grandmother, Jane Perceval Marsh, founded a children's hospital, and her great-great aunt Mary Maurice a school for governesses. Her most distinguished forebear was her great grandfather Frederick Denison Maurice, a leading man of letters in Victorian England, one of the founders of the Society of Apostles at Cambridge, a founder of Christian socialism, and at the end of his life Knightbridge professor of casuistry, moral theology, and moral philosophy at Cambridge. Joan Maurice was perhaps the only student of her day to pass a bust of her paternal great-grandfather in her visits to the university library (S. 1921–22, 97–105).

19 Robinson knew that Macmillan had asked Keynes to give an opinion on her book, and she was quite satisfied with the result. As she wrote Austin on December 7, Keynes had given her "a very good chit." She was especially pleased that he found the book easy to read. It is not clear whether Robinson had Keynes's report or an edited account of it (EAGR/Box 8/2/1/13/132–35).

20 The contributions of Kahn, Meade, Sraffa, and Austin Robinson have all been documented. See Aslanbeigui and Oakes 2002; Kahn 1984, 1985; Moggridge 1973; Moggridge in Keynes 1973a, 337–43; Ranchetti 2005, 125–30; Robinson 1977, 1985; and Robinson 1979, xi-xiv. There are no accounts of Robinson's contribution. According to Moggridge, Keynes mentioned an argument he had with Kahn and Robinson about purchasing power on May 10, 1931 (Moggridge in Keynes 1979, 48).

21 Letter from Keynes to Robinson, 10/16/32, quoted in Marcuzzo 2003, 551.

22 Letter from Robinson to Keynes, 3/26/34, JMK/UA/5/3/124–30.

23 Letter from Robinson to Kahn, 1/23/33, RFK/13/90/1/73–75.

24 Either Robinson or Keynes was mistaken about the date of this visit. He records it as January 22, she dates it January 23.

25 Letter from Robinson to Kahn, 2/17/33, RFK/13/90/1/127–30. Robinson's bemused account of this incident illuminates the extent to which Cambridge economists enjoyed privileged access to the *Economic Journal*. The 1930 symposiasts were all Cambridge theoreticians. Keynes accepted Robinson's paper on the symposium even though it was submitted more than two years after the original set of papers had appeared. Keynes and Shove seemed to regard it as self-evident that his note on her paper would be published. Keynes's reluctance to publish her counternote was based not on an excessive representation of Cambridge authors in the journal but on the length of the issue. On brief reconsideration, he decided to give her space for a short reply.

26 Letter from Robinson to Kahn, 2/17/33, RFK/13/90/1/127–30.

27 Ibid. Following her dismissive remarks about "poor old Gerald," Robinson noted that the cliché according to which women cannot take impartial and detached positions because of the female tendency to see all questions in

personal and subjective terms is mistaken. What conclusions did she draw from the Shove incident? "I begin to think that the conventional view is all wrong + that only women can take an impersonal interest in things because they have no ambition" (2/20/33, RFK/13/90/I/127–30). This observation seems strikingly incongruous on the part of a woman who shortly before had deserted her dinner guests in order to defend her interests in a scholarly dispute of quite modest dimensions. It rests on the assumption that she had no ambitions, from which it followed that her positions were detached from her personal interests. The premises of this reasoning are not consistent with Robinson's correspondence, which is filled with reflections on her interior life and her sense of herself. As this study documents, she was motivated by the ambitions of a professional academic careerist and attempted to achieve success both at Cambridge and in the cosmopolitan world of economics. As early as 1932, her work in economics, including her supervisions and lectures, was willfully tendentious, making her a source of increasingly abrasive conflicts in the Cambridge economics faculty. This was not a disposition she failed to recognize on other occasions. Less than a month after the Shove incident, she wrote Kahn on the pleasure she took in teaching as a way of pleading a case that her students would find persuasive: "I feel the sense of a definite point of view which is worthwhile to convey to the young" (3/16–18/33, RFK/13/90/I/191–97). And in August 1935, in the midst of her conflicts with Robertson, she wrote Kahn that she enjoyed coaching a certain Miss R for the tripos: "She is a devotee of Dennis but prepared to admit that what I say sounds convincing" (8/9/35, RFK/13/9/0/2/135–36). In the 1930s, Robinson seems to have seen economics as a field of contestation in which impersonal interests had no place.

28 Letter from Robinson to Kahn, 2/18/33, RFK/13/90/I/123–26.

29 Letter from Kahn to Robinson, 3/2/33, RFK/13/90/I/163–67. Kahn chaffed under the burden of Keynes's dependence. In spite of his status as "favorite pupil," he seems to have ascribed no great significance to his unique place in the Keynesian cosmos. Quite to the contrary, as he wrote Robinson on March 30, 1933: "Maynard has certainly accomplished a great revolution. He seems very excited about it all. He writes apologizing for a slip he made in the first article [in the *Times*] and putting it down to my absence. It is really absurd to go on in this kind of way. Do you remember what happened when I went to the Lakes (as a matter of fact I don't but I know it was something silly)? My place in the scheme of things is apparently to correct errors in arithmetic" (RFK/13/90/I/209–12).

30 Letter from Robinson to Kahn, 2/23–24/33, RFK/13/90/I/139–56.

31 Letter from Robinson to Kahn, 3/16–18/33, RFK/13/90/I/191–97.

32 See Keynes 1973a, 633–34; Keynes 1936, 213–15.

33 3/29/34, in Keynes 1973a, 422.

34 Letter from Pigou to Robinson, circa June-July 1933, JVR/vii/347/6.

35 Letters from Robinson to Kahn, 8/14/34, RFK/13/90/2/34–37; 8/26–27/34, RFK/13/90/2/97–98.

36 Letter from Robinson to Kahn, 8/30/34, RFK/13/90/2/64–71.

37 Note from Robinson to Kahn, circa 8/30/34, RFK/13/90/2/69–71.

38 Letter from Robinson to Kahn, 8/26–27/34, RFK/13/90/2/97–98.

39 Letter from Robinson to Kahn, 9/4/34, RFK/13/90/2/85–88.

40 Letter from Robinson to Kahn, 2/29/34, RFK/13/90/2/17–19.

41 Letter from Robinson to Kahn, 9/5–6/34, RFK/13/90/2/94–95.

42 *Cambridge University Reporter*, 3/25/30, 823–28.

43 "The Children" was Robinson's name for a group of young economists— some still research students—at Cambridge, Oxford, and LSE who held occasional conferences to discuss their work and were associated with the *Review of Economic Studies*. As editor of the *Economic Journal*, Keynes could offer the *Review* reduced terms for an advertisement.

44 *Cambridge University Reporter*, 11/27/34, 379.

45 2/18/35, FB/Min.V.118.

46 Letter from Keynes to Fay, 3/5/35, JMK/UA/5/3/140–42.

47 Wynne Plumptre (b. 1907), a University of Toronto graduate and lecturer, spent two years (1928–30) at King's College, Cambridge, where he was supervised by Keynes and became familiar with his work on the *Treatise*. In Easter 1936, he lectured at Cambridge in his field of expertise: "Recent Banking and Monetary Developments in the Dominions" (*Cambridge University Reporter*, 4/10/35, 88; Plumptre 1947, 366; Macgregor 1978).

48 In 1932, Pigou gave Robbins a lesson in the Cambridge etiquette of micro-social conflict resolution. At the time, both were members of the Committee of Economists appointed by Prime Minister Ramsay MacDonald to diagnose Britain's current economic problems. As chairman, Keynes had the task of drafting its report. When he advocated a tariff on imported manufactured goods as the only realistic emergency measure for increasing investment, Robbins, a doctrinaire free trader, rebelled and insisted on writing his own report. Pigou rebuked him in the following terms: "One never does that . . . one tries to reach the greatest possible measure of agreement and then, if necessary add a minute of dissent on particular points" (in Skidelsky 1992, 376).

49 Letter from Fay to Pigou, Keynes, and Shove, 3/2/35, JMK/UA/5/3/137–38.

50 Ibid.

51 Ibid.

52 Fay recalled that "in 1932 a similar difficulty threatened to arise on a small scale." Robinson had circulated a letter to supervisors in which she offered to lecture on theory over the long vacation in the summer to prepare students for their lectures in Part II of the tripos. Fay called Pigou, who resolved the matter in Fay's favor (ibid.).

53 Ibid.

54 JMK/UA/5/3/140–42. Recall that Tappan-Holland made a quite different argument against threats to the liberal intellectual culture of the Marshallian guild. What was pushing Cambridge in the direction of a regime that would decide academic matters on the basis of theoretical loyalties? It was Robinson's insistence to teach on doctrinaire Keynesian premises (letter from Tappan-Holland to Robinson, 10/16/32, JVR/vii/208/12). Her cautionary note to Robinson assumed that sectarian divisions—which Keynes saw only as a dangerous but erroneous impression—had already been formed.

55 Letter from Keynes to Fay, 3/5/35, JMK/UA/5/3/140–42.

56 Letter from Keynes to Shove, 3/5/35, JMK/UA/5/3/139.

57 Letter from Pigou to Robinson, circa June–July 1933, JVR/vii/347/6.

58 In her reminiscences of this period, Robinson recalled that in the dispute over her lecturing proposal Pigou ruled "in favor of free speech" (Robinson 1979, xiv).

59 Letter from Fay to Keynes, 3/6/35, JMK/UA/5/4/31–32.

60 For the full exchanges between Keynes and Robertson on the galleys of *The General Theory*, see Keynes 1973a, 493–523.

61 Robertson was not prepared to resume the dialogue later in the year. In October, when Keynes suggested he send a complete set of revised proofs, Robertson demurred. Since he could do no more than suggest "purely verbal changes," he would wait to see the book in print (in Keynes 1973a, 523–24).

62 In Keynes 1973a, 646. This observation confirms that Kahn kept Robinson up to date on developments in Keynes's thought.

63 Robinson's note on liquidity together with many comments on the galleys follow this letter (in Keynes 1973a, 646–50).

64 A letter from Keynes to Lydia indicates that this dinner took place on September 12 (JMK/PP/45/190/7).

65 This paper seems to have been either "The Long-Period Theory of Employment" or "Disguised Unemployment," both of which extended Keynes's framework.

66 Letter from Keynes to Lydia, 5/17/36, JMK/PP/45/190/7; Keynes 1973b, 87.

67 Letter from Robinson to Kahn, 8/15/34, RFK/13/90/2/39–40.

68 In their discussion of her essay on the mobility of labor, Robinson criticized Keynes's analysis of full employment, apparently to good effect. Although he did not find her critique persuasive, on October 18 he mentioned her work in a letter to Lydia for the first time. Kahn was apparently arguing with Keynes on Robinson's behalf. "Alexander is trying to come to the rescue of Joan's article. But it is no good. They will have to retreat on that chapter. The rest is very good" (JMK/PP/45/190/7).

69 See the *Cambridge University Reporter*, 7/18/36, 1279–80.

70 Letter from Kahn to Dobb, 6/2/36, JMK/UA/5/4/9/10–11.

71 Letter from Robertson to Keynes, 6/6/36, JMK/UA/5/4/11–12.

72 Letter from Keynes to Robertson, 9/20/36, DHR/CO/5/13.

73 Kahn sent a copy of this letter to Keynes: "JMK I thought you might like to see a copy of my letter to Dobb, which is to be discussed by the Lecture List Committee on Saturday" (JMK/UA/5/4/9/10–11).

74 Letter from Robertson to Keynes, 6/6/36, JMK/UA/5/4/9/11–12.

75 Ibid.

76 Letter from Keynes to Robertson, 9/20/36, DHR/CO/5/13.

77 Letter from Keynes to Kahn, 2/19/38, JMK/L/K/94–96.

78 Archival evidence sheds little light on Robertson's reasons for agreeing to recommend Robinson for a university lectureship. In view of their long-standing adversarial relationship, his decision seems peculiar. The following considerations, although speculative, are reasonable inferences from the evidence. (1) As chairman of the board, he may have felt obligated to take a more impartial position. This would not call for an unqualified or enthusiastic endorsement on his part. (2) Keynes was still seriously ill with cardiac disease, the reason he was not in Cambridge to participate in the board deliberations on Robinson's appointment. Robertson would not want to upset him. (3) Pigou, who was an advocate of Robinson and a guardian of academic liberalism, may have persuaded Robertson that opposition to the appointment was indefensible. (4) By 1938, Robertson's objections to *The General Theory* had caused him considerable distress, straining his relations with Keynes and producing friction with younger colleagues. If he opposed Robinson's appointment, he could expect to be the object of further animus and—in Keynes's metaphor—might face "armed insurrection."

79 Letter from Kahn to Keynes, 2/14–18/38, JMK/L/K/89–93.

80 16/2/38, GB/Min.V.118 (emphasis added).

81 5/25/36, FB/Min.V.118.

82 Letter from Kahn to Keynes, 2/14–18/38, JMK/L/K/89–93. Kahn's letter concerning the board meeting of February 14 began with two short paragraphs on its discussion of a revision in the tripos. Then he wrote extensively on Robinson's appointment. Although Keynes was dispirited by the manner in which his colleagues approved the appointment, his main worries over the Cambridge economics faculty lay elsewhere. After a perfunctory paragraph on the Robinson lectureship and his regret that he had not been on hand to support Kahn, he offered a much more comprehensive *tour d'horizon*, considering the reorganization of the tripos, the unhappy state of economics at Cambridge—"The School is going to pieces before our eyes"—and how these problems should be handled (letter from Keynes to Kahn, 2/19/38, JMK/L/K/94–96).

"WHO IS JOAN ROBINSON?"

1 See Latour 1987, 1988; Law 1986. Studies of scientific laboratories undertaken over the past thirty years take a parallel course. Scientists who win recognition are able to succeed by building alliances and gaining privileged

access to resources. See Fujimora 1996; Knorr-Cetina 1981; Kohler 1994; Latour and Woolgar 1976; Lynch 1985.

2 Letter from Robinson to Kahn, 11/5/52, RFK/13/90/5.

3 She returned the favor by pushing him to publish, drafting notes and memoranda on problems he was investigating in the 1930s. See, for example, the following letters from Robinson to Kahn: 1/16/33, RFK/13/90/1/55–56; 1/23/33, RFK/13/90/1/73–77; 3/18/33, RFK/13/90/1/98–99; 9/12/33, RFK/13/90/1/249–51; circa 1934, RFK/13/90/2/21–22; 9/2/34, RFK/13/90/2/76–83. However, he seems to have made little use of her as a theoretical resource.

4 See the following letters from Robinson to Austin: circa August 1928, EAGR/Box 8/2/1/13/26–32; circa August/September 1928, EAGR/Box 8/2/1/13/33–44; 9/27/28, EAGR/Box 8/2/1/13/45–50.

5 12/22/38, EAGR/Box 9/2/1/21/20–28.

6 Letter from Viner to Robinson, 9/2/33, JVR/vii/457/1–2.

7 Letter from Douglas to Robinson, 1/30/35, JVR/vii/123/1.

8 Letter from Durbin to Robinson, 2/10/38, JVR/vii/127/3.

9 Letter from Henderson to Robinson, 4/3/36, JVR/vii/197/3–4.

10 Letter from Henderson to Robinson, 4/7/36, JVR/vii/197/5–8.

11 See also Shove 1933; Kaldor 1934; Schumpeter 1934; Ellsworth 1938.

12 Letter from Douglas to Robinson, 1/30/35, JVR/vii/123/1, quoted in Aslanbeigui and Oakes 2008.

13 See the following letters from Robinson to Kahn: 1/18/33, RFK 13/90/1/57–58; 1/20/33, RFK/13/90/1/64–66; 2/23–24/33, RFK/13/90/1/139–46.

14 Letter from Robinson to Kahn, 3/16–18/33, RFK/13/90/1/191–97.

15 Letter from Keynes to Fay, 3/5/35, JMK/UA/5/3/140–42.

16 Letter from Haberler to Kahn, circa December 1932, JVR/ii/181/1.

17 Letter from Robinson to Austin, 10/20–24/32, EAGR/Box 8/2/1/13.

† BIBLIOGRAPHY †

ARCHIVAL SOURCES

Ragnar Frisch Papers (RF), The National Library of Norway, Oslo, Norway.

Richard F. Kahn Papers (RFK), Modern Archives, King's College, Cambridge University, Cambridge, England.

John Maynard Keynes Papers (JMK), Modern Archives, King's College, Cambridge University, Cambridge, England.

Dennis Holmes Robertson Papers (DHR), Wren Library, Trinity College, Cambridge University, Cambridge, England.

Austin Robinson Papers (EAGR), Marshall Library of Economics, Cambridge University, Cambridge, England.

Joan Violet Robinson Papers (JVR), Modern Archives, King's College, Cambridge University, Cambridge, England.

Minutes of the Meetings of the Faculty Board of Economics and Politics (FB), Cambridge University Library, Cambridge, England.

Minutes of the Meetings of the General Board of the Faculties (GB), Cambridge University Library, Cambridge, England.

PUBLISHED WORKS

Allen, Robert L. 1994a. *Europe*. Volume 1 of *Opening Doors: The Life and Work of Joseph Schumpeter*. New Brunswick, N.J.: Transaction.

———. 1994b. *America*. Volume 2 of *Opening Doors: The Life and Work of Joseph Schumpeter*. New Brunswick, N.J.: Transaction.

Ambrosi, G. Michael. 2003. *Keynes, Pigou and Cambridge Keynesians. Authenticity and Analytical Perspective in the Keynes-Classics Debate*. New York: Palgrave Macmillan.

Annan, Noel. 1999. *The Dons: Mentors, Eccentrics and Geniuses*. Chicago: University of Chicago Press.

Anonymous. 1948. "Adrian Leslie Stephen 1883–1948." *International Journal of Psycho-Analysis* 29: 4–6.

Aslanbeigui, Nahid. 1997. "Rethinking Pigou's Misogyny." *Eastern Economic Journal* 23.3: 301–16.

———. 2002. Introduction. In *The Economics of Welfare*, by A. C. Pigou. New Brunswick, N.J.: Transaction.

Aslanbeigui, Nahid, and Michele I. Naples. 1997. "Scissors and Horizon: Neoclassical Debates about Returns to Scale, Costs, and Long-Run Supply, 1926–1942." *Southern Economic Journal* 64.2: 517–30.

Aslanbeigui, Nahid, and Guy Oakes. 2002. "The Theory Arsenal: The Cambridge Circus and the Origins of the Keynesian Revolution." *Journal of the History of Economic Thought* 24.1: 5–37.

———. 2006. "Joan Robinson's 'Secret Document': A Passage from the Autobiography of an Analytical Economist." *Journal of the History of Economic Thought* 28.4: 413–26.

———. 2007. "The Twilight of the Marshallian Guild: The Culture of Cambridge Economists Circa 1930." *Journal of the History of Economic Thought* 29.2: 255–61.

———. 2008. "The Importance of Being at Cambridge: Joan Robinson and the Origins of the Theory of Imperfect Competition." In *Soziologie als Möglichkeit*, edited by Christian Papilloud. Weisbaden: VS Verlag.

Baehr, Peter. 2002. *Founders, Classics, Canons: Modern Disputes over the Origins and Appraisal of Sociology's Heritage*. New Brunswick, N.J.: Transaction.

Barber, Bernard. 1990. *Social Studies of Science*. New Brunswick, N.J.: Transaction.

Beard, Mary. 2000. *The Invention of Jane Harrison*. Cambridge, Mass.: Harvard University Press.

Berg, Maxine. 1996. *A Woman in History: Eileen Power, 1889–1940*. New York: Cambridge University Press.

Biagioli, M. 1993. *Galileo, Courtier: The Practice of Science in the Culture of Absolutism*. Chicago: University of Chicago Press.

Blitch, Charles P. 1985. "The Genesis of Chamberlinian Monopolistic Competition Theory: Addendum." *History of Political Economy* 17.3: 395–400.

Bradbrook, M. C. 1969. *'That Infidel Place': A Short History of Girton College, 1869–1969*. London: Chatto and Windus.

Burstyn, J. N. 1984. *Victorian Education and the Ideal of Womanhood*. New Brunswick, N.J.: Rutgers University Press.

Burtt, Edwin A. 1932. *The Metaphysical Foundations of Modern Science*. London: Routledge and Kegan Paul.

Butterfield, Herbert. 1957. *The Origins of Modern Science, 1300–1800*. New York: Free Press.

Cairncross, Alec. 1993. *Austin Robinson: The Life of an Economic Advisor*. New York: St. Martin's Press.

Caldwell, Bruce. 2005. *Hayek's Challenge: An Intellectual Biography of F. A. Hayek*. Chicago: University of Chicago Press.

Cambridge Journal of Economics. 7. 3/4. 1983.

Cambridge Journal of Economics. 18. 1. 1994.

Cambridge University Reporter. Various issues.

Cavalieri, Duccio. 2001. "On Some Controversial Aspects of Sraffa's Theoretical System in the Second Half of the 1920s." In *Piero Sraffa's Political Economy: A Centenary Estimate*, edited by Terenzio Cozzi and Roberto Marchionatti. New York: Routledge.

Chamberlin, Edward H. 1929. "Duopoly: Value Where Sellers Are Few." *Quarterly Journal of Economics* 44.1: 63–100.

———. 1933. *The Theory of Monopolistic Competition*. Cambridge, Mass.: Harvard University Press.

———. 1961. "The Origin and Early Development of Monopolistic Competition Theory." *Quarterly Journal of Economics* 75.4: 515–43.

Clapham, John H. 1922. "Of Empty Economic Boxes." *Economic Journal* 32.127: 305–14.

Coase, R. H. 1972. "The Appointment of Pigou as Marshall's Successor." *Journal of Law and Economics* 15.2: 473–85.

Coats, A. W. 1968. "Political Economy and the Tariff Reform Campaign of 1903." *Journal of Law and Economics* 11.1: 181–229.

———. 1972. "The Appointment of Pigou as Marshall's Successor." *Journal of Law and Economics* 15.2: 487–95.

Cole, Stephen. 1992. *Making Science: Between Nature and Society*. Cambridge, Mass.: Harvard University Press.

Collard, David A. 1990. "Cambridge after Marshall." In *Centenary Essays on Alfred Marshall*, edited by John K. Whittaker. Cambridge: Cambridge University Press.

Cozzi, Terenzio, and Roberto Marchionatti, eds. 2001. *Piero Sraffa's Political Economy: A Centenary Estimate*. New York: Routledge.

Dardi, Marco. 2001. "Why Did Sraffa Lose Interest in Imperfect Competition? A Comment on Marcuzzo." In *Piero Sraffa's Political Economy: A Centenary Estimate*, edited by Terenzio Cozzi and Roberto Marchionatti. New York: Routledge.

Deane, Phyllis. 2001. *The Life and Times of J. Neville Keynes: A Beacon in the Tempest*. Cheltenham: Edward Elgar.

Dennison, S. R., and John Presley, eds. 1992. *Robertson on Economic Policy*. New York: St. Martin's Press.

Deslandes, Paul R. 2005. *Oxbridge Men: British Masculinity and the Undergraduate Experience*. Bloomington: Indiana University Press.

Dickinson, G. Lowes. 1973. *The Autobiography of G. Lowes Dickinson and other Unpublished Writings*, edited by Dennis Proctor. London: Duckworth.

Dijksterhuis, E. J. 1961. *The Mechanization of the World Picture*. New York: Oxford University Press.

The Directorate of the Chamber's Special Organization. 1929. *The British Crown and the Indian States: An Outline Sketch Drawn up on behalf of the Standing Committee of the Chamber of Princes*. London: P. S. King and Son.

Dobb, Maurice. 1925. *Capitalist Enterprise and Social Progress*. George Routledge and Sons.

Douglas, Roy. 1983. "Chamberlain and Appeasement." In *The Fascist Challenge and the Policy of Appeasement*, edited by Wolfgang J. Mommsen and Lothar Kettenacker. London: HarperCollins.

Dyhause, Carol. 1995. *No Distinction of Sex? Women in British Universities 1870–1939*. London: UCL Press.

Egremont, Max. 1997. *Under Two Flags: The Life of Major-General Sir Edward Spears*. London: Weidenfeld and Nicolson.

Ellsworth, P. T. 1938. "Introduction to the Theory of Employment." *Journal of Political Economy* 46.5: 730.

Emmett, Ross B. 1998. "Entrenching Disciplinary Competence: The Role of General Education and Graduate Study in Chicago Economics." In *From Interwar Pluralism to Postwar Neoclassicism*, edited by Mary S. Morgan and Malcolm Rutherford. Durham, N.C.: Duke University Press.

European Journal of the History of Economic Thought. 2005. 12.3.

Evans, Richard J. 2005. *The Third Reich in Power 1933–1939*. New York: Penguin.

Feiwel, George R., ed. 1989a. *The Economics of Imperfect Competition and Employment*. New York: New York University Press.

———. 1989b. *Joan Robinson and Modern Economic Theory*. New York: New York University Press.

Fitzgerald, F. Scott. 1956. *The Crack-up*. New York: New Directions.

Fletcher, Gordon A. 2000. *Understanding Dennis Robertson: The Man and His Work*. Aldershot: Edward Elgar.

Forster, E. M. [1907] 1988. *The Longest Journey*. New York: Penguin Books.

———. 1934. *Goldsworthy Lowes Dickinson*. New York: Harcourt Brace Jovanovich.

Friedman, Milton. 1986. "Milton Friedman." In *Lives of the Laureates: Seven Nobel Economists*, edited by William Breit and Roger W. Spencer. Cambridge, Mass.: MIT Press.

Fujimura, Joan. 1996. *Crafting Science: A Sociohistory of the Quest for Genetics of Cancer*. Cambridge, Mass.: Harvard University Press.

Garegnani, Pierangelo. 2005. "On a Turning Point in Sraffa's Theoretical and Interpretive Position in the Late 1920s." *European Journal of the History of Economic Thought* 12.3: 453–92.

Geertz, Clifford. 1973. *The Interpretation of Cultures: Selected Essays*. New York: Basic Books.

———. 1983. *Local Knowledge: Further Essays in Interpretive Anthropology*. New York: Basic Books.

Gibson, Bill, ed. 2005. *Joan Robinson's Economics: A Centennial Celebration*. Aldershot: Edward Elgar.

Gilbert, Martin, and Richard Gott. 1963. *The Appeasers*. London: Weidenfeld and Nicolson.

Glendinning, Victoria. 2006. *Leonard Woolf: A Biography*. New York: Free Press.

Goffman, Erving. 1956. "The Nature of Deference and Demeanor." *American Anthropologist* 58.3: 473–502.

———. 1959. *The Presentation of Self in Everyday Life*. Garden City, N.Y.: Doubleday.

———. 1969. *Strategic Interaction*. Philadelphia: University of Pennsylvania Press.

Golinski, Jan. 1998. *Making Natural Knowledge: Constructivism and the History of Science*. New York: Cambridge University Press.

Goodwin, R. M. 1989. "Joan Robinson—Passionate Seeker after Truth." In *Joan Robinson and Modern Economic Theory*, edited by George R. Feiwel. New York: New York University Press.

Groenenwegen, Peter. 1995. *A Soaring Eagle: Alfred Marshall 1842–1924*. Aldershot: Edward Elgar.

Haffenden, John. 2005. *William Empson: Among the Mandarins*. New York: Oxford University Press.

Hall, Robert I., and C. J. Hitch. 1939. "Price Theory and Business Behaviour." *Oxford Economic Papers* 2: 12–45.

Harcourt, Geoffrey C. 1972. *Some Cambridge Controversies in the Theory of Capital*. Cambridge: Cambridge University Press.

———. 1990. "Joan Robinson's Early Views on Method." *History of Political Economy* 22.3: 411–27.

———. 1994. "Kahn and Keynes and the Making of *The General Theory*." *Cambridge Journal of Economics* 18.1: 11–23.

———. 1995. "Obituary: Joan Robinson 1903–1983." *Economic Journal* 105.432: 1228–43.

Harrod, Roy F. 1930. "Notes on Supply." *Economic Journal* 40.158: 232–41.

———. 1936. *The Trade Cycle: An Essay*. Oxford: Oxford University Press.

———. 1937a. "Mr Keynes and Traditional Theory." *Econometrica* 5.1: 74–86.

———. 1937b. "Review of *Essays in the Theory of Employment*." *Economic Journal* 47.186: 326–30.

———. 1951. *The Life of John Maynard Keynes*. New York: W. W. Norton.

Hayek, F. A. 1931a. *Prices and Production*. London: George Routledge and Sons.

———. 1931b. "Reflections on the Pure Theory of Money of Mr. J. M. Keynes." *Economica* 33: 270–95.

———. 1931c. "A Rejoinder to Mr. Keynes." *Economica* 31: 398–403.

———. 1932. "Reflections on the Pure Theory of Money of Mr. J. M. Keynes (continued)." *Economica* 35: 22–44.

———. 1995. *Contra Keynes and Cambridge: Essays, Correspondence*. Volume 9 of *The Collected Works of F. A. Hayek*, edited by Bruce Caldwell. Chicago: University of Chicago Press.

Henderson, Hubert D. 1940. "Obituary: Marjorie Eve Robinson." *Economic Journal* 50.197: 161–62.

Hicks, J. R. 1932. *The Theory of Wages*. London: Macmillan.

———. 1934. "A Reconsideration of the Theory of Value, Part I." *Economica* 1.1: 52–76.

———. 1937. "Mr Keynes and the 'Classics'; A Suggested Interpretation." *Econometrica* 5.2: 147–59.

Howarth, T. E. B. 1978. *Cambridge between Two Wars*. London: Collins.

Howson, Susan. 2004. "The Origins of Lionel Robbins's *Essay on the Nature and Significance of Economic Science*." *History of Political Economy* 36.3: 413–43.

Hull, David L. 1988. *Science as Process*. Chicago: University of Chicago Press.

Jones, T. W. 1978. "The Appointment of Pigou as Marshall's Successor: The Other Side of the Coin." *Journal of Law and Economics* 21.1: 235–43.

Kadish, Alon. 1982. *The Oxford Economists in the Late Nineteenth Century*. Oxford: Clarendon Press.

Kahn, Richard F. 1931. "The Relation of Home Investment to Unemployment." *Economic Journal* 41.162: 173–98.

———. 1933. "Public Works and Inflation." *Journal of the American Statistical Association, Supplement: Proceedings of the American Statistical Association* 28.181: 168–73.

———. 1935. "Some Notes on Ideal Output." *Economic Journal* 45.177: 1–35.

———. 1937. "The Problem of Duopoly." *Economic Journal* 47.185: 1–20.

———. 1984. *The Making of Keynes' General Theory*. Cambridge: Cambridge University Press.

———.1985. "The Cambridge 'Circus' (1)." In *Keynes and His Contemporaries: The Sixth and Centennial Keynes Seminar held at the University of Kent at Canterbury, 1983*, edited by Geoffrey C. Harcourt. New York: St. Martin's Press.

———. 1987. "Shove, Gerald Frank." In *The New Palgrave: A Dictionary of Economics*. Volume 4, edited by John Eatwell, Murray Milgate, and Peter Newman. New York: Palgrave.

———. 1989. *The Economics of the Short Period*. New York: St. Martin's Press.

Kaldor, Nicholas. 1934. "Mrs. Robinson's 'Economics of Imperfect Competition.'" *Economica* 1.3: 335–41.

Kennedy, John. 1951–60. "Maurice, Sir Frederick Barton." In *Dictionary of National Biography 1951–1960 Supplement*. Volume 20, edited by Leslie Stephen and Sidney Lee. London: Oxford University Press.

Kerr, Prue, and Geoffrey C. Harcourt, eds. 2002. *Joan Robinson: Critical Assessment of Leading Economists*. 5 volumes. New York: Routledge.

Kershaw, Ian. 2000. *Hitler 1936–45: Nemesis*. New York: Norton.

Keynes, J. M. 1920. *The Economic Consequences of the Peace*. New York: Harcourt, Brace and Howe.

———. 1925. *The Economic Consequences of Mr. Churchill*. London: Hogarth Press.

———. 1930. *A Treatise on Money*. Volumes 1 and 2. London: Macmillan.

———. 1931. "The Pure Theory of Money. A Reply to Dr. Hayek." *Economica* 31: 387–97.

———. [1936] 1964. *The General Theory of Employment, Interest, and Money*. New York: Harcourt Brace Jovanovich.

———. 1951. *Essays in Biography*. Edited by Geoffrey Keynes. New York: Horizon Press.

———. 1973a. *The General Theory and After: Part I Preparation*. Volume 13 of *The Collected Writings of John Maynard Keynes*, edited by Donald Moggridge. London: Macmillan.

———. 1973b. *The General Theory and After: Part II Defence and Development*. Volume 14 of *The Collected Writings of John Maynard Keynes*, edited by Donald Moggridge. London: Macmillan.

———. 1979. *The General Theory and After: A Supplement*. Volume 29 of *The Collected Writings of John Maynard Keynes*, edited by Donald Moggridge. London: Macmillan.

———. 1983. *Economic Articles and Correspondence: Investment and Editorial*. Volume 12 of *The Collected Writings of John Maynard Keynes*, edited by Donald Moggridge. London: Macmillan.

Keynes, J. M., and Hubert Henderson. 1929. "Can Lloyd George Do IT?" *Nation and Athenaeum*.

Kitch, Edmund W. 1983. "The Fire of Truth: A Remembrance of Law and Economics at Chicago, 1932–1970." *Journal of Law and Economics* 26.1: 163–234.

Knight, Frank. 1924. "Some Fallacies in the Interpretation of Social Cost." *Quarterly Journal of Economics* 38.4: 582–606.

Knorr-Cetina, Karin. 1981. *The Manufacture of Knowledge: An Essay on the Constructivist and Contextual Nature of Science*. Oxford: Pergamon Press.

Kohler, Robert E. 1994. *Lords of the Fly: Drosophilia Genetics and the Experimental Life*. Chicago: University of Chicago Press.

Koyré, Alexander. 1957. *From the Closed World to the Infinite Universe*. Baltimore: Johns Hopkins University Press.

Kurz, Heinz D. 2008. *Piero Sraffa: The Man and the Scholar. Exploring His Unpublished Papers*. London: Routledge.

Kurz, Heinz D., and Neri Salvadori. 2005. "Representing the Production and Circulation of Commodities in Material Terms: On Sraffa's Objectivism." *Review of Political Economy* 17.3: 413–41.

Latour, Bruno. 1987. *Science in Action: How to Follow Scientists and Engineers through Society*. Cambridge, Mass.: Harvard University Press.

———. 1988. *The Pasteurization of France*. Cambridge, Mass.: Harvard University Press.

———. 1999. *Pandora's Hope: Essays on the Reality of Science Studies*. Cambridge, Mass.: Harvard University Press.

Latour, Bruno, and Steve Woolgar. 1976. *Laboratory Life: The Social Construction of Scientific Fact*. Beverly Hills: Sage.

Law, John, ed. 1986. *Power, Action, and Belief*. London: Routledge.

Lee, Frederic S. 1981. "The Oxford Challenge to Marshallian Supply and Demand: The History of the Oxford Economists' Research Group." *Oxford Economic Papers* 33.3: 339–51.

Lévi-Strauss, Claude. 1983. *The Raw and the Cooked: Mythologiques*. Volume 1. Chicago: University of Chicago Press.

Levy, Paul. 1981. *G. E. Moore and the Cambridge Apostles*. New York: Oxford University Press.

Livingstone, David N. 2003. *Putting Knowledge in Its Place: Geographies of Scientific Knowledge*. Chicago: University of Chicago Press.

———. 2007. "Science, Site and Speech: Scientific Knowledge and Spaces of Rhetoric." *History of the Human Sciences* 20: 71–98.

Lux, David S. 1989. *Patronage and Science in Seventeenth-Century France*. Ithaca: Cornell University Press.

Lynch, Michael. 1985. *Art and Artifact in Laboratory Science: A Study of Shop Work and Shop Talk in a Research Laboratory*. London: Routledge.

MacGregor, Donald. 1978. "In Memoriam: Arthur Fistzwalter Wynne Plumptre, 1907–1977." *Canadian Journal of Economics* 11.4: 714–18.

Madge, Charles, and Tom Harrison. 1939. *Britain by Mass-Observation*. Aarmondsworth: Penguin.

Maneschi, Andrea. 1986. "A Comparative Evaluation of Sraffa's 'The Laws of Returns under Competitive Conditions' and its Italian Precursor." *Cambridge Journal of Economics* 10.1: 1–12.

Marchionatti, Roberto. 2001. "Sraffa and the Criticism of Marshall in the 1920s." In *Piero Sraffa's Political Economy: A Centenary Estimate*, edited by Terenzio Cozzi and Roberto Marchionatti. New York: Routledge.

Marcuzzo, M. Cristina. 1994. "R. F. Kahn and Imperfect Competition." *Cambridge Journal of Economics* 18.1: 25–39.

———. 1996. "The Writings of Joan Robinson." In *The Economics of Joan Robinson*, edited by Maria Cristina Marcuzzo, Luigi L. Pasinetti, and Alessandro Roncaglia. New York: Routledge.

———. 2001. "Sraffa and Cambridge Economics, 1928–1931." In *Piero Sraffa's Political Economy: A Centenary Estimate*, edited by Terenzio Cozzi and Roberto Marchionatti. New York: Routledge.

———. 2002. "The Collaboration between J. M. Keynes and R. F. Kahn from the *Treatise* to the *General Theory*." *History of Political Economy* 34.2: 421–47.

———. 2003. "Joan Robinson and the Three Cambridge Revolutions." *Review of Political Economy*. 15.4: 545–60.

———. 2005. "Piero Sraffa at the University of Cambridge." *European Journal of the History of Economic Thought* 12.3: 425–52.

Marcuzzo, M. Cristina, Luigi L. Pasinetti, and Alessandro Ronraglia, eds. 1996. *The Economics of Joan Robinson*. New York: Routledge.

Marcuzzo, M. Cristina, and Annalisa Rosselli, eds. 2005. *Economists in Cambridge: A Study through their Correspondence, 1907–1946*. London: Routledge.

Marcuzzo, M. Cristina, and Claudio Sardoni. 2005. "Fighting for Keynesian Revolution: The Correspondence between Keynes and J. Robinson." In *Economists in Cambridge: A Study through Their Correspondence, 1907–1946*, edited by M. Cristina Marcuzzo and Annalisa Rosselli. London: Routledge.

Marion, Mathieu. 2005. "Sraffa and Wittgenstein: Physicalism and Constructivism." *Review of Political Economy* 17.3: 381–406.

Marshall, Alfred. 1890. *Principles of Economics*. London: Macmillan.

Matthews, R. C. O. 1989. "Joan Robinson and Cambridge—A Theorist and Her Milieu: An Interview." In *Joan Robinson and Modern Economic Theory*, edited by George R. Feiwel. New York: New York University Press.

McGraw, Thomas K. 2007. *Prophet of Innovation: Joseph Schumpeter and Creative Destruction*. Cambridge, Mass.: Harvard University Press.

McWilliams Tullberg, Rita. 1990. "Alfred Marshall and the 'Woman's Question' at Cambridge." *Revue d'èconomie appliqué* 63.1: 209–30.

———. 1995. "Marshall's Contributions to the Women's Higher Education Movement." In *Alfred Marshall's Lectures to Women*, edited by Tiziano Raffaelli, Eugenio Biagini, and Rita McWilliams Tullberg. Aldershot: Edward Elgar.

———. 1998. *Women at Cambridge*. Revised ed. New York: Cambridge University Press.

Meek, Ronald L. 1977. "Maurice Herbert Dobb." *Proceedings of the British Academy* 53: 333–44.

Merton, Robert K. 1957. "Priorities in Scientific Discovery: A Chapter in the Sociology of Science." *American Sociological Review*, 22.6: 635–59.

———. 1968. "The Matthew Effect in Science." *Science* 159.3810: 56–63.

———. 1973. *The Sociology of Science*. Chicago: University of Chicago Press.

———. 1979. *The Sociology of Science: An Episodic Memoir*. Carbondale: Southern Illinois University Press.

Milner, Marion. 1954. "Karin Stephen 1889–1953." *International Journal of Psycho-Analysis* 35: 432–34.

Mitchell, Brian R. 1978. *European Historical Statistics 1750–1970*. New York: Columbia University Press.

Moggridge, Donald E. 1973. "From the *Treatise* to *The General Theory*: An Exercise in Chronology." *History of Political Economy* Spring: 72–88.

———. 1992. *Maynard Keynes: An Economist's Biography*. New York: Routledge.

Mongiovi, Gary. 1996. "Sraffa's Critique of Marshall: A Reassessment." *Cambridge Journal of Economics* 20.2: 207–24.

Moore, G. E. [1903] 1959. *Principia Ethica*. New York: Cambridge University Press.

Moran, Bruce T. 1991. *The Alchemical World of the German Court: Occult Philosophy and Chemical Medicine in the Circle of Moritz of Hessen (1572–1632)*. Stuttgart: Franz Steiner Verlag.

Mulkay, Michael. 1991. *Sociology of Science: A Sociological Pilgrimage*. Philadelphia: Open University Press.

Naldi, Nerio. 2005. "Piero Sraffa: Emigration and Scientific Activity (1921–45)." *European Journal of the History of Economic Thought*. 12.3: 379–402.

Nisticò, Sergio, and Girogio Rodono. 2005. "Reflections on Sraffa's Legacy in Economics: A Review Essay." *Review of Political Economy* 17.3: 471–87.

Oakes, Guy, and Arthur J. Vidich. 1999. *Collaboration, Reputation, and Ethics in American Academic Life: Hans H. Gerth and C. Wright Mills*. Urbana: University of Illinois Press.

Olesko, Kathryn M. 1991. *Physics as a Calling: Discipline and Practice in the Koenigsburg Seminar for Physics*. Ithaca: Cornell University Press.

Ophir, Adir, and Steven Shapin. 1991. "The Place of Knowledge: A Methodological Survey." *Science in Context* 4: 3–21.

O'Shaughnessy, T. J. 1994. "Kahn on the Economics of the Short Period." *Cambridge Journal of Economics* 18.1: 41–54.

Outram, Dorinda. 1984. *Georges Cuvier: Vocation, Science, and Authority in Post-Revolutionary France*. Manchester: Manchester University Press.

Pasinetti, Luigi L. 1987. "Robinson, Joan Violet." In *The New Palgrave: A Dictionary of Economics*. Volume 4, edited by John Eatwell, Murray Milgate, and Peter Newman. New York: Palgrave.

Peace Pledge Union. 2005. "The Royal British Legion—An Unofficial View." Available at: www.ppu.org.uk (March 11).

Pigou, Arthur Cecil. 1920. *The Economics of Welfare*. London: Macmillan.

———. 1922. "Empty Economic Boxes: A Reply." *Economic Journal* 32.128: 458–65.

———. 1924. *The Economics of Welfare*. 2d ed. London: Macmillan.

———. 1925. "In Memoriam: Alfred Marshall." In *Memorials of Alfred Marshall*, edited by A. C. Pigou. London: Macmillan.

———. 1927. "The Laws of Diminishing and Increasing Cost." *Economic Journal* 37.146: 188–97.

———. 1928. "An Analysis of Supply." *Economic Journal* 38.150: 238–57.

———. 1929. *The Economics of Welfare*. 3rd ed. London: Macmillan.

———. [1932] 1952. *The Economics of Welfare*. 4th ed. London: Macmillan.

———. 1933. *The Theory of Unemployment*. London: Macmillan.

———. 1936. "Mr. J. M. Keynes' General Theory of Employment, Interest, and Money." *Economica* 3.10: 115–32.

———. 1939. "Presidential Address." *Economic Journal* 49.194: 215–21.

Plumptre, A. F. Wynne. 1947. "Keynes in Cambridge." *Canadian Journal of Economics and Political Science* 13.3: 366–71.

Potier, Jean-Pierre. 1987. *Piero Sraffa, Unorthodox Economist (1898–1983): A Biographical Essay*. London: Routledge.

Raffaelli, Tiziano. 2007. "Marshall's Metaphors on Method." *Journal of the History of Economic Thought* 29.2: 135–51.

Ranchetti, Fabio. 2005. "Communication and Intellectual Integrity. The Correspondence between Keynes and Sraffa." In *Economists in Cambridge: A Study through Their Correspondence, 1907–1946*, edited by M. Cristina Marcuzzo and Annalisa Rosselli. London: Routledge.

Reder, Melvin W. 1982. "Chicago Economics: Permanence and Change." *Journal of Economic Literature* 20.1: 1–38.

Reinwald, Thomas P. 1977. "The Genesis of Chamberlinian Monopolistic Competition Theory." *History of Political Economy* 9.4: 522–34.

Review of Political Economy. 2003. Special Issue Commemorating Joan Robinson's Centenary 15.4.

Review of Political Economy. 2005. Special Conference Issue: "Piero Sraffa 1898–1983," edited by Neri Salvadori, 17.3.

Rima, Ingrid H., ed. 1991. *The Joan Robinson Legacy*. New York: M. E. Sharpe.

Robbins, Keith. 1968. *Munich 1938*. London: Cassell.

Robbins, Lionel. 1928. "The Representative Firm." *Economic Journal* 38.151: 387–404.

———. 1932. *An Essay on the Nature & Significance of Economics Science*. London: Macmillan.

Robertson, Dennis H. 1915. *A Study of Industrial Fluctuations*. London: P. S. King and Son.

———. 1923. "Women and Cambridge University." *Nation and Athenaeum*, July 7.

———. 1924. "Those Empty Boxes." *Economic Journal* 34.133: 16–30.

———. 1930. "The Trees of the Forest." *Economic Journal* 40.157: 79–116.

———. 1952. *Utility and All That*. London: George Allen and Unwin.

Robinson, E. Austin G. R. 1931. *The Structure of Competitive Industry*. London: Nisbet.

———. 1941. *Monopoly*. London: Nisbet.

———. 1947. "John Maynard Keynes, 1883–1946." *Economic Journal* 57.225: 1–68.

———. 1963. "Could There Have Been a 'General Theory' without Keynes?" In *Keynes's General Theory: Reports of Three Decades*, edited by Robert Lekachman. New York: St. Martin's Press.

———. 1977. "Keynes and His Cambridge Colleagues." In *Keynes, Cambridge and the General Theory: The Process of Criticism and Discussion Connected with the Development of the General Theory*, edited by Don Patinkin and J. Clark Leith. London: Macmillan.

———. 1985. "The Cambridge 'Circus' (2)." In *Keynes and His Contemporaries. The Sixth and Centennial Keynes Seminar Held at the University of Kent at Canterbury, 1983*, edited by Geoffrey C. Harcourt. New York: St. Martin's Press.

————. 1990. "Fifty-five Years on the Royal Economic Society Council." In *A Century of Economics: 100 Years of the Royal Economic Society and the* Economic Journal, edited by John D. Hey and Donald Winch. Oxford: Basil Blackwell.

————. 1994. "Richard Kahn in the 1930s." *Cambridge Journal of Economics* 18.1: 7–10.

Robinson, Joan V. 1932a. *Economics Is a Serious Subject: The Apologia of an Economist to the Mathematician, the Scientist and the Plain Man.* Cambridge: Heffer.

————. 1932b. "Imperfect Competition and Falling Supply Price." *Economic Journal* 42.168: 544–54.

————. 1933a. "A Parable on Saving and Investment." *Economica* 39: 75–84.

————. 1933b. "Comments on G. F. Shove's 'The Imperfection of the Market: A Further Note.'" *Economic Journal* 43.169: 124–25.

————. 1933c. "Review of *The Theory of Unemployment.*" *New Statesman and Nation* 6.131 (August 26): 240–41.

————. 1933d. *The Economics of Imperfect Competition.* London: Macmillan.

————. 1933e. "The Theory of Money and the Analysis of Output." *Review of Economic Studies* 1.1: 22–26.

————. 1934a. "Euler's Theorem and the Problem of Distribution." *Economic Journal* 44.175: 398–414.

————. 1934b. "What Is Perfect Competition?" *Quarterly Journal of Economics* 49.1: 104–20.

————. 1936a. "Disguised Unemployment." *Economic Journal* 46.182: 225–37.

————. 1936b. "The Long-Period Theory of Employment." *Zeitschrift für Nationalökonomie* 7: 74–93.

————. 1937a. *Essays in the Theory of Employment.* London: Macmillan.

————. 1937b. *Introduction to the Theory of Employment.* London: Macmillan.

————. 1941. "Rising Supply Price." *Economica* 8.1: 1–8.

————. 1951. *Collected Economic Papers.* New York: Augustus M. Kelley.

————. 1953. "Imperfect Competition Revisited." *Economic Journal* 63.251: 579–93.

————. 1956. *The Accumulation of Capital.* London: Macmillan.

————. 1979. *Contributions to Modern Economics.* Oxford: Basil Blackwell.

Rosselli, Annalisa. 2005a. "An Enduring Partnership: The Correspondence between Kahn and J. Robinson." In *Economists in Cambridge: A Study through Their Correspondence, 1907–1946*, edited by M. Cristina Marcuzzo and Annalisa Rosselli. London: Routledge.

————. 2005b. "Sraffa and the Marshallian Tradition." *European Journal of the History of Economic Thought* 12.3: 403–23.

————. 2005c. "The Defender of the Marshallian Tradition: Shove and the Correspondence with Kahn, J. Robinson and Sraffa." In *Economists in*

Cambridge: A Study through Their Correspondence, 1907–1946, edited by M. Cristina Marcuzzo and Annalisa Rosselli. London: Routledge.

Rudwick, Martin J. S. 1985. *The Great Devonian Controversy: The Shaping of Scientific Knowledge among Gentlemanly Specialists*. Chicago: University of Chicago Press.

Russell, Bertrand. 1967. *The Autobiography of Bertrand Russell, 1872–1914*. Boston: Little, Brown.

S., L. 1921–22. "Maurice, Frederick Denison." In *Dictionary of National Biography*. Volume 3, edited by Leslie Stephen and Sidney Lee. London: Oxford University Press.

Saltmarsh, John, and Patrick Wilkinson. 1960. *Arthur Cecil Pigou, 1877–1959*. Cambridge: Printed for King's College.

Samuelson, Paul A. 1970. *Readings in Economics*. New York: McGraw-Hill.

———. 1989. "Remembering Joan." In *Joan Robinson and Modern Economic Theory*, edited by George R. Feiwel. New York: New York University Press.

Schnädelbach, Herbert. 1984. *Philosophy in Germany, 1931–1933*. Translated by Eric Matthews. New York: Cambridge University Press.

Schumpeter, Joseph A. 1928. "The Instability of Capitalism." *Economic Journal* 38.151: 361–86.

———. 1934. "Robinson's Economics of Imperfect Competition." *Journal of Political Economy* 42.2: 249–57.

———. 1954. *History of Economic Analysis*. New York: Oxford University Press.

———. 2000. *Briefe/Letters*. Edited by Ulrich Hedtke and Richard Swedberg. Tübingen: Mohr Siebeck.

Schumpeter, Joseph A., Theodore O. Yntema, Edward H. Chamberlin, William Jaffe, L. A. Morrison, and A. J. Nichol. 1934. "Roundtable Conference: Imperfect Competition." *American Economic Review* 24.1: 21–32.

Shapin, Steven. 1994. *A Social History of Truth*. Chicago: University of Chicago Press.

———. 1998. "Placing the View from Nowhere: Historical and Sociological Problems in the Location of Science." *Transactions of the Institute of British Geographers* 23: 5–12.

Shapin, Steven, and Simon Schaffer. 1985. *Leviathan and the Air Pump: Hobbes, Boyle and the Experimental Life*. Princeton: Princeton University Press, 1985.

Shove, Gerald F. 1928. "Varying Costs and Marginal Net Products." *Economic Journal* 38.151: 258–66.

———. 1930. "The Representative Firm and Increasing Returns." *Economic Journal* 40.157: 94–116.

———. 1933a. "The Economics of Imperfect Competition." *Economic Journal* 43.172: 657–61.

———. 1933b. "The Imperfection of the Market. A Further Note." *Economic Journal* 43.169: 113–124.

Signorino, Rodolfo. 2005. "Piero Sraffa's Lectures on the Advanced Theory of Value 1928–31 and the Rediscovery of the Classical Approach." *Review of Political Economy* 17.3: 359–80.

Sisman, Adam. 2006. *The Friendship: Wordsworth and Coleridge*. New York: Viking.

Skidelsky, Robert. 1983. *John Maynard Keynes: Hopes Betrayed, 1883–1920*. London: Macmillan.

———. 1992. *John Maynard Keynes: The Economist as Saviour, 1920–1937*. London: Macmillan.

———. 2000. *John Maynard Keynes: Fighting for Britain, 1937–1946*. London: Macmillan.

Smith, Pamela H. 1994. *The Business of Alchemy: Science and Culture in the Holy Roman Empire*. Princeton: Princeton University Press.

Solow, Robert M. 1989. "An Interview." In *The Economics of Imperfect Competition and Employment*, edited by George R. Feiwel. New York: New York University Press.

Sraffa, Piero. 1925. "Sulle relazioni fra costo e quantità prodotta." *Annali di Economia* 2: 277–328.

———. 1926. "The Laws of Returns under Competitive Conditions." *Economic Journal* 36.144: 535–50.

———. 1930a. "A Criticism." *Economic Journal* 40.157: 89–92.

———. 1930b. "Rejoinder." *Economic Journal* 40.157: 93.

———. 1932. "Dr. Hayek on Money and Capital." *Economic Journal*, 42.165: 42–53.

Stigler, George J. 1942. *The Theory of Competitive Price*. New York: Macmillan.

Stolper, Wolfgang, F. 1994. *Joseph Alois Schumpeter: The Public Life of a Private Man*. Princeton: Princeton University Press.

Storer, Norman. 1966. *The Social System of Science*. New York: Holt, Rinehart, and Winston.

Sutherland, Gillian. 1992. "'Nasty Forward Minxes': Cambridge and the Higher Education of Women." In *Cambridge Contributions*, edited by Sarah J. Ormrod. New York: Cambridge University Press.

Swedberg, Richard, ed. 1991. *Joseph A. Schumpeter: The Economics and Sociology of Capitalism*. Princeton: Princeton University Press.

Sweezy, Paul M. 1939. "Demand under Conditions of Oligopoly." *Journal of Political Economy* 47.4: 568–73.

Traweek, Sharon. 1988. *Beamtimes and Lifetimes: The World of High Energy Physicists*. Cambridge, Mass.: Harvard University Press.

Turner, Marjorie S. 1989. *Joan Robinson and the Americans*. Armonk, N.Y.: M. E. Sharpe.

University of Toronto Library. 2002. Representative Poetry Online. Available online at http://rpo.library.utoronto.ca/poem/1056.html.

Walsh, Vivian. 1989. "A View of Joan Robinson's Last Decade." In *Joan Robinson and Modern Economic Theory*, edited by George R. Feiwel. New York: New York University Press.

Warwick, Andrew. 2003. *Masters of Theory: Cambridge and the Rise of Mathematical Physics*. Chicago: University of Chicago Press.

Weber, Max. 1946. *From Max Weber: Essays in Sociology*. Edited by H. H. Gerth and C. Wright Mills. New York: Oxford University Press.

———. 1978. *Economy and Society*. Volumes 1 and 2. Edited by Guenther Roth and Claus Wittich. Berkeley: University of California Press.

Weintraub, E. Roy. 2005. "Autobiographical Memory and the Historiography of Economics." *Journal of the History of Economic Thought* 27.1: 1–11.

Westfall, Richard S. 1981. *Never at Rest: A Biography of Isaac Newton*. New York: Cambridge University Press.

Whitaker, J. K. 1972. "Alfred Marshall: The Years 1877 to 1885." *History of Political Economy* 4: 1–61.

Wittgenstein, Ludwig. 1953. *Philosophical Investigations*. New York: Macmillan.

———. 1971. "Remarks on Frazer's *Golden Bough*." In *Wittgenstein: Sources and Perspectives*, edited by C. G. Luckhardt. Sussex: Harvester.

Woolf, Leonard. 1960. *Sowing: An Autobiography of the Years 1880 to 1904*. New York: Harcourt Brace Jovanovich.

Woolf, Virginia. [1929] 1993. *A Room of One's Own and Three Guineas*. London: Penguin Books.

Yntema, Theodore O. 1928. "The Influence of Dumping on Monopoly Price." *Journal of Political Economy* 36.6: 686–98.

Young, Allyn. 1913. "Pigou's Wealth and Welfare." *Quarterly Journal of Economics* 27.4: 672–86.

———. 1928. "Increasing Returns and Economic Progress." *Economic Journal* 38.152: 527–42.

Young, Warren. 1987. *Interpreting Mr. Keynes: The IS-LM Enigma*. Boulder: Westview Press.

Zuckerman, Harriet. 1977. *Scientific Elites: Nobel Laureates in the United States*. New York: Free Press.

Coleridge, Samuel Taylor, 258 n. 47

"common pool": Schumpeter on, 134–35, 148; Shove on, 143

contingencies: in formation of Robinson's early career, 14, 237; Keynes on, 223–24

Cornford, Francis, 250 n. 16

Cournot, Antoine Augustine, 89, 122, 129, 262–63 n. 17

credit and priority claims in Cambridge economics: character of, 135–36; Kahn on, 134–35; of research on imperfect competition, 135; Robinson vs. Kahn over, 136–39; Robinson vs. Shove over, 139–48; Schumpeter on, 134–35; Shove vs. Kahn over, 149–50

dialogue: functions of, in Marshallian guild, 115–16; as research practice in Cambridge economics, 13, 99–100; Robinson's embrace of, 5, 65, 103

Dickinson, Goldsworthy Lowes, 135, 149, 269 n. 105

Dictionary of the Treatise (Robinson), 189

"Disguised Unemployment" (Robinson), 21, 213, 276 n. 65

Dobb, Maurice, 34, 227; on Marshall's preeminence at Cambridge, 261 n. 4

Douglas, Paul, 238–39, 244

"Duopoly: Value Where Sellers Are Few" (Chamberlin), 128–29

Durbin, Evan, 239–40

Economic Consequences of Mr. Churchill, The (Henderson and Keynes), 194

Economic Consequences of the Peace, The (Keynes), 18, 119

economic genius, Robinson's conception of, 38–41, 252 n. 45

Economics Is a Serious Subject (Robinson), 41–45, 49, 58, 187; Robbins's *An Essay on the Nature and Signifi-* *cance of Economic Science* and, 253–54 n. 53

Economics of Imperfect Competition, The (Robinson), 2, 3, 8; Austin's account of origin of, 36–37; critical success of, 19–20; epistolary account of origin of, 45–49; foundation of Robinson's professional identity and, 45–48; Kahn's role in origin of, 36–38; Robinson's account of origin of, 37–38; Sraffa and origin of, 18–19. *See also* credit and priority claims in Cambridge economics

Economics of Welfare, The (Pigou), 38–40, 96, 108

Economics Tripos, 22–25, 30, 66, 120, 152, 213, 228, 242; reform of, 191–92

Edgeworth, Francis, 94, 119

Empson, William, dismissal of, 255 n. 7

epistolary anthropology, 12

Essays in Persuasion (Keynes), 202

Essays in the Theory of Employment (Robinson), 2, 9, 21, 100; Keynes's qualified blessing of, 220; Robinson and Keynes and proofs of, 14, 214–17, 243

"Euler's Theorem and the Problem of Distribution" (Robinson), 65, 67, 190, 269 n. 106

Faculty Board of Economics and Politics (Cambridge University), 23–24, 90, 175, 238; grant of Robinson fellowship allowance by, 260 n. 65; recommendation of Robinson for university lectureship by, 17–18. *See also* university lectureship, Robinson's appointment to

Fay, C. R., 151, 202, 230, 275 n. 52; on Robinson, 6, 8; Robinson's appointment and, 197–201

"flesh, the + the devil," 86

Florence, Philip Sargant, 34

footnoting, ethics of, 138

"Foreign Exchanges, The" (Robinson), 215–17

Frazer, James, 250 n. 16

Friedman, Milton, 3–4

Frisch, Ragnar, 125–26, 133, 269 n. 99

"Full Employment" (Robinson), 216

General Board of the Faculties (Cambridge University), 23, 226, 230–33, 248 n. 1. *See also* university lectureship, Robinson's appointment to

General Theory of Employment, Interest, and Money, The (Keynes), 2, 15, 18, 22; Kahn's role in writing of, 97, 186, 189; Keynes's meta-interpretation of, 207–8, 219, 223–26; original rhetorical strategy of, 186–87, 202–3, 211; origin of, 20–21; Robinson's conception of ideal rhetorical strategy for, 212–13, 219; Robinson's understanding of, 206–8, 224–25

Gifford, Charles, 36–38, 109

Goffman, Erving, 11

Graduate Economics Club (Harvard University), 130, 263 n. 17

Grand Scheme (Robinson), 192–94, 201; Fay's response to, 196–99, 201; implications of, for Robertson's lectures, 194–95; Keynes's response to, 194, 199–202

Guillebaud, Claude, 49, 106, 129, 192, 256 n. 12

Haberler, Gottfried, 245–46

Haldane, J. B. S., "gross immorality" of, 255–56 n. 7

Hall, Robert, 111

Harcourt, Geoffrey, 1, 253 n. 51

Harrison, James, 250 n. 16

Harrod, Roy, 9, 38, 207; on Keynes's Marshallian credentials, 93, 95; review of Robinson's *Essays in the Theory of Employment* by, 21–22

Hawtrey, Ralph, 64; comments of, on galleys of *The General Theory*, 209–10

Hayek, F. A., 133; review of Keynes's *Treatise* by, 163–68. *See also* "Parable on Saving and Investment, A"

Henderson, Hubert, 194, 241–42

Hicks, J. R., 120, 195; academic credentials of, 18

Hitch, C. J., 111

Hitler, Adolf, 68–72, 76

Hoskyns, John, 256–57 n. 24

imperfect competition, 2; American Economic Association roundtable on, 132; conditions at Cambridge for Robinson's work on, 14, 96–99; Sraffa's article on, 95–96

"Imperfect Competition and Falling Supply Price" (Robinson), 58, 112–13, 119, 243; controversy with Shove over, 182–84

"Imperfect Competition and the Marginal Principle" (Kahn), 136–39

"Influence of Dumping and Monopoly Price, The" (Yntema), 36

"intellectual aristocracy" (Annan), Robinson's membership in, 272–73 n. 18

Introduction to the Theory of Employment (Robinson), 2, 9, 22, 239–40; initial reservations of Keynes about, 221–22; intentions of Robinson in writing, 221–23; Keynes's endorsement of, 223

Jevons, Stanley, 89

Kahn, Richard F., 4; at American Statistical Association meeting, 121; early Cambridge success of, 120; fellowship dissertation of, 7–8; Harvard University and, 60–61, 100–102, 125–33; impressions of, on economics in United States, 121; impressions of, on Schultz, 121–24; impressions of, on Viner, 121–24; on kinked demand curve, 111; observations of, on Robinson's dialogue with Pigou,

Robertson, Dennis H. (*cont.*)
and, 47; response of, to *The General
Theory*, 211; Robinson's appointment
to lectureship and, 34, 277 n. 78

Robinson, Austin: in Africa for research, 56–57; Cambridge lectureship of, 33–34; in India for work, 33;
interest of, in academic administration, 152–53; in Marshallian guild,
151; on Robinson's ambitions, 6; as
secretary of faculty board, 46, 152;
support of, for Robinson's career,
151–55; as tutor to maharajah of
Gwalior, 151–52

Robinson, Joan: as academic career
strategist, 237–40; as advocate of
simplicity in economic theory,
242–45; as anonymous reviewer of
Pigou's *The Theory of Unemployment*,
186–89; application of, for university
lectureship, 194–95; appointment
of, to part-time probationary faculty
lectureship, 191, 248 n. 1; attempt
of, to gain access to Keynes, 181–85;
comment of, on *The General Theory*
galleys and correspondence about,
206–7, 210–11; competition of, with
Chamberlin over priority, 128–35;
conflicts of, with Robertson, 8;
conflicts of, with Shove over credit
for research on imperfect competition, 4–5; dialogue of, with Pigou
on "Imperfect Competition and
Falling Supply Price," 114–20,
240–41; differences of, with Keynes,
over character of economic theory,
216–20; drafting of *The Economics
of Imperfect Competition* by, 105–7;
early career intentions of, 32; early
institutional marginality at Cambridge and, 35, 49–50; early philosophy of, on economic science, 7; early
relationship of, with Robertson, 238;
failure of, to acknowledge Kahn's

fellowship dissertation in *The Economics of Imperfect Competition*, 108;
financial dependence of, on Austin,
151–55; first research program of, 7–8;
galleys of *The General Theory* and,
205–6; imp as aspect of character
of, 84–85, 245; impression management skills of, 240–42; "inferiority
complex of an intelligent woman"
and, 245; Keynes's *Treatise* and, 20,
189–91; limited knowledge of, on
literature in economic theory, 108–9;
memorandum of, for Schumpeter
on teaching economics, 242; as
mother, 66–67; outline of unwritten
novel by, 58–59; Nobel Prize in economics and, 3; as propagandist for
The General Theory, 162–63, 213–20;
proposed lectures of, on applications
of monetary theory, 191–92; pursuit
of, of Keynes's patronage, 8–9, 14,
162–63, 172, 186; refusal of, to learn
advanced mathematics, 105, 114–17;
reputation of, 1–4; restrictions on
women at Cambridge and, 29–30;
rewards of teaching at Cambridge
and, 245; reporting on princely
states of India and, 33–35; role of,
in Keynes's controversy with
Hayek, 163, 168–72; role of, in
securing Cambridge lectureship for
Austin, 33–35; state of mind of, in
writing *Economics Is a Serious Subject*, 258 n. 47; strategies of, of academic career production, 4–10,
13–14; tendentious views of, on
economics, 273–74 n. 27; undergraduate credentials of, 23; use of Kahn's
ideas in *The Economics of Imperfect
Competition* by, 109–10, 111–12;
use of Sraffa in gaining access to
Keynes by, 185; as winner in conflict with Robertson, 240. *See
also* Maurice, Joan; professional

tangency condition, 112, 116

Tappan-Holland, Marjorie (née Tappan): critique of Robinson's "gospel view of economics" by, 176–78, 276 n. 54; critique of Robinson's supervision of first-year students by, 175–76; Kahn and Robinson's view of, 250 n. 18; as Robinson's second supervisor, 30–31

Taussig, Frank, 244–45

"Theory of Money and the Analysis of Output, The" (Robinson), 20, 41, 251 n. 37

Theory of Monopolistic Competition, The (Chamberlin), 101

Theory of Unemployment, The (Pigou), 185–88

tractability (in *Economics Is a Serious Subject*), 43

Treatise on Money, A (Keynes), 9, 31, 121, 124, 203; Cambridge Circus critique of, 54, 120; Hayek's review of, 163–65, 204; origin of *The General Theory* and, 20, 222; Robinson's conception of, 39–41, 171, 224–25; Robinson's efforts to understand, 14, 169, 180; study of, by Robinson in 1934, 189–91, 205, 239

unconscious plagiarism, of Robinson by Kahn, 138

university lectureship, Robinson's appointment to: Kahn's perception of, 232–33; minutes of faculty board meeting on, 232; Pigou's role in, 230; Robertson's role in, 230–31; Shove's role in, 231

Viner, Jacob, 100, 109, 238; Cambridge economics, view of, 121–24

Wanderjahre, and Cambridge economics students, 91

Weber, Max, 11, 151

"What Is Perfect Competition?" (Robinson), 65, 244

women at Cambridge University: chaperonage and, 29; denial of rights to receive degrees by, 25–26, 249 n. 13; granting of rights to titular degrees to, 27–28, 249–50 n. 15

Woolf, Leonard, 149

Woolf, Virginia, 24, 73–74, 102, 153, 250 n. 19, 258 n. 48

Workers' Educational Association, 222

Yntema, Theodore, 36, 109, 265 n. 39

NAHID ASLANBEIGUI is professor of economics and the Chair of Economics and Finance, Monmouth University. She is the co-editor of *Rethinking Economic Principles: Critical Essays on Introductory Textbooks* (1996), *Borderlands of Economics: Essays in Honour of Daniel R. Fusfeld* (1997), and *Women in the Age of Economic Transformation: Gender Impact of Reforms in Post-Socialist and Developing Countries* (1994).

GUY OAKES is professor of philosophy and Jack T. Kvernland Professor in the School of Business, Monmouth University. He is the author of *The Imaginary War: Civil Defense and American Cold War Culture* (1994), *The Soul of the Salesman: The Moral Ethos of Personal Sales* (1990), and *Weber and Rickert: Concept Formation in the Cultural Sciences* (1988), and coauthor of *Collaboration, Reputation, and Ethics in American Academic Life: Hans H. Gerth and C. Wright Mills* (1999).

LIBRARY OF CONGRESS CATALOGING-IN-PUBLICATION DATA

Aslanbeigui, Nahid.
The provocative Joan Robinson : the making of a Cambridge economist / Nahid Aslanbeigui and Guy Oakes.
p. cm. — (Science and cultural theory)
Includes bibliographical references and index.
ISBN 978-0-8223-4521-3 (cloth : alk. paper)
ISBN 978-0-8223-4538-1 (pbk. : alk. paper)
1.   Robinson, Joan, 1903–1983.
2.   Neoclassical school of economics.
3.   Keynesian economics.
4.   Economists—Great Britain.
I.   Oakes, Guy.
II. Title.
III. Series: Science and cultural theory.
HB103.R63A85 2009
330.15'6092—dc22
2009003265